AGRARIAN
CRISIS IN INDIA

Thank you for choosing a SAGE product!
If you have any comment, observation or feedback,
I would like to personally hear from you.

Please write to me at **contactceo@sagepub.in**

Vivek Mehra, Managing Director and CEO, SAGE India.

AGRARIAN
CRISIS IN INDIA

Status, Dimensions and
Mitigation Strategies

EDITED BY

M. Dinesh Kumar
M. V. K. Sivamohan
Nitin Bassi

Los Angeles | London | New Delhi
Singapore | Washington DC | Melbourne

First published in 2022 by

SAGE Publications India Pvt Ltd
B1/I-1 Mohan Cooperative Industrial Area
Mathura Road, New Delhi 110 044, India
www.sagepub.in

SAGE Publications Inc
2455 Teller Road
Thousand Oaks, California 91320, USA

SAGE Publications Ltd
1 Oliver's Yard, 55 City Road
London EC1Y 1SP, United Kingdom

SAGE Publications Asia-Pacific Pte Ltd
18 Cross Street #10-10/11/12
China Square Central
Singapore 048423

Published by Vivek Mehra for SAGE Publications India Pvt Ltd. Typeset in 10.5/13 pt Bembo by Zaza Eunice, Hosur, Tamil Nadu, India.

Library of Congress Control Number: 2022905528

ISBN: 978-93-5479-454-4 (HB)

SAGE Team: Amrita Dutta, Satvinder Kaur and Kanika Mathur

Contents

Part I: The Changing Characteristics of India's Agricultural Sector

Part II: Findings and Insights from Field Research

             M. V. K. Sivamohan, V. Niranjan,
             M. Dinesh Kumar and Nitin Bassi

             5.1. Introduction   135
             5.2. Agriculture in West Bengal   138
             5.3. The Study Location   143
             5.4. Results and Discussions   148
             5.5. Summary and Findings   160
             References   162

Chapter 6   Agricultural Growth in Gujarat   164
             M. Dinesh Kumar, Nitin Bassi and V. Niranjan

             6.1. Introduction   164
             6.2. Agriculture in Gujarat: Recent Experience 166
             6.3. The Study Location   172
             6.4. Results and Discussion   176
             6.5. Summary and Findings   188
             References   190

Chapter 7   Agricultural Growth in Coastal
             Andhra Pradesh   192
             V. Niranjan, K. Siva Rama Kishan,
             M. V. K. Sivamohan and Nitin Bassi

             7.1. Introduction   192
             7.2. Changes in Agricultural Landscape of
                  Andhra Pradesh since the 1970s   193
             7.3. The Study Location   204
             7.4. Results and Discussion   208
             7.5. Summary and Findings   216
             References   220

Chapter 8   Agricultural Changes in Maharashtra   222
             Nitin Bassi, K. Siva Rama Kishan,
             M. Dinesh Kumar and M. V. K. Sivamohan

             8.1. Introduction   222
             8.2. Agriculture in Maharashtra   224
             8.4. Results and Discussion   233
             8.5. Summary and Findings   244
             References   246

Part III: Mitigating the Agrarian Crisis

List of Illustrations

FIGURES

TABLES

List of Abbreviations

ASCI	Administrative Staff College of India
BCCI	Bengal Chamber of Commerce and Industry
CB	Cross-breeding
CSRE	Crash Scheme for Rural Employment
DFID	Department for International Development
EIA	Environmental impact assessment
GBM	Ganges–Brahmaputra–Meghna
GCA	Gross cropped area
GGRC	Gujarat Green Revolution Company
GIA	Gross irrigated area
GIS	Geographic information system
GSDP	Gross state domestic product
HE	High endowment
HVCs	High-value crops
HYVP	High-yielding variety programme
HYVs	High-yielding varieties
IAAP	Intensive Agriculture Area Programme
IADP	Intensive Agriculture Development Programme
ICSSR	Indian Council of Social Science Research
IGNP	Indira Gandhi Nahar Project
IMD	India Meteorological Department
IRAP	Institute for Resource Analysis and Policy
IWMI	International Water Management Institute
LE	Low endowment
ME	Medium endowment
MFAL	Marginal Farmers and Agricultural Labourers
MGNREGS	Mahatma Gandhi National Rural Employment Guarantee Scheme
Mha	Million hectare

MMP	Mission mode project
MSFD	Multi-stage flash distillation
MSP	Minimum support price
NABARD	National Bank for Agriculture and Rural Development
NDVI	Normalized Difference Vegetation Index
NeGP	National e-Governance Programme
NMC	Narmada Main Canal
NREGA	National Rural Employment Guarantee Act
NREGS	National Rural Employment Guarantee Scheme
NSA	Net sown area
NSDP	Net state domestic product
NSSO	National Sample Survey Office
PDS	Public distribution system
PIREP	Pilot Intensive Rural Employment Project
PMKSY	Pradhan Mantri Krishi Sinchayee Yojana
SFDA	Small Farmers Development Agency
SRE	Super rich endowment
SSP	Sardar Sarovar Project
TE	Triennium ending
TFP	Total factor productivity
VHE	Very high endowment

Preface

Indian agriculture is in a state of transition. While every year some parts of the country witness droughts, floods, heatwaves or effects of cyclones, farmers across the country have shown great resilience to the challenges posed by these weather extremes by adopting efficient irrigation technologies and practices and hybrid seed varieties, and exploring new markets to get best returns for their produce. Parallelly, Central and various state governments have improved physical infrastructure in rural areas, including roads, electricity distribution network and storage facilities, for supporting agriculture production, storage and transportation. However, millions of marginal and small farmers who have limited access to land, water, capital, technology and information are unable to take advantage of the opportunity which comes with this transition, as with the existing productivity levels, they are unable to cover the costs of their inputs which are constantly on the rise. This has precipitated into a sort of crisis where the proportion of farmers incurring losses from agriculture is on the rise. Farmer suicides are attracting media attention and are becoming politically sensitive issues.

In the past, agrarian change in general and agrarian crisis in particular had been analysed by many scholars, but from the perspective of modes of production and agrarian structure, largely corresponding to the colonial and pre-colonial era. There has been too little comprehensive work looking at the problems from the perspective of limits induced by land scarcity and water stress, changing dynamics with respect to cost of various inputs affected by changing subsidy structure and externalities induced by the changing environmental and market conditions. Such analysis requires systematic engagement with sociology and agricultural economics and is also important to understand the nature and extent of agrarian crisis. This edited book intends to undertake such comprehensive assessment.

The vast differences in agro-climatic conditions, resource endowment, socio-economic conditions and landholding pattern among regions, and more importantly the differences in growth trajectory witnessed by these regions, make it imperative that research on agrarian crisis in the sector looked at individual regions rather than the aggregate-level scenario of the country. Thus, this volume presents a comparative analysis of the situation in regions with distinct physical (agro-ecology, water availability, land availability and climate) and socio-economic environment (overall economic conditions of the farmers, and infrastructure and market conditions), as all of them have bearing on the profitability of farming. The collection of chapters in this volume goes deep into the factors causing the crisis by analysing the vast amount of primary data collected from four different agro-ecological regions in the country and secondary data at regional and national levels.

The book offers significant lessons for policymakers on the agrarian change from a historical perspective; the regions that need to receive greater attention; the changes that are occurring in the characteristics of India's farming systems; the strategies that need to be adopted on the physical, institutional and policy fronts to mitigate the crisis; and the measures to be adopted to sustain agricultural growth in different regions. We sincerely hope that this volume helps the scholars, academics, practitioners and policymakers to deepen their understanding of the key characteristics of India's agriculture sector, which need to be kept in mind while analysing agriculture-related problems.

Acknowledgements

First of all, we are thankful to the Indian Council of Social Science Research (ICSSR), Ministry of Human Resource Development, Government of India, New Delhi, for providing grant-in-aid to the Institute for Resource Analysis and Policy (IRAP), Hyderabad, for undertaking a research study 'The Factors Causing the Agrarian Crisis in India: A Study from Four Agro-ecological Regions in Four States'. This study inspired us to do this edited volume and provided the material for at least five of the chapters included in the volume.

The authors are extremely grateful to Ms Vaishnavi Potharaju, Research Officer, IRAP, for her support in extensively reviewing published literature and updating secondary data sets which were immensely helpful in finalizing certain chapters of the manuscript. Further, we are thankful to Ms Archana Dineshkumar Manhachery, Consultant, Science Editing, for patiently reading and meticulously editing the manuscript for scientific accuracy, consistency, language and readability. We are also highly thankful to Mr Ajath Sanjeev, Executive Assistant to Director, IRAP, for rigorously carrying out the reference check and preparing the 'Table of Contents' and 'List of Abbreviations' of the manuscript.

We are indebted to the ardent efforts of our field coordinators and investigators for collecting primary data from the four agro-ecological regions in India. We would specifically like to express our special thanks to Dr Partha Sarathi Banerjee (Field Coordinator, West Bengal) and Mr Jitendra Chaudhary (Field Coordinator, Gujarat).

We extend our sincere thanks to the farmers and rural households in the four agro-ecological regions who spared their time to patiently listen to our study requirements and provided responses to the queries posed by the field investigators.

We are grateful to the individual contributors, who are responsible for drafting, revising and finalizing the contents of their respective chapters, for having collaborated with us in this effort. The book project would not have been possible without the contributions of other individual staff members of IRAP and the organization at large. For us, they are invaluable.

PART I

The Changing Characteristics of India's Agricultural Sector

Chapter 1

Development of Indian Agriculture
An Overview

M. V. K. Sivamohan, M. Dinesh Kumar
and Nitin Bassi

1.1. INTRODUCTION

India is the second most populous country in the world. Although it is one of the fastest growing economies, it is still a middle-income country in terms of per capita income. While agriculture accounts for only 12 per cent (GoI, 2014) of the national GDP, the majority of the people in rural areas (nearly 55%), wherein nearly 68 per cent of the country's population lives, are directly dependent on this sector as a major source of livelihood. This makes it nearly 520 million people, nearly twice the population of the United States. While the economy continues to grow, the agricultural component of the GDP has been falling consistently since Independence.[1] This is because the proportion of population living on farming has not reduced steadily. The primary sector of India's economy is therefore in a crisis. Some scholars believe that by the time India becomes a developed economy, a large proportion of the rural population would have eventually moved to

---

[1] It consistently dropped from 51.4 per cent of the total GDP in 1950–51 to 15.5 per cent of the GDP in 2010–11 (MoA, 2012).

cities and towns, and only a small fraction of the people living in rural areas would be engaged in farming, a phenomenon observed in many developed countries, and that the overdependence is only a temporary phenomenon.

Many developed and industrialized nations around the world have experienced major structural changes in their economy from agriculture to the manufacturing and service sectors and have seen a remarkable shift in the occupational profile of their people. However, assuming a similar trajectory for India would be problematic. There are two vital reasons for this. First of all, it took a couple of centuries for this transition to happen in the case of most developed countries of the West. Second, if the manufacturing sector has to absorb a vast majority of these people (500+ million), the scale of industrialization required would be massive, and this would be hard to achieve in the next few decades. More so, such a growth in that sector will have to be primarily driven by growth in domestic consumption and not exports.[2] On the other hand, given the fact that the size of average per capita landholding in the most backward regions (Bihar, West Bengal, Assam, Odisha and Uttar Pradesh) is very small (Kumar et al., 2012) and is constantly on the decline, the ability of a large section of the rural people dependent on farming directly or indirectly to generate surplus and get the necessary skills to move up the economic ladder and increase their purchasing power in the near future is highly questionable.

This scenario suggests that a vast majority of the people would continue to live in rural areas with low incomes. This can threaten the sustainability of the very growth, which is witnessed in the country's economy in the past two decades, as it will not be broad-based. Therefore, the crisis may not be temporary and cannot be ignored.

---

[2] This is in lieu of the fact that most of the countries where the consumption levels are very high are already highly industrialized and India has to compete with these countries in terms of advanced technologies. The only possibility is that the underdeveloped countries of Africa grow rapidly to become major importers of manufacturing from India. This is also very unlikely.

1.2. EVOLUTIONARY DEVELOPMENT

From the Neolithic age (10000–800 BC) to neoliberal times of 1991 onwards, agriculture in India occupied a crucial place in the lives of the people and the development of its economy. Apart from providing food grains to the nation, it released labour, generated savings and promoted the markets of individual goods. In present times, agriculture has been instrumental in earning foreign exchange. This is the brighter as well as dark side of the country's economic growth.

Important chronological documentation of events and dates in early Indian history was poor. Sanskrit *sanhitas, puranas'* archaeological evidence and travelogues of foreign travellers form the basis of interpretations. India under the British rule got a chronology of historical events written by the Europeans, which after 1947 was corrected by several Indian scholars. This bears testimony to the existence of agriculture in the Indian subcontinent ever since 9000 BC with the domestication of wheat and barley plants and animals such as sheep, goats and elephants. A variety of tropical fruits such as muskmelon and mango were indigenous to India (Gulati, 2006). Rice was cultivated in the Indus Valley Civilisation (Dev, 2006). The *Encyclopedia Britannica* mentions that in the later Vedic texts (1000–500 BCE), references are replete on the cultivation of a wide range of cereals, vegetables and fruits. Milk and milk products were part of the diet. Animal husbandry was an important activity. The Vedic period had two segments: the first was the Bronze Age (3300–1300 BCE) which was the early Vedic period and the other was the Iron Age (1200–26 BC). In Rigveda, the economy was said to have been sustained (Basham, 2008) by the twin activities of pastoralism and agriculture.

The Indus Valley Civilisation, more correctly called the Indian–Saraswati River civilization, (Nene, 2012a) flourished in the current-day India and Pakistan. This civilization was most prosperous, produced surplus grain, and traded with countries in West Asia and North and East Africa (Kalyanaraman, 2000). Kautilya (321–296 BC) authored *Arthashastra*, a great remarkable treatise of the times on statecraft. It contains the *Varta*, the science of agriculture and animal husbandry, as one of the four sciences included in the book. The art of management of crops, sowing and plant protection, in addition to describing the advancements made in agriculture during those times, and the organizational roles of the agriculture administrators were all detailed in the book. References to agriculture were not restricted to the northern parts of the country but also extended to the southern region. *Tirukkural* (70 BC), a famous Tamil classic, had several comments on agriculture. With the decline of the Mauryan Empire, the Gupta dynasty ruled the country. Varahamihira wrote *Brihat-Samhita* (505–587 AD), which contains modes of detecting groundwater resources, predicting rainfall and guidelines for crop choices which were widely acclaimed by scholars.

Further, several texts in Sanskrit and other languages dealt with agriculture, horticulture and fauna. Irrigation and storage systems were built in India like in Mesopotamia, Egypt, Iran, China and Sri Lanka from the early period. Thus, glimpses of the fascinating accounts of the development of agriculture, which had parallels and adoptions in India from the advancements made elsewhere, show that it kept pace with the march of history.

The Arab Agricultural Revolution from 700 AD bloomed with a rapidly expanding Arab empire. The global economy brought in by Muslim traders across the old world enabled the diffusion of many crop and farming techniques among different parts of the Islamic world. The adoption of several crops such as mangoes, rice, cotton and sugarcane picked up throughout the Muslim-ruled areas. The revolution continued until 1300 AD.

The medieval period (200–1757 AD) saw economic prosperity during its early phase because of agriculture and export of agricultural products. In the early Middle Ages (200–1200 CE), methodical ploughing, weeding, manuring irrigation and crop safeguard were implemented for sustained agriculture (Stein, 2010). Frequent internal wars between states and losses incurred because of militants in the north and central regions adversely affected agriculture during the later phase. The zamindari system was developed as a state right into the king's superior ownership of the entire domain, but the concurrent, hereditary, permanent and long-established right of *khudkasta raiyats* (permanent resident cultivators of the village) was recognized during

Muslim rule. Land revenue was collected by local chiefs and lieges in addition to the officials of the state. Land revenue collection was initiated with Sher Shah Suri (1540–1545) and was perfected under the emperor Akbar (1556–1605; Mamoria, 1973).

The East India Company, which entered as a trading company, ruled India from 1757 to 1857. It was not interested in developing agriculture and was callous towards the country. It was mainly concerned with commerce and the collection of '*kappam*', a form of ransom from local rulers. This compelled Britain to take the reins in 1857. After a series of famines that haunted the country, the British Government established Famine Commissions (1880, 1898 and 1902) and Irrigation Commission (1903). Thus, some positive economic changes followed.

Since the early 18th century, there has been a gradual development in agricultural machinery, fertilizers, and the recognition of plant diseases. Indians from the late 17th century AD had used manure that they had innovated called '*Kunjapajala*' (Nene, 2012b). The latter Indian economic history provides pointers on the long-term dynamics of agricultural growth in the south Asia region. However, the 18th and 19th centuries saw sluggish growth of agriculture compared to the earlier growth in the preceding forty years.

The shift in the trajectory of economic growth and development efforts is worth recalling.

According to the best estimates available, India's national income increased between 1870 and 1914 at a rate of 1–2 percent per year, and per capita income at the rate of 0.5–1 percent per year. Simon Kuznet's calculations showed that the growth rate of national income ranged between 1.5 and 3.1 percent annually among the industrializing countries (except US, Japan, and Canada) in the late 19th century. Pre-war India was not far behind this standard. What made these other countries special was that growth was sustained there for a much longer period than in India. During the interwar period, India's rate of growth of per capita income declined to near zero. (Roy, 2006)

This resulted in a shift in economic growth in the second decade of the 20th century.

The growth of the manufacturing industry compensated for the slump in the agricultural growth to an extent that after the First World War, it was too small to offset the stagnation. The reminisces of early colonial rule were seen in the writings of freedom fighters, tourists, and some socialists. In the later period of British rule, they brought in some structural changes in Indian agriculture. This was reflected in the collection of the government share of revenue payment in cash. Major agriculture production was controlled by zamindars. Gradually, the British, in order to ward off neglect and high-handedness on their part, hurled the tenants into increased poverty. As part of reforms, the British also renovated a few irrigation canals and established a banking system to help farmers. A few agricultural research institutions and 95 agricultural colleges were established by them, including the Indian Agricultural Research Institute, Pusa, in 1936 (Mamoria, 1973).

Thus, the establishment of colleges and research institutes, providing lending facilities to farmers through banks and renovation of irrigation canals were some of the positive interventions the Britishers made towards improvements in the agricultural sector. However, the role of the British government remained as administrator and revenue collector, with no social responsibility and welfare concerns.

It took five years for India after Independence to slowly gear up for development activities in 1951. The Planning Commission was established to initiate planned development. During the first decade after 1951, the emphasis was laid on welfare goals and infrastructural works for rural development. The Community Development Programme was launched in 1952. The programme envisaged the development of rural areas through a concentration of efforts on individuals and primary cultivators and some changes in government administration at the district level and below. The programme's origin was in the early experiments, especially the Etawah project and Nilokheri Experiment of S. K. Dey in rehabilitating the refugees from Pakistan. Its thrust was the promotion of welfare in the villages. It was implemented along with National Extension Service to bring about a progressive outlook among people, promote cooperative action and enhance increased production and employment in rural areas. Thus, the first phase of development efforts focused on creating an egalitarian rural society. The strategy adopted was based on the recognition of the need for structural changes such as land reforms.

The model as it was implemented, however, was of low political intervention with a reformist thrust against an essentially semi-feudal, pro-capitalist peasant society. Therefore, without a radical transformation of the rural society, the Community Development Programme, National Extension Service and cooperatives did not make a substantive impact on rural life. Ideology was quite strong as reflected in the strategy, but lukewarm commitment at the implementation level minimized good results trickling from the programme. In the second phase of developmental efforts, during the 1960s, productivity goals dominated the planning. As the growth rate in the agricultural sector was not found satisfactory, in 1958, the Government of India approached Ford Foundation to examine the ways and means of increasing food production in the country. Their report entitled *India's Food Crisis and Steps to Meet It* identified pitfalls in food production. It suggested a programme entitled Intensive Agriculture Development Programme (IADP) to be introduced in 18 selected districts, based on a set of criteria (Taylor et al., 1965). This report, according to American and Indian experts, accurately hit every bull's eye of the programme or programmes which India needed if it was to attain the increase in agricultural production which it sought. These suggestions changed the direction and structure of development efforts by making them function on the basis of dominant goals.

While the community development strategy spread the resources thinly across all the areas, the IADP strategy was based on an intensive approach to maximize the gains through integrated efforts at the administrative, technical and financial fronts on areas which do not achieve a rapid increase in the levels of agricultural production. In only 3 of the 18 selected districts, perceptible changes in food grain yields were noticed (Brown, 1971). The lessons from IADP showed that creating irrigation potential and providing extension support were not sufficient to step up agricultural production (Mukherji, 1961). Hence, a high-yielding variety programme (HYVP) was introduced in IADP as a component of IADP, wherein seeds of high-yielding varieties (HYVs), chemical fertilizers, etc., were also provided as a package. Around this time, local pressures were building up in districts where IADP was not introduced for launching an identical agricultural development programme. These pressures resulted in starting the Intensive Agriculture Area Programme (IAAP) in as many as 114 districts, with an identical philosophy and approach to that of IADP.

The second decade, thus, saw the emergence of area-based programmes such as IADP, HYVP and IAAP, all aimed at accelerating technological change to induce output and productivity in the agricultural sector. The approach proved correct and resulted in the spread of the Green Revolution. The Green Revolution, a technological breakthrough in Indian agriculture, started in 1960 and with its success, the country attained food sufficiency within a decade. Around that time, new seed fertilizer irrigation technologies started to diffuse in tropical developing countries. The HYVs (Mexican semi-dwarf varieties) developed in CIMMYT in Mexico came in handy and were suitable for the climatic conditions in Punjab in northern India. The socio-economic conditions prevalent in the land consolidation programmes and private tube wells coming into existence have also given impetus to the Green Revolution. This was known as the first wave of the Green Revolution in India (Fujita, 2010). However, the 'lost decades' as they were called during the mid-1960s–mid-1980s (due to shortage of foreign exchange for import-substituting industrial sector and the earlier negligence of agriculture until the mid-1960s) made India pay a huge cost, which was considered as the 'Ricardian trap' in development economics (Hayami, 1997). Further, the first wave of the Green Revolution, though successful, could benefit only the wheat-growing areas of northern India such as Punjab, Haryana and western parts of Uttar Pradesh. The rural areas continued to be poor (Fujita, 2010).

The second wave of the Green Revolution in the 1980s witnessed impressive agricultural growth in India involving all crops, including rice, in the entire country. The major change had been the improvement of irrigation systems, with upstream storages allowing the cultivation of crops in the dry season, which in turn enabled intensification and specialization in the Green Revolution agriculture.

Then came the third phase of developmental efforts, where focused attention was given to those who could not derive benefit from the earlier developmental programmes. In 1970, a special agency called the Small Farmers Development Agency (SFDA) was established in 46 districts, following the advice of the All India Credit Rural Review Committee of the Reserve Bank of India. This programme was, in several ways, different from the earlier programmes. First, the difference was in the largely group-oriented approach. Second, in this programme, loans with a subsidy as financial assistance were given. Lastly, the focus of attention was to enable the small landholders to become viable, an approach which was not found in the past development efforts. Marginal farmers and landless labourers were also concurrently catered through yet another development programme called Marginal Farmers and Agricultural Labourers (MFAL) programme. The activities included under SFDA and MFAL programmes were minor irrigation schemes (wells), agricultural development, sheep rearing, goat rearing, fisheries, sericulture, dairying and the like. During the 1970s, attempts were made through development programmes to generate employment in rural areas. During 1971–1972, a Crash Scheme for Rural Employment (CSRE) was launched, which was later intensified under the Pilot Intensive Rural Employment Project (PIREP).

However, from the 1930s to the mid-1970s, real agricultural wages showed continued stagnation and the number of agricultural labourers increased. The historiographical explanations of class-cum-capital arguments could not shed much light on the agrarian crisis of the 1920s. Shrinking of the extent of land availability on the one hand and growing population on the other were attributed by some scholars as the reason for the looming crisis in the economic growth during this period. However, the interwar crisis was over by the late 1950s, when area, land productivity and cropping intensity were growing at a much better rate than in the earlier period. The trajectory of agricultural growth was accentuated with the development process and initiatives from the government in the 1950s through the 1970s (Sivamohan, 1990).

Further, ever since 1947 up till 1991, India chose an inward-looking restrictive form of governance, which in turn placed it in complete solitude. The economic crisis faced by the country by 1991 with depleted foreign currency reserves, inflation, Gulf War and oil shock crisis, all added up to a crisis of confidence among investors and even among government circles. The confronting debt default forced the then government to seek loans from IMF and World Bank on the latter's terms and conditions. Thus, the adoption of structural adjustment became imminent in the economic programmes of the time.

1.3. THE ERA OF PLANNING

Economic planning began in 1951; overall, 12 Five-Year Plans were prepared. Sixty-five years had achieved a spectacular development on the agricultural front in the country. The national Five-Year Plans and the planning process in the planned era reflect the policy approach of the government towards agriculture from time to time. A brief analysis of the approach in different plans shows how they also contributed to furthering agrarian crises. The First Plan (1951–1956) laid emphasis on agricultural development with a focus on avoiding farmers' exploitation, increasing the productivity of agriculture and initiating land reforms. This plan was said to be based on the Harrod–Domar model. The aim during the First Plan was to improve the living standards of people. The attention was on agriculture, irrigation and energy for restoring the disequilibrium created as a consequence of the Second World War.

The Second Plan period (1956–1961) saw the top priority given to industrial development. The impressive achievements of food grain production during the First Plan period left planners with a false notion that the country had already solved the food problem. For achieving balanced growth, prioritization of the industrial sector was considered. However, agriculture did not perform as well as the industry, which was also met with shortfalls. The meagre effort at agricultural development during this period led to a hoard of problems in the Indian economy. The Second Five-Year Plan was popularly known as the 'Mahalanobis plan'.

The initial phase of development in Indian agriculture witnessed large initiatives in agrarian reforms, institutional changes, construction of some major irrigation projects and cooperative credit made available to farmers. The second phase in the Indian agricultural development unfolded in the 1960s with the adoption of 'Green Revolution'. The Third Plan period (1961–1966) was in the context of shortfall in food grains and their continued imports. Thus, the plan's goal was fixed to create a self-reliant and self-generating economy. Hence, the focus fell in favour of the agricultural sector and targeted at doubling the growth rate in the production of food crops for internal consumption and commercial crops for increased exports. The Third Five-Year Plan was popularly known as 'Gadgil Yojana'.

However, the agricultural production expectations were severely hampered by unfavourable weather conditions during 1965–1969. The overall economy of the country suffered a severe setback because of two hostile wars that the nation faced: the first one with China (1962) and the other with Pakistan (1965). Drought conditions in several parts of the country also accentuated the economic crisis. These events delayed the planning process, and intermediate annual plans were formulated before the Fourth Five-Year Plan (1969–1974) came into operation. The three-year period (1966–1969) was declared as plan holiday to rectify the shortfalls that occurred in previous plan periods. The Fourth Plan (1969–1974) had two goals for agriculture: first to step up production and second to make small farmers, dry land farmers and agricultural labourers inclusive in the development process. Institutions were created to cater to target groups and areas as pointed earlier. The Fourth Plan period saw the nationalization of 14 private banks for expanding the functioning of the banking sector.

The Fifth Five-Year Plan (1974–1978) was formulated when the country was in a severe inflationary grip. This period started witnessing diversification, which resulted in fast growth in milk, fishery, poultry, and vegetable and fruit production, which accelerated growth in agricultural GDP (Chand, 2003). During this period, the 20-point programme was initiated in 1975 to boost development among various components in the agricultural sector. Boosting up agricultural production, irrigation level, soil and water conservation, flood control, fertilizer use, subsidies and rural roads were the components which found priority in the programme. Fertilizer subsidies were extended from the nitrogenous fertilizer to phosphatic and other complex fertilizers by 1979. The focus of the further plan was 'Garibi Hatao' (eradicate poverty), economic justice and agricultural development. Again, then came two annual plans under the name 'Rolling Plan'. However, this was discussed in 1980, and the Sixth Five-Year Plan was formulated (1980–1985). The Sixth Plan (1980–1985) prepared by the Indian National Congress after the change of government from Janata Party focused on poverty reduction to extend conditions for expanding the economy. Infrastructure development for agriculture and industry was sought to be strengthened.

A systems approach was adopted to deal with related aspects and a growth rate of 5.2 per cent per annum was anticipated and 5.4 per cent was achieved. The focus was on cash and non-cash crops and promotion of scientific use of land and water resources. The National Bank for Agriculture and Rural Development (NABARD) was established in 1982 for catering to credit for agriculture. The main focus of the Seventh Plan (1985–1990) was on policies and programmes for accelerating food grain production and increasing employment and per hectare yield. The programmes like Jawahar Rozgar Yojana and National Watershed Development Programme for Rainfed Areas were initiated and, for the first time, the private sector was given priority over the public sector in planning. The Eighth Five-Year Plan period (1992–1997) was for consolidation of gains made over the years and to look for agricultural efforts which were sustainable and promote exports. The use of fertilizer and extending benefits of the Green Revolution were given a big boost for expanding rainfed agriculture. This was a period in the worldwide philosophy of growth guided by market forces and liberal policies. The plan put emphasis on development of human resources.

The Ninth Plan period (1997–2002) targeted needed productive employment, poverty eradication, price stability, food and nutritional security to all, safe drinking water and promotion of rural public bodies for agriculture and rural development. The attention was on growth with justice and equity. The Tenth Plan (2002–2007), as far as agriculture is concerned, focused on the efficient use of soil and water and their conservation. Opportunities were provided for the promotion of agricultural exports in the wake of liberalization. The plan aimed to double per capita income in 10 years.

However, agriculture and allied sectors registered a mixed performance during this time. The objective of doubling the growth rate achieved in the Tenth Plan posed a challenge during the Eleventh Plan period to attain the target. The Eleventh Five-Year Plan (2007–2012) also gave priority to rainfed agriculture for increasing productivity to match strides with irrigated agriculture. Further, it aimed at rapid and more inclusive growth. An important target of the Twelfth Plan was to improve the efficiency of major and minor irrigation projects by 36 per cent (they were assessed to already have attained 30% efficiency) along with further reduction in the gap between irrigation potential created and utilized (GoI, 2011). It is clearly laid out in the last two Five-Year Plans that for the economy to grow at 9 per cent, it is necessary that agriculture should grow by at least 4 per cent per annum.

1.4. REVOLUTIONARY CHANGES IN AGRICULTURE

The policy of the new agricultural strategy devised by the government in the 1960s revolutionized agricultural production in India. India was among the first developing countries to adopt the Green Revolution in the mid-1960s. The decision to adopt this policy was triggered by severe drought conditions in 1966, which resembled a situation like in the early Independence days. Limited foreign exchange compelled India to seek grains and food from friendly countries. There were a host of factors responsible for the success of the Green Revolution which are as follows.

1. Irrigation potential was increased through the construction of major and medium irrigation projects. Dams were built to arrest large volumes of monsoon water, which until then were wasted and simple irrigation techniques were used to water the fields. This practice contributed to increased production in agriculture. The two decades of development which followed 1951 saw the creation of considerable irrigation potential through the construction of several major and medium irrigation projects.

   At the beginning of the planned era, the irrigation potential created through major and medium irrigation projects was 9.7 million hectare (Mha), and by the end of annual plans (1966–1969), it was 18.1 Mha.

Although this growth in irrigation potential was still inadequate in terms of the country's irrigation requirements, the rate of growth was most impressive, as it constituted over one-tenth of the world's total irrigated area (Jensen et al., 1990) at that time. The irrigation potential created in respect of major and medium projects increased from 9.70 Mha in the pre-plan period to 46.24 Mha (tentative), including 4.60 Mha anticipated to be created in the Eleventh Plan. In the corresponding period, the potential utilization has increased from 9.70 Mha to 35.10 Mha.

2. Adoption of HYVs of seeds provided the main scientific base for the success of the Green Revolution. Their discovery and use considerably raised crop productivity.

3. Improvement in cropping intensity (double-cropped area) was another important feature which appeared because of the Green Revolution. This was made possible on account of the early maturity of the HYV seeds which enabled the possibility of raising two or three crops in the same plot of land which was previously used for only one crop. While one season for the growth of crops was provided by the monsoon, the other came from the irrigation facilities.

4. Increased use of fertilizers helped significantly in increasing agricultural output.

5. Improved credit flow helped the farmers in need of timely financial requirements. Increased expenditure on inputs such as fertilizers and seeds warranted financial help to the farmer.

6. Plant protection measures by using pesticides were another important factor for the success of the Green Revolution. Under the plant protection scheme, the area increased from 17 Mha in 1965–1966 to 66 Mha in 1991–1992.

7. Expansion of area under cultivation was also an important factor which contributed to the success of the Green Revolution.

The major success of the Green Revolution was in the attainment of food self-sufficiency in India within a decade. The first Green Revolution which preceded the 1980s, according to some scholars

(Fujita, 2010), had critical importance as seen by the high growth rate registered. However, the first wave of the Green Revolution was confined to mainly the wheat crop in northern India such as Punjab, resulting in a limited contribution to the overall economic development of the country. On the contrary, the second wave of the Green Revolution saw growth in almost all crops and covered the whole country. This resulted in raising rural income and alleviation of poverty substantially. This raise of rural India as a market for non-agricultural products and services was vital for rapid economic growth after the 1990s.

The 'blow-hot, blow-cold' approaches taken by the Planning Commission towards issues in the agricultural sector in India have often led to crises situations in agricultural development. The following problems manifest this crisis.

1. The First Five-Year Plan was a success mainly because of agriculture, favourable monsoons, and the emphasis and priority given to agriculture. Its success developed complacency among the planners.
2. Quick yielding projects were not given the required impetus, and minor irrigation works did not receive adequate attention.
3. Plans provided for more unproductive expenditure.
4. Provision of inadequate rural credit haunted farmers. While the annual credit requirement of Indian farmers was estimated at ₹10,000–₹12,000 million, the provision made was only ₹35,000 million.
5. There was no coordinated provision for agricultural inputs for simultaneous production of inputs such as fertilizers, pesticides and cement.
6. New farming techniques were not enforced, and farming practices were not standardized.
7. There was a lack of a suitable price policy for farm output.
8. India was passing through a crisis of confidence. Planners did not provide any concrete measures to keep up the morale of the people.
9. Unrealistic planning was reflected in the non-realization of targets set for agriculture during the planning era.
10. There was an inordinate delay in undertaking land reforms.

1.5. POST-LIBERALIZATION EXPANSION

The recent phase of post-economic reforms is characterized by deregulation, reduced participation of government in economic activities and liberalization. However, the agricultural sector was affected by the devaluation of exchange rate, liberalization of external trade and withdrawal of protection to industry. During this period, opening up the domestic market due to a new international trade accord and WTO was another change which affected agriculture (Tripathi & Prasad, 2009). Because of the challenges imminent in this context, the new agricultural policy was launched in 2000 by the Government of India.

Since the inception of reforms, the Indian economy has achieved a tremendous growth rate. It is due to the excellent performance of the service sector and improvements in the secondary sector. However, this growth process bypassed the agricultural growth rate which recorded sharp deceleration. The Second Green Revolution mentioned earlier showed pathways towards this trend.

Reforms in the agricultural sector, in particular, came under severe criticism in the late 1990s, when 221 farmers in the South Indian state of Andhra Pradesh committed suicide. Agriculture employs 58 per cent of the Indian population today, yet its contribution to GDP is poor. Agricultural production fell by 12.6 per cent in 2003, one of the sharpest drops in independent India's history. Agricultural growth slowed from 4.69 per cent in 1991 to 2.6 per cent in 1997–1998 and 1.1 per cent in 2002–2003 (Directorate of Economics and Statistics, n.d.). This slowdown in agriculture is in contrast to the 6 per cent growth rate of the Indian economy for almost the whole of the past decade. Farmer suicides were 12 per cent of the total suicides in the country in 2000, the highest ever in independent India's history (unofficial estimates put them as high as 100,000 across the country, while government estimates are much lower at 25,000). This is largely because only those who hold the land title in their names are considered farmers, and this ignores women farmers who rarely hold land titles and other family members who run the farms.

Agriculture seems to be at an advanced stage of the crisis, with its most extreme manifestation in the rise in the number of suicides among farmers. Following are the probable reasons (Ahoy, 2016) for the same.

1. Seeds are crucial input for farmers and were purchased by them from government institutions across the country. The institutions were responsible for the quality, quantity, price and supply even to the hinterlands. With liberalization, markets were allowed to deal in seeds and, as a result, prices shot up. The presence of terminator seeds in the HYV seeds marketed prevented harvested seeds in the farms from germinating.

2. Farmers were encouraged to shift from growing a mixture of traditional crops to export-oriented cash crops. This required fertilizers whose prices soared by up to 300 per cent.

3. To open up India's markets, the reforms also withdrew duties and tariffs on imports.

4. There was non-availability of loans after 1991 and changes in lending pattern of commercial banks.

5. Overall, there is a reduction in government investments for rural development.

6. As a constituent of neoliberal policy, the government restricted public distribution system (PDS) by creating two groups—below and above poverty line—and continuously increased prices.

7. The government acquired 5 Mha of (often) fertile land for special economic zones as part of the economic reforms. These lands are intended for commercial and industrial purposes.

The agrarian sector in India is also at the root of other socio-economic crises that the country has seen. The examples cited by the magazine (*Resurgent India*, 2016) are struggles over the Land Acquisition Act and uprisings by caste-based communities dependent on a stagnating agricultural sector such as the Jat agitation in Haryana and Maratha region in Maharashtra. The Dalit agitation is also assuming economic proportions, as the causes of unrest among Dalits are increasingly being linked to the deprivation of their land titles. In terms of environmental factors, the agricultural sector is the worst affected by the current environmental crisis, be it the crisis of water, climate change or land degradation.

1.6. RATIONALE FOR THE BOOK

Agrarian change in India has been analysed in the past from various perspectives. They include problems and challenges induced by different agrarian structures (feudal, ryotwari, permanent settlement, etc.); various modes of production (feudal, capitalist and socialist); challenges posed by unfavourable situation vis-à-vis various factors of production such as water scarcity, land scarcity, limited access to inputs and production technologies; environmental externalities inducted on production; externalities induced by the changing market conditions; and growing risks and indebtedness among farmers.

Notwithstanding their limitations, there has been an enormous volume of scholarly work done during the past five decades, looking at the agrarian change from the perspective of modes of production and agrarian structure, largely corresponding to the colonial and pre-colonial era. However, there has been too little comprehensive work looking at the problems from the perspective of limits induced by land scarcity and water stress, changing dynamics with respect to the cost of various inputs affected by changing subsidy structure, and externalities induced by the changing environmental and market conditions.

While the former (i.e., looking at agrarian change from the perspective of modes of production and agrarian structure) required the use of disciplines such as sociology and anthropology, the latter required systematic engagement with agricultural economics. The latter also required comparative analysis of regions with distinct physical (agroecology, water availability, land availability and climate), socio-economic environment (overall economic conditions of the farmers and infrastructure and market conditions), as all of them have bearing on the profitability of farming.

Vast differences in agro-climatic conditions, resource endowment, socio-economic conditions and landholding pattern among regions, and more importantly the differences in growth trajectory witnessed by these regions, make it imperative that research on agrarian crisis in the sector looked at individual regions rather than the aggregate-level scenario of the country. The dairy sector emerged as a major contributor to agricultural growth in India. Its contribution to farm income, especially that of small and marginal farmers, should be assessed and considered carefully. More importantly, the role of livestock in making the farming system resilient to production and market risks and averting crisis in farm sector needs to be carefully analysed. Obviously, analysis carried out for one region will not hold good for another region. The extensive review of published literature validates this argument about the disciplinary bias and lack of regional focus in research on agrarian transformation.

1.7. OBJECTIVES AND SCOPE OF THE BOOK

Currently, the following features characterize the picture of growing agrarian crisis in India. First, the overall profitability in farming is reported to be declining. Second, farming is increasingly becoming a risky enterprise, with increasing production, technology, credit and market-related risks. Third, with the declining size of operational holding, the average potential surplus from farming is becoming insignificant. Fourth, there is growing disinterest and lack of motivation among the rural youth in farming, with a resultant increase in the average age of population engaged in farming and consequent lack of ability to make 'state-of-the-art' technologies and equipment for farm modernization. There is a need to examine the root cause of this vexing phenomenon.

Investigating deep into the causes of the crisis, the analyses presented in the book are not only based mainly on primary data collected from four different agroecological regions in the country, from four major states, namely West Bengal, Gujarat, Andhra Pradesh and Maharashtra, but are also backed by analysis of macro-level secondary data on the changing characteristics of Indian agriculture. Using the analysis, five chapters of the book (Chapters 5–9) together address the following research questions: 1. To what extent have physical factors such as resource depletion and degradation of primary productivity of land

and changing weather patterns contributed to the current agrarian crisis in India? 2. To what extent have socio-economic factors such as increasing employment opportunities in the non-farm occupations in the rural as well as urban areas and outward movement of people from rural areas to urban areas as a result of better education and declining size of operational holdings and better wages contributed to the crisis? 3. To what extent have the institutional and policy factors such as reduction in input subsidies, globalization of agriculture and creation of non-farm employment through legislative measures and crop insurance precipitated or reduced the crisis?

In the wake of the current transformation of the agricultural sector, the book also discusses the drivers of future agricultural growth and the key features of the emerging farming systems; the technologies that act as drivers of change in agricultural output and are capable of improving the input use efficiency and reducing the production related risks and their cost implications; the institutional approaches which can reduce the market risks associated with the emerging farming systems; and the role of financial sector in boosting technology adoption and reducing market risks in farming. The book then explores the broad physical strategies for sustaining agricultural growth in India which are centred on low-cost irrigation development in water-abundant regions, increasing the effective availability of water for agriculture through water transfers, water harvesting in the naturally water-rich hilly regions and water productivity improvements in agriculture. It also looks at institutional measures for changing the trajectory of water use in agriculture.

1.8. CONTENTS OF THE BOOK

The book has 12 chapters. In Chapter 2, we present the results of extensive analysis of secondary data with regard to the changing characteristics of India's agricultural sector since the early 1950s with regard to some key attributes. They are per capita land and water availability, land use, average growth rates in agriculture, cropping pattern, level of seed production, levels of fertilizer use for various crops, degree of farm mechanization and labour use, real wage rates, extent of agricultural subsidies, electricity consumption in agriculture, average crop and milk yields and value of agricultural outputs in real terms. The purpose of the analysis was to identify the different points of occurrence of crisis in the history of agriculture post Independence, as well the opportunities for boosting agricultural growth in the country.

The analyses based mainly on the primary data collected from four different agroecological regions in the country, from four major states, namely West Bengal, Gujarat, Andhra Pradesh and Maharashtra, address the following research questions: 1. To what extent have physical factors such as resource depletion and degradation, primary productivity of land and changing weather patterns contributed to the current agrarian crisis in India? 2. To what extent have socio-economic factors such as increasing employment opportunities in the non-farm occupations in the rural as well as urban areas and outward movement of people from rural areas to urban areas as a result of better education and declining size of operational holdings and better wages contributed to the crisis? 3. To what extent have the institutional and policy factors such as reduction in input subsidies, globalization of agriculture and creation of non-farm employment through legislative measures and crop insurance precipitated or reduced the crisis? 3. To what extent does the very nature of the crisis in agriculture change from region to region?

In the wake of the current transformation of the agricultural sector, the book also discusses the drivers of future agricultural growth and the key features of the emerging farming systems; the technologies which act as drivers of change in agricultural output and are capable of improving the input use efficiency and reducing the production related risks and their cost implications; the institutional approaches which can reduce the market risks associated with the emerging farming systems; and the role of the financial sector in boosting technology adoption and reducing market risks in farming. The book then explores the broad physical strategies for sustaining agricultural growth in India which are centred on low-cost irrigation development in water-abundant regions, increasing the effective availability of water for agriculture through water transfers, water harvesting in the naturally water-rich hilly regions and water productivity improvements in agriculture. It also looks at institutional measures for changing the trajectory of water use in agriculture.

But before venturing into the empirical research on the agrarian crisis, we investigated the primary factors driving annual agricultural growth rates in the country. Such an investigation was found necessary as a lot of emphasis has been placed on annual agricultural growth rates. More importantly, much has been made out of the exceptionally high agricultural growth rates witnessed over short time periods in certain Indian states such as Gujarat and Madhya Pradesh, with some researchers and policymakers calling them 'miracle growth' due to institutional and policy reforms in the sector and calling out other states to emulate. The main point of enquiry here was whether there are factors other than these which determine short-term growth rates and to what extent those factors can influence long-term growth rates. The results of these analyses are presented in Chapter 3 of the book.

Chapter 4 of the book is based on an extensive review of published literature on the performance of post-Independence Indian agriculture. It presents the outcomes of the review in a structured manner, synthesizes them and identifies some of the key knowledge gaps vis-à-vis the changing scenario of agriculture as an enterprise, that is, changing profitability of farming. While undertaking the review, highly localized studies which consider a few districts or a state as the unit of analysis and also those not done on a significant time scale are excluded. This is followed by description of the approach, methodology and analytical procedures used for the field studies in the next section.

Chapters 5–8 of the book are based on the extensive field research conducted by the Institute for Resource Analysis and Policy in 2014–2015. The study involved the use of a new conceptual framework and empirical methods. It was grounded in four agroecological regions from four states in India, namely Gujarat, Andhra Pradesh, Maharashtra and West Bengal, on the theme of agrarian crisis. The locations covered were Palanpur district in semi-arid and alluvial north Gujarat; districts of Hooghly and North 24 Parganas in West Bengal; West Godavari district of Coastal Andhra Pradesh; and Chandrapur district in the semi-arid, hard rock area of Vidarbha region in Maharashtra.

From these four regions, five districts were selected for undertaking a household survey for collecting socio-economic data and details of the farming enterprise, including inputs, outputs and prices. Among selected districts, the highest geographical area is for district Banaskantha (12,703 km²) followed by Chandrapur (10,695 km²), West Godavari (7,742 km²), North 24 Parganas (4,094 km²) and Hooghly (3,149 km²). The district of North 24 Parganas had the highest population density. Low population density was observed in Banaskantha and Chandrapur. While the former is a semi-arid and naturally water-scarce region, the latter is a dry and physically water-scarce region. However, Banaskantha has registered the highest decadal (from 2001 to 2011) population growth rate (19.6%) among the selected districts.

Longitudinal analysis involving time-series data of farm inputs, outputs and throughputs at the level of individual farms was carried out to understand the changes in agricultural production situation from the point of view of farming as an economic enterprise. Each of the four regions had a unique 'agro-climatic and socio-economic setting' which enabled analysis of the influence of these factors on the nature and magnitude of the crisis. The time frame considered was 35 years, beginning in 1980. The time-series data were obtained from the farm households using recall method. From each region, a total of five villages were chosen for the field investigation. A total of 526 households were chosen for the survey. The five villages from each location were selected in such a way that they together represent the unique characteristics of the region by capturing the variations in agro-climate, geo-hydrology, land holdings and overall socio-economic conditions.

A range of analytical procedures was used to estimate the changes in net income from farming over time; opportunity cost of engaging in farming operations for the farm households; size of operational holdings of farmers over time; and risk involved in farming. The study went beyond assessing the economics of major crops, covered all the crops grown by the surveyed farmers, and also analysed the inputs, outputs and return from dairy farming, which is increasingly becoming an integral part of the farming activity in agriculturally prosperous regions.

The study assessed the magnitude of the crisis and the physical, socio-economic, institutional and policy factors causing it. Farming risks were assessed considering the physical and socio-economic factors causing a crisis in the sector in the selected regions. The impacts of institutional and policy factors on the cost of inputs, improvement in infrastructure on procurement and marketing, and legislative measures on the creation of non-farm employment were also analysed. Based on these analyses, the institutional and policy measures for mitigating the crisis were suggested for each region.

Chapter 9 of the book synthesizes the main results from the four location studies, compares the agricultural performance of these states, distils the key findings and draws useful conclusions. The findings are with regard to the regions that face the most severe crisis and the physical, socio-economic, institutional and policy factors causing an agrarian crisis. The conclusions drawn are in terms of the key strategic interventions for improving the sustainability of agricultural production in distinct agroecological regions.

Chapter 10 discusses the strategies for improving the efficiency of use of inputs, including irrigation water in agriculture and institutional mechanisms for achieving them. It particularly looks at the specific technological and institutional interventions required to reduce production and market risks in farming in the wake of the transformation in the farming system characterized by a shift towards high-value fruits and vegetables and cash crops. It closely examines the role of the financial institutions for raising technology adoption and reducing market risks through farm loans linked to crop insurance, insurance products designed on the basis of market risks and subsidies linked to adoption of efficient technology and resource use.

Chapter 11 first takes a look at some of the current priorities of the government by examining its policies and programmes and identifies the lacuna. It then discusses the long-term strategies for promoting sustainable agricultural growth in India, with a focus on regions that are agroecologically very distinct. The strategies explored are physical/technical, institutional and policy-related in nature.

The concluding chapter (Chapter 12) summarizes the key findings from each chapter.

REFERENCES

Ahoy, P. (2016). Agrarian crises in India: An aftermath of the new economic reforms. *International Journal of Sociology and Social Anthropology, 1(*1), 91–98.

Basham, A. L. (2008). *The wonder that was India: A survey of the history and culture of the Indian subcontinent before the coming of Muslims.* Scholarly Publishing Office, University of Michigan.

Brown, D. D. (1971). *Agricultural development in India's districts.* Harvard University Press.

Chand, R. (2003). *Government intervention in food grain markets in changing context* [Policy Paper No. 19]. National Centre for Agricultural Economics and Policy Research.

Dev, S. M. (2006). Agricultural labour and wages since 1950. In S. Wolpert (Ed.), *Encyclopaedia of India* (Vol. 1). Thomson Gale.

Directorate of Economics and Statistics. (n.d.) http://eands.dacnet.nic.in/latest_AT_Glance.htm

Fujita, K. (2010). *The Green Revolution and its significance for economic development: Implications for sub-Saharan Africa.* Japan International Cooperative Agency.

GoI. (2011). *Report of working group on major and medium irrigation and command area development for the XII plan (2012–17).*

GoI. (2014). *Economic survey of India 2013.* Ministry of Finance.

Gulati, A. (2006). Agricultural growth and diversification since 1991. In S. Wolpert (Ed.), *Encyclopaedia of India* (Vol. 1). Thomson Gale.

Hayami, Y. (1997). *Development economics: From poverty to the wealth of nations.* Oxford University Press.

Jensen, M. E., Rangeley W. R., & Dieleman P. J. (1990). Irrigation trends in world agriculture. In: Irrigation of Agricultural Crops. American Society of Agronomy, Madison, Wisconsin, pp. 31-67.

Kalyanaraman, S. (2000). *Sarasvati.* Babasaheb (Umakant Keshav) Apte Samarak Samiti.

Kumar, M. D., Sivamohan, M. V. K., & Bassi, N. (Eds.). (2012). *Water management, food security and sustainable agriculture in developing economies.* Routledge.

Mamoria, C. B. (1973). *Agriculture problems in India.* Kitab Mahal.

Mukherji, B. (1961). *Community development in India.* Orient Longmans.

Nene, Y. L. (2012a). Environment and spiritualism: Integral parts of ancient Indian literature on agriculture. *Asian Agri-History, 16(*2), 123–141.

Nene, Y. L. (2012b). Significant milestones in evolution of agriculture in the world. *Asian Agri-History, 16(3),* 219–235.

Resurgent India. (2016). *The Agrarian Crisis in India: Introduction.* new.resurgentindia.org/the-agrarian-crisis-in-India-indroduction/, October issue.

Roy, T. (2006). Roots of agrarian crisis in interwar India: Retrieving a narrative. *Economic & Political Weekly, 41(52),* 5389–5400.

Sivamohan, M. V. K. (1990). *Management process in development, with reference to Nagarjuna Sagar Right Canal Command Area Development Authority* [PhD Thesis]. Nagpur University, Nagpur.

Stein, B. (2010). *A history of India* (2nd ed., revised and edited by D. Arnold). Wiley-Blackwell.

Taylor, C. C., Ensminger, D., Johnson, H. W., & Joyce, J. (1965). *India's roots of democracy: A sociological analysis of rural India's experience in planned development since Independence*. Orient Longman.

Tripathi, A., & Prasad, A. R. (2009). Agricultural development in India since Independence: A study on progress, performance, and determinants. *Journal of Emerging Knowledge on Emerging Markets, 1*(1), 63–92.

Chapter 2

Changing Landscapes in Indian Agriculture

V. Niranjan, M. Dinesh Kumar,
M. V. K. Sivamohan and Saurabh Kumar

2.1. INTRODUCTION

A lot has changed in Indian agriculture since Independence. The
changes are related to the following: the ecological environment
(condition of water and land resources); the socio-economic environment governing agricultural production (production relations, labour
supply and real wage rates, average size of landholdings, and access
to irrigation facilities, various input technologies and technologies to
control production environment), processing (various post-harvest
technologies), storage (cold storages) and marketing (types and sizes
of produce markets and ease in accessing the markets); institutional
environment governing input supply (supply outlets for seeds, fertilizers
and pesticides, and agencies supplying electricity and irrigation water),
production and marketing (institutional avenues available for selling the
produce and the laws that are in force); and the policy environment
relating to input supply, input prices (water pricing policy, electricity pricing policy, fertilizer pricing policy, etc.) and marketing of the
crop produce.

The purpose of this chapter is to discuss the changing parameters
of agricultural production in India since Independence, especially after
1950–1951, the resultant outcome in terms of quantum of food grain

and other agricultural outputs, and the value of agricultural production. The analysis considered several variables at the macro level such as per capita arable land, per capita renewable water resource, irrigation facilities, farm mechanization, input use (seed, labour, machines, fertilizers and irrigation), cropped area and cropping pattern, livestock population, extent of irrigation, crop technologies, energy consumption, farm wage rates, yield of major crops, especially cereals, and milk yield, and agricultural outputs, especially food grain outputs and average growth rates in agricultural GDP.

2.2. NATURAL RESOURCE ENDOWMENT AND LAND USE PATTERN

Land and water are two important natural resources essential for the very living of beings. In India, the distribution of water and land resources has wide interregional variation. An annual conference of Cornell and Syracuse on 'Agrarian Crisis in India' held at Cornell University (Cornell University, 2013) aptly put the importance of land and water in the agrarian crisis. Much of the agrarian discourse is about the land in terms of control, methods of cultivation, interconnections with social standing and power, dependence on state structures, and help. Yet water is equally vital and central to all these issues. Land does not disappear, whereas water often does. Water shows clear signs of crisis due to droughts, floods and cyclones.

The land, soils and water are classified into low endowment (LE), medium endowment (ME), high endowment (HE), very high endowment (VHE) and super rich endowment (SRE) categories based on the geographical characteristics of their respective distribution in India (Karennavar & Haremath, 1990). The classification is presented in Table 2.1.

Further, six of the important classified soil groups and their distribution in India along with their dominant features are presented in Table 2.2.

The net sown area (NSA) had risen by 18.44 per cent from 1950–1951 to 2000–2001. It was only 46 per cent of the total reporting area by 2000 and slightly decreased to 45.81 per cent during 2009–2010.

Table 2.1 *Distribution and Endowments of Natural Resources in India*

Endowment	Water	Land	Soil
Very high endowment (VHE)	Maharashtra	Andhra Pradesh	Rajasthan
			Andhra Pradesh
High endowment (HE)	Bihar	Assam	Meghalaya
	Karnataka	Jammu and Kashmir	Nagaland
		Tamil Nadu	Tripura
		West Bengal	Uttar Pradesh
		Union Territory	Assam
			Himachal Pradesh
			Jammu and Kashmir
			Kerala
			Manipur
Medium endowment (ME)	Andhra Pradesh	Bihar	Bihar
	Gujarat	Gujarat	Gujarat
	West Bengal	Karnataka	Karnataka
		Odisha	
Low endowment (LE)	Punjab	Haryana	Odisha
	Meghalaya	Himachal Pradesh	Punjab
	Nagaland	Kerala	West Bengal
	Odisha	Manipur	Haryana
	Sikkim	Meghalaya	
	Tamil Nadu	Nagaland	
	Tripura	Punjab	
	Kerala	Sikkim	
	Manipur	Tripura	

(Continued)

Table 2.1 *(Continued)*

Endowment	Water	Land	Soil
	Jammu and Kashmir		
	Himachal Pradesh		
	Haryana		
	Assam		
Super rich endowment (SRE)	Union Territory	Madhya Pradesh	Madhya Pradesh
	Uttar Pradesh	Rajasthan	Uttar Pradesh
	Madhya Pradesh	Uttar Pradesh	Maharashtra

Source: Based on Karennavar and Haremath (1990).

The barren and uncultivable land shrunk from 37,484 thousand hectares to 17,709. Both the cultivable and fallow land had also decreased during this period. Yet the total available cultivable waste and fallow lands are 4.4 per cent and 4.8 per cent in the total reported land, indicating that there is a scope to further increase the NSA. The fallow lands are distributed across the country but have a great concentration in the states of Bihar, Andhra Pradesh, Rajasthan and Karnataka. The changes in the temporal and spatial distribution of fallow land are explained as occurring due to variability in precipitation and irrigation water and low level of mechanization (Pandey & Ranganathan, 2018). However, a marginal increase seen in the land area under cultivation is at the cost of the undesirable consequences for the ecological sector which is observed due to the expansion of land for non-agricultural uses mostly diverted from ecological uses. The interstate sectoral changes show such patterns in Haryana, Karnataka, Kerala, Maharashtra, Uttar Pradesh, West Bengal and Himachal Pradesh. In Odisha and Himachal Pradesh, the changes were at the cost of either ecological or non-agricultural sectors or both. The expansion of fallow lands was seen as a consequence of erratic rainfall and poor mechanization.

Table 2.2 *Distribution of Soils in India*

Soil	Area (Mha)	States	Features
Alluvial	142.5	Northern areas extending from Rajasthan to West Bengal	Generally suitable for irrigation
Black	60.3	Madhya Pradesh, Maharashtra, Karnataka, Andhra Pradesh, Tamil Nadu and Odisha; also found in West Bengal, Bihar, Uttar Pradesh and Rajasthan	Have high water-retaining capacity; some of them tend to become alkaline and saline after the introduction of irrigation
Red	49.8	Tamil Nadu, Karnataka, Andhra Pradesh, Madhya Pradesh, Bihar and Odisha	Low in moisture, retaining capacity and good permeability; react well to irrigation
Desert	14.6	Western Rajasthan	Sandy and poor in fertility
Laterites	12.1	In heavy rainfall areas of Kerala, Madhya Pradesh, Andhra Pradesh, Assam, Bihar and Odisha	Have relatively low organic matter content, low primary minerals and accumulation of sesquioxide
Forest soils	28.1	Madhya Pradesh, Andhra Pradesh, Bihar and Maharashtra	Deposition of organic matter

Source: Siddiqui, S. A., and Fatima, N. (2017).

2.3. PER CAPITA LAND AND WATER AVAILABILITY

The per capita land and water availability are declining alarmingly in India (Figure 2.1 and Figure 2.2, respectively). While the important reasons for the continuous decline are population growth, urbanization, non-availability of land and water, and land for other growing needs, land degradation and water depletion are commonly experienced problems in ecologically and environmentally stressed parts of the country. From 1951 to 2001, the per capita land availability consistently declined from 0.9 ha to 0.3 ha. By 2035, it is projected to be at 0.1 ha. The per capita water availability trend is no better than land availability scenarios from 1951 to 2001; it reduced from 5,177 m³ per year to 1,820 m³ per year. The average annual per capita water availability in the year 2011 was assessed to be 1545 cubic meters (Ministry of Jal Shakti, 2021). Many water-rich areas have very low per capita arable land and vice versa. While this is the average figure, what is more important is the regional variation. There are many regions where per capita renewable water availability is very low, and where 70 per cent of the water is concentrated in the Ganges–Brahmaputra–Meghna (GBM) basin (Kumar et al., 2012).

As per a report of the Central Ground Water Board (CGWB) on groundwater resource assessment and irrigation potential in India, the regions facing problems of groundwater over-exploitation are mostly concentrated in: (i) the north western part of the country including parts of Punjab, Haryana, Delhi and Western Uttar Pradesh where even though the replenishable resources are abundant, there has been indiscriminate withdrawal of ground water leading to over-exploitation; (ii) the western part of the country, particularly in parts of Rajasthan and Gujarat, where due to arid climate, ground water recharge itself is limited, leading to stress on the resource and (iii) the southern part of peninsular India including parts of Karnataka, Andhra Pradesh, Telangana and Tamil Nadu where due to inherent aquifer properties of crystalline aquifers, the ground water availability is low (CGWB, 2019). The naturally water-rich regions are those which experience medium to high rainfall and low evaporation. Hence, Eastern India, the eastern part of Central India, Western Ghats and the Northeast come into this category. Their water demands would be driven by the total

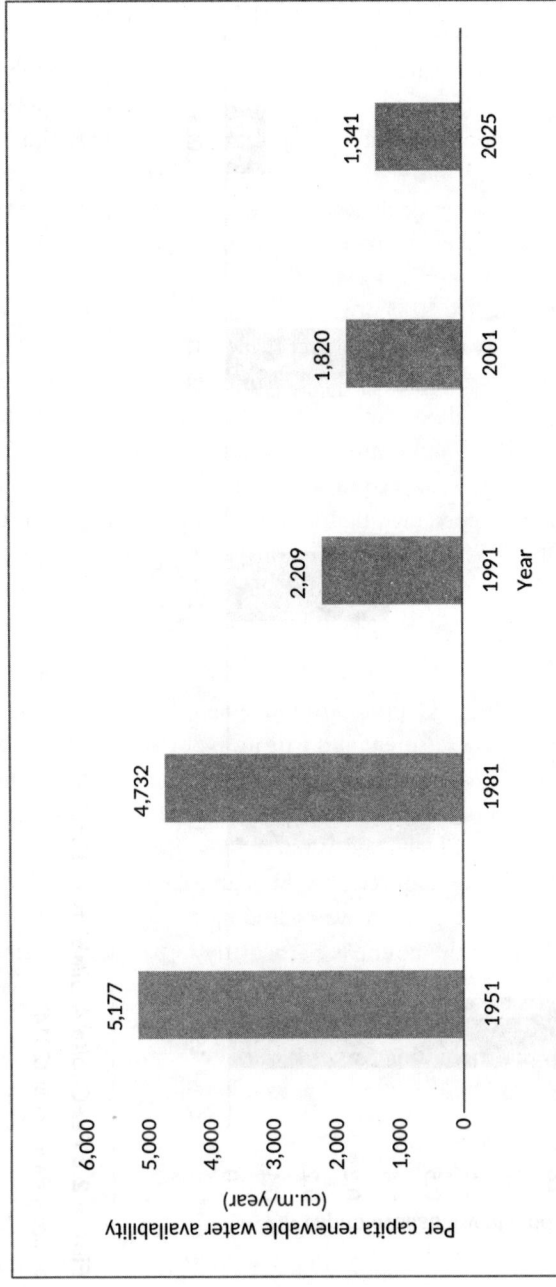

Figure 2.1 *Per Capita Renewable Water Availability in India*

Source: Ministry of Jal Shakti (2021). Per Capita Availability of Water, Posted on 25th March, 2021 by PIB, Delhi. https://pib.gov.in/PressReleaseIframePage.aspx?PRID=1707522

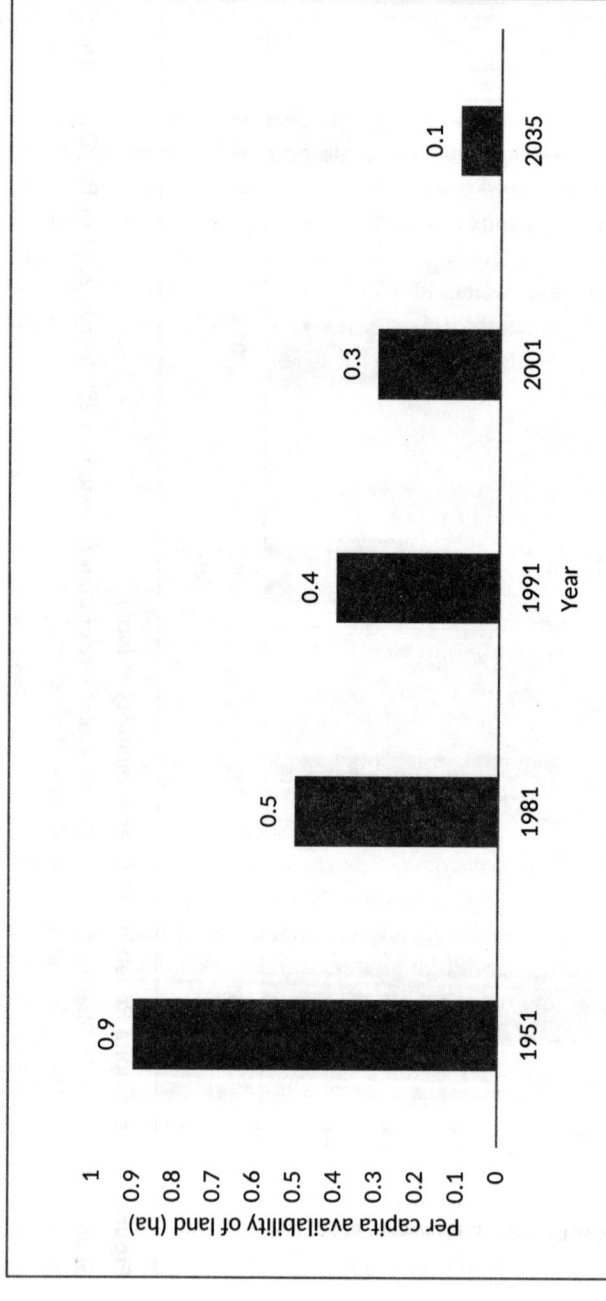

Figure 2.2 *Per Capita Availability of Land (Ha)*
Source: Ravisankar (2014).

amount of arable land and the number of times it can be put to use in a year, rather than the total food demand. The reason for this is that land, rather than water, is the limiting factor. Aggregate demand for water in agriculture in these regions is a function of the land available for cultivation. If we assume the same cropping pattern, reference evapotranspiration can be a good basis for comparison (Kumar et al., 2012). The area per capita of cultivated land is high in regions which are physically water-scarce and low in regions which are water-rich. For instance, the per capita cultivated land in the water-scarce states of Rajasthan, Punjab and Karnataka are 0.38 ha, 0.334 and 0.233 ha, respectively, whereas in the water-rich states of Bihar and Kerala, it is only 0.09 ha (Kumar, 2003).

The policy decision of the West Bengal government to offer subsidized power connections to farmers is an illustrative example of how misguided policies could produce unintended outcomes. It was based on the aggressive lobbying by some researchers that the abundant groundwater in West Bengal and other parts of Eastern India could be exploited by the many millions of small and marginal farmers who do not have direct access to wells for irrigation, that it would bring about agrarian change and poverty reduction (Mukherji, 2003, 2006, 2008; Mukherji et al., 2012; Shah, 2001) and that limiting exploitation of groundwater has a huge opportunity cost (Mukherji et al., 2012). However, due to the limited amount of arable land and with a much smaller proportion of it lying unirrigated and the high rainfall, there are major limitations on the extent to which groundwater use for agriculture could be intensified in West Bengal. This aspect has been completely ignored by these researchers. Kumar et al. (2014) had shown that such subsidized power connections without targeting the poor would only benefit the large diesel well owners, who could replace their old diesel engines with electric pumps, thereby being able to pump groundwater at much lower costs and sell at prohibitive prices to the small and marginal farmers in their neighbourhood to make large profits.

Yet further exploitation of groundwater in West Bengal should be done with utmost care. The reason is that a small increase in groundwater pumping can play havoc with the region's water ecology, as thousands of wetlands also receive their inflows from shallow aquifers. Lowering of the water table of shallow aquifers during winter–summer seasons, when agricultural water demand actually picks up, can result in the temporary drying up of the shallow wetlands. This will have a huge impact on very poor families. The reason as pointed out by Mukherjee et al. (2010) is that the poor farmers depend on these water bodies not only for domestic water supplies and irrigation but also for fish, which is a major source of protein. Clearly, the negative externalities of such approaches were ignored. Hence, if the policy of subsidized power connections for agriculture is implemented in West Bengal, it would become the classical case of private benefits at huge public costs.

Arguments about recharging the aquifers during monsoon using schemes such as the National Rural Employment Guarantee Scheme (Verma & Shah, 2012) do not hold much water, as the aquifers are fully replenished and do not have much storage space during monsoon months. In a state which is endowed with a large number of small water bodies (wetlands) which function as natural recharge systems, why should one invest so much money for exploiting groundwater and then recharging? Instead, if these wetlands are well managed, the poor farmers can tap water from these small water bodies for irrigation at a much lower cost. The obsession with the idea of achieving 100 per cent utilization of natural recharge can only be attributed to the poor understanding of how groundwater systems interact with wetlands. As is now understood, the concept of 'groundwater overdevelopment' is complex and linked to various 'undesirable consequences' which are physical, social, economic, ecological, environmental and ethical in nature (Custodio, 2000). Therefore, an assessment of groundwater overdevelopment involves hydrological, hydrodynamic, economic, social and ethical considerations (Kumar & Singh, 2008; Kumar et al., 2012).

2.4. AGRICULTURAL GROWTH

Figure 2.3 presents the trends in agricultural GDP in India from 1954–1955 to 2012–2013 and the changing contribution of agriculture to India's overall GDP during that period. The agricultural outputs in value

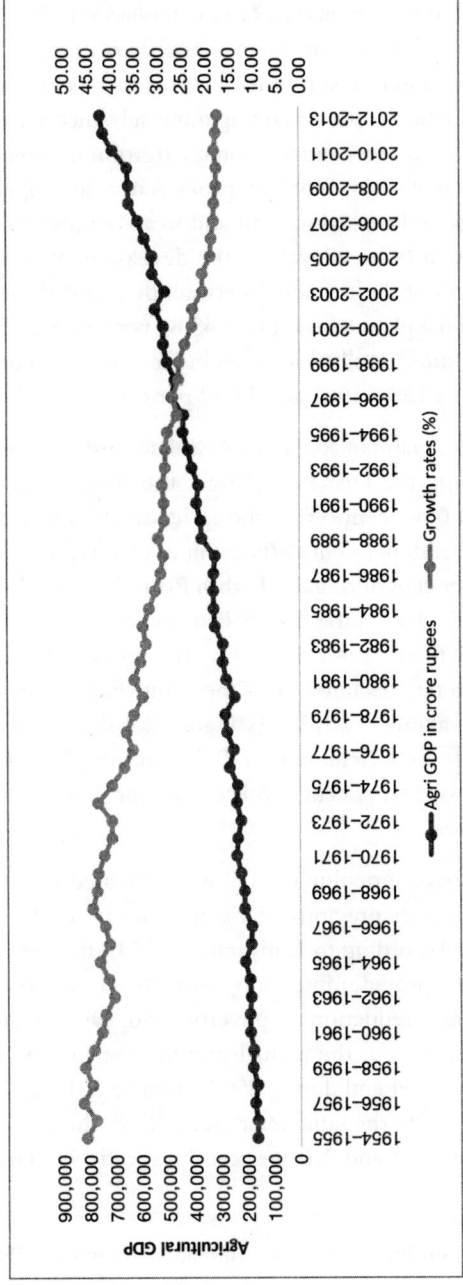

Figure 2.3 *Agricultural GDP and Contribution of Agriculture to India's GDP*

Source: Ministry of Statistics and Programme Implementation (2021).

terms grew from ₹1683.61 billion to ₹7645.10 billion[1] in 2012–2013 in
real terms, with significant variations in annual growth rates (Kumar et
al., 2019). The creation of institutional support and technology interventions through hybrid seeds, providing input subsidies (for fertilizers,
pesticides, water, seeds, etc.) and widening irrigation facilities through
the operationalizing of major irrigation projects have all helped to stem
the deceleration of agricultural growth and steadily build it up till the
early 20th century in India. However, the development of secondary
and territory sectors of the economy persistently eclipsed the share of
agriculture during the planned era. From 45.86 per cent in 1955–1956,
the share of agriculture and allied activities in GDP at factor costs dipped
to 35.39 per cent in 1980–1981 and 17.52 per cent in 2012–2013.

As regards growth rates in agricultural GDP against the overall GDP
growth rates, during the First Plan period, the annual average GDP
growth rate was 3.6 per cent, while the agricultural GDP growth rate
was a little less at 2.88 per cent. While the overall GDP growth rate
increased to 6.7 per cent during the Eighth Plan, the agricultural GDP
was 4.78 per cent. During the Tenth Plan period, while the annual
average GDP growth rate was 7.8 per cent, the agricultural GDP average annual growth rate declined to 2.5 per cent (Figure 2.4, based on
Sharma, 2012; Sivakumar, 2013). As Figure 2.4 shows, overall, the
annual growth rate in agricultural GDP (during the Five-Year Plan
periods) never crossed 6 per cent, while during the Third Plan period,
it was even negative.

The growth rate of agricultural GDP was estimated at 1.9 per cent
during 2012–2013 over previous year's growth rate of 3.6 per cent
(NCAER, 2013). According to Rangarajan (2014), the period 1993–
1994 to 2011–2012 provides interesting insights into the relationship
between growth and reduction in poverty ratio. During the period
1993–1994 to 2004–2005, the annual growth rate in the per capita
income was 6.9 per cent and during 2004–2005 to 2011–2012, it was
10.55 per cent.[2] During the same reference period, the poverty ratios
declined by 0.7 per cent and 2.18 per cent, respectively. The Second

---

[1] US$1 equals to ₹70.

[2] Estimates based on https://www.macrotrends.net/countries/IND/india/
gdp-per-capita

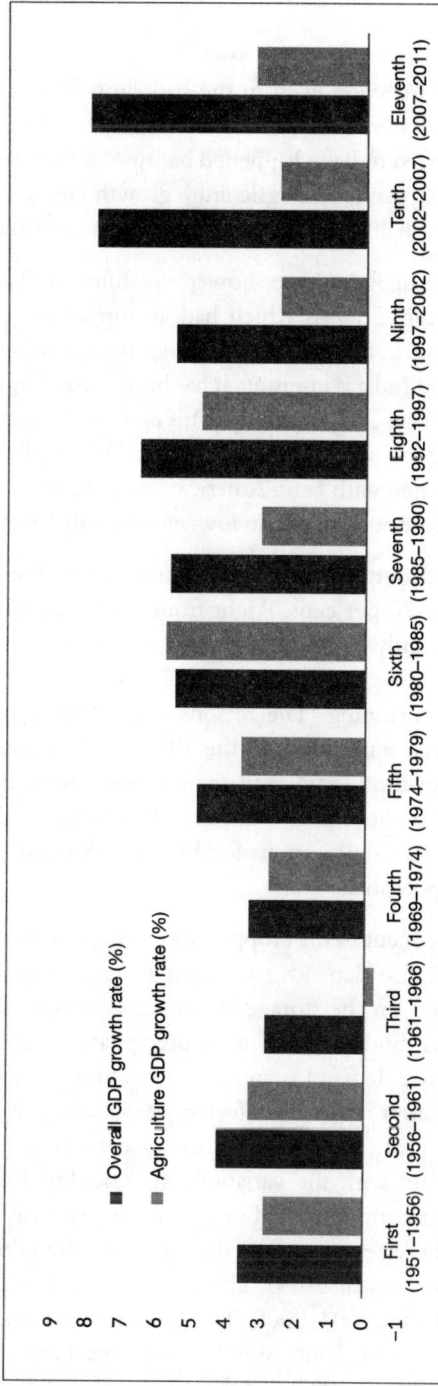

Figure 2.4 *'India's GDP and Agricultural GDP Growth Rates over Plan Periods*

Source: Based on Sharma, 2012; Sivakumar, 2013.

Plan period shows a decline even in the backdrop of an unchanged inequality in rural areas and an increase in urban areas. The decline in poverty can be inferred to have happened because of the faster growth rate which was taking place. The agriculture growth rate was also picking up in the second half of the period in all the states of India.

The growth rate in agriculture showed volatility in different plan periods due to various reasons which had an impact on the overall economic growth rate in the country. Although the agricultural growth rate as experienced in India is inspiring, it has been marred by substantial divergence (Pingali et al., 2019, p. 368). This divergence was driven by the high growth of the urban economy in states like Delhi and Goa, which can be compared with Latin America; states like Bihar and Uttar Pradesh are now more comparable to low-income sub-Saharan Africa.

Out of the total output of the agriculture sector, the crop segment accounted for 70 per cent. Right from the Ninth Plan period, it remained significantly lower than the targets. The crop subsector registered an impressive growth rate (3.1%) during the first decade of India's five-year planning. The reasons were already discussed in Chapter 1. The deceleration during the 1960s (1.7%), coupled with a severe shortage of food grains and their imports from the United States, along with conditionality attached to their supplies, forced the Government of India to increase its food grain production and build massive irrigation potential.

More than 50 per cent of the cropped area in the country is rainfed. Irrigation potential also depends to a great extent on precipitation, as irrigation depends on the storage in surface reservoirs and annual recharge to aquifers, both dependent on precipitation. On the other hand, irrigation water demand is an inverse function of rainfall in an area. Thus, crop output is directly affected by rainfall in two different ways. As a recent study has indicated, the year-to-year fluctuations in rainfall correspond with the variations in agricultural GDP. The agricultural GDP growth witnessed in a year was primarily explained by the difference between rainfall of that year and the rainfall of the preceding year (Kumar et al., 2019). There are, however, some changes in growth patterns after 2004–2005. The growth rate as measured by the average annual rate of change was 4.33 per cent during the Eighth Plan (1992–1993 to 1996–1997) and then declined to 2.25 per cent in

Table 2.3 *Annual Growth Rate in Output of Various Subsectors of Agriculture at 1999–2000 Prices, 1950–1951 to 2016–2017 (%)*

Period	Crop Sector	Livestock	Fisheries	Horticulture Crops	Cereals
1950–1951 to 1959–1960	3.06	1.42	5.79	0.74	3.95
1960–1961 to 1969–1970	1.70	0.41	4.00	4.87	2.10
1970–1971 to 1979–1980	1.79	3.92	2.90	2.86	2.40
1980–1981 to 1989–1990	2.24	4.91	5.67	2.63	2.89
1990–1991 to 1999–2000	3.02	3.79	5.36	5.95	2.24
2000–2001 to 2010–2011	2.85	4.29	3.63	3.78	1.83
2011–2012 to 2016–2017	0.98	5.30	7.49	3.88	0.26

Source: MOA & FW, 2019.

the Tenth Plan (2002–2003 to 2006–2007). There was some growth in crop output during the Eleventh Plan. Further, resilience to the severe drought of 2009–2010 was noticed in the moderate effect compared to earlier ones (GoI, 2011). Table 2.3 provides the trend in the annual rate of change in crop output (at 1999–2000 constant prices).

The Economic Survey 2017–18 (GoI, 2018) pointed that the impact of climate change in terms of temperature and rainfall is not linear. When temperatures are higher, subsequent rainfall will be significantly lower and dry days are relatively more than normal. The extreme climate shocks are twice as high in unirrigated lands when compared to the irrigated agriculture. The survey further estimated that extreme shocks of temperatures reduced agricultural yield by 4 per cent and 4.7 per cent for kharif and rabi, whereas extreme rainfall shocks reduced yields by 12.8 per cent and 6.7 per cent for the respective farming seasons.

The crop sector output also showed a deceleration in growth like that in agricultural GDP after 1996–1997. Some growth pattern is observed during 2004–2005. The growth rate change was 4.33 per cent during the Eighth Plan (1993–1997) and it declined to 2.25 per cent. The deceleration continued during the Tenth Plan (2003–2007). As pointed out earlier, the effect of the 2009–2010 drought was moderate, and there was also some growth rate of crop output during the Eleventh Plan period (GoI, 2011). Around this time, India witnessed a phenomenal growth in milk production. Afterwards, in the 1970s, Verghese Kurien steered India from a milk-deficit country to the largest milk producer in the world. Milk production increased from 17 million ton in 1950–1951 to 84.6 million ton in 2001–2002 and was 132.4 million ton in 2012–2013 (GoI, 2013).

The growth in livestock, which was 1.4 per cent per annum till the 1950s and as low as 0.4 per cent per annum in the 1960s, went up to 3.9 per cent in the 1970s. Ever since then, its growth rate was higher than the crop sector and touched 4.9 per cent in the 1980s and maintained above 4 per cent afterwards. In general, buffaloes have higher yield than indigenous cows. However, crossbreed cows are more productive. The average milk production of local cows is highest in Haryana (4.11 kg/day), followed by Punjab (2.88 kg/day) and Gujarat (2.84 kg/day). For crossbreed cows, it is highest in Punjab (8.36 kg/day), followed by Gujarat (7.96 kg/day) and West Bengal (7.82 kg/day). The highest milk yield of buffaloes is in West Bengal (6.26 kg/day), followed by Haryana (5.64 kg/day) and Punjab (5.62 kg/day). In the global context, the Indian dairy sector is very impressive in terms of livestock population and total milk production but extremely poor in productivity (GoI, 2003).

The other important indicators of agricultural performance are the production and yield growth rates. The growth rate of all crops was halved to 1.58 per cent from the 1990s. Table 2.4 shows all-India compound growth rates of area, production and yield of major crops.

Table 2.4 All-India Compound Growth Rates of Area, Production and Yield of Major Crops

Crop	1950–1951 to 1966–1967			1967–1968 to 1980–1981			1981–1982 to 2011–2012		
	Area	Production	Yield	Area	Production	Yield	Area	Production	Yield
Cereals	−0.01	2.39	2.15	0.38	2.46	1.47	−0.08	2.09	2.00
Pulses	0.06	0.80	0.74	0.42	−0.53	−0.95	0.02	0.82	0.80
Food grains	−0.04	2.22	2.26	0.39	2.27	1.87	−0.14	1.89	2.03
Oilseeds	1.46	3.39	1.90	1.12	1.66	0.53	1.22	3.20	1.96
Fibres	0.52	2.69	2.11	0.26	2.53	1.20	1.00	3.25	2.16
Non-food grains	1.17	3.00	2.01	0.81	2.18	0.83	1.15	3.21	2.07
All crops	0.20	2.37	2.17	0.46	2.25	1.43	0.12	2.14	2.05

Source: Directorate of Economics and Statistics (2012).

The area under crops also showed negative growth of –0.25 per cent per annum. This may be due to landlessness among peasants and transfer of land for non-agricultural purposes and more so due to neoliberalism. However, there is some marginal improvement in the production and area of food grains which calls for a careful explanation (Jha, 2007). Some researchers analysed the variations in production data (Kannan & Sundaram, 2011) from 1967 to 2008 considering various sources. Their findings suggest that the cropping pattern in India has undergone significant changes over time. There is a marked shift from the cultivation of food grains to commercial crops. Further, among food grains, the area under coarse cereals declined by 13.3 per cent between 1971 and 2008.

It is to be noted here that the per capita food grain availability in India has been declining alarmingly since 2001, with a major reduction in the production of cereals and pulses. On the other hand, the per capita demand for food grains is growing due to changing consumption patterns. At the same time, the average per capita demand for cereals for animal feed is growing owing to increased demand for animal products such as milk, beef, mutton, pork, poultry products, eggs and freshwater fish (Amarasinghe et al., 2007). The combined effect of rising per capita demand and declining per capita availability has resulted in food crisis, which is manifested by the rising price of cereals and pulses in the market (Kumar et al., 2012).

2.5. CHANGING CROPPING PATTERNS AND LIVESTOCK HOLDING

Among several issues in agriculture, the changing cropping patterns assumed much interest among researchers, as it has a significant say on agricultural productivity and the volume of output of different crops. The cropping pattern in India has undergone significant changes over time. As the cultivated area remains more or less constant, the increased demand for food because of an increase in population and urbanization has put agricultural land under stress and thus resulted in crop intensification and substitution of food crops with commercial crops (Kannan & Sundaram, 2011).

The area under rice, as a proportion of the total area, declined marginally from 23.02 per cent in 1970–1971 to 22.57 per cent in

2007–2008. In the case of wheat, the area increased from 10.42 per cent in 1970–1971 to 14.18 per cent in 2007–2008. As regards the total area under food grains, it declined from 75.54 per cent in 1970–1971 to 63.52 per cent in 2007–2008, which is remarkable. There was a sharp decline in the proportion of area under coarse grains, which include bajra and jowar, from 24.48 per cent to 15.14 per cent. As a result, the total area under cereals declined—from 61.9 per cent to 51.9 per cent. Interestingly, the total area under oilseed crops increased from 9.85 per cent (in 1970–1971) to 13.93 per cent in 2007–2008. An increase in area under sugarcane as a proportion of the total cropped area was observed during the reporting period. Similarly, the total area under 'non-food grain crops' also increased from 19.39 per cent to 26.41 per cent.

Nevertheless, a reduction in percentage area under a crop does not mean that the absolute area under that crop had reduced, particularly given the fact that the gross cropped area (GCA) had increased by almost 50 per cent from 131.9 Mha to 192.2 Mha. Overall, the cultivated area under cereals increased from 78.23 Mha in 1950–1951 to 96.69 Mha in 2012–2013. The area under paddy went up from 30.81 Mha in 1950–1951 to 44.71 Mha in 2010–2011 and then came down to 42.41 Mha in 2012–2013. The area under wheat went up from 9.75 Mha (1970–1971) to 29.65 Mha (2012–2013). The area under coarse cereals was 45.95 Mha in 1970–1971 but came down sharply to 24.64 Mha in 2012–2013. The highest area under cultivation for coarse cereals was in 1970–1971 (45.95 Mha). The area cultivated under pulses increased from 19.09 Mha in 1950–1951 to 23.47 Mha in 2012–2013.

The total area under food grain crops (fine cereals, millets and pulses) therefore actually increased, that is, from 97.32 Mha to 121.16 Mha, though a smaller percentage of the GCA is under food crops. While the increase in area is only 22 per cent against a much larger increase in population during the reporting period of four decades, important is the increase in crop productivity (yields per unit area) which enabled much larger production from a smaller area. This has been discussed in the next section of the chapter. This increase in crop yields was achieved mainly through an increase in irrigation and the adoption of high-yielding varieties, particularly in paddy, wheat and maize sectors.

But the adoption of high-yielding varieties was also enabled by access to irrigation facilities. Much of the fine cereals (rice and wheat) are irrigated today. The total area under irrigated rice and wheat went up from 24.26 Mha to 53.18 Mha. The irrigated area under fine and coarse cereals went up from 28.09 Mha to 57.26 Mha and that of total food crops from 30.12 Mha to 61.08 Mha.

A similar trend was found in sugarcane and oilseeds. The irrigated area under oilseeds went up from 1.87 Mha to 4.89 Mha and for sugarcane from 1.09 Mha to 7.3 Mha.

The reality is contrary to the findings of some researchers that in the post-economic reform period, many farmers in rural areas moved away from agriculture, seeking non-farm activities, leading to a fall in agricultural productivity and output. While it is true that the observed trend among farmers is that they are moving to more remunerative commercial crops in place of traditional cash crops, however, the preference for food crops continues to increase as could be seen by the increase in agriculture outputs.

Bidyadhar and Kumar (2018) analysed the NSSO data of the 59th round (2002–2003) and 70th round (2012–2013) and found that an increasing number of farmers were cultivating fruits and vegetables and sugarcane and other cash crops in various regions, while the number of those engaged in the cultivation of cereals and pulses declined. The proportion of high concentration of cultivation areas has slightly decreased, but the dependency of farm workers on cultivation has increased during that period in different agro-climatic regions of India. This trend of farmers' engagement is given in Annexure 2.3.

The most remarkable is the change in area under crops, which increased from 118.8 Mha to 140 Mha. It constituted 42.6 per cent of the total geographical area in 2009–2010. The NSA peaked in 1990–1991, with 143 Mha under different crops. More importantly, there has been a steady increase in the intensity of land use, with area cropped more than once increasing as a result of an increase in irrigation facilities. The net irrigated area increased by 42.4 Mha from 20.9 Mha to 63.3 Mha. The gross irrigated area (GIA) increased by 63.8 Mha from 22.6 Mha to 86.4 Mha. However, the increase in GIA (63.8 Mha) did not result in a proportional increase in GCA due to the reason that the net (maximum) sown area which must have been under purely rain-fed cultivation was only 109.3 Mha in 1970–1971 against the NSA of 118.8 Mha, and it further reduced to 105.8 Mha by 2010–2011, if we assume that there is no double cropping under rainfed conditions. This means that there is a significant amount of area in India which receives irrigation water for the first crop itself, and its proportion to the total cropped area is on a steady rise. This area was a minimum of 9.5 Mha in 1970–1971 and went up to 34.2 Mha (i.e., 140–105.8).[3] In other words, even the expansion in NSA was possible with expansion in irrigation, with a minimum of around 25 Mha of additional irrigation (of 63.8 Mha) going to the first crop itself. In addition to the multipronged demands on agricultural land, its decline is a resultant of the rapid growth of population and more so because of urbanization, industrialization, and residential, commercial and infrastructural development.

However, rainfed agriculture contributes to 40 per cent of the country's food production (Table 2.5). Even after achieving the ultimate irrigation potential, a substantial portion of the land will continue to be under rainfed conditions. A large portion of the acreage under coarse cereals (85%), pulses (83%), oilseeds (70%), rice (42%) and cotton (60%) area is under rainfed conditions (Venkateswarlu & Prasad, 2012). Different estimates are available with regard to the area covered under rainfed conditions. It was estimated in 2012–2013 that more than half of agricultural sown land, that is, '53 per cent', is dependent on rain-fed irrigation. Rainfed irrigation is dependent on rainwater and is not supplemented by water from any other source (*Resurgent India*, 2017).

Rainfed agriculture helps in contributing significantly to the carrying capacity of Indian agriculture, namely the capacity to support the number of people and livestock on a sustainable basis. The production of coarse cereals and others showed yield gains during 2008–2009. However, large yield gaps are evident, which need to be addressed in rainfed agriculture.

---

[3] However, we still do not know how much the actual is, and the figure can only be higher than the estimates because of the fact that there is no data on the area which is double-cropped and under rain-fed conditions. As a matter of fact, in many high rainfall areas such as West Bengal, Assam and Kerala, two crops are raised under rainfed conditions.

Table 2.5 *Area Sown under Various Rainfed Crops and Percentage of Rainfed Area during 2008–2009*

Crop	Area Sown (Mha)	Rainfed Area (%)
Rice	45.5	42
Coarse cereals	27.5	85
Jowar	7.5	91
Bajra	8.7	91
Maize	8.2	75
Pulses	22.1	83
Red gram	3.4	96
Bengal gram	7.9	67
Oilseeds	27.6	70
Groundnut	6.2	79
Rapeseed and mustard	6.3	27
Soya bean	9.5	99
Sunflower	1.8	69
Cotton	9.4	65

Source: Venkateswarlu, B., & Prasad, J. V. N. S. (2012).

Over nearly the past 40 years, farm practices in India have changed dramatically. This change essentially came from expansion in irrigation facilities, mainly gravity irrigation from canals and well irrigation. In the early 1970s, a small percentage of the total area was under irrigation, that is, only 20 Mha out of the 118 Mha of the NSA was under irrigation. Today, a little more than 63 out of the 140 Mha of the sown area is under irrigation, which makes it to 45 per cent. This means that 55 per cent of the farmed area does not use irrigation facilities (known as the rainfed area). As we have seen earlier, this doesn't mean that the rainfed crop area is only 55 per cent. In fact, as per our estimates, it is 105 Mha, which is nearly 75 per cent of the NSA. A much larger percentage of the NSA is under rainfed crops during the rainy season either because of sufficient amount of rainfall (like in Kerala, Assam and

West Bengal) or due to the lack of access to irrigation water during that particular season (like in western Rajasthan and some hard rock areas of Gujarat, Maharashtra and peninsular India). The figures, therefore, indicate that the maximum area that can be brought under irrigation in a given season is only 45 per cent. These figures also do not suggest that the 55 per cent of the NSA, which is left out without irrigation facilities, actually requires irrigation. However, unfortunately, this is one of the major misconceptions that exist in the sector.

In fact, many of the regions which do not have irrigation facilities may not require irrigation for crop production in most parts of the year owing to the excessively high rainfall which again lasts for several months starting from June to December, followed by winter and summer rains. Investment in irrigation may not be economically viable in such areas, as returns would be very low. Therefore, what comes out from the foregoing analysis is that the area which actually requires irrigation could be lower than 74 Mha. However, the distinction between rainfed areas which actually require irrigation for better crop growth due to moisture stress during the growing season and the rainfed areas which remain as rainfed by virtue of having a sufficient amount of soil moisture from rainfall for crop growth is hardly ever made by the official agencies dealing with rainfed areas (see, for instance, NRAA, 2011).[4] Therefore, the differential risk faced by farmers from these two distinct regions is never considered for agricultural policies.

That said, a significantly large area is under irrigation in India even during the rainy season, which was estimated to be around 34.2 Mha as on 2010–2011. The area receiving such irrigation was only 9.5 Mha during 1970–1971. Probably, owing to the access to well irrigation, which is widespread regionally, farmers in the low and medium rainfall regions are able to provide supplementary irrigation to their

---

[4] As a result of this, the criteria used for classification of 'rainfed areas' in India, based on the extent of irrigation as a percentage of the NSA in the district, put both Kerala and western Rajasthan under the same category as one with more than 70 per cent of area under rainfed conditions and the same type of recommendation is made in terms of measures to improve crop productivity. It fails to make the distinction between the two regions in terms of incidence of moisture stress during the growing season.

long-duration kharif crops (like irrigated cotton and castor), which replaced their shorter duration rainfed counterparts.

India has the world's largest livestock population, which includes cattle, buffaloes, goats and sheep as the most important ones. The cattle population increased from 155.3 million in 1951 to 199.08 million units in 2007. The adult female cattle population increased from 54.4 million in 1950–1951 to 72.95 million units in 2007. Similarly, the population of buffalo, adult female buffalo, sheep and goats also increased gradually from 1950–1951 to 2007. The total number of livestock units (comprising cattle, goat and sheep) went up from 285 million units to 516.5 million units. What is most interesting is the changing composition of livestock. First, the proportion of small ruminants in the livestock population has steadily increased from 31.5 per cent to 41.1 per cent. Second, the proportion of buffaloes in the bovine population has increased from 24.4 per cent to 34.6 per cent. Third, the proportion of cows in the cattle population has also increased, that is, from 30 per cent to 36.6 per cent. The reason for the first trend could be the rising price of meat; the reason for the second could be the higher milk yield from buffaloes; and that for the third could be the reducing preference for draught animals in rural areas for carrying out agricultural operations, which is replaced by machine power.

2.6. SEED PRODUCTION IN AGRICULTURE

Seeds carry the genetic potential of crop species for agriculture production. Crop improvement and delivery are of critical importance to the farmers for improved yields, meeting environmental challenges and food security. Seeds account for a 20–25 per cent share in the productivity of crops. The Department of Agriculture, Co-operation and Farmers' Welfare implements the central sector scheme 'development and strengthening of infrastructure facilities for production and distribution of quality seeds'. A major restructuring of the seed industry by the Government of India through National Seed Project Phase-I (1977–1978), Phase-II (1978–1979) and Phase-III (1990–1991) strengthened the much-needed seed infrastructure development. A new seed development policy was launched in 1988–1989, which was another important initiative of the government which transformed the seed sector. It gave impetus for private individuals, MNCs and corporate segments in India's seed sector to establish a strong R&D base for product development. In each of the seed companies, emphasis was laid on high-value hybrid seeds of cereals, vegetables and hi-tech products such as Bt cotton (GoI, 2020). During the last four decades, seed production technologies have changed and new technologies such as transgenics, tissue culture, soil-less agriculture and verti culture have emerged. In the liberalized and changed environment, India is increasingly engaging in the import and export of seeds and planting materials.

In addition to the public sector producing seeds in the country, for agricultural development, the private sector also contributes significantly to the production of seeds in India (Table 2.6). The private sector took major strides in the production of seeds which also propelled the public sector to overtake the former in the production of quality seeds. Till 2001–2002, the private sector developed 150 hybrid seeds of cotton compared to 15 by the public sector. Similarly, in maize, the number of hybrid varieties developed was 67, against 3 in the public sector. The public sector increased its productivity from 8 per cent to 19 per cent in cotton, from 4 per cent to 40 per cent in maize and from 25 per cent to 58 per cent in rice (Singh & Chand, 2011). The agriculture research innovations in this regard seemed to show a semblance of 'national science innovation systems' model with partnerships among academia, private sector and public sector (Hall et al., 2001).

Table 2.7 presents the trend of the production of certified seeds. The seed production programme is highly vibrant, the seeds are exported to

Table 2.6 *Seed Production and Share of Private Sector in India*

Year of Production	Total Seed Production (Lakh Quintals)	Share of Private Sector (%)
2003–2004	132.27	47.48
2004–2005	140.51	45.02
2005–2006	148.18	46.80
2006–2007	194.31	41.00

Source: GoI (2020).

Table 2.7 Crop-wise Distribution of Certified/Quality Seeds (Lakh Quintals)

Crop	2007–2008	2008–2009	2009–2010	2010–2011	2011–2012	2012–2013	2013–2014
Wheat	63.25	74.83	90.66	97.83	97.61	116.47	93.75
Paddy	48.93	58.18	60.95	69.34	74.41	72.14	72.45
Maize	5.80	7.94	7.74	8.94	9.35	9.07	11.20
Jowar	2.38	2.41	2.24	2.16	1.99	2.29	2.06
Bajra	1.90	2.20	1.74	2.31	2.27	2.14	2.20
Ragi	0.27	0.25	0.05	0.26	0.26	0.29	0.29
Barley	1.27	1.62	1.77	1.79	3.80	1.97	1.08
Cereals Total	**123.80**	**147.43**	**165.15**	**182.62**	**189.96**	**204.37**	**183.03**
Gram	6.73	8.60	12.32	12.50	13.16	14.83	17.48
Lentil	0.56	0.59	0.55	0.74	0.66	0.70	1.28
Peas	1.10	1.29	2.07	1.47	1.36	1.79	3.17
Urd bean	1.40	1.37	1.61	1.96	2.31	2.33	1.64
Mung bean	1.34	1.23	1.29	1.76	2.00	2.13	1.95
Pigeon pea	1.18	1.09	1.37	1.52	1.92	1.80	1.73
Cowpea	0.10	0.16	0.20	0.33	0.32	0.45	0.24
Others	0.16	0.15	0.28	0.56	0.53	0.48	0.31
Pulses Total	**12.57**	**14.48**	**19.69**	**20.83**	**22.26**	**24.51**	**27.80**

Groundnut	14.43	15.90	18.86	21.79	20.02	23.16	19.39
Rapeseed	1.71	1.63	2.09	2.07	2.56	1.88	1.63
Sesame	0.22	0.18	0.18	0.20	0.23	0.20	0.18
Sunflower	0.92	0.80	0.76	0.55	0.29	0.35	0.32
Soya bean	16.52	20.89	28.44	25.55	37.60	32.08	38.94
Linseed	0.02	0.01	0.01	0.04	0.02	0.02	0.05
Castor	0.42	0.42	0.29	0.31	0.67	0.68	0.51
Safflower	0.08	0.09	0.07	0.08	0.09	0.04	0.06
Others	0.01	–	0.01	0.01	0.01	–	0.01
Oilseeds Total	34.33	39.92	50.71	50.61	61.49	58.41	61.09
Cotton	1.89	2.27	2.36	2.33	2.53	2.50	2.28
Jute	0.24	0.28	0.27	0.27	0.32	0.30	0.30
Mesta/others	0.50	0.03	0.02	0.04	0.24	0.15	0.29
Fibres Total	2.63	2.58	2.65	2.64	3.09	2.95	2.87
Others	5.72	11.40	18.91	20.63	18.32	23.20	26.60
Grand Total	179.05	215.81	257.11	277.34	294.85	313.44	301.39

Source: Directorate of Economics and Statistics (2021).

different neighbouring and developing countries successfully. India is producing quality seeds suiting diverse tropical, temperate and subtropical varieties in sufficient qualities. This has become possible because of the presence of diverse agro-climate geographical zones in the country to test seeds before exporting.

2.7. CHANGING FERTILIZER CONSUMPTION

Fertilizer consumption in India has been increasing over the years and, today, India is one of the largest producers and consumers of fertilizers in the world. By 2009–2010, total fertilizer consumption in the country was 26.49 million nutrient ton (Jaga & Patel, 2012). Usage of fertilizers also grew, as an increasing number of farmers started applying fertilizers to their crops and with increased their dosage. The gap between consumption and production is met through imports.[5]

With limited arable land[6] and the burden of increasing population, efficient use of inputs plays an important role in sustaining food security in India. Therefore, the only way to improve food production is to increase crop yields through the scientific use of fertilizers along with other inputs such as high-yielding variety seeds and irrigation, using the limited arable land, with an emphasis on protecting the environment. The government has been consistently pursuing policies conducive to increased supply and consumption of fertilizers (Jaga & Patel, 2012).

Several researchers analysed the pattern of usage of chemical fertilizers and flood grain production (Singh, 2013). A study of biofertilizer use and agriculture production relationships indicated that for achieving sustainable agriculture, biofertilizers are very useful compared to chemical fertilizers (Mazid & Khan, 2015).

Sharma and Thaker (2011) examined various determinants of fertilizer consumption and concluded that the non-price factor (better seeds, irrigation, credit) plays a more important role in determining the

---

[5] India is the largest importer of urea, MAP and DAP; second largest of ammonia and fourth largest of potash fertilizers in the world (Sharma and Thaker, 2010).

[6] See Kumar et al. (2014).

demand of fertilizers compared to the price of fertilizers. Hence, the government, they argued, should pay more attention to the former. Infrastructural development, with a focus on agricultural R&D along with fertilizers, increases production and productivity in agriculture.

Over the last six decades, the production and consumption of fertilizers have increased in India significantly. The total fertilizer consumption in 1950–1951 was 0.69 lakh ton. A consistent increase in consumption was observed during 1950–1951 to 2011–2012. During 2011—2012, the fertilizer consumption was 277.4 lakh ton (increased by nearly 402 times from 1950–1951 levels). In terms of consumption per unit of NSA, the fertilizer use during 1950–1951 was only 0.58 kg/ha. Over the years, the consumption increased to a whooping level of 189.1kg/ha of NSA. For a hectare of GCA, the consumption went up from 0.52 kg to 137 kg during the reporting period. The increased use of fertilizers had resulted in a substantial increase in crop yields in the Green Revolution areas. But the intensive use of land resources for cultivation with two–three crops through the help of irrigation water had also resulted in a loss of primary productivity of soils. This is forcing farmers to apply a higher dosage of fertilizers to maintain yield levels.

Table 2.8 presents the trends in consumption of chemical fertilizers and the food grain production in India before and after the announcement of the Agricultural Policy 2000.

However, criticism is rampant regarding the use of chemical fertilizers for the sake of increased agricultural production and exports. The close consequences of consumption of the fertilizers proved fatal to the quality of soil, crops and water and people's health too. The excessive use of chemical fertilizers gave a false feeling of excessive production of food grains. But 'we are living in an age of severe food scarcity and nothing has changed from the situation in 1960s' (*Resurgent India*, 2016). With the introduction of New Agricultural Policy, greater emphasis was given to the promotion of organic cultivation (Kumar et al., 2017). There was a considerable reduction in the growth rate of chemical fertilizer consumption after 2000–2001.

Table 2.8 Fertilizer Consumption (Lakh Ton) and Food Grains (Million Ton)

Year	Fertilizer Consumption	Food Grain Production	Year	Fertilizer Consumption	Food Grain Production
Before the Announcement of Agriculture Policy			After the Announcement of Agriculture Policy		
1986–1987	86.45	143.42	2000–2001	167.02	196.81
1988–1989	110.40	169.92	2002–2003	160.94	174.78
1990–1991	125.46	176.39	2004–2005	183.99	198.36
1992–1993	121.55	179.48	2006–2007	216.51	217.28
1994–1995	135.63	191.50	2008–2009	249.09	234.47
1996–1997	143.77	199.43	2010–2011	281.20	244.49
1998–1999	167.98	203.61	2012–2013	258.04	257.13
1999–2000	180.69	209.80	2013–2014	239.59	264.77
			2014–2015	255.81	252.00
			2015–2016	267.52	251.60
			2016–2017	259.49	275.10
			2017–2018	265.93	284.80

Source: Based on Directorate of Economics and Statistics, 2010; Directorate of Economics and Statistics, 2021.

Notes: Total food grains include cereals (rice, wheat), coarse cereals and pulses. Total fertilizer consumption includes N, P, K fertilizers.

2.8. CHANGING DEGREE OF FARM MECHANIZATION AND LABOUR USE

Draught animals were the major source of power for farming operations till 1971–1972. This was followed by the use of diesel engines, electric engines and human labour. But, gradually, this is being replaced by machines, in the form of tractors, tillers, and electric and diesel pumps for irrigation, which was enabled by easy access to drilling technologies, pump sets, electricity supply, diesel, machines, tractors and tillers in rural areas and access to finance for the purchase of agricultural equipment. The biggest change has come in the use of tractors, which currently account for 42 per cent of the total power use in farming, from a meagre 8.5 per cent in 1971 1972. The tractors have essentially replaced the use of human labour and draught animals for ploughing. Diesel engines and electric pumps have replaced draught animals and human labour in lifting water from wells and ponds. Electric motors supply 25 per cent of the total power requirements in farming. The level of mechanization is highest in harvesting and threshing (as high as 60%–70%), followed by soil working and seedbed preparation (40%) and irrigation (37%). The total power use in farming operations has also gone up from 0.424 kW/ha to 1.658 kW/ha. However, full utilization of available power for agricultural operations requires a sufficient amount of land to operate and availability of water.

Economies of scale are obtained in farm mechanization if large and contiguous pieces of land are operated. However, reducing the average size of operational holdings and increasing the number of parcels (fragmentation) would pose big challenges to farm mechanization.

There are different types of agricultural labours in India.

1. Those attached to landlords, who are also called bonded labourers
2. Landless labourers who are independent and who work exclusively for others
3. Petty farmers with tiny landholdings who have one or more sons working for prosperous farmers
4. Labourers migrating from less endowed areas to other places and neighbouring states

As mentioned above, the scale of operations is limiting the use of machines. The human labour still remains significantly in Indian agriculture.

2.9. CHANGES IN REAL WAGE RATES IN INDIAN FARMS

The increased employment opportunities in the non-farm sector and outmigration of people seeking non-farm employment from rural areas to cities and towns have been pushing the real wage rates in agriculture in the recent past. A look at the wage rates for ploughing (male), sowing (male), transplanting (male), transplanting (female), weeding (male), harvesting (male) and harvesting (female) shows that there are significant regional variations in real wage rates. The highest wage rates were observed in Kerala for most occupations, followed by the north-western states of Jammu and Kashmir, Himachal Pradesh, Punjab and Haryana. These five states almost invariably have been at the top throughout the period. Wage rates are very low in Madhya Pradesh, Bihar, Odisha, Uttar Pradesh and Karnataka.

However, in states, namely Karnataka, Maharashtra, Uttar Pradesh and West Bengal, though wage rates for non-agricultural occupations grew, the agricultural wages either remained stagnant or declined (Usami, 2011). This could be due to the fact that the growth in agriculture sector has been very sluggish in these states, with the result that new jobs are not created in the farms, whereas the rural sector failed to supply sufficient skilled labour to the areas where it was required, which resulted in widening demand–supply gap in the non-agricultural sector.

On the other hand, wage rates for non-farm occupations declined or remained stagnant in Punjab, Haryana, Jammu and Kashmir, Gujarat, Rajasthan and Madhya Pradesh (Usami, 2011). This might be probably because the increased demand from the non-farm sector is being met by an increased outflow of people from rural areas, seeking employment in the non-farm sector in cities and towns. It is important to note that states such as Punjab, Gujarat and Rajasthan experience large-scale migration of rural workforce to cities, as agricultural mechanization has replaced labour force in farms. Interestingly, the labour demand in agriculture in a few states such as Haryana, Rajasthan and Punjab is being met by migrant labourers from Bihar.

2.10. AGRICULTURAL SUBSIDIES

While farming is a private enterprise in India, the government plays a vital role in agricultural development. Government interventions are diverse and varied and include providing self-sufficiency, creating employment, supporting small-scale producers for adopting modern technologies and inputs, reducing price instability and improving the income of farm households (Salunke & Deshmukh, 2012). An agricultural subsidy is governmental financial support paid to farmers and agribusinesses to supplement their income, manage the supply of agricultural commodities, and influence the cost and supply of such commodities. Inputs such as fertilizers, irrigation water and electricity account for a significant share of the agricultural subsidies in India, and fertilizer and electricity subsidies have attracted much attention from policymakers and researchers in the recent past. It is often argued that the heavy input subsidies encourage wasteful use of resources such as nutrients, water and electricity in agriculture.

Table 2.9 presents the year-wise increase in the total amount of subsidies provided in the agriculture sector. In 1980–1981, subsidy amounted to ₹1,228.5 crore which subsequently increased to ₹115,952.20 crore by 2008–2009. In the year 1980–1981, the GCA was about 173 Mha, which increased to about 188 Mha by 1996–1997, and then to 195.35 Mha by 2008–2009. Adjusting to inflation, with an assumed average annual inflation rate of 9 per cent, the agriculture subsidies in real times increased manifold from 1980–1981 to 2008–2009, both in aggregate terms (8.45 times from ₹1,228.5 crore to ₹10,383 crore) and per ha of GCA (7.5 times from ₹70.9 to ₹531). Currently, the subsidy in agriculture (2008–2009) stands at ₹5,935/ha of GCA at current prices.

Subsidies make positive as well as negative impacts on the agriculture sector of India. However, agricultural subsidies play a vital role in achieving agricultural growth in India, and without subsidies, development is very difficult. Due to widespread corruption and ineffective management of subsidies, and low literacy rate among farmers, they are unable to receive subsidies and are facing a financial crisis (Salunke & Deshmukh, 2012).

Table 2.9 *Distribution of Total Subsidies and GCA in India (1980–1981 to 2008–2009)*

Subsidies	Fertilizers (in ₹ Crores)	Electricity (in ₹ Crores)	Irrigation (in ₹ Crores)	Total Subsidies (in ₹ Crores)	Gross Cropped Area (in '000 Hectares)
1980–1981	471.88 (38.41)	357.56 (29.10)	399.10 (32.49)	1,228.5 (100.00)	173,324
1985–1986	1,804.80 (37.63)	1,324.15 (27.61)	1,667.21 (34.76)	4,796.2 (100.00)	177,526
1990–1991	4,638.56 (35.20)	4,621.00 (35.07)	3,917.41 (29.73)	13,177.0 (100.00)	185,403
1996–1997	8,148.41 23.86)	15,594.00 (45.67)	10,404.73 (30.47)	34,147.1 (100.00)	188,601
2000–2001	13,724.05 (24.80)	26,904.00 (48.62)	14,711.71 (26.58)	55,339.8 (100.00)	186,565
2008–2009	101,180.68 (87.26)	14,771.52 (12.74)	–	115,952.2 (100.00)	195,350

Sources: The Fertiliser Association of India (n.d.); Ministry of Power (n.d.).

Table 2.10 *Growth of Farm Machinery in India*

Agriculture Operation/Machine	No. of Lakhs[a] 1992	No. of Lakhs[a] 2003	Area Commanded as Percentage of Net Area Sown
Tractors	12.22	23.61	25.00
Seed drill			
1. Tractor drawn	3.90	73.50	11.15
2. Animal drawn	51.03	23.77	12.06
Thresher			
1. Wheat	10.76	7.26	17.00
2. Paddy	0.35	1.61	2.21
3. Multicrop	1.68	6.81	5.76
Plant protection equipment	29.56	58.31	48.39

Source: Mehta (2007).

Table 2.10 shows that the number of farm machinery appliances consistently increased from 1992 to 2003. These increased numbers reflect more use of advanced technology in the agriculture sector. These changes were made possible only through government subsidies available for purchasing machinery required for agriculture production. The government provided up to 30 per cent of subsidies on purchasing farm equipment in India. This benefit encourages farmers to buy more farm equipment for farming (Salunke & Deshmukh, 2012).

2.11. CHANGES IN ELECTRICITY CONSUMPTION IN AGRICULTURE

Per capita annual energy consumption is a widely accepted indicator of development. Indian agriculture has become more energy-intensive and fossil-fuel-based over the years. The total electricity consumption in India increased from 4,182 GWh in 1947 to 852,903 GWh in 2012–2013, which is nearly a 204 times increase. Electricity consumption for agriculture increased by a staggering 1,225 times from 125 million units in 1947 to 153 billion units in 2012–2013. The total electricity consumption in 1947 was 4,182 million Units, of which only 3 per cent was for agriculture. However, by 2012–2013, the electricity consumption in agriculture was nearly 18 per cent of the total electricity consumption, a clear indication of how agriculture is becoming increasingly mechanized and dependent on fossil fuel.

Irrigation is the major energy-consuming area in crop and dairy farming and agricultural processing. The electricity consumption per unit of GIA increased four times from 7 kWh/ha in 1950–1951 to 30 kWh/ha in 1960–1961. Since surface irrigation does not require much energy, the analysis was done in relation to the net well-irrigated area. The same rate of increase was seen in the case of net irrigated area by wells. Interestingly, the consumption went on to increase 160 times to 1,154 kWh/ha of GIA in 2006–2007. If we consider the net irrigated area by wells, the electricity consumption increased by 100 times to 2,758 kWh/ha during the same time period. This drastic increase in the electricity consumption can be mainly attributed to the increased number of wells and electric pump sets, whose proportion of the total area under irrigation has been consistently increasing over the past four decades to become nearly 65 per cent of the net irrigated area in the country. Over and above an increase in the amount of groundwater pumped for irrigation, the energy consumption per unit of groundwater pumped has been increasing in many semi-arid and arid areas owing to a decline in groundwater levels.

The total commercial energy input in Indian agriculture increased from 425.4×10^9 megajoule in 1980–1981 to $2,592.8 \times 10^9$ megajoules in 2006–2007. The shift coupled with increasing commercialization and diversification towards high-value crops will require more commercial energy (Jha et al., 2012). Energy in agriculture can be divided into two categories—direct and indirect. The direct use is in pumping and mechanists (tractors, motors, power tillers, etc.) and indirect use is in the form of fertilizers and pesticides. Table 2.11 (a and b together) present the temporal change in commercial energy use in Indian agriculture. Table 2.11a gives details of energy use in agriculture through

Table 2.11a *Trends in Fertilizer Consumption in Terms of Nutrients and Energy in Indian Agriculture*

Phase	Year	Nitrogen (N)		Phosphorus (P2O5)		Potash (K2O)		Total NPK			
		Quantity (000 ton)	Energy Giga Joule (GJ)	Quantity (000 ton)	Energy Giga Joule (GJ)	Quantity (000 ton)	Energy Giga Joule (GJ)	Quantity (000 ton)	Energy Giga Joule (GJ)	Total NPK kg/ha	Growth Rate (%)
I	1960–1969	508.91	30.84	147.19	8.92	71.80	4.35	727.90	44.12	4.61	23.71
II	1970–1979	2,483.73	150.53	740.95	44.91	418.14	25.34	3,642.81	220.78	21.65	10.29
III	1980–1989	5,330.68	353.37	2,132.46	129.24	889.48	53.91	8,852.61	536.52	50.07	8.58
IV	1990–1999	10,086.89	611.33	3,392.90	205.63	1,185.64	71.86	14,665.41	888.81	78.20	4.14
V	2000–2009	13,106.35	794.32	5,351.48	324.33	2,448.66	148.40	20,906.10	1,267.04	110.46	5.26
VI	2010–2013	13,282.38	804.99	5,534.10	335.40	2,330.55	141.25	21,146.87	1,281.63	108.08	−4.71
CAGR (%)		8.97[a]		9.93[a]		8.72[a]		9.16[a]		–	

Source: Directorate of Economics and Statistics, 2010; Directorate of Economics and Statistics, 2021.

Notes: [a]Significant at 5 per cent level

Table 2.11b *Use of Electricity for Agricultural Purposes*

S. No.	Year	Consumption for Agricultural Purposes		Total Consumption in GWh	% Share of Agricultural Consumption to Total Consumption
		Total Consumption in GWh	kWh/ha		
1	1970–1971	4,470	26.96	43,724	10.22
2	1980–1981	14,489	83.93	82,367	17.59
3	1990–1991	23,422	126.10	123,099	19.03
4	2000–2001	85,732	462.57	277,029	30.95
5	2010–2011	120,209	609.21	612,645	19.62
6	2011–2012	131,967	675.89	694,392	19.00
7	2012–2013	147,462	758.59	824,301	17.89
	CAGR (%)	8.90[a]	8.47[a]	7.42[a]	1.36[a]

Source: Based on data from Ministry of Statistics and Programme Implementation (n.d.).

Notes: [a]Significant at 5 per cent level

fertilizer consumption (from 1960 to 2013), and Table 2.11b gives the details of use of electricity in agriculture (from 1970 to 2013).

2.12. RISING CROP AND MILK YIELDS

Remarkable yield improvements were observed across all crop sectors. The analysis of the trend in yield of various crops (including rice, wheat, coarse cereals, pulses, oilseeds, sugarcane and other commercial crops) show the following: Rice yield improved significantly from 668 kg/ha in 1950–1951 to 2,462 kg/ha in 2012–2013, witnessing a fourfold increase. The wheat yield increased from 663 kg/ha in 1950–1951 to 3,119 kg/ha in 2012–2013, which is nearly five times. However, the regional variations in yield are very high, with the highest yields in paddy and wheat obtained in Punjab and Haryana and lowest in the eastern state of Bihar (Ladha et al., 2000). The yield in coarse cereals also showed an increasing trend from 408 kg/ha in 1950–1951 to 1,626 kg/ha in 2012–2013. In the case of pulses, the yield increased from 441 kg/ha in 1950–1951 to 786 kg/ha in 2012–2013.

Among oilseeds, groundnut had a yield of 775 kg/ha in the year 1950–1951 which increased up to 1,268 kg/ha in 2011–2012 and then came down to 996 kg/ha. Similarly, the yield of rapeseed and mustard increased from 368 kg/ha in 1950–1951 to 1,234 kg/ha in 2012–2013. No cultivation of soya bean was reported until 1960–1961. The yield of soya bean was 426 kg/ha in 1970–1971, which increased threefold to 1,354 kg/ha by 2012–2013. The average yield of oilseeds increased from 481 kg/ha in 1950–1951 to 1,169 kg/ha in 2012–2013.

The average sugarcane yields increased from 33.4 ton/ha in 1950–1951 to 67 ton/ha in 2012–2013, though there is wide variation across the region—from the lowest in the subtropical areas of Uttar Pradesh and Bihar to the highest in the hot and semi-arid areas of Tamil Nadu. This increase is nearly two times. The cotton yield also increased five-fold from 88 kg/ha in 1950–1951 to 483 kg/ha in 2012–2013. Other commercial crops such as tea, coffee, jute and tobacco also had shown an increasing trend in the terms of yield.

The availability of high-yielding varieties of wheat and paddy in the late 1960s, along with technology and new institutional structures (agricultural extension, access to crop technology and procurement system), enabled the farmers to adopt improved methods of cultivation. This was followed by the provision of better irrigation facilities and input subsidies. There was relatively higher growth in the yield of all major crops during the Green Revolution period. It indicates that crops other than rice and wheat shared technology benefits (Kannan & Sundaram, 2011).

Although the total crop production globally needs to be doubled by 2050 to sustain demands from a rising population, studies suggest that yields may no longer be increasing in different parts of the globe (Ray et al., 2013). Rice areas with doubling yield rates are found in some local areas within Afghanistan, India, Bangladesh, Laos Vietnam and Cambodia. However, significant yield declines are found in per capita in a few parts, especially Uttar Pradesh, Maharashtra and Tamil Nadu (Ray et al., 2013). A study by Kumar et al. (2019) found that in India,

1. A significant positive correlation existed between Normalized Difference Vegetation Index (NDVI) and the crop yields during the study period 1951–2012.
2. Rice, maize and jowar yields will not have the required incremental rate of growth, while wheat and bajra yields will be able to meet the expectations by 2050. More efforts were to be given to improve the yield rates of rice according to the study.

India is home to a large number of indigenous varieties of cattle and buffaloes, many of which are low yielding. To improve the productivity of local cattle and buffaloes, a massive programme for cross-breeding (CB) of local non-descript cows with exotic ones (Holstein Friesian and Jersey) and upgrading of local buffaloes with better dairy breeds like Murrah buffalo and Mehsana buffalo varieties are being done for quite some time. However, results of CB of buffaloes using artificial insemination have not been very good. Over the years, the proportion of the CB cows and buffaloes has increased, replacing the low-yielding non-descript animals. As a result of these efforts, the average daily milk yield of non-descript cows has increased by 440 g (26.5%), crossbreds by 850 g (15%), and buffaloes by 830 g (23.2%) since 1993–1994 (Directorate of Economics and Statistics, 2012).

As a result of continuous rise in the area of operation and yield levels of all crops, the total agricultural outputs have constantly grown during the past several decades, with the exception of drought years. Rice production increased from 20.58 million ton in 1950–1951 to 104.4 million ton in 2012–2013. The increase was nearly fivefold. Wheat production increased 14 times from 6.46 million ton in 1950–1951 to 92.46 million ton in 2012–2013. The coarse cereal production also had shown an increasing trend from 1950–1951 to 2012–2013, from 15.38 million ton in 1950–1951 to 40.06 million ton in the year 2012–2013, in spite of a significant reduction in area under these crops, by 13 Mha. The total cereal production increased six times during the reporting period. The production of pulses increased from 8.41 million ton in 1950–1951 to 18.45 million ton in 2012–2013.

The total food grain production (fine and coarse cereals and pulses) recorded a fivefold increase from 50.83 million ton in 1950–1951 to 25.36 million ton in 2012–2013, though the increase in area under these crops was only to the tune of 24 per cent during this period.

Among oilseeds, groundnut production increased from 3.48 million ton in 1950–1951 to 4.75 million ton in 2012–2013, with a slight increase in area. The rapeseed and mustard production increased 10 times from 0.76 million ton in 1950–1951, while the area recorded a threefold increase. Production of soya bean witnessed significant growth from a mere 0.01 million ton in 1970–1971 to 14.68 million ton in 2012–2013. Overall, the total oilseed production increased six times, from 5.16 million ton in 1950–1951 to 31.01 million ton in 2012–2013, while the increase in area under these crops was to the tune of nearly 150 per cent—from 10.73 Mha to 26.53 Mha.

As regards commercial crops, coffee production increased from 0.110 million ton in 1970–1971 to 0.318 million ton in 2012–2013. Cotton (lint) production increased from 3.4 million ton in 1950–1951 to 34 million ton in 2012–2013. Sugarcane production increased from 57.05 million ton in 1950–1951 to 338.96 million ton in 2012–2013. Production of tea also increased from 0.419 million ton in 1970–1971 to 1.135 million ton in 2012–2013. Tobacco also maintained steady growth in terms of production.

Milk production, which was only 17 million ton in the year 1950–1951, increased more than seven times to 127.9 million ton, by 2011–2012, to make India the largest producer of milk in the world. The per capita availability of milk also increased from 130 g/day in 1950–1951 to 290 g/day in 2011–2012, though the per capita milk production was lowest during 1968–1969, with the figure touching 112 g/day. Such an impressive growth was made possible through the introduction of high-yielding breeds of cattle (cows and buffaloes), most of which happened under the Operation Flood programme, also known as White Revolution, which continues even today. The population of indigenous varieties of cattle, which are low yielding, had drastically reduced over the past few decades in India.

2.13. CHANGES IN VALUE OF AGRICULTURAL OUTPUTS IN REAL TERMS

For many crops (cereals, pulses, a few oilseeds and sugarcane), there is government intervention in procurement which controls the market price of the produce. So the prices are administered. For common paddy and coarse cereals, the minimum support price (MSP) was ₹74/quintal in 1975–1976 and ₹1,310/quintal in 2013–2014. In the case of wheat, the MSP was ₹105/quintal in 1975–1976 and ₹1,350/quintal in 2012–2013. Gram had an MSP of ₹90/quintal in 1975–1976 and ₹3,000/quintal in 2012–2013. The MSP of sugarcane increased from ₹13/quintal in 1980–1981 to ₹210/quintal in 2013–2014. Cotton had an MSP of ₹135/quintal in the year 1975–1976 and ₹4,000/quintal in the year 2013–2014. The MSP for groundnut went up from ₹26/quintal in 1980–1981 to ₹4,000/quintal in 2013–2014. Black soya bean and yellow soya bean had MSPs at ₹183 and ₹198/quintal, respectively, in the year 1980–1981 and ₹2,500 and ₹2,560/quintal, respectively, in the year 2013–2014. The sunflower seed had an MSP of ₹183/quintal in the year 1980–1981 and ₹3,700/quintal in the year 2013–2014. Both rapeseed/mustard and sunflower had an MSP of ₹400/quintal in the year 1985–1986 and ₹3,000/quintal and ₹2,800/quintal, respectively, in the year 2012–2013.

The real prices of agricultural commodities were computed from the values of the Consumer Price Index, for two reference years, that is, 1965 and 1985. As per the estimates, the real price for paddy was ₹22/quintal

in 1975–1976, which increased to ₹26/quintal in 1995–1996. It also
went up marginally from ₹167/quintal in 2000–2001 to ₹186/quintal
in 2012–2013. In the case of wheat, the real price decreased from ₹31/
quintal to ₹28/quintal during 1975–1976 and 1995–1996. The price
was almost stable during 2000–2001 and 2012–2013 (Table 2.12).
For all oilseed crops (groundnut, rapeseed mustard, sunflower and
soya bean), the real price increased marginally during 1996–1997 and
2012–2013. The price rise was significant for pulses during the latter
period, that is, 1996–1997 and 2012–2013. For pigeon pea, the increase
was to the tune of 46 per cent—from ₹393 to ₹573/quintal. For black

Table 2.12 *Real Price of Food Grains (₹/Quintal)*

Year	Paddy Common	Coarse Cereals	Wheat	Gram	Pigeon Pea	Green Gram	Black Gram
1975–1976	22	22	31	26	0	0	0
1980–1981	27	27	33	0	48	51	51
1985–1986	26	24	30	48	55	55	55
1990–1991	27	24	30	60	64	64	64
1995–1996	26	22	28	51	58	58	58
2000–2001	167	146	200	361	393	393	393
2005–2006	161	149	184	407	397	431	431
2010–2011	177	156	207	372	621	651	603
2012–2013	186	175	201	446	573	655	640

Source: ICSSR, 2015.

Note: From 1975–1976 to 1995–1996, base 1960–1961 = 100; from
1996–1997 to 2012–2013, base 1986–1987 = +100

gram, the increase was to the tune of 63 per cent. These changes may be attributed to the increasing demand owing to improvement in the purchasing power and decline in domestic production.

2.14. CONCLUSION

India is bestowed with a rich endowment of land. Although large areas of western Rajasthan and some parts of Kachchh have desert soils, the soil profile in India, on the whole, shows that it is highly congenial for irrigated agriculture and there is still scope for increasing the NSA, provided water is available to irrigate the crops. Due to a sharp increase in population during the past seven plus decades, the per capita arable land and renewable water availability declined sharply in the country during this period.

While the agricultural GDP in value terms at constant prices increased 4.5 times during 1954–1955 to 2011–2012, the average growth rate in agricultural GDP varied between various plan periods. The crop sector output also showed variation in growth and deceleration in the growth similar to that in agricultural GDP. The growth rate in livestock population was impressive and kept a constant pace of about 4 per cent after the 1970s. The milk production had increased impressively, though there were wide variations among different states. However, the per capita food grain production has declined significantly since 2001. It could also be seen that the total area under irrigated agriculture under food crops, sugarcane and oilseeds expanded. The NSA in the country peaked at 143 Mha along with steadily increasing intensity of land use.

During the period, from 522 kg/ha in 1950–1951 to 2,462 kg/ha in 2012–2013, growth in the yield of major cereals was very impressive— from 668 kg/ha in 1950–1951 to 2,462 kg/ha in 2012–2013 for rice and from 663 kg/ha in 1950–1951 to 3,119 kg/ha in 2012–2013 for wheat. But to achieve this, along with the use of new varieties, the input use in agriculture had to be increased substantially. For instance, for a hectare of GCA, the use of fertilizers went up from 0.52 kg to

137 kg during the same period. The electricity consumption per unit of GIA increased 160 times from 7 kWh/ha in 1950–1951 to 1,154 kWh/ha of GIA in 2006–2007. The extent of agricultural subsidies in real terms increased manifold from 1980–1981 to 2008–2009, both in aggregate terms (8.45 times) and per ha of GCA (7.5 times).

The last four decades witnessed a giant leap in seed production and with the onset of new technologies such as transgenics tissue culture, soil-less agriculture and verti culture, likewise, fertilizer consumption has been increasing and, as of now, India is one of the major producers as well as consumers of fertilizers in the world. While the farm mechanization is increasing in Indian agriculture, the limited scale of operations could not reduce human labour which is on a rising scale. All subsidies are not bad, and India's agricultural subsidies revolve around electricity, fertilizers and irrigation water. The agricultural energy consumption increased from 125 million units in 1947 to 153 billion units in 2012–2013.

Table 2A.1 Changes in Land Use Pattern in India (Million Hectare)

Category	1950–1951	1960–1961	1970–1971	1980–1981	1990–1991	2000–2001	2001–2002	2002–2003	2003–2004	2004–2005	2005–2006	2006–2007	2007–2008	2008–2009 (P)	2009–2010 (P)	2010–2011 (P)	2011–2012 (P)	2012–2013 (P)	2013–2014 (P)	2014–2015 (P)	2015–2016 (P)
Geographic Area	328.73	328.73	328.73	328.73	328.73	328.73	328.73	328.73	328.73	328.73	328.73	328.73	328.73	328.73	328.73	328.73	328.73	328.73	328.73	328.73	328.73
Reporting/Area for land use	284.32	298.46	303.75	304.16	304.86	305.19	305.13	305.36	305.57	305.59	306.88	307.09	307.23	307.41	307.41	307.48	307.39	307.49	307.8	307.78	307.75
Area under non-agricultural use	9.36	14.84	16.48	19.60	21.09	23.75	23.91	24.12	24.52	24.76	24.99	25.45	25.88	26.21	26.16	26.40	26.31	26.50	26.91	26.94	27.08
Barren and uncultivable land	38.16	35.91	28.13	19.96	19.39	17.48	17.41	17.52	17.47	17.47	17.33	17.29	17.02	16.85	17.18	17.18	17.22	17.07	16.94	16.99	16.94
Net sown area	118.75	133.20	140.86	140.29	142.87	141.34	140.73	131.94	140.71	140.64	141.16	139.82	141.02	141.90	139.17	141.56	140.98	139.93	141.43	140.13	139.51
Gross sown area	131.89	152.77	165.79	172.63	185.74	185.34	188.01	173.89	189.66	191.10	192.74	192.38	195.22	195.33	189.19	197.68	195.80	194.22	200.95	198.38	197.05
Cropping Intensity	111.07	114.69	117.70	123.05	130.01	131.13	133.60	131.79	134.79	135.88	136.54	137.59	138.44	137.65	135.94	139.64	138.88	138.79	142.09	141.57	141.25
Forest land under good tree cover	14.24	18.11	21.01	22.18	22.24	22.88	22.85	22.87	22.90	22.89	23.28	23.27	23.28	23.27	23.28	23.28	23.29	23.28	23.34	23.31	23.35

Misc tree crops and groves	19.83	4.46	4.37	3.58	3.82	3.44	3.44	3.43	3.38	3.36	3.39	3.35	3.40	3.34	3.21	3.20	3.16	3.18	3.19	3.10	3.09
Cultivable waste lands	22.94	19.21	17.50	16.74	15.00	13.63	13.52	13.65	13.24	13.27	13.22	13.27	13.04	12.73	12.95	12.65	12.64	12.64	12.39	12.42	12.29
Current fallows	10.68	11.64	10.60	14.83	13.70	14.78	15.34	22.46	14.49	14.79	14.21	15.51	14.65	14.19	16.01	14.28	14.51	15.29	14.16	15.09	15.41
Old fallows	17.45	11.18	8.73	9.72	9.66	10.27	10.51	11.97	11.31	10.88	10.70	10.52	10.33	10.29	10.84	10.32	10.67	11.04	10.69	11.09	11.31
Permanent pastures and grazing lands	6.68	13.97	13.26	11.99	11.40	10.66	10.53	10.45	10.48	10.45	10.44	10.42	10.36	10.34	10.34	10.30	10.31	10.26	10.26	10.26	10.26

Source: Directorate of Economics & Statistics (2019).

Notes: 1. Percentages worked out over the reported area.

2. In 2009–2010, there was a significant decline in total cropped area and NSA due to decline in NSA in the states of Andhra Pradesh, Bihar, Jharkhand, Rajasthan, Tamil Nadu, Uttar Pradesh and West Bengal. This was mainly due to deficient rainfall.

3. P = Provisional

4. Cropping intensity is the percentage of the GCA to the NSA.

Table 2A.2 Area under Major Crops in India (in Terms of %)

	1970–1971	1980–1981	1990–1991	2000–2001	2010–2011 (P)	2011–2012 (P)	2012–2013 (P)	2013–2014 (P)	2014–2015 (P)
Rice	22.5	23.3	23.0	24.2	21.9	22.3	22.0	22.1	22.3
Wheat	11.0	12.9	12.9	13.9	15.2	15.4	15.7	15.6	16.2
Coarse cereals	3.0	2.3	1.3	0.8	0.4	0.4	0.4	0.4	0.3
Total cereals	61.4	60.8	55.5	54.7	51.4	51.1	50.7	50.4	51.3
Pulses	13.9	13.2	13.4	11.5	12.8	12.0	11.3	11.8	10.9
Total food grains	75.3	73.9	68.9	66.2	64.3	63.1	62.0	62.3	62.3
Total oilseeds	8.9	9.1	13.5	13.3	14.6	14.3	14.9	15.0	14.3
Groundnut	4.6	3.9	4.5	3.6	2.9	2.7	2.7	2.7	2.6
Cotton	4.7	4.5	4.1	4.6	5.5	6.2	6.1	5.9	6.4
Jute	0.5	0.5	0.4	0.5	0.4	0.4	0.4	0.4	0.4
Total fibre	5.5	5.3	4.7	5.2	6.0	6.7	6.6	6.4	6.8

Sugarcane	1.6	1.7	2.1	2.5	2.6	2.8	2.8	2.7	2.8
Tobacco	0.3	0.3	0.2	0.2	0.2	0.2	0.2	0.2	0.2
Condiments and spices	1.1	1.2	1.3	1.5	1.7	1.9	1.7	1.6	1.7
Potatoes									
Onions									
Total fruits and vegetables	2.2	2.9	3.6	4.4	4.8	4.9	4.9	4.9	5.0
Fodder crops	4.2	4.7	4.5	5.0	3.9	4.0	4.8	4.9	4.6
Total non-food grains	19.6	20.2	24.1	25.3	26.6	27.3	28.5	28.3	28.0
Gross cropped area	100.0	100.0	100.0	100.0	100.0	100.0	100.0	100.0	100.0

Source: Directorate of Economics & Statistics (2017).

Note: P = Provisional

Table 2A.3 Cropping Pattern in Different Agro-climate Regions in India (% of Farmers)

Agro-climate Region	Cereal		Pulse		Sugar Product		Spices		Fruits and Vegetables		Oilseeds		Fibres		Others	
	NSS 59th Round	NSS 70th Round	NSS 59th Round	NSS 70th Round	NSS 59th Round	NSS 70th Round	NSS 59th Round	NSS 70th Round	NSS 59th Round	NSS 70th Round	NSS 59th Round	NSS 70th Round	NSS 59th Round	NSS 70th Round	NSS 59th Round	NSS 70th Round
Western	61.6	51.8	10.4	8.6	0.5	2.3	1.7	5.6	21.5	24.5	1.4	1.4	0.0	0.0	2.8	5.7
Himalayan Eastern	55.0	49.0	1.3	0.6	0.1	0.2	7.6	10.3	31.4	35.5	0.9	0.7	1.1	0.3	2.6	3.5
Himalayan Lower Gangetic	72.7	65.1	0.6	1.2	0.1	0.1	0.9	2.4	11.1	14.9	1.4	2.4	11.7	11.8	1.6	2.2
Plains Middle Gangetic	76.8	81.4	4.1	3.3	7.2	5.5	0.3	0.2	5.7	4.3	0.8	1.6	1.3	0.4	3.8	3.3
Plains Upper Gangetic	56.5	48.5	10.4	10.6	13.0	13.9	0.5	0.1	5.0	7.3	3.5	1.0	0.2	0.0	10.8	18.6
Plains Trans Gangetic	50.3	51.0	3.4	1.4	3.2	0.9	0.1	0.1	1.9	1.4	0.6	0.2	7.3	13.5	33.1	31.5

Region																
Plains Eastern Gangetic	78.6	79.7	7.5	4.8	0.3	0.1	0.3	0.5	11.1	10.9	1.6	2.7	0.3	1.1	0.2	0.0
Hills Central Plateau	62.4	52.5	16.5	15.3	0.2	2.3	0.5	0.4	2.7	1.4	12.7	17.8	1.7	3.2	3.4	7.0
Hills Western Plateau	38.4	33.4	25.5	18.0	5.0	6.7	1.0	0.7	4.6	2.5	10.2	18.9	13.2	19.3	2.0	0.5
Hills Southern Plateau	48.7	43.4	11.4	13.6	1.8	3.7	2.6	2.3	5.6	6.0	19.1	15.2	6.7	13.6	4.2	2.2
Hills East Coast	69.2	67.5	4.5	2.3	2.7	1.5	1.9	2.1	7.9	11.4	9.0	8.5	2.7	3.6	2.1	3.2
Western Coast	24.9	27.2	2.3	1.2	0.1	0.1	14.6	17.2	21.6	19.7	24.3	23.5	0.8	0.1	11.3	11.0
Gujarat Plains	89.0	48.9	9.3	11.2	0.4	0.4	0.0	0.4	0.9	3.1	0.1	8.5	0.0	20.0	0.4	7.4
Western Dry	45.7	44.1	23.0	23.4	0.0	0.0	0.0	0.3	0.6	0.2	2.0	10.1	7.9	0.6	20.7	21.3
India	58.7	55.1	9.8	8.9	3.3	3.2	2.0	2.5	8.5	9.1	8.2	9.2	4.1	5.9	5.3	6.1

Source: Directorate of Economics & Statistics, 2017.

Note: (P) = Provisional

REFERENCES

Amarasinghe, U. A., Shah, T., & Singh, O. P. (2007). *Changing consumption patterns: Implications on food and water demand in India* (Vol. 119). International Water Management Institute.

Bidyadhar, M., & Kumar. A. (2018). Changing cropping pattern in Indian agriculture. *Journal of Economic and Social Development, 14*(1).

Central Ground Water Board (2019). National Compilation on Dynamic Groundwater Resources of India, 2017. Government of India, Ministry of Jal Shakti, Department of Water Resources, RD & GR, Central Ground Water Board, Faridabad. http://cgwb.gov.in/GW-Assessment/GWRA-2017-National-Compilation.pdf

Cornell University. (2013). *Agrarian crisis in India.* Paper presented at the Annual Conference of the Cornell/Syracuse on South Asian Consortium, US Department of Education.

Custodio, E. (2000). *The complex concept of overexploited aquifer* (2nd ed.). Fundación Marcelino Botín.

Directorate of Economics and Statistics. (2010). *Agricultural statistics at a glance.* Dept. of Agriculture and Cooperation, Ministry of Agriculture, New Delhi, September 2010. http://desagri.gov.in/documents-reports/agricultural-statistics-at-a-glance/agricultural-statistics-at-a-glance-2010/

Directorate of Economics and Statistics. (2012). *Agricultural statistics at a glance.* Directorate of Economics and Statistics, Department of Cooperation, Ministry of Agriculture, Government of India, November 2012.

Directorate of Economics and Statistics. (2017). *Land use statistics 2014–15.* Department of Agriculture Cooperation and Farmers Welfare.

Directorate of Economics and Statistics. (2019). *Agricultural statistics at a glance.* Department of Agriculture Cooperation and Farmers Welfare.

Directorate of Economics and Statistics. (2021). *Agricultural statistics at a glance.* Dept. of Agriculture and Cooperation, Ministry of Agriculture, New Delhi, May 2021.

GoI. (2003). *Economic survey 2002–2003.* Economic Division Ministry of Finance, Government of India.

GoI. (2011). *Report of working group on major and medium irrigation and command area development for XII Five-Year Plan* (2012–2017).

GoI. (2013). *Annual report* (2012–2013). Department of Animal Husbandry, Dairying and Fisheries.

GoI. (2018). *Economic survey 2017–2018.*

GoI. (2020). Indian seed sector. https://agricoop.nic.in/en

Hall, A., Bockett, G., Taylor, S., Sivamohan, M. V. K., & Clark, N. (2001). Why research partnerships really matter: Innovation theory, institutional arrangements and implications for developing new technology for the poor. *World Development, 29*(5), 783–797.

Jaga, P. K., & Patel, Y. (2012). An overview of fertilizers consumption in India: Determinants and outlook for 2020—A review. *International Journal of Scientific Engineering and Technology*, 1(6), 285–291.

Jha, G. K., Pal, S., & Singh, A. (2012). Changing energy use pattern and the demand projection for Indian agriculture. *Agricultural Economics Review*, 25(1), 61–68.

Jha, P. (2007). Some aspects of the well-being of India's agricultural labour in the context of contemporary agrarian crisis. *Indian Journal of Labour Economics*, 49(4), 741–764.

Kannan, E., & Sundaram, S. (2011). *Analysis of trends in India's agricultural growth*. Institute for Social and Economic Change.

Karennavar M. F., & Haremath, S. S. (1990). Natural Resource endowment regions in India. In Mandal, R. B., *Patterns of Regional Geography*, vol 2, Concept Publishing, New Delhi.

Kumar, L. P., Indira, M., & Gangothri, M. (2017). Trends in fertilizer consumption and foodgrain production in India: A co-integration analysis. *SDMIMD Journal of Management*, 8(2), 45–50.

Kumar, M. D. (2003). *Food security and sustainable agriculture in India: The water management challenge* (Vol. 60). International Water Management Institute.

Kumar, M. D., Bassi, N., Sivamohan, M. V. K., & Venkatachalam, L., (2014). Breaking the agrarian impasse in eastern India. In: Kumar, M. D., Bassi, N., Narayanamoorthy, A., Sivamohan, M. V. K., (Eds.). *Water, Energy and Food Security Nexus: Lessons from India for Development*. Routledge/Earthscan, London, UK.

Kumar, M. D., Ganguli, A., & Sivamohan, M. V. K. (2019). *What drives annual agricultural growth rates in India*. Institute for Resource Analysis and Policy.

Kumar, M. D., & Singh, O. P. (2008). How serious are groundwater over-exploitation problems in India? A fresh investigation into an old issue. In M. D. Kumar (Ed.), *Managing water ion the face of growing scarcity, inequity and declining returns: Exploring fresh approaches*. 7th Annual Partners' meet of IWMI–Tata Water Policy Research Program, ICRISAT, Patancheru, 2–4 April.

Kumar, M. D., Sivamohan, M. V. K., & Bassi, N. (Eds.). (2012). *Water management, food security and sustainable agriculture in developing economies*. Routledge.

Kumar, T. V. L., Barbosa, H. M., & Rao, K. K. (2019). Current livestock production statistics of India. *Sustainability II*, 4657.

Ladha, J. K., Fischer, K. S., Hossain, M., Hobbs, P. R., & Hardy, B. (Eds.) (2000). *Improving the oproductivity and sustainability of rice–wheat systems of the Indo-Gangetic plains: A synthesis of NARS–IRRI partnership research* [Discussion Paper No. 40]. International Rice Research Institute, Los Baños.

Mazid, M., & Khan, T. A. (2015). Future of bio-fertilizers in Indian agriculture: An overview. *International Journal of Agricultural and Food Research*, 3(3), 10–23.

Mehta, M. M. (2007). Public-Private Partnership in Mechanising Indian Agriculture for Second Green Revolution. In: S. Ayyappan, P. Chandra and

S. K. Tandon (Eds.), *Agricultural Transformation through Public–private Partnership–An interface*. ICAR. March, 19–20.

Ministry of Agriculture and Farmer Welfare (2019). Agricultural Statistics at a Glance, Directorate of Economics and Statistics, Dept. of Agriculture, Cooperation and Farmer Welfare, Ministry of Agriculture and Farmer Welfare, Govt. of India, New Delhi, January 2019.

Ministry of Jal Shakti (2021). Per Capita Availability of Water, Posted on 25th March, 2021 by PIB, Delhi. https://pib.gov.in/PressReleaseIframePage.aspx?PRID=1707522

Ministry of Statistics and Programme Implementation (2021). Sector-Wise GDP of India, https://statisticstimes.com/economy/country/india-gdp-sectorwise.php, accessed on November 28, 2021.

Mukherjee, S., Shah, Z., & Kumar, M. D. (2010). Sustaining urban water supplies in India: Increasing role of large reservoirs. *Water Resources Management, 24*(10), 2035–2055.

Mukherji, A. (2003). *Groundwater development and agrarian change in Eastern India* [IWMI–Tata Comment No. 9, based on V. Ballabh, K. Chaudhary, S. Pandey, & S. Mishra]. IWMI–Tata Water Policy Research Program, Anand.

Ministry of Power (n.d.). Various Annual Reports from 1990–91 to 2020–21: https://powermin.gov.in/en/content/annual-reports-year-wise-ministry

Mukherji, A. (2006). Political ecology of groundwater: The contrasting case of water-abundant West Bengal and water-scarce Gujarat, India. *Hydrogeology Journal, 14*(3), 392–406.

Ministry of Statistics and Programme Implementation (n.d.). India Electricity Consumption: Utilities: Agriculture. https://www.ceicdata.com/en/india/electricity-consumption-utilities/electricity-consumption-utilities-agriculture

Mukherji, A. (2008). Spatio-temporal analysis of markets for groundwater irrigation services in India: 1976–1977 to 1997–1998. *Hydrogeology Journal, 16*(6), 1077–1087.

Mukherji, A., Shah, T., & Banerjee, P. S. (2012). Kick-starting a second green revolution in Bengal. *Economic & Political Weekly, 47*(18), 27–30.

National Rain-Fed Area Authority (2011). Challenges of food security and its management. National Rain-Fed Area Authority, New Delhi.

NCAER (National Council of Applied Economic Research). (2013). *Agricultural outlook and situation analysis reports* [Quarterly Report April–June].

Pandey, G., & Ranganathan, T. (2018). Changing land-use pattern in India: Has there been an expansion of fallow lands? *Agricultural Economics Research Review, 31*(1), 113–122.

Pingali, P., Aiyar, A., Abraham, M., & Rahman, A. (2019). *Transforming food systems for a rising India*. Springer Nature.

Rangarajan, C. (2014). Growth and human development. Sri M. Ramakrishnayya memorial lecture organized by Sub-Hindustani Trust and Indian Institute of Management and Commerce, Hyderabad.

Ravishankar, T. (2014). *Monetizing modern land management practices.* National Remote Sensing Centre, ISRO (DOS).

Ray, V. D., Mueller, D. N., West, C. P., & Foly, A. J. (2013). Yield trends are insufficient to double global crop production by 2050. *PLOS One, 8*(6). https://doi.org/10.1371/Journal

Resurgent India. (2016). The agrarian crisis in India: Introduction (October). https://new.resurgentindia.org/the-agrarian-crisis-in-India-introduction/

Resurgent India. (2017). Status of rainfed agriculture in India (November). new.resurgentindia.org/status-of-rainfed-agriculture-in-India

Salunkhe, H. A., & Deshmush, B. B. (2012). The overview of government subsidies to agriculture sector in India. *IOSR Journal of Agriculture and Veterinary Science,* 1(5), 43–47.

Shah, T. (2001). *Wells and welfare in the Ganga basin: Public policy and private initiative in eastern Uttar Pradesh, India* (Vol. 54). International Water Management Institute.

Sharma, V. P. (2012). India's agricultural development under the new economic regime: Policy perspective and strategy for the 12th Five-Year Plan. *Indian Journal of Agricultural Economics, 67*(1), 46–78.

Sharma, V. P., & Thaker, H. (2011). Demand for fertilisers in India: Determinants and outlook for 2020. *Indian Journal of Agricultural Economics, 66*(4), 638–661.

Siddiqui, S. A., & Fatima, N. (2017). Indian soils: identification and classification. *Earth Science India, 10* (III), 1–14.

Singh, H., & Chand, R. (2011). The Seeds Bill, 2011: Some reflections. *Economic & Political Weekly, 46*(51), 22–25.

Singh, J. (2013). Demand projection of chemical fertilizer's consumption in India: Determinants and outlook for 2020. *International Journal of Transformations in Business Management, 2*(3), 62–64.

Sivakumar, M. (2013). Gross capital formation and GDP growth in Indian agriculture sector [Munich Personal RePEc Archive, Paper No. 46946]. https://mpra.ub.uni-muenchen.de/46946/

The Fertiliser Association of India (n.d.). All-India Consumption of Fertiliser Nutrients—1950–51 to 2020–21. https://www.faidelhi.org/statistics/statistical-database

Usami, Y. (2011). A note on recent trends in wage rates in rural India. *Review of Agrarian Studies, 1*(1), 149–182.

Venkateswarlu, B., & Prasad, J. V. N. S. (2012). Carrying capacity of Indian agriculture: Issues related to rainfed agriculture. *Current Science, 102*(6), 882–888.

Verma, S., & Shah, T. 2012. *Beyond digging and filling holes: Lessons from case studies of best-performing MGNREGA assets* [Water Policy Research Highlight No. 42]. IWMI–Tata Water Policy Program, Anand.

Chapter 3

Annual Growth Rate*
What Drives Agricultural Growth?

M. Dinesh Kumar, Nitin Bassi, Arijit Ganguly and M. V. K. Sivamohan

3.1. INTRODUCTION

In India, the practice of predicting agricultural growth rates is as old as its independence. The predictions are made before the onset of monsoon, once the India Meteorological Department (IMD) forecasts of the country's rainfall become available. The agricultural growth prediction for the ensuing crop year mainly takes into consideration whether the rainfall would be normal or above or below normal. Since it is a widely believed fact that agriculture in India is still a 'gamble with monsoon', the short-term (mainly annual) agricultural growth rate is linked to annual rainfall, suggesting that a good monsoon would ensure a high agricultural growth rate during the year concerned. An extension of this logic was that a low annual growth rate in the agriculture sector is attributed to the failure of the monsoon during that year. More strangely, an impressive growth rate in agriculture in the medium term is attributed to the high performance of the sector in terms of technology adoption, policy frameworks and institutional interventions.

But two questions remain unanswered. First, is it appropriate to link the performance of the agriculture sector in terms of growth rate to

---

* This chapter is a revised version of the article Kumar et al., (2019) published in *Economic and Political Weekly*.

the aggregate predictions of monsoon rainfall in a country like India? Here, the underlying argument is that India has several rainfall zones (IMD itself had defined 36 rainfall zones). The mean annual rainfall in India varies widely spatially from as low as 200 mm in Jaisalmer to as high as 11,000 mm in Cherrapunji and, therefore, large downward deviation of rainfall in one low rainfall region (like the north-western part of India) can be made up by a small upward deviation of rainfall in a high rainfall zone (like the northeast or Western Ghats). Second, even if the rainfall does influence agricultural growth rates, how can the average rainfall of a single year alone cause wide year-to-year fluctuations in the agricultural growth rate noticed in the country?

In the past, the absence of long-term data on (spatial) average annual rainfall made it difficult to develop a more nuanced and empirical understanding of this vexed issue. Now such data are available for a considerably long time duration from IMD. In this chapter, we first analyse the historical agricultural growth trends and trends in (spatial) average annual rainfall in India and examine whether any useful inferences on annual agricultural growth rate during a year can be drawn on the basis of the annual rainfall data. Thereafter, we explore the key factors which actually drive short-term agricultural growth rates and draw implications for analysing the impact of national agricultural policies. Prior to doing that, we first provide a theoretical perspective on agricultural growth, discussing the drivers of change in agricultural outputs in value terms.

The hypothesis pertaining to annual agricultural growth rates was also tested for Gujarat, which is an agriculturally very dynamic state, experiencing very significant year-to-year variations in annual rainfalls and high volatility in annual agricultural growth performance. Considering the fact that there will be a differential effect of a certain degree of departure of annual rainfall from the normal values on agricultural outputs with a difference in mean annual rainfall and contribution to the overall agricultural output,[1] such analyses become very

---

[1] The effect of a 25 per cent decline in annual rainfall from normal values on agricultural output in a region with a mean annual rainfall of 1,600–2,000 mm will be much less than that caused by the same degree of departure in a region where the annual rainfall is in the range of 400–500 mm and which contributes more significantly to the agricultural output in value terms.

crucial for regions where the effects of such variations on the trends in agricultural growth rate are likely to be less. Although the state shows regional variation in the magnitude of mean annual rainfall, water resources endowment and irrigation facilities (Kumar & Perry, 2019), these variations are much less as compared to the variations that exist at the national level.

3.2. AGRICULTURAL GROWTH: SOME THEORETICAL PERSPECTIVES

Agricultural growth in any region can occur because of (a) growth in crop output; (b) increase in value of the given output; and (c) diversification of agriculture towards high-valued crops and livestock products (Bhalla & Singh, 2009). Here, the growth in output can result from three major phenomena. First, the output of a crop can increase due to a variety of reasons, including crop technology adoption, irrigation supplement to rainfed crop, precision irrigation, availability of adequate soil moisture due to rains and better soil nutrient management or increase in area under the given crop. Second, the value of the given output in the market can increase due to changes in the demand–supply situation, which is particularly important in the case of non-cereal crops and perishable products such as fruits and vegetables, and where the sufficient infrastructure for storage is either absent or economically unviable. Third, the farmers can shift to high-valued crops or livestock, which give higher returns from a unit of land and unit of livestock, respectively. Such a shift can be often subject to high crop risk or market risk (Kumar & Amarasinghe, 2009). But availability of good credit facilities, marketing infrastructure, research and extension services and technical inputs can fasten this process.

Hence, several factors can drive agricultural growth, namely environmental factors; institutional factors, including those which are market-related (Bhalla & Singh, 2009; Gulati, 2002); policy factors; infrastructural factors (Bhalla & Singh, 2009; Shah et al., 2009); and science/technology-related factors (Bhalla & Singh, 2009). Some of the environmental factors here are the availability or failure of rains and snow, changes in atmospheric temperature, humidity, wind speed and sunshine (exogenous), and changes in soil moisture regime and soil nutrient regime (endogenous). The infrastructure-related factors are the presence of irrigation facility, presence of roads for transport, presence of storage and market infrastructure, and precision irrigation technology. That said, it is important to consider that both creation of irrigation infrastructure (wells, reservoirs—both small and large—canals and pumps) and installation of precision water application technologies will have their effect, only if the resource availability situation is good or does not get altered. In the face of resource depletion (like reduced inflows into irrigation reservoirs or groundwater depletion, showing up in declining well yields), the potential benefits of extended irrigation infrastructure in the form of expansion in the irrigated area cannot be derived.

The input price policy can be one which encourages efficient use or one which encourages wasteful use of input resources such as water, fertilizers and pesticides. For the first one to happen, the price has to be raised to reflect the value of the resource and, for the second one, the price has to be lowered or input subsidy is raised. While the positive impact of the first one will be both long term and short term (Pearce & Warford, 1993), that of the second one will be short term. Conversely, the negative effects of the first measure, if any, would be rather short-lived and that of the second measure would be long term. The best example is electricity pricing for groundwater pumping.

Institutional factors such as property rights in land and water will have long-term impacts on the equity, efficiency and sustainability of resource use (Pearce & Warford, 1993; Thobani, 1997). Similarly, good extension services will have both short- and long-term impacts on yield by encouraging farmers to adopt better crop varieties, better input use technologies or better agronomic practices. Produce price regulations, particularly through enforcement of minimum support prices, will have a significant impact on the allocation of land for a particular crop (Bhalla & Singh, 2009). Also, agricultural trade can have severe effects on the market value of crops, which the trade affects. But, in the long run, the volume of production of that crop itself can change. In which direction the change takes place depends on whether the trade policy encourages import or export of the commodity in question and the comparative advantage of the region in question in terms of producing that crop.

Lastly, science and technology can have far-reaching consequences and can often overcome the constraints induced by the environmental factors. This has been adequately demonstrated in India, which experienced the impacts of high-yielding varieties of major cereal crops, brought in by the Green Revolution. The introduction of a new high-yielding variety or a drought-resistant variety can have both short-term and long-term effects on crop productivity, depending on the environmental factors. In a region that is highly vulnerable to droughts, a drought-resistant variety of a dominant crop will have a significant impact on both the area under the crop and the yield of the crop, if significant drought-proofing measures are not in place. But in the face of deteriorating soil quality (or primary productivity of soils), the potential benefits from high-yielding varieties cannot be derived. This is called 'technology fatigue'.

All these lead us to the point that the drivers of growth in agriculture could be too many, and the final outcome of the introduction of these drivers would be a result of the interplay of different drivers. A policy to boost groundwater irrigation will not make the desired effects on irrigated areas unless sufficient groundwater is available for exploitation or sufficient arable land is available for expansion of cropped areas. To sum up, it would be meaningless to make linear or even unidirectional projections of the impacts of one set of interventions, be it policy-related, institutional, market, technology-related or infrastructure-related, without knowing the interactions among various actors.

3.3. HISTORICAL AGRICULTURAL GROWTH TRENDS

Following is the analysis of historical growth rates in agricultural GDP of India since 1955–1956. The agricultural outputs in value terms grew from ₹1,683.61 billion to ₹7645.10 billion[2] in 2012–2013 in real terms (Figure 3.1). The annual agricultural growth rates ranged from −12.77 per cent during 1979–1980 to a highest of 15.24 per cent during 1988–1989 (Figure 3.1). The analysis shows that the variation in annual agricultural growth rates is wide. While there had been

---

[2] US$1 equals to ₹70.

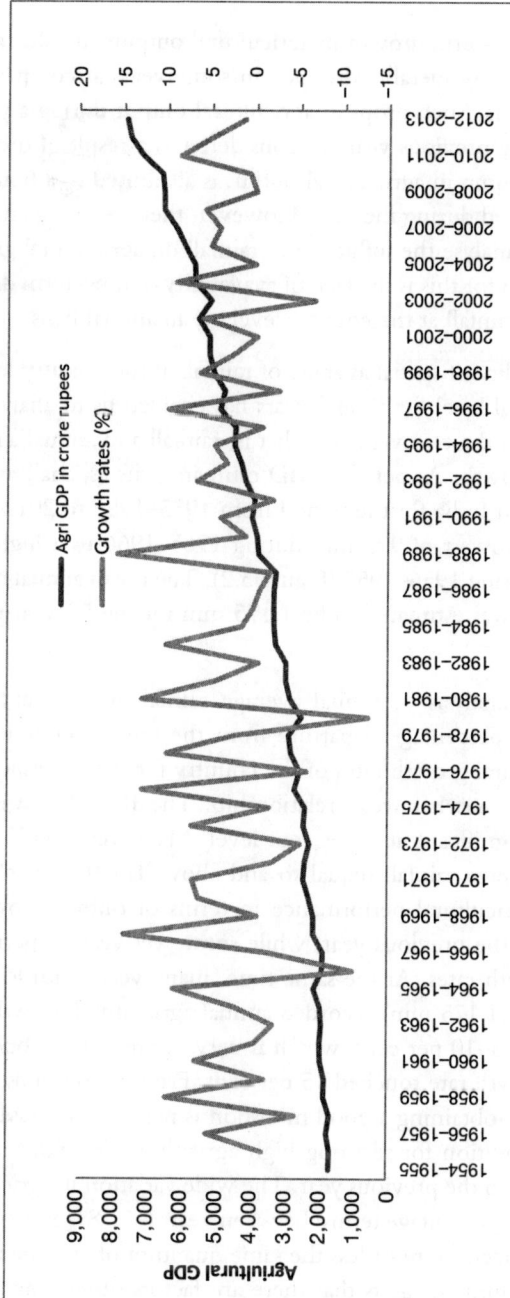

Figure 3.1 *Agricultural GDP and the Growth Rates in India*

Source: https://tradingeconomics.com/india/gdp-from-agriculture

considerable long-term growth in agricultural outputs in value terms, the outputs had considerably dropped in some years as compared to the previous years. Such drops in agricultural output during a year as compared to the previous year are considered as a result of drought, and any major jump in agricultural output is attributed to a bountiful monsoon received during the year. However, there were no attempts so far to really analyse the influence of rainfall on agricultural growth rate. One reason for this is the lack of availability of long-term data on average spatial rainfall at the country level on an annual basis.

The availability of spatial average of rainfall at the country level as well as divisional level for several years has enabled us to analyse the linkage between the two variables, that is, rainfall and annual agricultural output growth. As per the IMD estimates, the (spatial) average annual rainfall in India for the period from 1955–1956 to 2012–2013 ranged from a lowest of 925 mm during 1965–1966 to a highest of 1,380.5 mm during 1956–1957 (Figure 3.2). The mean annual rainfall of the country was estimated to be 1,175 mm for the 58-year period considered.

Regression analysis of annual average rainfall in different years (expressed as a percentage departure from the mean value) and the annual agricultural growth rates of the country for the corresponding years show a somewhat weak relationship. The R^2 value was only 0.31, though significant at 5 per cent level. Many years with excessively high average rainfall (equal to and above 1,300 mm) clocked very dismal agricultural performance in terms of output growth in comparison to the previous year, while some wet years experienced two-digit growth rates. At the same time, many years with less than normal rainfall (1,175 mm) recorded annual agricultural growth rates in the range of 5–10 per cent, which is very impressive. In one case, the annual growth rate touched 15 per cent. From such trends, it can be inferred that obtaining a good monsoon is neither a necessary nor a sufficient condition for securing high agricultural growth during a year in relation to the previous year. The wide variation in agricultural growth rates (in percentage terms) between years (−5.78% and 14.75%) which experienced more or less the same quantum of average rainfall (around 1,150 mm) suggests that there are factors other than annual rainfall which influence the agricultural growth rates.

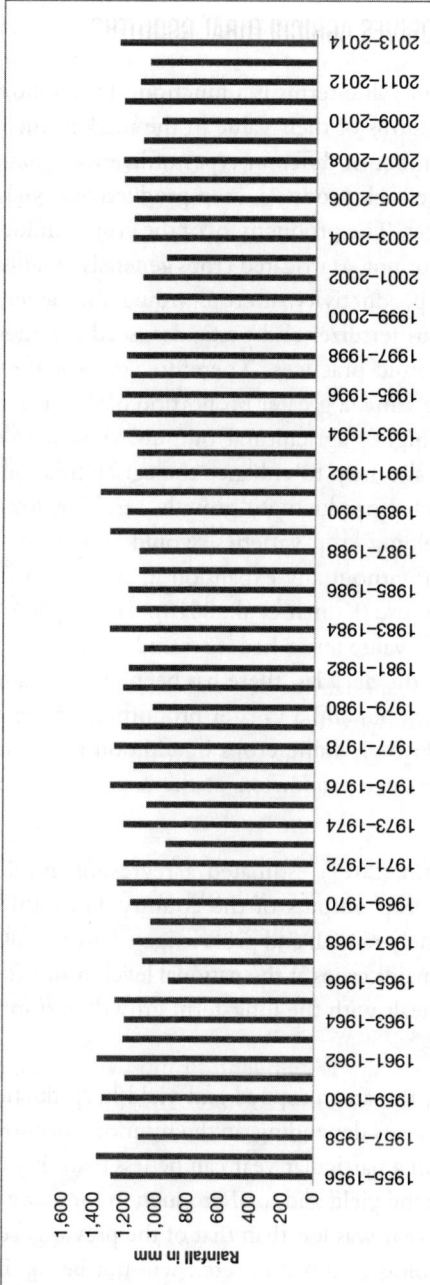

Figure 3.2 *Average Annual Rainfall of India: 1955–1956 to 2013–2014*

Source: https://imdpune.gov.in/library/public/e-book110.pdf

3.4. WHAT DRIVES AGRICULTURAL GROWTH?

The agricultural output in value terms is a function of the following: types of crops grown in terms of their value in the market; total area under each crop; the number of different types of livestock and their productivity; price of livestock products; crop productivity (yield per ha); and the produce prices. The productivity of the crop is influenced by whether it is irrigated or not, as irrigated crops generally yield higher than rainfed crops. The productivity of crops would also depend on the level of inputs such as fertilizer and pesticides, seed varieties and labour inputs for agronomic practices. Therefore, even if the total cropped area remains the same, a greater proportion of the area under irrigation would mean higher agricultural outputs. A shift towards high-value crops would also help to enhance the agricultural outputs in value terms. Total factor productivity growth, resulting from the introduction of high-yielding crop varieties, would also ensure high agricultural growth even without any expansion in area under irrigation and increase in input use (Kumar et al., 2010). This explains how the agricultural outputs in value terms had increased substantially over the years. Basically, over the decades, there has been greater adoption of high-yielding crop varieties and a greater proportion of the cultivated area brought under high-value crops in addition to expansion in cropped area and a greater proportion of the area coming under irrigation.

Kannan and Sundaram (2011) estimated a regression model for predicting the value of crop outputs of the country and found that two key parameters, namely rainfall and gross irrigated area, explained growth performance of major crops at the national level to an extent of 70 per cent. The study dealt with the long-term growth performance of the crop sector.

But in the short run, the area cropped and yield keep fluctuating for many crops between years depending on the monsoon occurrence. The gross cropped area in a particular year can be less than that of the previous year, and so are the yield and total production for many crops if the rainfall during the year was less than that of the previous year, as the effect of crop technology, crop shift, etc., will not be significant during such short time spans. Vice versa can happen if a particular year happens to be wetter than the previous year. For certain high-value crops, the prices can fluctuate between years depending on the market conditions influenced by the supply of produce and the demand situation. Hence, short-term trends can be different from long-term trends and can be influenced by the situation in the current year vis-à-vis rainfall, market conditions, etc., in the previous year.

A univariate regression analysis was carried out to assess the influence of the rainfall of the previous year as well as the current year on agricultural output growth rates. For this, the 'increase/decrease in rainfall in a particular year over the previous year as a percentage of the previous year's rainfall' was estimated for all the years from 1956–1957 onwards. The percentage increase in rainfall varied from (–)26.83 to (+)28.60. Hence, the range in annual rainfall change is very wide. The annual agricultural growth rate varied from (–)12.77 to (+)15.24. Here again, we find that the fluctuation in the growth rate is wide.

The analysis shows that the rate of growth in annual agricultural output in a particular year is heavily influenced by the percentage difference in rainfall of that year over the previous year. The rainfall difference (from the previous year) as a percentage of the previous year's rainfall explained the change in annual agricultural growth rate to an extent of 51 per cent (Figure 3.3).

The regression model is $Y = 0.328 \times X + 2.727$, where 'Y' is the annual growth in agricultural output (%) and 'X' is the percentage change in rainfall.

A high percentage increase in rainfall over the previous year results in high agricultural growth, and a high percentage decline results in very low growth, often resulting in negative growth. This is quite comprehensible, as good monsoon rainfall ensures sufficient soil moisture for the production of kharif (monsoon) crops without irrigation and good recharge of aquifers and sufficient inflows into reservoirs that can be used for intensifying cropping during the subsequent seasons. Nevertheless, it is important to observe that there was never a situation in which there was a negative growth in annual agricultural output even with a positive change in rainfall, while vice versa was observed.

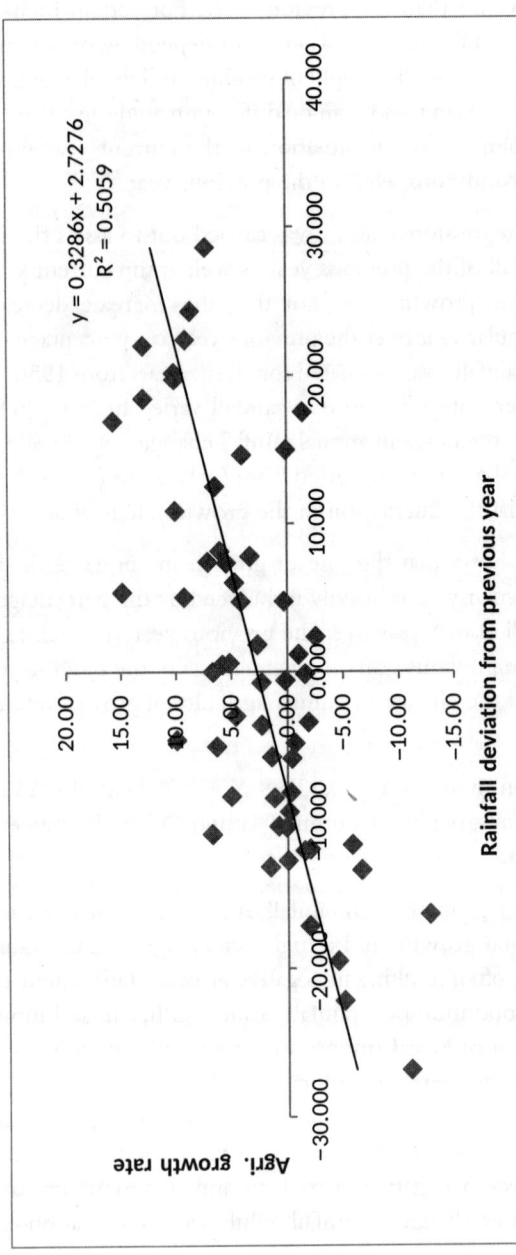

Figure 3.3 *Annual Agricultural Growth Rate vs Rainfall Deviation from Previous Year in India*

Source: Authors' own analysis based on: (i) https://imdpune.gov.in/library/public/e-book110.pdf; and (ii) https://trading-economics.com/india/gdp-from-agriculture

In many years, the agricultural growth rate was impressive in spite of them not being high rainfall years. This was because the preceding years were very low rainfall or drought years. Likewise, many wet years did not experience high agricultural growth rates as they were preceded by equally wet years or normal years. Also, there are some years in which the agricultural growth rate was positive in spite of the percentage change in rainfall over the previous year being negative. This is in line with the model prediction. As per the model, when the decline in rainfall becomes very large (above 8.29%), the growth becomes negative.

Needless to say, there are many complex factors which, if put together, should explain the remaining 49 per cent. One of them is spatial variation in rainfall. As regards the potential effect of this on the accuracy of model predictions, it is quite possible that even at the aggregate level, the country receives very good monsoon, some of the regions contributing significant agricultural outputs might have experienced below-normal rainfall, and this 'anomaly' can reduce the effect of increase in aggregate rainfall. What matters is in which region the rainfall departure actually takes place and the contribution of that region to the overall agricultural output of the country in value terms. A 100–200 mm downward deviation in annual rainfall from the normal value in north-western India, which receives low to medium rainfall (450–600 mm) but has high agricultural productivity, will have a much larger impact on the overall agricultural output of the country than a 100–200 mm downward deviation in rainfall in eastern India which receives very high rainfall but has low agricultural productivity. Every year, the regions which experience rainfall departure in India can keep changing, making the relationship between average annual rainfall and agricultural output more complex. These nuances are not captured in the weighted average of rainfall available for the country as a whole from IMD.

Nevertheless, it is very unlikely that the trend in the spatial average rainfall at the country level does not conform to the rainfall trend in the majority of the geographical area. That being the case, we have theoretically explained how an increase in rainfall from the previous year contributes to higher agricultural output.

The other factors that can drive agricultural growth are agricultural inputs (seeds, irrigation water, labour/machinery, fertilizers and pesticides), crop diversification, especially adoption of high-value crops, and adoption of new crop technologies (with high-yielding varieties). A positive change in these factors helps maintain a low annual agricultural growth rate even when the change in rainfall is negative.

That said, it is also important to note that it is with good monsoon or with improved access to irrigation water that the farmers are encouraged to apply optimum dosage of fertilizers and pesticides, use good seed varieties, and put in sufficient labour, as without water from precipitation or irrigation to crops, none of these inputs will have an effect on agricultural outputs. As a result, in the statistical analysis, the effect of many of these independent variables gets subsumed as the effect of change in 'rainfall', which is the primary driver of agricultural growth. It is only in situations when the farmers previously did not have sufficient knowledge of the importance of using optimum levels of inputs such as fertilizers and agronomic practices and have now started accruing and using such knowledge or while introducing some new high-yielding varieties that their 'differential effects' on agricultural output growth would be pronounced.

Analysis was also carried out to assess the influence of irrigation on agricultural growth rate, which showed a statistically significant influence of irrigation growth (estimated as the percentage increase in gross irrigated area in a particular year over the previous year irrigated area). The R^2 value was 0.17 (Figure 3.4). Subsequently, a multivariate analysis was performed using rainfall departure (in percentage terms) and irrigation growth (in percentage terms) as independent variables against agricultural growth rates as a dependent variable. The R^2 value increased to 0.55, and both the parameters were found to be significant at 5 per cent level (Table 3.1). The model was found to be quite significant statistically. The estimated regression equation is as follows:

Annual agricultural growth rate = 1.6245 + 0.476 × Irrigation Growth (%) + 0.3075 × Percentage Difference in Annual Rainfall from the Previous Year.

One reason for the only marginal improvement in R^2 value is that a large part of the possible variation in irrigated area between two

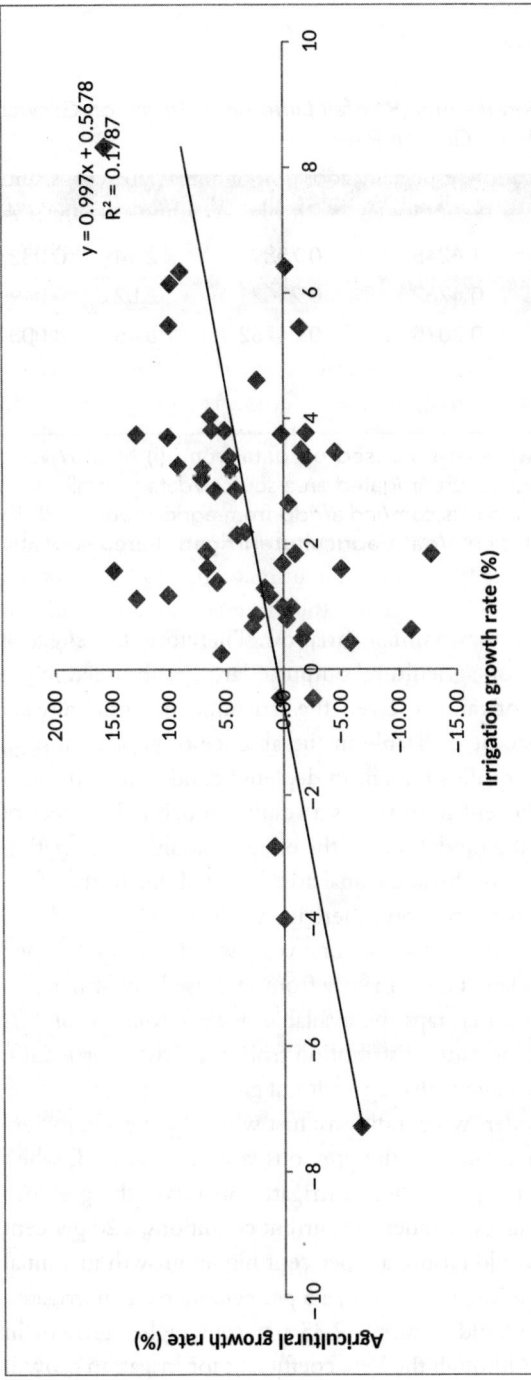

Figure 3.4 *Agricultural Growth Rate vs Irrigation Growth Rate in India*

Source: Authors' own analysis based on: (i) https://www.indiastat.com/data/agriculture/irrigated-area-sources/data-year/all-years; and (ii) https://tradingeconomics.com/india/gdp-from-agriculture

Table 3.1 *Regression Results (Rainfall Difference, Irrigation Growth and Annual Agricultural Growth Rate)*

Predictor	Coefficient	SE Coefficient	T Value	P
Constant	1.6245	0.7589	2.14	0.032
Irrigation growth	0.4762	0.2362	2.02	0.049
Difference in average rainfall over the previous year	0.3075	0.04762	6.46	0.000

Source: Authors' own analysis based on data from: (i) https://www.indiastat.com/data/agriculture/irrigated-area-sources/data-year/all-years; (ii) https://tradingeconomics.com/india/gdp-from-agriculturei); and (iii) https://www.indiastat.com/data/agriculture/irrigated-area-sources/data-year/all-years

consecutive years is due to rainfall variation. Therefore, the effect of irrigated area change on agricultural output is largely subsumed in the model as the effect of rainfall. Even the irrigation potential already created does not become utilizable in the absence of good monsoon precipitation, as the aquifers remain in depleted condition, and reservoirs do not get sufficient inflows. As a result, probably the effect of irrigation shown by the model is only the effect of additional irrigation potential created and not the additional area irrigated due to the effect of rainfall. Only in a few situations, there is an increase in irrigated area over a short time period (in this case, one year) which is not explained by an increase in rainfall. This is mainly from increased investment for building infrastructure that taps the available water resources for irrigation expansion or for water distribution from the existing irrigation system. The analysis suggests that agricultural growth rates can become significant or high under two conditions: first when there is a high percentage increase in rainfall over the previous year And, second, when there is a high percentage increase in irrigated area over the previous year. As the model suggests, under the current conditions, a 20 per cent increase in rainfall would ensure a 6 per cent higher growth in annual agricultural outputs in India. Similarly, a 5 per cent increase in irrigated area over one year would ensure a 2.35 per cent higher growth in agricultural output. Although the beta coefficient for irrigation growth is higher than that of rainfall difference (+ive), a careful look at the historical growth rates in irrigation in India shows that the maximum value of annual irrigation growth rate ever obtained was 8.6 per cent (during 1988–1989), whereas the maximum value for increase in rainfall obtained was 28.6 per cent (1973–1974). Hence, in reality, the extent to which the rainfall fluctuations drive agricultural growth rates up and down is much higher than that of change in irrigated area.

Further multivariate analysis was done with two more variables, namely average annual rainfall (expressed as a percentage departure from mean value) and the actual gross irrigated area. All four variables were found significant at 5 per cent level. However, this improved the R^2 value only marginally to 0.573. More importantly, 'percentage departure of rainfall from normal' had a much lower effect on the agricultural growth rate, with a beta coefficient of 0.10, than 'percentage increase in rainfall over the previous year' which had a beta coefficient of 0.25. Further, as one would expect, the extent to which the rainfall can depart from the normal value was lower than that of departure from the previous year value. The departure of annual rainfall from mean value ranged from –20.25 per cent to 17.50 per cent. Hence, its actual effect on the agricultural growth rate would be much less. The coefficient for irrigation growth in the new model was 0.48. The least significant variable was the gross irrigated area of the year, with a beta coefficient of 0.000040.

3.5. EXPLAINING AGRICULTURAL GROWTH IN GUJARAT

Gujarat is one state which experiences high volatility in agricultural performance with very high year-to-year variation in annual growth rates of agricultural GDP (Kumar et al., 2010). It is also a state which experiences high year to year variation in annual rainfalls. There is also a large regional variation in the average annual rainfall (Kumar & Perry, 2019). It is evident from Table 3.2, which shows differences in mean annual rainfall between regions, namely North Gujarat, Saurashtra and South Gujarat, and also within regions—between Banaskantha and Sabarkantha in North Gujarat, between Rajkot and Junagadh

Table 3.2 *Interregional Variation in Rainfall in North Gujarat*

Name of Region	Years of Record	Rainfall (mm)			No. of Rainy Days		
		STD	Mean	CV (%)	STD	Mean	CV (%)
North Gujarat							
A. Banaskantha							
Palanpur	83	353.60	682.20	51.83	11.73	30.43	38.54
Vav	28	251.62	346.94	73.53	8.55	15.57	54.90
B. Sabarkantha							
Idar	83	428.77	920.34	46.55	13.67	37.77	36.19
Prantij	83	336.48	740.01	45.57	11.52	33.47	34.42
South Gujarat							
A. Valsad							
Gandevi	28	761.53	2,063.61	36.90	15.76	60.39	26.10
Navsari	35	668.79	1,442.12	46.38	20.20	50.09	40.34
B. Panchmahals							
Jambughoda	85	492.35	1,172.83	41.98	14.43	48.15	29.98
Zalod	83	302.13	834.98	36.18	10.93	38.52	28.38
Saurashtra							
A. Junagadh							
Junagadh AM	78	487.80	863.01	56.52	14.70	37.43	39.28
Porbandar	78	377.08	564.82	66.76	10.06	23.54	42.74
B. Rajkot							
Jasdan	68	247.49	547.48	45.20	11.96	28.29	42.28
Rajkot	78	296.74	605.03	49.05	10.49	28.49	36.83

Source: Kumar (2002).

in Saurashtra and between Valsad and Panchmahals in South Gujarat (Kumar, 2002).

The wide differences in water resources endowment and irrigation facilities are also significant (Jagadeesan & Kumar, 2015), though much less as compared to the variations that exist at the national level, and therefore the anomaly caused by such variations in defining the effect of change in rainfall on agricultural growth rates will be less.

Since 2002–2003, Gujarat has achieved an average annual growth rate of 9 per cent (at 2011–2012 constant prices) in its agricultural GDP. Several narratives have been presented to explain this trend. One of these attributes to the increase in gross cropped area, which was an outcome of the availability of water for supplementary irrigation from the numerous small water-harvesting structures in the state and the highly productive well irrigation (Shah et al., 2009). However, data and analysis presented by them in favour of their arguments were insufficient to drive any meaningful inference. For instance, Shah et al. (2009) explained agricultural growth in Gujarat by comparing agricultural output in a drought year (2000) with the seven-year period post 2002, four of which either received normal rainfall or were wet years. But Kumar et al. (2010) found that the growth trend observed by Shah et al. (2009) was actually a good recovery from a major dip in production that occurred during the drought years of 1999 and 2000, facilitated by higher rainfall and introduction of large volumes of water for irrigation from Sardar Sarovar project, which began in 2002. The analysis presented by Kumar and Perry (2019) re-emphasized the role of rainfall in improving groundwater conditions in the state almost during the same period, which in their opinion had influenced the agricultural performance of the state. However, it was necessary to explain empirically the extent to which annual rainfall fluctuations influence annual agricultural growth rates.

In this analysis, we tried to extend the hypothesis established at the national level for explaining the agricultural growth trend in Gujarat. For the statistical model, data sets for the value of annual agricultural output from 1961–1962 to 2013–2014 (at factor cost) obtained from the Reserve Bank of India (2019) report and Dholakia and Sapre (2013) were adjusted to 2011–2012 constant prices (the latest series). Thereafter, the annual growth rates in state agricultural GDP were estimated. Also, the values of spatial average annual rainfall from 1961–1962 to 2013–2014 were estimated using the monthly rainfall figures from two different regions in Gujarat, namely mainland Gujarat and Saurashtra and Kachchh. The contribution of each region to the state's annual rainfall was ascribed in proportion to the area covered by each region. The annual agricultural GDP of Gujarat for the period from 1960–1961 to 2012–2013, adjusted to 2011–2012 prices, is presented in Figure 3.5.

A regression model between the annual agricultural growth rate (as dependent variable) and percentage difference in annual rainfall from the previous year (as independent variable) returned an $R2$ value of 0.83 (Figure 3.6). This means that a change in rainfall explained the variation in the annual agricultural growth rate in Gujarat to an extent of 83 per cent. The relationship between percentage change in rainfall between two consecutive years and the growth rate in agricultural GDP between the two years is stronger for Gujarat. This is as per the expectations as the regional variations in rainfall and water endowment, which have the potential to eclipse the effect of rainfall change on agricultural growth rates and cause an anomaly in the relationship, which is much less in Gujarat as compared to the variations at the national level. For instance, in Gujarat, the mean annual rainfall varies from 350 mm in Kachchh to around 2,000 mm in Dangs and Valsad in South Gujarat. At the national level, however, the rainfall varies from as low as 200 mm in Jaisalmer (western Rajasthan) to around 11,000 mm in certain pockets of Meghalaya in the northeast, with most parts of northeast receiving more than 3,000 mm of annual precipitation. The climate varies from hyper-arid in western Rajasthan to cold and humid in most parts of the northeast.

As in the case of national-level aggregate analysis, the model was expanded to include the change in gross irrigated area over the previous year as the second independent variable. Since the data for the gross irrigated area in Gujarat was available for 1985–1986 to 2013–2014, the other two variables were also adjusted for the same time period. The multiple regression model shows that the relationships between annual agricultural growth rate and the change in rainfall and change in gross irrigated area are statistically significant, and the p-values for the independent variables are less than the 5 per cent significance level (Table 3.3). Further, the R^2 value increased to 0.92, confirming that the regression model is robust with the considered variables. The poor effect of annual growth in irrigation (gross irrigated area) on agricultural

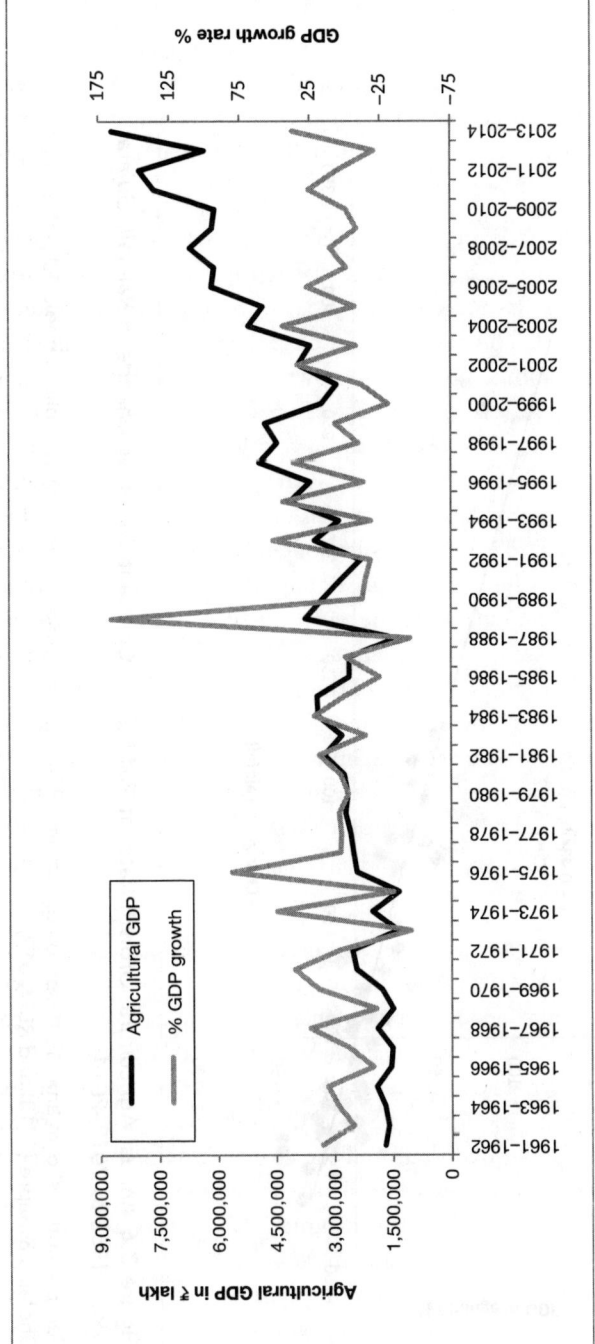

Figure 3.5 Gujarat State's Agricultural GDP and the Growth Rate (Adjusted to 2011–2012 Prices)

Source: Authors' own analysis based on Dholakia & Sapre (2013) and RBI (2019).

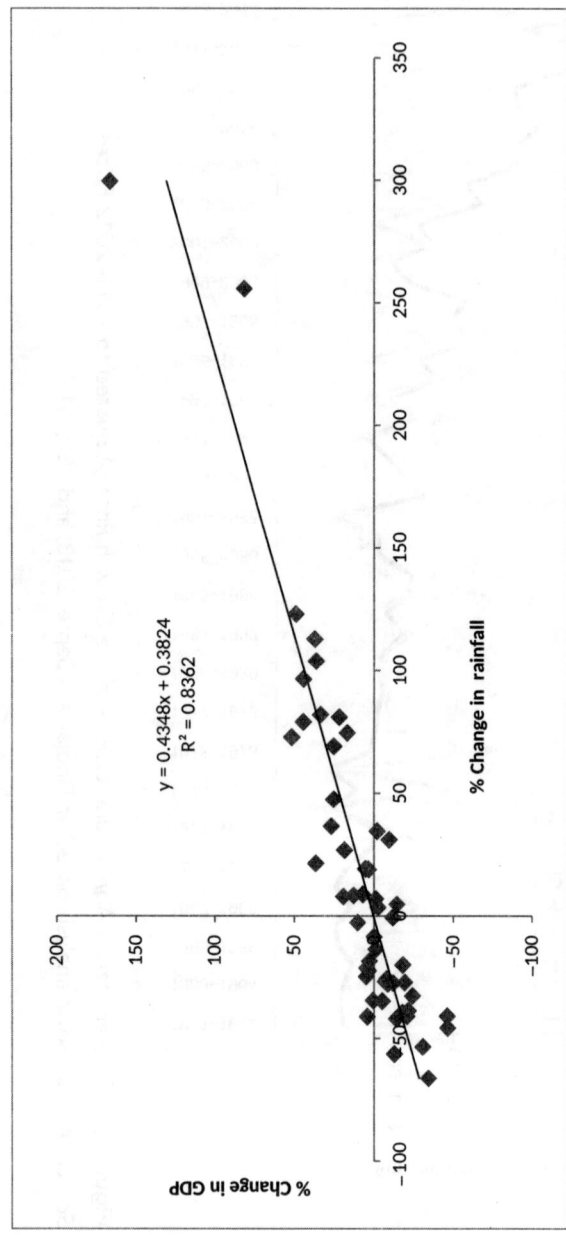

Figure 3.6 *Annual Agricultural Growth Rate (at 2011–2012 Constant Prices) vs Change in Rainfall, Gujarat (1961–1962 to 2013–2014)*

Source: Authors' own analysis based on data from: (i) https://imdpune.gov.in/library/public/e-book110.pdf; and (ii) Dholakia & Sapre (2013) and RBI (2019).

Table 3.3 *Results from the Regression Analysis*

	Coefficients	Standard Error	t Stat	P-value
Intercept	−1.24442	2.210276	−0.56301	0.578249
X Variable 1 (difference in average rainfall over the previous year)	0.393819	0.052009	7.57209	4.88×10^{-8}
X Variable 2 (irrigation growth)	1.022592	0.355157	2.87927	0.007874

Source: Authors' own analysis based on data from: (i) https://imdpune. gov.in/library/public/e-book110.pdf; (ii) https://www.indiastat.com/data/ agriculture/irrigated-area-sources/data-year/all-years; and (iii) Dholakia & Sapre (2013) and RBI (2019).

growth rate could be because the rainfall variation causes a similar variation in actual irrigated area, and the effect of changes in the irrigated area is largely captured by the effect of change in rainfall. The state of Gujarat had experienced a very high degree of water resources development over the past many decades, on both the groundwater front and surface waterfront. As a result, higher rainfall resulting in a higher amount of recharge increases the potential of the wells. Similarly, higher rainfall, resulting in a larger volume of inflows into existing minor, medium and major reservoirs of the state, results in a larger proportion of the existing surface command area being brought under irrigation. In low rainfall years, just the opposite happens. Having said that, the differential effect of irrigation (5%) can be explained by the additional irrigation facilities built during the year in areas where resource endowment is favourable, increasing the irrigation potential created.

3.6. CONCLUSIONS

For long, agricultural economists and planners in India believed that the quantum of monsoon rainfall in a particular year (or its departure from mean values) would mainly determine the annual agricultural growth rate that the country would achieve in that year. This was basically the logical extension of the valid concept that the agricultural output of the country in a particular year can change with the monsoon rainfall which ensures sufficient moisture for the kharif (monsoon) crops and adequate inflows in reservoirs and replenishment of aquifers for irrigation. The absence of long-term data on average annual rainfall on the country's landmass, however, made it difficult to test this hypothesis. But such views ignore the fact that at times there can be wide fluctuations in agricultural outputs between two consecutive years due to large variations in the corresponding rainfall, and as a result, the value of agricultural outputs can be less than that of the previous year. Poor agricultural growth performance observed in certain years was attributed to the inadequate rainfall of that year and high growth rates observed in certain other years were attributed to effective policy interventions and good monsoon. The influence of the preceding year's rainfall in determining the agricultural growth performance of a year was largely ignored.

Our analysis suggests that obtaining a good monsoon is neither a necessary nor a sufficient condition for securing high agricultural growth during a year in relation to the previous year. The wide variation in agricultural growth rates between years which experienced more or less the same quantum of rainfall suggests that there are factors other than annual rainfall which influence the agricultural growth rates.

Further analysis suggests that the annual agricultural growth performance (rate) of the country is mainly explained by two key factors: (a) the percentage difference in average rainfall of the year under consideration from the previous year and (b) the percentage increase in gross irrigated area over the previous year. These two variables explain agricultural growth performance to an extent of 55 per cent at the national level. This was further validated by similar analyses carried out for Gujarat, in which case, rainfall change explained the annual agricultural growth rate to the extent of 92 per cent. The factors such as level of agricultural inputs, crop diversification and introduction of new high-yielding varieties along with the spatial variation in rainfall should explain the remaining. Higher the percentage increase in average annual rainfall of a year over the previous year, higher the chances of obtaining high growth rates. Higher the percentage increase in gross irrigated area over the previous year, again higher would be the chances of obtaining high agricultural growth rates during the year. The average rainfall of the year (expressed as percentage departure from mean value) has a much smaller effect on annual agricultural growth rates in reality.

Based on this analysis, we argue that too much is made out of the annual agricultural growth rates in planning and policy circles. Poor agricultural growth performance in a year may not be because of the poor performance of the monsoon during that year. Instead, it can as well be due to the very good performance of monsoon or abnormally wet conditions during the previous year. Likewise, very high agricultural growth performance (agricultural growth rate) during a year may neither be because of good monsoon performance nor because of any policy reforms. It may be due to the poor performance of monsoon during the previous year.

Given the wide fluctuations in average annual rainfall in the country, the estimates of annual agricultural growth rates can often be misleading when they are used for drawing inferences on agricultural sector performance, at both national and state levels. The future focus should be on assessing medium-term growth rates, which carefully pick up the base year in which the magnitude of annual rainfall is quite close to that of normal rainfall.

REFERENCES

Bhalla, G. S., & Singh, G. (2009). Economic liberalisation and Indian agriculture: A state-wise analysis. *Economic & Political Weekly*, *44*(52), 34–44.

Dholakia, R. H., & Sapre, A. A. (2013). *Inter-sectoral terms of trade and aggregate supply response in Gujarat and Indian agriculture* [Working Paper No. 2013-07-02]. Indian Institute of Management, Ahmedabad.

Gulati, A. (2002). *Challenges to Punjab agriculture in a globalizing world.* Presentation at the Policy Dialogue on Challenges to Punjab Agriculture in a Globalizing World, IFPRI and ICRIER, New Delhi.

https://www.indiastat.com/data/agriculture/irrigated-area-sources/data-year/all-years

https://tradingeconomics.com/india/gdp-from-agriculturei)

https://imdpune.gov.in/library/public/e-book110.pdf

Jagadeesan, S., & Kumar, M. D. (2015). *The Sardar Sarovar project: Assessing economic and social impacts.* SAGE Publications.

Kannan, E., & Sundaram, S. (2011). *Analysis of trends in India's agricultural growth* [Working Paper No. 276]. Institute of Social and Economic Change, Bangalore.

Kumar, M. D. (2002). *Reconciling water use and environment: Water resources management in Gujarat resource, problems, issues, options, strategies and framework for action.* Report of the Hydrological Regime Subcomponent of the State Environmental Action Programme supported by the World Bank. Gujarat Ecology Commission.

Kumar, M. D., & Amarasinghe, U. (2009). *Water productivity improvements in Indian agriculture: Potentials, constraints and prospects* [National River Linking Project Series 4]. Challenge Program on Water and Food, International Water Management Institute, Colombo.

Kumar, M. D., Ganguly, A., & Sivamohan, M. V. K. (2019). What drives annual agricultural growth rates in India? *Economic & Political Weekly, 54*(1), 33–36.

Kumar, M. D., Narayanamoorthy, A., Singh, O. P., Sivamohan, M. V. K., Sharma, M. K., & Bassi, N. (2010). *Gujarat's agricultural growth story: Exploding some myths* [Occasional Paper No.]). Institute for Resource Analysis and Policy, Hyderabad.

Kumar, M. D., & Perry, C. J. (2019). What can explain groundwater rejuvenation in Gujarat in recent years? *International Journal of Water Resources Development, 35*(5), 891–906.

Pearce, D. W., & Warford, J. J. (1993). *World without end: Economics, environment, and sustainable development.* Oxford University Press.

Reserve Bank of India. (2019). *Handbook of statistics on Indian states.*

Shah, T., Gulati, A., Shreedhar, G., & Jain, R. C. (2009). Secret of Gujarat's agrarian miracle after 2000. *Economic & Political Weekly, 44*(52), 45–55.

Thobani, M. (1997). Formal water markets: Why, when, and how to introduce tradable water rights. *The World Bank Research Observer, 12*(2), 161–179.

Chapter 4

Past Studies on Agrarian Change and the Significance of the Current Work

M. Dinesh Kumar and Saurabh Kumar

4.1. INTRODUCTION

Agrarian change in India has been analysed in the past from various perspectives. They include problems and challenges induced by different agrarian structures (feudal, ryotwari, permanent settlement, etc.); various modes of production (feudal, capitalist and socialist; see Arnold, 2005; Chakrabarty, 2013; Chatterjee & Rudra, 1989; Habib, 1999; Omvedt, 1983); challenges posed by unfavourable situation vis-à-vis various factors of production such as water scarcity (see Dev, 2016; Mishra, 2008; Reserve Bank of India, 2006), land scarcity (see Gulati et al., 2020; Mishra, 2008), limited access to inputs and production technologies (see Mishra, 2008); environmental externalities inducted on production (Selvaraj & Ramasamy, 2006; Tripathi & Sindhi, 2020); externalities induced by the changing market conditions (see Gulati et al., 2020; Singh, 2018); and growing risks and indebtedness, among farmers (Mishra, 2008).

Notwithstanding their serious limitation, there has been an enormous volume of scholarly work done during the past five decades or so, looking at the agrarian change from the perspective of modes of production and agrarian structure, largely corresponding to the colonial and pre-colonial era.[1] However, there has been too little comprehensive work looking at the problems from the perspective of limits induced by land scarcity and water stress, changing dynamics with respect to the cost of various inputs affected by changing subsidy structure, and externalities induced by the changing environmental and market conditions. It will not be an exaggeration if one says that, often, aesthetic taste, value-based judgements and romanticism driven by disciplinary biases dominated the 'academic exchanges' which were devoid of objectivity and empirical rigour.

While the former (i.e., looking at agrarian change from the perspective of modes of production and agrarian structure) required the use of disciplines such as sociology and anthropology, the latter required systematic engagement with agricultural economics. The latter also required comparative analysis of regions with distinct physical (agroecology, water availability, land availability and climate), socio-economic environment (overall economic conditions of the farmers and infrastructure and market conditions), as all of them have bearing on the profitability of farming. Obviously, analysis carried out for one region, no matter how rigorous it is, will not hold well for another region.

The extensive review of published literature carried out by us and presented in a synthesized form in this chapter basically validates this argument. However, highly localized studies which consider a few districts or a state as the unit of analysis and also studies which are not done on a significant time scale are excluded from the review. The review provided the basis for the empirical research undertaken in four distinct regions of India, covering West Bengal, Andhra Pradesh, Gujarat and Maharashtra, on agrarian change and the phenomenon largely termed as 'agrarian crisis' by researchers and scholars, involving longitudinal analysis. In the subsequent section of this chapter, the outcomes of the review are presented in a structured manner. This is

---

[1] Chatterjee and Rudra (1989) had described the historical sources on production relations which existed during those eras as those related to the acts of revenue collection, and not as those related to the 'acts of production', and that the economic history is largely a history of revenue collection and not of production relations.

followed by a description of the approach, methodology and analytical procedures used for the field studies in the next section.

4.2. REVIEW OF PAST RESEARCH ON AGRARIAN CHANGE

The Indian economy has undergone transformative changes since Independence, with a decline in the share of agriculture in the GDP. Despite a fall in its share from 55.1 per cent in 1950–1951 to 17.32 per cent in 2018–2019, the importance of the agricultural sector and its growth cannot be undermined in augmenting the growth of the rural economy and associated allied activities, as agriculture is the primary source of livelihood for nearly half of India's population.

After Independence, during the span of seven decades, Indian agriculture has witnessed wide variations in its growth. India achieved self-sufficiency in food grain production (particularly in rice and wheat) after adopting Green Revolution technologies during the late 1960s such as the use of hybrid seeds, improvement in irrigation facilities and improved farm mechanization. India has the 10th largest arable land resource in the world.

With 20 agro-climatic regions, all the 15 major climates in the world exist in India. The country also has 46 of the 60 soil types in the world. India is the largest producer of spices, pulses, milk, tea, cashew and jute, and the second largest producer of wheat, rice, fruits and vegetables, sugarcane, cotton and oilseeds. Further, India is second in the global production of fruits and vegetables and is the largest producer of mango and banana (IBEF, 2021).

Despite high levels of production, agricultural yield in India is lower when compared to other countries such as the United States, China and Brazil. The agricultural yield of food grains has increased by more than four times since 1950–1951 and was 2,070 kg/ha in 2014–2015 (Directorate of Economics & Statistics, 2015). Although India is the second highest producer of paddy (rice) in the world (as of 2013), its yield is lower than that of China, Brazil and the United States. It is also the leading producer of pulses, but its yield is the lowest (Directorate of Economics & Statistics, 2015; FAO, n.d.).

Many studies have been done on the development, growth and performance of Indian agriculture (Balakrishnan et al., 2008; Bhalla & Singh, 2009; Chand et al., 2007; Reddy & Mishra, 2009; Vaidyanathan, 2010). Systematic efforts were also made by many researchers to analyse growth in crop output and its elements through decomposition analysis (Joshi et al., 2006; Majumdar & Basu, 2005; Minhas & Vaidyanathan, 1965; Sagar, 1977, 1980; Sarma & Subrahmanyam, 1984). Some studies also analysed the historical aspects of agricultural growth, disparity and impact on farmers' income (Bhalla & Singh, 2001, 2009; Radhakrishna, 2002; Rao, 1998; Sawant & Achuthan, 1995; Vaidyanathan, 2010).

Kannan and Sundaram (2011) discussed the trends and patterns in the growth of the crop sector at the national and state levels. They found that the cropping pattern in India had undergone significant changes, with a significant shift from the cultivation of food grains to commercial crops. The area under coarse cereals, which is generally cultivated in dry regions, has declined by 13.3 per cent between triennium ending (TE) 1970–1971 and TE 2007–2008. The performance of pulses in terms of area and output was not impressive during the study period. They also observed that technological and institutional support for a few crops such as rice and wheat had brought significant changes in crop area and output composition in some regions. Rice accounted for only 15.4 per cent of gross cropped area (GCA) in TE 1962–1965 and increased to 23 per cent in TE 2003–2006 in Northwest India. Similarly, wheat area almost doubled in these periods. The expansion of area under these two crops resulted in a contraction of the area under coarse cereals, pulses and oilseeds in that region. In the central region, the share of cotton increased in the 1980s and constituted about 10 per cent of the total value of crop output in recent years. Apart from this, the annual growth in yield during 1967–1968 to 2007–2008 for major crops was worked out to be low.

On the one hand, Green Revolution made India self-sufficient and freed it from vagaries of famines and other natural calamities; however, on the other hand, it also increased the disparities between different states/regions within the country, as it helped those regions which were under good irrigation as compared to rainfed areas.

Regional disparities, instability and sharp variations in agricultural productivity have remained a matter of deep concern in the area of agricultural economics in India. Such regional variations are due to disparities in natural resource endowments, topography, climatic conditions and also socio-economic and institutional factors. Many authors have conducted studies on the effects of new technologies such as seed fertilizer technology and high-yielding varieties on production instability in agriculture (Hazell, 1982; Mehra, 1981). But Ray (1983) and Rao et al. (1988), on the one hand, strongly refute the impact of Green Revolution technology on variations in output for some crops and, on the other hand, ascribe it to the increase in sensitivity of production to variation in rainfall and complementarity of new technology with irrigation.

Mahendra Dev (1987) distinguishes between the effects of technology and rainfall variations on fluctuations in output by analysing weather-adjusted and -unadjusted growth rates in food grain output for all the major states of the country. Based on the standard deviation in the year-to-year change in output, the study concluded that there was a progressive but marginal decline in instability at the all-India level. At the state level, there was a decline in some cases and an increase in some other states. Larson et al. (2004) and Sharma et al. (2006) also analysed this issue for the period beyond the mid-1980s, and both have reported contradictory results, as Larson et al. (2004) reported a rise in the instability over time, whereas Sharma et al. (2006) reported a decline in instability over time. More recently, Chand et al. (2011) also studied instability and regional variations in agricultural outputs and argued that when a longer period which involves the spread of improved technology to a large area is considered, the inference on increase in agricultural instability due to the adoption of new technology gets totally negated at the country level.

However, with so many studies conducted on production instability, the literature reveals that there is still no consensus on these issues in relation to the impact of adoption of new technologies.

Attempts have also been made to assess interstate variations over time in terms of the performance of overall agriculture. It is found that in the short run, states exhibit a tendency to converge to a single rate of growth but, in the longer run, there are two divergent patterns; states with better irrigation spread tend to converge to a higher rate of growth, whereas states with a lower proportion of crop area under irrigation tend to converge to a lower rate of growth (Bhide et al., 1998).

Chand and Chauhan (1999) examined the trend in agricultural productivity, output growth and regional divergence in per rural person and per hectare net state domestic product (NSDP) from agriculture during the period 1980–1981 to 1996–1997. They found clear evidence to the effect that since 1980–1981, regional differences in agricultural productivity and income have grown and the gap between underdeveloped and developed and poor and rich states has increased. This has happened despite special efforts made to reduce interstate disparities by promoting similar level of agricultural development in underdeveloped states. They argued for a need to make more vigorous efforts on technological, institutional and infrastructural fronts to raise productivity and to accelerate growth rate not only of crop sector but also of livestock and other subsectors of agriculture in underdeveloped states. A special and immediate focus is needed for eastern states, namely Bihar, Odisha and Assam, hill regions and eastern Uttar Pradesh.

The need to increase the food production to become self-reliant and to cut the food grain imports was so pressing after Independence that the Indian agriculture and Green Revolution technologies heavily favoured paddy and wheat more than other crops. But slowly it was realized that agricultural diversification was important for the overall growth of the agriculture sector. The agricultural diversification can be based on high-value crops (HVCs) and livestock (Gulati et al., 2020; Joshi et al., 2004, 2006).

While agriculture continues to have excessive employment pressure, past trends indicate limited opportunities for a rapid transfer of labour to non-farm sectors (Chadha, 2008). With a tardy shift of labour towards non-farm sectors, within agriculture, crop diversification out of staples towards HVCs such as fruits, vegetables, condiments and spices, aromatic and medicinal plants, flowers and plantation crops like coffee and tea is one of the alternatives that can augment incomes, generate employment and reduce poverty (Ali & Abedullah, 2002; Barghouti et al., 2004; Birthal et al., 2013; Joshi et al., 2004; Weinberger & Lumpkin, 2007).

Birthal et al. (2015) established that households diversifying towards HVCs are less likely to be poor, the biggest impact being for small-holders. Furthermore, using continuous treatment matching, they established the relationship between the degree of diversification (share of area dedicated to HVC) and poverty. They showed that growers of HVCs needed to allocate at least 50 per cent area to HVCs to escape poverty. The effect of diversification on poverty is, in general, positive, but it withers after a threshold probably because of constraints, that is, capital on smaller farms and labour on larger ones.

Livestock farming has emerged as a supplementary source of income in India with the increased number of marginal farmers with ever-reducing farm sizes. In India, it is part of a composite farming system characterized by crop–livestock interactions (Kumar and van Dam, 2013; Singh, 2004). Evidence from the National Sample Survey Office's (NSSO) 70th round survey showed that more than one-fifth (23%) of agricultural households with very small parcels of land (less than 0.01 ha) reported livestock as their principal source of income. Farming households with some cattle head are better able to withstand distress due to extreme weather conditions (DoAHD, n.d.).

As per National Account Statistics 2019, the value of the output of milk in 2017–2018 was ₹701,530 crore (at current prices), surpassing the total value of output from the top two food grains, ₹272,221 crore for paddy and ₹173,984 crore for wheat (MoSPI, 2019). With the value of agricultural and allied sectors estimated at around ₹28 lakh crore, this means that contribution of the dairy sector is more than 25 per cent of India's agricultural output in value terms (FICCI, 2020).

Dairying has become an important secondary source of income for millions of rural families and has assumed the most important role in providing employment and income-generating opportunities, particu-larly for marginal and women farmers. Most of the milk is produced by animals reared by small, marginal farmers and landless labourers. Of the total milk production in India, about 48 per cent milk is either consumed at the producer level or sold to non-producers in the rural area. The balance 52 per cent of the milk is a marketable surplus available for sale to consumers in urban areas. Out of marketable surplus, it is estimated that about 40 per cent of the milk sold is handled by the organized sector (i.e., 20% each by cooperative and private dairies) and the remaining 60 per cent by the unorganized sector (DoAHD, n.d.). Although livestock farming is part of a composite farming system with crop–livestock interactions, livestock farming has not attracted much attention from researchers working on agrarian change, agricultural growth and farming risks.

Ghosh et al. (2017) argued that milk production in India still remains largely a subsistence activity, and producing milk for sale is not always profitable. Their findings also raise serious concerns about the commercial prospects of dairy farmers, especially in the eastern region and among the labour classes and others who practise dairy as a subsidiary economic activity. However, Kumar and Singh (2017) have a different view about the growth of the dairy sector and do not comply with Ghosh et al. (2017) and argue with the help of various decadal data and Government of India reports that dairy production is the only subsector of the farm sector in India which has been growing steadily over the past couple of decades, whereas the cash crop sector, though growing, shows a high degree of erraticism. They also argue that the analysis of the dairy sector requires a more comprehensive approach, as it is part of a composite farming system which provides rural employment and family nutrition for small and marginal farmers.

From the days of the Green Revolution, agriculture sector in India has come a long way. Green Revolution technologies freed India from the clutches of food grain import and mass-scale poverty. But many regions in the country still face low growth and disparity, owing to various political, socio-economic and climatic conditions. India's agriculture policy has focused on achieving food security for the nation, and now that this goal has been achieved, there is a need to ease pressure on the production of two major staple food grains, that is, paddy and wheat, and shift towards agriculture diversification in the form of livestock (dairy sector), forestry and other allied sectors such as fisheries, which can reduce poverty and increase incomes for small and marginal farmers. Rapid urbanization, increased income and changing food consumption can provide good opportunities and new markets for HVCs and the livestock sector.

The outcomes of the review can be synthesized as follows. As a result of several factors, including irrigation and technology advancements, a marginal decline in the instability of agricultural output is observed at the national level. However, there were significant regional differences in agricultural productivity growth, owing to differences in the level of use of inputs and adoption of crop technologies (like high-yielding varieties) and agroecological factors, and this had culminated in major differences in the average yield of crops among regions. During the period from 1980–1981 to 1996–1997, the regional differences in agricultural productivity and income have grown, and the gap between underdeveloped and developed and poor and rich states has increased. During nearly four decades from 1970–1971 to 2007–2008, Indian agriculture had witnessed crop diversification with a shift towards HVCs (cotton, etc.) and reduction in area under coarse cereals, while technological and institutional support for crops such as rice and wheat had resulted in an increase in area and output composition of these crops.

With limited potential for absorption of rural workforce in the rural non-farm sector, crop diversification can be an opportunity to increase farm revenues, as studies show that diversification to HVCs reduces poverty of farm households, especially smallholders. Nevertheless, its impact on farming risk from the point of view of technology, production and market is not yet fully understood. The strong and inverse relationship between farm size and farm income at the aggregate level shows the potential negative impact the increasing rural population will have on the income of the average agricultural households as a result of reducing the size of the landholding with time, unless there is large scale shifting of rural populations out of agriculture or significant opportunities generated in the rural non-farm sector for absorbing this workforce.

With the apparently vast differences in agro-climatic conditions, resource endowment, socio-economic conditions (especially poverty rates, labour availability and wage rates) and landholding pattern among regions, and more importantly the differences in the growth trajectory of these regions (rural population growth, irrigation expansion, urban growth and rate of industrialization), it is imperative that research on agrarian transformation and crisis in the sector should look at individual regions rather than the aggregate-level scenario of the country. With the dairy sector now accounting for 25 per cent of the total value of agricultural outputs in India, systematic research is needed to understand its contribution to farm income, especially that of small and marginal farmers. More importantly, the role of the livestock in making the farming system resilient to production and market risks and averting crises in the farm sector needs to be carefully analysed.

4.3. OBJECTIVES OF THE RESEARCH ON AGRARIAN CRISIS

The study addressed the following key research questions:

1. To what extent do the physical factors such as resource depletion and degradation, primary productivity of land and changing weather patterns contribute to the current agrarian crisis in India?
2. To what extent do the socio-economic factors such as increasing employment opportunities in the non-farm sector in the rural as well as urban areas and outward movement of people from rural areas to urban areas as a result of better education and declining size of operational holdings and better wages contribute to the crisis?
3. To what extent do the institutional and policy factors such as reduction in input subsidies, globalization of agriculture and creation of non-farm employment through legislative measures and crop insurance precipitate or reduce the crisis?
4. How far does the nature of crisis in agriculture change from region to region?

4.4. APPROACH, METHODOLOGY AND ANALYTICAL TOOLS

4.4.1. The Approach

The study involved a longitudinal analysis involving time series data of farm inputs, outputs and throughputs at the level of individual farms to understand the changes in agricultural production situation from the point of view of farming as an economic enterprise. The study comprised of four distinct regions, each one characterized by a unique 'agro-climatic and socio-economic setting', to enable the influence of these factors on the nature and magnitude of the crisis. The time frame considered was 35 years, beginning 1980. The time series data were obtained from the farm households using the recall method. From each region, a total of five villages were chosen for the field investigation. A total of 526 households were chosen for the survey. The five villages from each location were selected in such a way that they together represent the unique characteristics of the region by capturing the variations in agro-climate, geo-hydrology and landholdings and overall socio-economic conditions.

A range of analytical procedures was used to estimate the changes in net income from farming at the farm level over time, changes in opportunity cost of engaging in farming operations for the farm households, changes in the size of operational holdings of farmers over time and changes in the risk involved in farming. The study assessed the magnitude of the crisis and the physical, socio-economic, institutional and policy factors causing it. Based on the identification of these factors, the institutional and policy measures were suggested for each region.

4.4.2. Methods and Analytical Tools

A questionnaire was designed to collect data from sample households on the following: (a) extent of use of farm inputs and farm outputs; (b) market price of inputs; (c) farm gate price of farm outputs; (d) time series data on historical changes in the use of inputs and volume of outputs produced for crops and livestock; and (e) time series data on historical changes in the price of inputs, farm gate price of produce and wage rates for farm labourers. A separate questionnaire was also designed to collect data at the village level for sample villages on the following: (a) total number of operational holdings at present; (b) total number of farmers; (c) landholding pattern (number of farmers under each holding category); (d) total number of wage labourers engaged in farming operations; (e) wage rates in the non-farm sector; (f) market price of agricultural land in the village; and (g) time series data on historical changes in all of the above.

Secondary data was collected from each region on the overall physical environment (rainfall and weather patterns), socio-economic conditions including agricultural scenario, migration, non-farm employment, wage rates in the farm sector and non-farm sector, education, market dynamics in agriculture, and government interventions in the agriculture sector.

Net income from farming at any given point of time was estimated by considering the following: (a) net return from each crop per household and (b) percentage area under each crop considering all the crops grown during the year. Further, revenue from dairying was separately estimated using (a) the milk yield from each category of livestock per livestock unit and its selling rate and (b) the number of animals under each livestock type. All the income figures were adjusted to real prices (2013–2014 prices) using Consumer Price Index for comparison.

The net income from farming was estimated using the following equation.

Let us assume that the farmers grow a total of m crops. Then the average net income from crop production per unit of land can be estimated ($\varnothing$) as:

$$\varnothing = \left\{ \frac{\left[\sum_{i=1}^{m} A_i \times ICROP_i \right]}{\sum_{i=1}^{m} A_i} \right\} \tag{1}$$

Here, A_i is the area under crop i; $ICROP_i$ is the income per unit area of land from crop i.

Now, let us assume that the farmers keep a total of n types of livestock. N_j is the total number of livestock in the jth category. Then the average incremental income from dairy production per unit of livestock (β) can be estimated as:

$$\beta = \left\{ \frac{\left[\sum_{j=1}^{n} N_j \times ILSTOCK_j \right]}{\sum_{j=1}^{n} N_j} \right\} \tag{2}$$

Here, $ILSTOCK_j$ is the income from livestock category j.

The average income from crop production can be estimated as:

$$\emptyset = \sum_{i=1}^{m} A_i \times ICROP_i \tag{3}$$

Likewise, the average income from livestock production (β) can be estimated as:

$$\beta - \sum_{j=1}^{n} N_j \times ILSTOCK_j \tag{4}$$

Incremental farm surplus ($FARM_{SURPLUS}$) was estimated by using the following variables: average net income from crop production per hectare of the gross (sample) cropped area $\emptyset$; current GCA (A_{GROSS}); average holding of different types of livestock of the (sample) farmers at present (N); and average income per unit of livestock (β) as:

$$FARM_{SURPLUS} = A_{GROSS} \times \emptyset + Nx\,\beta \tag{5}$$

Farming risks were assessed considering the physical factors (such as resource scarcity and variable climate) and socio-economic factors (such as declining per capita landholding, migration to urban areas and low availability of farm labour) causing a crisis in the agriculture sector in the selected regions. The impact of institutional and policy factors on reduction in input cost (through subsidies), improvement in infrastructure for procurement and marketing, and creation of non-farm employment through legislative measures are also analysed.

4.4.3. Profile of the Surveyed Households

Demographic details of surveyed households are presented in Table 4.1. Households in North Gujarat support more people as indicated by its high family size among households in other regions. Further, North Gujarat has the highest proportion of households belonging to other backward castes. Only Vidarbha was found to have substantial

Table 4.1 *Demographic Details of the Surveyed Households*

Region	Selected Districts	No. of Households Surveyed	Households Size (No./Household)	Proportion of Households under Different Caste Category				Proportion of Households with BPL Card
				General	SC	ST	OBC	
Coastal Andhra	West Godavari	135	3.83	39	13	1	47	74
Gangetic Plains	Hooghly and North 24 Parganas	150	4.55	81	12	–	7	37
North Gujarat	Banaskantha	150	5.62	2	1	–	97	0
Vidarbha	Chandrapur	91	4.10	4	5	49	41	15

Source: Primary data from the field survey.

households with a tribal population who are mainly engaged in rainfed agriculture. Interestingly Coastal Andhra, which has a higher per capita agricultural income than Gangetic Plains and Vidarbha, was found to have the highest proportion of households below poverty line.

Compared to other regions, a high proportion of adult family members in surveyed households in North Gujarat were engaged in agriculture (including dairy) as their major livelihood activity (Table 4.2). In Coastal Andhra and Vidarbha, more than 75 per cent of female adult members were reported to be handling household works exclusively. However, our field survey suggests that in Vidarbha, a large proportion of such adult female members take up farm or non-farm labour work. Gangetic Plains had the highest proportion of unemployed people. Further, except for Vidarbha, a high proportion of children in the surveyed households were enrolled in schools (Table 4.2). Low registration of children in schools in Vidarbha may be due to their involvement in household work, as a high proportion of adult female members in the region were engaged in farm and non-farm labour work.

Nevertheless, as presented in Table 4.3, major household expenditure continued to be on food items and for purchasing agricultural inputs. However, in Chandrapur, the proportion of total expenditure on agri-inputs had increased substantially between 1980–1981 and 2013–2014. As a result, households were spending a lesser amount on food items and thus compromising on their food security. Nevertheless, in all the districts, there was an increase in the proportion of total income being spent on children's education, thus indicating their desire for a child's better future.

4.4.4. Changes in Landholding over Time

Between 1980–1981 and 2013–2014, average landholding with households in districts of Hooghly and North 24 Parganas had reduced by almost half (Table 4.4). Since these districts have a high population density, any growth in population ultimately leads to more land fragmentation and hence smaller landholdings. There was no change in average landholding per household in the districts of Banaskantha and Chandrapur during the same time period, though it has reduced a little

Table 4.2 *Major Occupation of the Surveyed Households*

S. No.	Region	Selected Districts	Major Occupation of Adult Members (% to Total)				Proportion of Children Studying
			Agriculture and Dairying	Farm Labour	Non-farm Labour	Unemployed	
1	Coastal Andhra	West Godavari	34	–	–	3	90
2	Gangetic Plains	Hooghly and North 24 Parganas	54	1	6	7	84
3	North Gujarat	Banaskantha	82	1	2	–	100
4	Vidarbha	Chandrapur	59	–	1	2	64

Source: Primary data from the field survey.

Table 4.3 Expenditure (Current Prices) on Major Items by Surveyed Households

S. No.	Particulars	Time Period	West Godavari	Hooghly & North 24 Parganas	Banaskantha	Chandrapur
				Average Expenditure per Household (% to Total)		
1	Food items	1980–81	29	24	21	46
		1990–91	27	21	13	41
		2000–01	17	18	14	38
		2010–11	15	18	16	42
		2013–14	18	21	16	28
2	Agricultural inputs	1980–81	40	55	21	14
		1990–91	28	53	25	8
		2000–01	23	43	25	10
		2010–11	14	39	21	12
		2013–14	19	44	23	32

(Continued)

Table 4.3 (Continued)

S. No.	Particulars	Time Period	Average Expenditure per Household (% to Total)			
			West Godavari	Hooghly & North 24 Parganas	Banaskantha	Chandrapur
3	Children education	1980–81	0	2	10	1
		1990–91	4	11	8	6
		2000–01	14	12	5	10
		2010–11	19	9	10	7
		2013–14	15	11	9	8
4	Health care	1980–81	15	14	9	4
		1990–91	18	15	14	12
		2000–01	12	11	12	10
		2010–11	8	8	5	8
		2013–14	11	9	9	9
5	HH items and durable goods	1980–81	7	8	15	9
		1990–91	5	6	18	10
		2000–01	23	20	23	11
		2010–11	40	23	29	12
		2013–14	29	8	25	11

Table 4.4 *Landholdings Details of Surveyed Households*

S. No.	Selected Districts	Average Area of Operational Landholding (Acre/Household)				
		1980–1981	1990–1991	2000–2001	2010–2011	2013–2014
1	West Godavari	3.07	3.05	3.01	2.91	2.91
2	Hooghly and North 24 Parganas	1.70	1.58	1.22	0.94	0.89
3	Banaskantha	4.84	4.84	4.84	4.84	4.84
4	Chandrapur	0.65	0.65	0.65	0.65	0.65

Source: Primary data from the field survey.

in West Godavari district. Households in Banaskantha, an agricultural prosperous region, have a significantly high average landholding in comparison to households in other surveyed districts.

4.4.5. Changes in Cropped and Irrigated Area

Cropped area in Hooghly and North 24 Parganas had almost decreased by half between 1980–1981 and 2013–2014 (Table 4.5). There can be several factors for that, including changing rainfall magnitude and pattern; limited access to irrigation; low land productivity; crop failure; low returns form; and low availability of farm labourers. Some of these are discussed further in the subsequent sections. However, cropped area in Banaskantha and Chandrapur has increased. Except for Banaskantha, a high proportion of cropped area in all the districts was under irrigation (Table 4.5). However, most of the surveyed households in Chandrapur provide only one–two supplementary irrigations during monsoon and not more than two–three irrigations during the winter season, as groundwater, which is the major resource of irrigation, is severely limited, whereas in Banaskantha, annual groundwater abstraction has gone beyond its annual natural recharge limits and thus there is no scope for bringing more land under irrigation. However, large farmers have adopted micro-irrigation technologies to make efficient use of the available water and to bring more cropped areas under irrigation.

Table 4.5 *Cropped and Irrigated Area of the Surveyed Households*

Selected Districts	Gross Cropped Area (Acres)				Irrigated Area as % of Cropped Area (Acres)				
	1980–1981	1990–1991	2000–2001	2010–2011	2013–2014	1980–1981	1990–1991	2000–2001	2010–2011	2013–2014
West Godavari	700	726	666	641	615	98	98	98	98	98
Hooghly and North 24 Parganas	554	544	435	336	291	65	75	85	94	95
Banaskantha	1,083	1,091	1,043	1,219	1,145	53	96	60	55	55
Chandrapur	365	361	361	405	591	99	100	100	96	87

Source: Primary data from the field survey.

4.5. CONCLUSIONS

Systematic studies on Indian agriculture have a long history, dating back to the colonial era, while documentation of the agrarian economy had begun much earlier. However, these studies displayed a disciplinary bias, with most of them looking at agrarian structures, modes of production or production relations and agrarian change. There was very limited comprehensive work looking at the problems from the perspective of factors of production and externalities. Academic debates were often dominated by aesthetic taste, value-based judgements and romanticism driven by disciplinary biases and were devoid of objectivity and empirical rigour. In this chapter, we attempted a review of the studies that look at agrarian change from an economic perspective to see whether they provided sufficient leads to validate the theory that Indian agriculture is undergoing a crisis.

Based on the review, we identified some key gaps in those studies. They mainly concern the following: (a) lack of ability to capture the regional variations in the agricultural situation and long-term change in farmer incomes in real terms and (b) limited attempt to capture the contribution of livestock production and dairy farming on farmer income. Based on these identified gaps, a longitudinal study was designed to develop a proper empirical understanding of the temporal changes in Indian agriculture from an economic perspective of changing farm incomes over a period of three plus decades (from 1980–1981 to 2012–2013), covering four distinct agroecologies of the country. The methodology and analytical tools were also discussed in the chapter.

REFERENCES

Ali, M., & Abedullah, M. (2002). Nutritional and economic benefits from enhanced vegetable production and consumption in developing countries. *Journal of Crop Production*, 6(1), 145–176.

Arnold, D. (2005). Agriculture and 'improvement' in early colonial India: A prehistory of development. *Journal of Agrarian Change*, 5(4), 505–525.

Balakrishnan, P., Golait, R., & Kumar, P. (2008). *Agricultural growth in India since 1991*. Department of Economic Analysis and Policy, Reserve Bank of India.

Barghouti, S., Kane, S., Sorby, K., & Ali, M. (2004). *Agricultural diversification for the poor: Guidelines for practitioners* (ARD Discussion Paper No. 1). The World Bank, Washington, DC.

Bhalla, G. S., & Singh, G. (2001). *Indian agriculture: Four decades of development.* SAGE Publications.

Bhalla, G. S., & Singh, G. (2009). Economic liberalization and Indian agriculture: A statewise analysis. *Economic & Political Weekly, 44*(52), 34–44.

Bhide, S., Kalirajan, K. P., & Shand, R. T. (1998). India's agricultural dynamics: Weak link in development. *Economic & Political Weekly, 33*(39), A118–A127.

Birthal, P. S., Joshi, P. K., Roy, D., & Thorat, A. (2013). Diversification in Indian agriculture toward high-value crops: The role of small farmers. *Canadian Journal of Agricultural Economics/Revue canadienne d'agroeconomie, 61*(1), 61–91.

Birthal, P. S., Roy, D., & Negi, D. S. (2015). Assessing the impact of crop diversification on farm poverty in India. *World Development, 72*(2015), 70–92.

Chadha, G. K. (2008). *Employment and poverty in rural India: Which way to go now?* [ILO Asia-Pacific Working Paper Series]. International Labour Organization, Geneva.

Chakrabarty, A. (2013). *Trends in agricultural productivity in post land reform period: A study of the impact of agricultural productivity on employment and the economy of West Bengal* [Thesis submitted for the Doctor of Philosophy in Economics]. University of North Bengal, Darjeeling.

Chand, R., & Chauhan, S. (1999). *Are disparities in Indian agriculture growing?* [Policy Brief No. 8]. National Centre for Agricultural Economics and Policy Research, New Delhi.

Chand, R., Raju, S. S., Garg, S., & Pandey, L. M. (2011). *Instability and regional variations in Indian agriculture* [Policy Paper No. 26]. National Centre for Agricultural Economics and Policy Research, New Delhi.

Chand, R., Raju, S. S., & Pandey, L. M. (2007). Growth crisis in agriculture: Severity and options at national and state levels. *Economic & Political Weekly, 42*(26), 2528–2533.

Chatterjee, S., & Rudra, A. (1989). Relations of production in pre-colonial India. *Economic & Political Weekly, 24*(21), 1171–1175.

Dev, S. M. (2016). Water management and resilience in agriculture. *Economic & Political Weekly, 51*(8), 21–24.

Directorate of Economics & Statistics. (2015). *Agricultural Statistics at a Glance 2015.* http://eands.dacnet.nic.in/PDF/Agricultural_Statistics_At_Glance-2015.pdf

DoAHD (Department of Animal Husbandry and Dairying). (n.d.). Cattle and dairy development. https://dahd.nic.in/about-us/divisions/cattle-and-dairy-development

FAO (Food and Agriculture Organization). (n.d.). FAOSTAT. http://www.fao.org/faostat/en/#compare

FICCI (Federation of Indian Chambers of Commerce and Industry). (2020). Development of dairy sector in India. http://ficci.in/spdocument/23304/Development-Dairy-Sector.pdf

Ghosh, N., Tripathi, A., Rajeshwor, M., & Singh, R. (2017). Do producers gain from selling milk? An economic assessment of dairy farming in contemporary India. *Economic & Political Weekly*, *52*(25/26). https://www.epw.in/journal/2017/25-26/special-articles/do-producers-gain-selling-milk.html

Gulati, A., Kapur, D., & Bouton, M. M. (2020). Reforming Indian agriculture. *Economic & Political Weekly*, *55*(11), 35–42.

Habib, I. (1999). *The agrarian system of Mughal India 1556–1707* (2nd revised ed.). Oxford University Press.

Hazell, P. B. R. (1982). *Instability in Indian foodgrain production* (Research Report No. 30). International Food Policy Research Institute, Washington, DC.

IBEF (India Brand Equity Foundation). (2021). Indian agriculture industry analysis https://www.ibef.org/industry/agriculture-presentation

Joshi, P. K., Birthal, P. S., & Minot, N. (2006). *Sources of agricultural growth in India: Role of diversification towards high value crops* (MTID Discussion Paper No. 98). International Food Policy Research Institute, Washington, DC.

Joshi, P. K., Gulati, A., Birthal, P. S., & Tewari, L. (2004). Agricultural diversification in South Asia: Patterns, determinants and policy implications. *Economic & Political Weekly*, *39*(24), 2457–2468.

Kannan, E., & Sundaram, S. (2011). *Analysis of trends in India's agricultural growth* (Working Paper No. 276). ISEC, Bangalore.

Kumar, M. D., & Singh, O. P. (2017). Economics of dairy farming in India. *Economic & Political Weekly*, *52*(41), 77–79.

Kumar, M. D., & van Dam, J. (2013). Drivers of change in agricultural water productivity and its improvement at basin scale in developing economies. *Water International*, *38*(3), 312–325.

Larson, D. W., Jones, E., Pannu, R. S., & Sheokand, R. S. (2004) Instability in Indian agriculture: A challenge to the Green Revolution technology. *Food Policy*, *29*(3), 257–273.

Mahendra Dev, S. (1987). Growth and instability in foodgrains production: An inter-state analysis. *Economic & Political Weekly*, *22*(39), A82–A92.

Majumdar, K., & Basu, P. (2005). Growth decomposition of foodgrains output in West Bengal: A district level study. *Indian Journal of Agricultural Economics*, *60*(2), 220–234.

Mehra, S. (1981). *Instability in Indian agriculture in the context of the new technology* (Research Report No. 25). International Food Policy Research Institute, Washington, DC.

Minhas, B. S., & Vaidyanathan, A. (1965). Growth in crop output in India, 1951–54 to 1958–61: An analysis by component elements. *Journal of Indian Society of Agricultural Statistics*, *17*(2), 230–252.

Mishra, S. (2008). Risks, farmers' suicides and agrarian crisis in India: Is there a way out? *Indian Journal of Agricultural Economics*, *63*(1), 38–54.

MoSPI (Ministry of Statistics and Programme Implementation). (2019). National accounts statistics 2019. http://www.mospi.gov.in/publication/national-accounts-statistics-2019

Omvedt, G. (1983). Capitalist agriculture and rural classes in India. *Bulletin of Concerned Asian Scholars, 15*(3), 30–54.

Radhakrishna, R. (2002). Agricultural growth, employment and poverty: A policy perspective. *Economic & Political Weekly, 37*(3), 243–250.

Rao, C. H. (1998). Agricultural growth, sustainability and poverty alleviation: Recent trends and major issues of reform. *Economic & Political Weekly, 33*(29 & 30), 1943–1948.

Rao, C. H., Ray, S. K., & Subbarao, K. (1988). *Unstable agriculture and droughts: Implications for policy*. Vikas Publishing House.

Ray, S. K. (1983). An empirical investigation of the nature and causes for growth and instability in Indian agriculture: 1950–80. *Indian Journal of Agricultural Economics, 38*(4), 459–474.

Reddy, D. N., & Mishra, S. (2009). Agriculture in the reforms regime. In D. N. Reddy & S. Mishra (Eds.), *Agrarian crisis in India*. Oxford University Press.

Reserve Bank of India. (2006). *Report of the working group to suggest measures to assist distressed farmers*.

Sagar, V. (1977). A component analysis of the growth of productivity and production in Rajasthan: 1956–61 to 1969–74. *Indian Journal of Agricultural Economics, 32*(1), 108–119.

Sagar, V. (1980). Decomposition of growth trends and certain related issues. *Indian Journal of Agricultural Economics, 35*(2), 42–59.

Sarma, P. V., & Subrahmanyam, S. (1984). A note on the decomposition of the growth rate of aggregate crop output. *Agricultural Situation in India, 39*(9), 691–694.

Sawant, S. D,. & Achuthan, C. V. (1995). Agricultural growth across crops and regions: Emerging trends and patterns. *Economic & Political Weekly, 30*(12), A2–A13.

Selvaraj, K. N., & Ramasamy, C. (2006). Drought, agricultural risk and rural income: Case of a water limiting rice production environment, Tamil Nadu. *Economic & Political Weekly, 41*(26), 2739–2746.

Sharma, H. R., Singh, K., & Kumari, S. (2006). Extent and source of instability in foodgrains production in India. *Indian Journal of Agricultural Economics, 61*(4), 648–666.

Singh, O. P. (2004). Water Productivity of Milk Production in North Gujarat, Western India. Proceedings of the 2nd Annual Conference of Asia Pacific Association of Hydrology and Water Resources, Suntec City, Singapore.

Singh, S. (2018). Reforming agricultural markets in India: A tale of two model acts. *Economic & Political Weekly, 53*(51), 15–18.

Tripathi, A. K., & Sindhi, S. (2020). Droughts, heatwaves and agricultural adaptation: A historical account for India. *Economic & Political Weekly, 55*(26 & 27), 5–12.

Vaidyanathan, A. (2010). *Agricultural growth in India: The role of technology, incentives, and institutions*. Oxford University Press.

Weinberger, K., & Lumpkin, T. A. (2007). Diversification into horticulture and poverty reduction: A research agenda. *World Development, 35*(8), 1464–1480.

PART II

Findings and Insights from Field Research

Chapter 5

Agricultural Transformation in West Bengal

M. V. K. Sivamohan, V. Niranjan,
M. Dinesh Kumar and Nitin Bassi

5.1. INTRODUCTION

The West Bengal and the Central Bengal regions are the oldest agricultural settlements in India (Chakrabarty, 2013). Except for the western part (Birbhum and Bankura), which contained laterite formation, the rest of West Bengal and Central Bengal was identified as 'semi-aquatic rice plain' (Bose, 1986, pp. 37–38). In fact, from the 17th century, the rivers of the region started to change their course towards the east, and from the 19th century, the shift gained momentum. This caused the silting up of the rivers and simultaneous fall in sub-soil water levels, which resulted in the decline of agriculture in West and Central Bengal. Foothills of the Himalayas as well as the districts of Maida, Dinajpur, part of Rajshahi and Bogra were also part of the alluvial zone. The crops of the old alluvial zone were aus rice, sugarcane, maize, jowar, millets, pulses, oilseeds, wheat, barley and, to a small extent, jute. It must be mentioned that aus rice, whose yield level was relatively poor, grows on relatively high land and requires less water than aman rice. As a consequence, a dominance of aus cultivation was witnessed in the alluvial zone of West Bengal, where there was no freshwater due to the salinity of the rivers. The loss of silt-laden red water resulted in a shift to inferior crops, and a drastic fall in yields was observed (Mukherjee,

1938, pp. 83–84). From the middle of the 19th century, the natural drainage system was also severely affected by the construction of rail and road embankments. As a consequence, stagnant water became a breeding ground for mosquitoes, which resulted in series of malaria epidemics. People were dying regularly in the districts of Jessore, Hooghly, 24 Parganas, Nadia, Burdwan, Birbhum and Howrah. This resulted in a decline in rural population and a sharp decline in cultivated land between 1891 and 1931 (Chaudhuri, 1970; Klein, 1972, pp. 132–160).

The growth in agriculture in Bengal slowed down after 1920 due to rapid population growth and stagnation in cropped area. Between 1920 and 1946, Bengal agriculture had reached equilibrium at low levels of production shown by the zero growth in cultivated area and near-zero growth in yield (Blyn, 1966, pp. 20–27; Islam, 1979, p. 203). In the settlement report of Dacca, in 1917, it was mentioned that the cultivated land as a percentage of cultivable land reached 92 per cent. Excessive population pressure in the fertile lands of East Bengal forced the people to move in search of new patches of land.[1]

Cultivation was even extended to the less fertile laterite region of districts of Bankura and Birbhum and also in Tamluk and Contai subdivisions of Midnapore. Therefore, expansion of population, cultivation was extended to lesser fertile zones. The operational holdings got subdivided and became smaller in size. Therefore, a slump in productivity and production was a natural and logical outcome in Bengal. It should

---

[1] http://14.139.211.59/bitstream/123456789/1507/8/08_chapter_02.pdf; Madhupur jungle located at the northeast of Dacca was reclaimed. Chunks of the agrarian community started moving up the Jamuna and the Assam valley up to Guwahati and along the left bank of Brahmaputra as far as Tejpur (Mukherjee, 1938, p. 275). People from Bakerganj, Jessore and Khulna started moving to the Sundarban region in search of livelihood. Between 1881 and 1901, the lands of the less fertile Barind area consisting of parts of the districts of Maida, Bogra and Rajshahi were brought into cultivation, and Santhal from Chota Nagpur area were engaged because of their experience in clearing jungle and forest land for cultivation (Cooper, 1988, p. 27). Forest land of the western Duars (Jalpaiguri district) was also brought under cultivation. People migrated from other parts of North Bengal and Chota Nagpur and started working as coolies in the tea gardens or as sharecroppers on agricultural lands (Chakrabarty, 2013).

further be noted that the rise in population and adverse Iand–man ratio accentuated sharecropping on newly reclaimed land and competition for land forced cultivators to accept exploitative tenancy arrangements such as 'share contract'. It was also observed that price fluctuations especially for rice and jute had a serious impact on Bengal's agriculture (Chakrabarty, 2013).

After several decades of stagnation, with the limited impact of Green Revolution, the agriculture of West Bengal gathered momentum in real terms during the decade of the 1980s. A decomposition analysis of agricultural growth rates in the state during 1970–1971 to 1979–1980, 1980–1981 to 1991–1992 and 1992–1993 to 2003–2004 showed a remarkable improvement in the yield growth, which acted as the main driver of growth during the 1980s. The growth rates in cultivated area and cropping pattern change showed the sign of improvement during the 1980s, but their relative contributions to output growth have declined in relation to the contribution of crop yields. A more or less similar pattern continued during the 1990s and onwards. However, the yield growth rates declined sharply during the 1990s (from 3.57% per annum to 1.54% per annum), as a result of which the output growth also declined significantly (Ghosh & Kuri, 2007).

The high growth rates in yield and hence the high output growth in West Bengal during the 1980s were mainly due to the combined effect of technological factors (Ghosh & Kuri, 2007; Sekar & Pal, 2012) and institutional reforms, mainly Operation Barga (Ghosh & Kuri, 2007). During the 1980s under the Left Front government, some institutional and technological advancements took place in rural West Bengal, which seem to have played a key role in the significant improvement in the 1980s, though it is still debatable. As analysed by Ghosh and Kuri (2007), the agricultural growth in West Bengal in the 1980s was also influenced by the growth in production of boro paddy through the extension of irrigation by shallow private tube wells. However, the growth rates in total agricultural output (in value terms) and production of important crops have declined significantly after the 1990s. The yield of most of the important crops has either stagnated or even declined. A declining trend has also been noticed in the growth of area, though not much serious as yield. In short, the state has experienced a slowing down of growth performance in agriculture in recent years (Ghosh & Kuri, 2007).

In spite of the significant decline in yield growth, the growth in paddy outputs during the economic reform period was mainly due to yield effects than the effect of area expansion, while both area expansion and yield growth contributed to output growth during the Green Revolution period (Sekar & Pal, 2012).[2] However, the biggest challenge that the state faces today in achieving sustainable growth in the farm sector is the declining size of the farm holdings, which reduces the ability to produce a surplus.

Following a quick review of the agricultural situation in distinct regions (developed and developing districts) vis-à-vis some key development indicators, the chapter analyses how the performance of the agricultural sector in the state has been changing over the three plus decades and examines how factors such as crop technology changes, change in cropping pattern and farming system modifications, irrigation expansion, changing input use and cost of inputs and changing market conditions contribute to this trend, based on primary data collected from two districts, namely 24 Parganas and Hooghly.

5.2. AGRICULTURE IN WEST BENGAL

West Bengal is primarily dependent on agriculture and medium industry. Rice and potato are the important food crops of the state. The agriculture sector contributed 18.7 per cent of gross state domestic product (GSDP) in 2009–2010. It is also the second-largest tea producing state in the country. It produced 329.3 million tons of tea in

---

[2] The rate of growth of rice productivity in IGP was around 3.2 per cent till 1980, which was impressive after the Green Revolution period. However, there had been a deceleration in the growth rate of rice productivity after the 1980s, which was particularly more evident during the 1990s (0.37%). According to Sekar and Pal (2012), the factors that might have contributed to the rapid decline in yield growth since the early 1980s is absence of any technological breakthrough after the mid-1960s. Since the introduction of IR8 in 1966, no major technological breakthrough had occurred, even though some early maturing varieties were developed (Sekar & Pal, 2012).

2014–2015. Fish production in the state during the corresponding year was 1.61 million tons. The state accounted for 10 per cent of the edible oil production in the country. While the compounded annual growth rate of employment increased by 3.55 per cent in urban areas, the rural areas saw a growth rate of 3.33 per cent in the state. Agricultural sector made impressive strides with 3.05 per cent per annum (GoWB, 2007).

In the post-globalization period, crop diversification seemed to occur in West Bengal in favour of high-value crops or crops fetching higher income to farmers aiding agricultural growth. The small and marginal farmers who are risk averters started allocating plots of land to non-food grain as well as food grain crops in order to mitigate risk. However, the process of diversification suffered a setback after 2000–2001, more specifically from 2005–2006 onwards, mainly due to lackadaisical expansion of irrigation facilities (Dasgupta & Bhaumik, 2014).

A study of the relationship between value of agricultural produce per hectare of net area sown and agricultural values (Sarkar & Ghosh, 2017) traced the roots to the pace of agricultural development. There is the coexistence of developed and developing districts in West Bengal. The changing patterns of association of agricultural development indicators for the decadal year of 1990–1991, 2000–2001 and 2010–2011 were analysed. Ten (10) variables were identified at the district level in West Bengal to analyse the level of agricultural development. The analysis showed the following pattern of development in the agricultural sector (Table 5.1).

The presence of sharp variation in development had been recognized and brought to focus in 1971 by the Bengal Chamber of Commerce and Industry, Calcutta (BCCI, 1971) when it stated:

While the Calcutta Metropolitan District or the district of Burdwan in the coal–iron ore belt represents a relatively high level of development, the outlying regions like Darjeeling–Cooch Behar–Jalpaiguri in the north or Purulia–Bankura–Murshidabad in the west reflect a sorry plight of stagnation and decay. Indeed, a greater degree of intra-state regional

Table 5.1 *Relative Levels of Agricultural Development and Districts in West Bengal, 2010–2011*

S. No.	Indicators	State Average	Developed Districts	Developing Districts
Agriculture Sector				
1	Gross value of agricultural produce per hectare of net area sown (₹)	34,523.73	Howrah, Hooghly, Nadia, Malda, 24 Parganas (N), Murshidabad, Darjeeling, Burdwan	Midnapore, Cooch Behar, Bankura, Dakshin Dinajpur, Jalpaiguri, 24 Parganas (S), Uttar Dinajpur, Birbhum, Purulia, Kolkata
2	Gross value of agricultural produce per capita of rural population (₹)	3,199.49	Darjeeling, Dakshin Dinajpur, Nadia, Burdwan, Hooghly, Jalpaiguri, Cooch Behar, Bankura, Malda, Midnapore, Uttar Dinajpur	24 Parganas (N), Murshidabad, Birbhum, Howrah, Purulia, 24 Parganas (S), Kolkata
3	Gross value of agricultural produce per agricultural worker (₹)	32,100.00	Darjeeling, Kolkata, Jalpaiguri, Nadia, Howrah	24 Parganas (N), Cooch Behar, Hooghly, Murshidabad, Malda, Dakshin Dinajpur, Midnapore, Burdwan, Bankura, Birbhum, Uttar Dinajpur, 24 Parganas (S), Purulia
4	Percentage of area under commercial crops to gross cropped area	17.35	Hooghly, Nadia, Murshidabad, Jalpaiguri, Cooch Behar, Uttar Dinajpur, 24 Parganas (N)	Darjeeling, Malda, Dakshin Dinajpur, Burdwan, Howrah, Birbhum, Midnapore, 24 Parganas (S), Bankura, Purulia, Kolkata
5	Percentage of net area sown to total geographical area	60.90	Uttar Dinajpur, Dakshin Dinajpur, Cooch Behar, Nadia, Birbhum, Murshidabad, Hooghly, Burdwan, 24 Parganas (N), Midnapore	Malda, Howrah, Jalpaiguri, Bankura, Purulia, Darjeeling, 24 Parganas (S), Kolkata

6	Cropping intensity	160.7	Darjeeling, Nadia, 24 Parganas (N), Murshidabad, Cooch Behar, Howrah, Uttar Dinajpur, Hooghly, Jalpaiguri, Burdwan, Midnapore	Dakshin Dinajpur, Bankura, 24 Parganas (S), Darjeeling, Birbhum, Purulia, Kolkata
7	Percentage of agricultural workers to total (main) workers	25.54	Uttar Dinajpur, Birbhum, Dakshin Dinajpur, Purulia, Bankura, Midnapore, Malda, Burdwan, Cooch Behar, Murshidabad, 24 Parganas (S)	Hooghly, Nadia, Jalpaiguri, 24 Parganas (N), Darjeeling, Howrah, Kolkata
8	Credit to agriculture (per capita)	97.00	Darjeeling, Birbhum, Hooghly, Midnapore, Burdwan, Nadia, Bankura, Malda, Cooch Behar	Murshidabad, 24 Parganas (N), 24 Parganas (S), Jalpaiguri, Purulia, Howrah, Uttar Dinajpur, Dakshin Dinajpur, Kolkata
9	Consumption of fertilizer per hectare of gross cropped area	127.91 (kg)	Howrah, Hooghly, Darjeeling, Burdwan, Purulia, Birbhum	24 Parganas (N), 24 Parganas (S), Cooch Behar, Midnapore, Bankura, Jalpaiguri, Malda, Uttar Dinajpur, Nadia, Murshidabad, Dakshin Dinajpur, Kolkata
10	Average size of holdings (in hectare)	0.785	Darjeeling, Jalpaiguri, Birbhum, Bankura, Burdwan, Cooch Behar, Nadia, Purulia, Malda	Murshidabad, 24 Parganas (N), Hooghly, Midnapore, 24 Parganas (S), Uttar Dinajpur, Howrah, Dakshin Dinajpur, Kolkata

Source: Sarkar and Ghosh (2017).

142 | M. V. K. Sivamohan et al.

imbalance is not witnessed in any other state of the Indian Union, as ... the data provided by the Census of India, reveals.

5.2.1. Production Performance of Agriculture in West Bengal

A great deal of discussion took place in recent years on the issue of production performance of agriculture in West Bengal. Boyce (1987) observed that the exponential growth rate of total agricultural output in West Bengal was 1.74 per cent per annum during the period 1949–1980, which was lower than the population growth rate. However, since the early 1980s, the situation changed dramatically so much so that the rate of growth of agricultural output far exceeded the growth rate of population in West Bengal. As reported by the CMIE (1993), the rate of growth of agricultural production in the states of eastern India increased rapidly during the 1980s, and the fastest growth has been recorded in West Bengal, particularly with regard to the food grains production (growing by 6.5% per annum during 1981–1982 to 1991–1992, while the all-India average was only 2.7% per annum). Saha and Swaminathan (1994) further reported that for the period 1981–1982 to 2000–2001, the exponential growth rate of all-crop production for West Bengal was 6.4 per cent per annum. This gave rise to the contention that the impasse in agriculture of West Bengal ended. To understand the scenarios, the following were put forward to appreciate the context.

During 1990–1991 to 1992–1993, the annual growth rate of food grains production in West Bengal was 4.99 per cent, which was far greater than the growth rate observed for all India (2.88%). During the same period, the annual growth rate of rice production was as high as 5.53 per cent in West Bengal as against 3.58 per cent for all India. Even for commercial crops such as jute and potatoes, West Bengal recorded a high growth rate of production during this period (Sarkar and Ghosh, 2017).

In both West Bengal and all India, the growth rate of food grains production decelerated significantly during 1993–1994 to 1999–2000.

During this period, annual growth rates of food grains production in West Bengal and all India were 2.45 per cent and 2.06 per cent, respectively. It is important to note that not only the annual growth rate of food grains production in West Bengal has been higher than the same for all India in the early years of economic reforms, but even the growth rate of food grains production exceeded the growth rate of population during this period (Sarkar and Ghosh, 2017).

As far as agricultural performance at the national level is concerned, the situation changed drastically after 1999–2000. During 1999–2000 to 2004–2005 (more matured phase of economic reforms), the growth rate of food grains production at the all India level became negative (–0.23% per annum), while the population grew at the rate of 1.96 per cent per annum. On the other hand, in West Bengal, food grains production grew at the rate of 2.06 per cent per annum even during this phase of agrarian crisis which was again higher than the population growth rate. The overall picture obtaining in West Bengal during 1999–2000 to 2004–05 appears to be quite satisfactory, particularly with regard to the growth rate of food grains production, when agriculture in many states, as well as in all India, suffered a setback (Sarkar and Ghosh, 2017).

5.3. THE STUDY LOCATION

5.3.1. Physiography

The state of West Bengal is divided into three distinct physiographic units: extra-peninsular region of the north, comprising mainly Himalayan foothills, falling in Darjeeling, Jalpaiguri and Cooch Behar districts; the peninsular mass of the south-west forming a fringe of Western Plateau, covering the entire district of Purulia, the western part of the districts of Bardhaman, Paschim Medinipur and Birbhum and the northern part of Bankura districts; and alluvial and deltaic plains of the south and east, comprising the deltaic zone falling in Sundarban area of the district of South 24 Parganas and a small part of North 24 Parganas districts and plain flat terrain falling in the remaining areas of the state.

5.3.2. Climate

Gangetic Plains in West Bengal are dry sub-humid to moist sub-humid with an average annual rainfall of about 1,400 mm in central alluvial plains and 1,600 mm in alluvial coastal saline plains. Major soils are red and yellow deltaic alluvium and red loamy types. In the coastal tract of the region, alluvium of recent to Pleistocene ages and the tertiary sediments form the principal aquifers. The aquifers in the porous alluvial formations in the region are characterized by a high groundwater potential with an average water yield of about 50–150 m³/hr. However, high salinity in groundwater occurs along the coastal tract. The stage of groundwater development is 73 per cent, and groundwater irrigation is mainly through the use of shallow tube wells. Major crops that are grown include rice, rapeseed and jute.

5.3.3. Demography

Gangetic Plains in West Bengal are in about 355 km wide area along the Bay of Bengal and covered by the network of streams forming the mouths of the Ganga and Brahmaputra rivers. The districts included in this region are Murshidabad, Nadia, North 24 Parganas and Hooghly. Sundarban coastal region is also a part of this region. The total population in the region is 2.8 crore, with a density of about 1,690 person per sq. km. It is among the most fertile regions in the world, and the major crops that are grown include jute, tea and rice. The demographic details of the two districts of the Gangetic Plains in West Bengal are given in Table 5.2.

5.3.4. Changing Land Use

5.3.4.1. Land Use of Hooghly District

The district has an area of 3,149 sq. km, which is about 3.55 per cent of the total geographical area of the state. In 2005, the reported area under land utilization statistics of the district was 312.22 sq. km, 71 per cent of which was sown, and 27 per cent under non-agricultural use. Forest area is negligible (less than 1%). The land utilization statistics

Table 5.2 *Demographic Details of Gangetic Plains*

Region Covered	District Selected	Population (Selected District)			
		2001 (in Lakh)	% to Region's Overall	2011 (in Lakh)	% to Region's Overall
Gangetic Plains (West Bengal)	Hooghly	50.42	20.62	55.20	19.80
	North 24 Parganas	89.34	36.54	100.83	36.17

Source: Authors' own analysis based on Census of India (2011).

Table 5.3 *Land Utilization Statistics of Hooghly District (in '000 ha)*

1	Reporting area	312.22
2	Forest area	0.53
3	Area under non-agricultural use	84.65
4	Barren and uncultivable land	0.61
5	Permanent pasture and other grazing land	0.06
6	Land under miscellaneous tree groves not included in net sown area	3.18
7	Cultivable waste land	1.83
8	Fallow land other than current fallow	0.55
9	Current fallow	1.08
10	Net sown area	219.73

Source: District Human Development Report, 2011.

of the district thus offer enough scopes for both agricultural and non-agricultural activities (Table 5.3).

5.3.4.2. Land Use of North 24 Parganas District

Agriculture is still a major source of livelihood in rural North 24 Parganas. The net cropped area of the district is 2.60 lakh ha with current fallow of 1,334 ha and land under miscellaneous tree groves of

Table 5.4 *Land Utilization Statistics of North 24 Parganas District (in '000 ha)*

1	Reporting area	386.52
2	Forest area	–
3	Area under non-agricultural use	119.7
4	Barren and uncultivable land	–
5	Permanent pasture and other grazing land	–
6	Land under miscellaneous tree groves not included in net sown area	4.44
7	Cultivable waste land	0.17
8	Fallow land other than current fallow	0.55
9	Current fallow	1.82
10	Net sown area	260.73

Source: District Human Development Report, 2010.

4,317 ha. Nearly 25 per cent of the total landmass of the district is now under non-agricultural use (Table 5.4). The reduction in agricultural land is to be explained mainly by the fact that increased utilization of land for non-agricultural purposes, particularly in the areas adjacent to Kolkata, changed the land use pattern of the district radically.

5.3.5. Changes in Operational Holding

Although there is an increase in the number of landholdings between 2000–2001 and 2010–2011, the total landholding had decreased (Table 5.5). The average size of landholding was found to be lowest in Gangetic Plains (0.7 ha), which is a water-rich region.

Agriculture in the Gangetic Plains is small-farmer-centric, with 97 per cent of the cultivators being small and marginal farmers. Marginal operational landholding accounts for 84 per cent of the total operational holdings (Table 5.6), whereas the number of operational holders belonging to the medium-sized category, as a proportion of the total number of operational holdings, is insignificant (0.2%). There are no

Table 5.5 *Agricultural Landholdings in Gangetic Plains*

Region	Total No. of Landholdings (in 000')		Total Area of Landholdings (in 000' ha)	
	2000–2001	2010–2011	2000–2001	2010–2011
Gangetic Plains	1,748	1,814	1,293	1,286

Source: ICSSR (2015).

Table 5.6 *Size Class-wise Details of the Operational Landholdings, Gangetic Plains of West Bengal*

S. No.	Landholding Size Class	Particulars	Gangetic Plains	
			2000–2001	2010–2011
1	Marginal	% to total no. of landholdings	81.1	84.0
		% to total area	52.9	58.3
		Avg. size (ha)	0.5	0.5
2	Small	% to total no. of landholdings	15.1	13.3
		% to total area	32.2	30.5
		Avg. size (ha)	1.6	1.6
3	Semi-medium	% to total no. of landholdings	3.4	2.6
		% to total area	12.4	10.0
		Avg. size (ha)	2.7	2.7
4	Medium	% to total no. of landholdings	0.4	0.2
		% to total area	2.4	1.1
		Avg. size (ha)	4.9	4.9
5	Large	% to total no. of landholdings	0.0	0.0
		% to total area	0.1	0.1
		Avg. size (ha)	25.7	16.0

Source: ICSSR (2015).

large farmers in the region. Like in AP, the proportion of operational holdings belonging to the marginal category has increased, and that belonging to other categories (small, semi-medium and medium) has reduced over the reporting period.

5.3.6. Agricultural Situation

5.3.6.1. Cropped Area and Irrigated Area

The gross cropped area of Gangetic Plains is 26.12 lakh ha, out of which 35 per cent is irrigated, and the groundwater irrigated area is 52 per cent to that of the gross irrigated area.

5.4. RESULTS AND DISCUSSIONS

5.4.1. Income and Expenditure

In the districts, namely Hooghly and North 24 Parganas, average household expenditure during 1980–1981 and 1990–1991 was more than the income, as agricultural productivity in the region was low due to lack of access to irrigation facilities. As a result, households have had to depend on private loans or government aids for their survival. However, with the increase in access to irrigation, improvement in crop productivity and emergence of employment opportunities outside the farm in the subsequent years, households were able to take care of their financial needs. In fact, in the 2010s, surveyed households could save 17–21 per cent of their annual income.

Table 5.7 shows the changes in average annual household income, the proportion of income from agriculture and annual expenditure as a percentage of the annual income over time (from 1980–1981 to 2013–2014). As Table 5.7 shows, while the average annual household income (at current prices) had increased consistently (from ₹28,463 to ₹144,996), the percentage of income from agriculture reduced (from 98% to 74%), and the expenditure as a percentage of the income consistently reduced. Further, while the percentage expenditure on agricultural inputs reduced consistently till 2010–2011, it increased on

Table 5.7 *Income and Expenditure (Current Prices) Pattern of Surveyed Households, Hooghly and North 24 Parganas*

			Districts Covered
S. No.	Time Period	Particulars (Average per Household)	Hooghly and North 24 Parganas
1	1980–1981	Average annual income (₹/HH)	28,463
		% agricultural income	98
		% expenditure	113
2	1990–1991	Average annual income (₹/HH)	52,449
		% agricultural income	95
		% expenditure	105
3	2000–2001	Average annual income (₹/HH)	96,356
		% agricultural income	87
		% expenditure	89
4	2010–2011	Average annual income (₹/HH)	144,390
		% agricultural income	75
		% expenditure	79
5	2013–2014	Average annual income (₹/HH)	144,996
		% agricultural income	76
		% expenditure	83

Source: ICSSR (2015).

durable goods. The latter can be taken as an indicator for an improvement in the family's living standard.

Nevertheless, as Table 5.8 shows, the major household expenditure continues to be on food items and for purchasing agricultural inputs. The expenditure on healthcare started to decrease from 2000 to 2014.

Table 5.8 *Expenditure (Current Prices) on Major Items by Surveyed Households, Hooghly and North 24 Parganas*

S. No.	Particulars	Time Period	Average Expenditure per Household (% to Total) Hooghly and North 24 Parganas
1	Food items	1980–1981	24
		1990–1991	21
		2000–2001	18
		2010–2011	18
		2013–2014	21
2	Agri inputs	1980–1981	55
		1990–1991	53
		2000–2001	43
		2010–2011	39
		2013–2014	44
3	Children education	1980–1981	2
		1990–1991	11
		2000–2001	12
		2010–2011	9
		2013–2014	11
4	Healthcare	1980–1981	14
		1990–1991	15
		2000–2001	11
		2010–2011	8
		2013–2014	9
5	Household items and durable goods	1980–1981	8
		1990–1991	6
		2000–2001	20
		2010–2011	23
		2013–2014	8

Source: ICSSR (2015).

5.4.2. Changes in Cropping and Irrigation Pattern

The cropping and irrigation pattern of surveyed households in Hooghly and North 24 Parganas is presented in Table 5.9. Between 1980–1981 and 2013–2014, the proportion of cropped area under monsoon crops has remained unchanged. However, it has increased for winter crops (from 28% to 34%), while for summer crops there is a significant decline, as the proportion of area under summer paddy has reduced substantially (13% to 9% for the latter). From 2000 onwards, new crops such as mustard, red lentil and coriander were introduced in the winter season.

Almost the entire cropped area (except for that under red lentil) during winter and summer seasons is irrigated. There was also substantial improvement in area irrigated during the monsoon season. Post 2000, almost the entire area under vegetables was irrigated. Also, the irrigated area for monsoon paddy increased by almost seven times between 1980–1981 and 2013–2014. However, most of this increase is due to one–two supplementary irrigations being provided to the paddy crop during the monsoon.

5.4.3. Changes in Agricultural Inputs

As Table 5.10 shows, between 1980–1981 and 2013–2014, the cost (adjusted to 2013–2014 prices) of agricultural inputs for all the crops except vegetables had gone up. Its graphical representation is given in Figure 5.1. For summer paddy, input cost increased to almost three times the 1980–1981 levels. One major reason for this increase is the substantial increase in expenditure on fertilizers. The average expenditure on fertilizers (adjusted to 2013–2014 prices) had increased from ₹5,563/acre in 1990–1991 to ₹7,417/acre in 2013–2014. Further, as the average landholding size of farmers in the region is low, they mostly depend on rental pumps to lift water for irrigation. Both the pump rent and cost of diesel had increased slightly from the 1980–1981 levels, which led to an increase in average cost (adjusted to 2013–2014 prices) of irrigation from ₹1,879/acre to about ₹2,700/acre during the period from 1980–1981 to 2013–2014.

Table 5.9 Cropping and Irrigation Pattern of Surveyed Households, Gangetic Plains of West Bengal

Season	Crop	Proportion of Cropped Area under Different Crops (%)					Proportion of Cropped Area Which Is Irrigated (%)				
		1980–1981	1990–1991	2000–2001	2010–2011	2013–2014	1980–1981	1990–1991	2000–2001	2010–2011	2013–2014
Monsoon	Paddy	37	37	34	35	38	13	35	59	86	91
	Vegetables	2	2	2	2	2	28	72	100	100	93
	Overall	39	39	37	37	40	13	37	61	91	90
Winter	Potato	26	24	25	25	26	100	99	100	100	100
	Vegetables	2	2	2	2	3	92	94	100	100	100
	Mustard	0	0	1	1	2	0	0	100	100	100
	Red lentil	0	0	1	1	1	0	0	0	0	8
	Coriander	0	0	1	1	1	0	0	100	100	100
	Overall	28	27	29	30	34	99	98	100	100	96
Summer	Vegetables	7	7	8	8	9	95	100	100	100	100
	Jute	3	3	3	2	2	94	100	100	100	100
	Sesame	11	11	11	13	14	94	100	100	100	100
	Paddy	13	14	12	9	8	100	100	100	100	100
	Overall	33	35	34	32	25	96	100	100	100	100

Source: ICSSR (2015).

Table 5.10 *Agri Input Cost at Real Prices (2013–2014) for the Surveyed Households, Gangetic Plains of West Bengal*

| Season | Crop | Input Cost (₹/Acre) | | | | |
		1980–1981	1990–1991	2000–2001	2010–2011	2013–2014
Monsoon	Paddy	19,273	16,135	24,560	24,787	26,061
	Vegetables	113,624	67,622	54,600	59,995	62,905
Winter	Potato	60,874	83,255	93,159	98,201	95,527
	Vegetables	140,309	86,247	73,337	68,626	70,679
	Mustard	–	–	9,155	13,434	14,519
	Red lentil	–	–	11,531	12,803	15,425
	Coriander	–	–	7,094	8,044	11,911
Summer	Vegetables	89,801	56,100	52,517	52,902	61,017
	Jute	88,633	89,164	81,799	95,022	95,342
	Sesame	10,704	13,964	12,728	11,702	12,803
	Paddy	12,218	11,490	18,425	28,720	30,924

Source: ICSSR (2015).

However, the average input cost for vegetables had come down substantially. For vegetables grown in monsoon and winter seasons, it reduced by almost half. One of the main reasons was the reduction in the expenditure (adjusted to 2013–2014 prices) on pesticides and insecticides, which had come down to almost half, that is, from an average of ₹4,267/acre in 1980–1981 to ₹2,237/acre in 2013–2014.

5.4.4. Changes in Crop Yield and Net Return

The overall yield of all the crops increased from 1980–1981 to 2013–2014 (Table 5.11). Average yield of monsoon paddy doubled while that of summer paddy increased to five times. Yield for potato and vegetables also went up substantially. This was mainly due to the increased application of fertilizer and irrigation. However, the average net return from paddy, which was the main staple crop in the region, had declined (Table 5.12). Reduction was more substantial

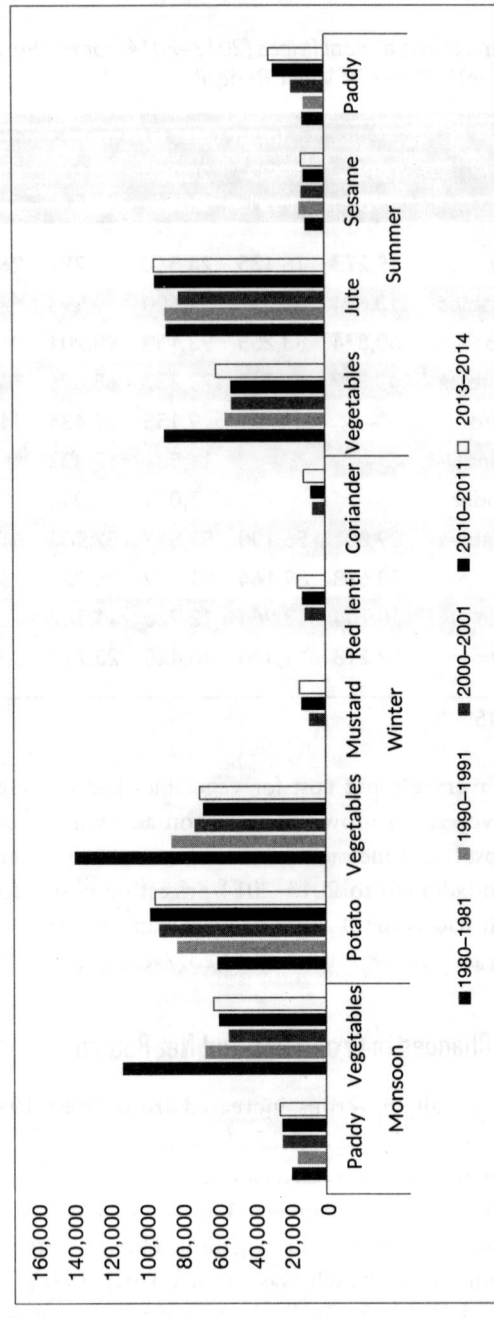

Figure 5.1 *Changing Input Costs over Time, West Bengal (₹/Acre)*

Source: Authors' own analysis based on primary data.

Table 5.11 Crop Yield for the Surveyed Households, Gangetic Plains of West Bengal

Season	Crop	Crop Yield (kg/Acre)				
		1980–1981	1990–1991	2000–2001	2010–2011	2013–2014
Monsoon	Paddy	903	959	1,400	2,276	1,913
	Vegetables	8,664	8,843	10,084	12,974	15,822
Winter	Potato	5,219	5,879	7,499	14,011	15,745
	Vegetables	10,188	10,847	12,435	14,515	14,571
	Mustard	–	–	588	1,019	810
	Red lentil	–	–	840	1,138	965
	Coriander	–	–	519	730	845
Summer	Vegetables	7,858	7,739	9,337	12,538	13,078
	Jute	1,961	1,889	2,287	3,178	2,933
	Sesame	576	489	731	848	887
	Paddy	584	752	1,203	2,071	2,600

Source: ICSSR (2015).

during monsoon season where farmers had even incurred losses in 2013–2014. Nevertheless, farmers still go for monsoon paddy, despite low profitability, as this is the only crop they can grow during that season because of heavy rains. Also, the fodder which they obtain from paddy is fed to the animals.

There was also a decline in income from the jute crop. This could be attributed to the high expenditure on purchasing agri inputs for these crops. Further, despite reduction in input cost for vegetables during the summer season, the net returns had declined. The probable reason could be damage to vegetable produce, a highly perishable item, during the summer season which is characterized usually by very warm and dry weather. For the rest of the crops, net returns increased between 1980–1981 and 2013–2014. Farmers were also able to get substantial earnings from mustard, red lentil and coriander, which were introduced only in the early 2000s.

Table 5.12 *Net Return from Various Crops at Real Prices (2013–2014) for the Surveyed Households, Gangetic Plains of West Bengal*

| Season | Crop | Net Return (₹/Acre) | | | | |
		1980–1981	1990–1991	2000–2001	2010–2011	2013–2014
Monsoon	Paddy	45,911	19,838	3,630	1,764	–1,293
	Vegetables	–	65,822	32,222	56,952	73,119
Winter	Potato	75,447	13,226	13,394	63,938	85,199
	Vegetables	–	–	87,262	67,345	64,733
	Mustard	–	–	5,619	15,630	9,788
	Red lentil	–	–	18,423	28,551	23,189
	Coriander	–	–	33,800	28,840	38,794
Summer	Vegetables	70,967	59,982	38,975	60,549	54,989
	Jute	67,819	52,600	30,605	21,137	6,188
	Sesame	–	21,344	25,260	17,151	26,001
	Paddy	14,503	12,091	6,836	3,494	7,821

Source: ICSSR (2015).

Figure 5.2 shows the graphical representation of the changes in net income per acre of land for various crops grown in the area over time (i.e., from 1980–1981 to 2013–2014).

5.4.5. Changes in Livestock Holding and Milk Yield

As presented in Table 5.13, the total number of livestock with surveyed households had reduced over the years. The number of indigenous cattle had reduced to nil. However, there was a significant increase in the number of crossbred cattle, which indicates household interest in dairy. Since the 1980s, the average milk yield per milch animal had also increased before coming down slightly in 2013. The average amount of milk sold by households had also shown the same trend. However, revenue from selling milk had reduced by almost half over the years. This may be due to the fact that the milk prices are determined by the fat content, which is generally low in cow's milk. As a result, the

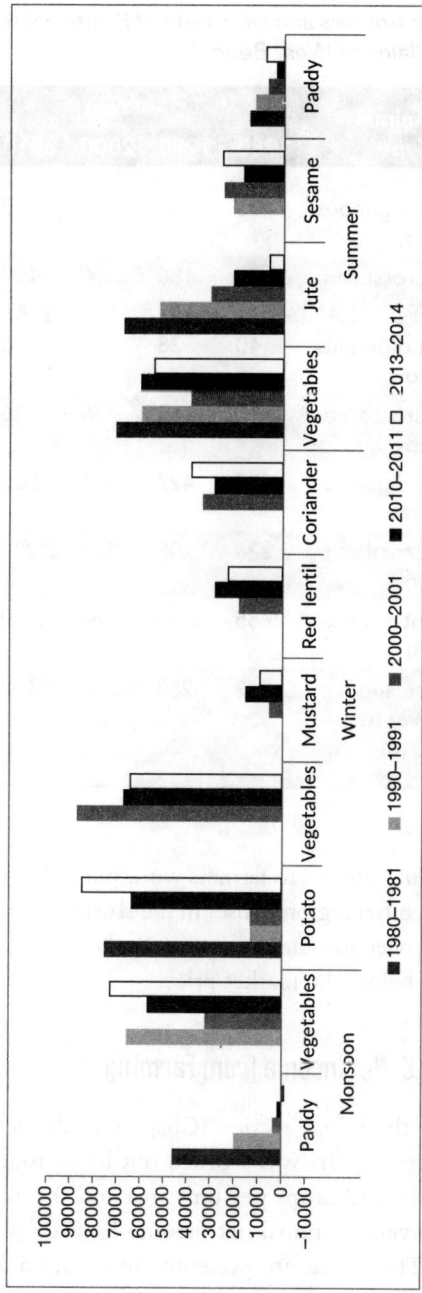

Figure 5.2 *Change in Average Net Return from Various Crops over Time, West Bengal (₹/Acre)*

Source: Authors' own analysis based on primary data.

Table 5.13 *Number of Animals and Milk Yield of Households Owning Livestock, Gangetic Plains of West Bengal*

S. No.	Particulars	Animal Type	Year 1980	1990	2000	2010	2013
1	No. of milch animals	Indigenous cow	53	52	7	2	0
		Crossbred cow	92	180	159	129	101
2	No. of non-milch animal	Indigenous cow	40	38	2	0	0
		Crossbred cow	40	83	39	26	43
3	Milk yield (lit/annum) per milch animal	Indigenous cow	427	427	495	360	–
		Crossbred cow	2,226	2,208	2,165	2,334	2,094
4	Average amount of milk sold (lit/day/HH)		5.55	6.76	7.64	7.29	7.22
5	Revenue from selling milk (₹/day/HH) at real prices (2013–2014)		343	283	230	167	155

Source: ICSSR (2015).

per litre milk price being offered to farmers work out to be below the procurement prices in other regions. Also, in the absence of any formal arrangement for milk collection and distribution at the local level, prices offered to farmers are below the market price.

5.4.6. Net Income from Farming

As discussed in the methodology section (Chapter 4), the net income from farming in different years was worked out by considering the net income from individual crops per unit area and the area under those crops plus the average annual net income from dairy production per household. The results are presented in Figure 5.3. As can

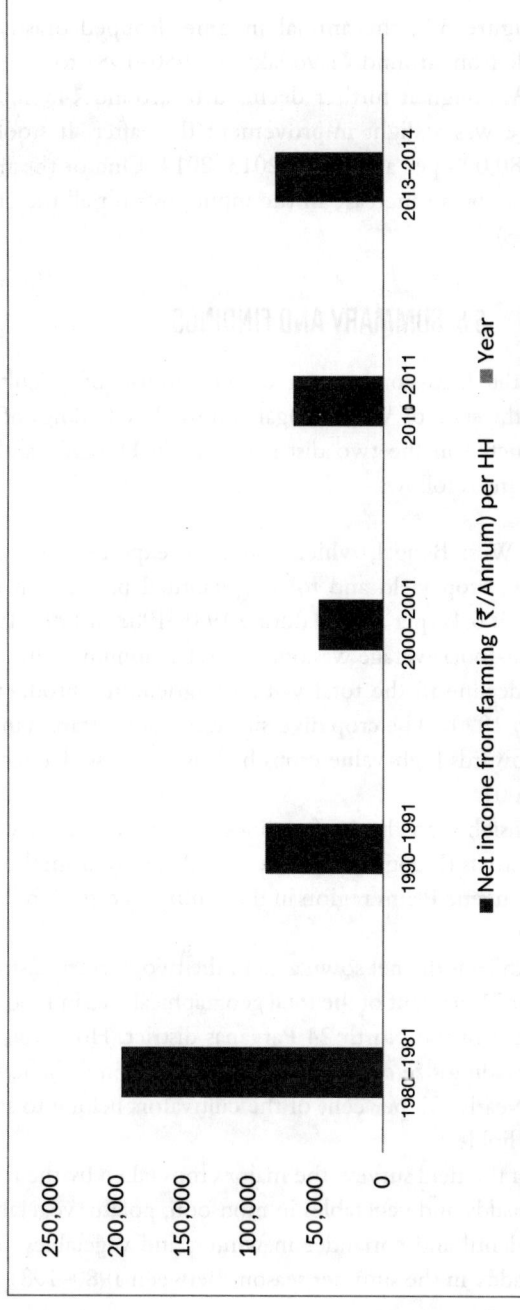

Figure 5.3 *Net Annual Income (₹) from Farming for the Surveyed Households in West Bengal (1980–1981 to 2013–2014)*

Source: Authors' own analysis based on primary data.

be seen from Figure 5.3, the annual income dropped drastically during the decade from around ₹1.96 lakh in 1980–1981 to ₹57,000 in 1990–1991. Although it further declined to around ₹48,000 by 2000–2001, there was a slight improvement thereafter. It stood at approximately ₹80,000 per annum in 2013–2014. One of the main reasons for this can be an increase in the input costs for all the crops (except vegetables).

5.5. SUMMARY AND FINDINGS

The summary of the discussions presented on the history of agricultural development in the state of West Bengal and the key findings of the field study conducted in the two districts, namely Hooghly and 24 North Parganas, are as follows:

1. The state of West Bengal, which had once experienced a high growth rate in crop yield and total agricultural production (the latter growing at 6.4% per annum during 1981–1982 to 1991–1992, whereas the all-India average was only 2.7% per annum), witnessed a significant decline in the total value of agricultural production since the early 1990s. The crop diversification which started in the early 1990s towards high-value crops had also witnessed a decline since 2000–2001.

2. For further insights on the performance of agriculture since the 1980s, two districts (Hooghly and North 24 Parganas) from the fertile alluvial Gangetic Plains region in the south and east of the state were selected.

3. About 4.4 lakh ha is the net sown area in the two selected districts, accounting for 71 per cent of the total geographical area in Hooghly and 75 per cent in the North 24 Parganas district. However, the average landholding size of the farmers in this region is the lowest in the state. Nearly, 97 per cent of the cultivators belong to small and marginal holders.

4. At the time of the field survey, the major crops taken by the farmers included paddy and vegetables in monsoon; potato, vegetables, mustard, red lentil and coriander in winter; and vegetables, jute, sesame and paddy in the summer season. Between 1980–1981 and

2013–2014, while the area under winter crops had increased, the area under summer crops decreased (mostly under paddy by about 38%). The high-value crops such as mustard, red lentil and coriander were introduced in the winter season. However, there was no change in the area under monsoon crops.

5. The entire cropped area during the winter and summer seasons is irrigated. Between 1980–1981 and 2013–2014, the irrigated area under paddy and vegetables during monsoon had increased by 6 and 2.5 times, respectively. Most of this increase was due to one–two supplementary irrigations provided during the monsoon.

6. Between 1980–1981 and 2013–2014, the cost (adjusted to 2013–2014 prices) of agricultural inputs for all the crops except vegetables had risen. This was mainly due to an increase in expenditure (adjusted to 2013–2014 prices) on fertilizers (by 33%) and irrigation (by 44%). For vegetables, the cost of cultivation had reduced due to a decline in the expenditure on pesticides and insecticides (by almost 50%).

7. Overall, the crop yields had increased from 1980–1981 to 2013–2014 due to increased dosage of fertilizer and irrigation. The yield had doubled for monsoon paddy (1,913 kg/acre in 2013–2014) and increased five times for the summer paddy (2,600 kg/acre in 2013–2014), though the cropped area for the latter had declined. Further, except for two crops (monsoon paddy and jute), net returns for all the crops had increased. Despite its low profitability (negative returns in 2013–2014), farmers still prefer monsoon paddy, as this is the only crop they can grow during that season, and the fodder from the crop is fed to the animals.

8. The two case study districts witnessed a significant increase in the number of crossbred cows, which indicates household interest in dairy. However, the price offered to farmers for the milk is low as it has low-fat content and there is no formal arrangement for its collection and distribution.

9. In spite of a shift in cropping pattern with the inclusion of high-value crops and an increase in the extent of dairy farming, the household's net annual income from farming (adjusted to 2013–2014 prices) declined by 71 per cent between 1980–1981 and 2013–2014. Further, during the same period, the proportion

of household's annual income from agriculture declined by about 22 per cent. However, the major expenditure for the surveyed households continues to be on purchasing agricultural inputs.

REFERENCES

BCCI (Bengal Chamber of Commerce and Industry). (1971). *West Bengal: An analytical study.* Oxford and IBH Publishing.

Blyn, G. (1966). Agricultural trends in India, 1891–1947: Output, availability, and productivity. *Economic Development and Cultural Change, 16*(3), 477–482.

Bose, S. (1986). *Agrarian Bengal: Economy, social structure and politics, 1919–1947.* Cambridge University Press.

Boyce, J. K. (1987). *Agrarian impasse in Bengal: Institutional constraints to technological change.* Oxford University Press.

Chakrabarty, A. (2013). *Trends in agricultural productivity in post land reform period: A study of the impact of agricultural productivity on employment and the economy of West Bengal* [Thesis submitted for the Doctor of Philosophy in Economics]. University of North Bengal, Darjeeling.

Chaudhuri, B. B. (1970). Growth of commercial agriculture in Bengal—1859–1885. *The Indian Economic & Social History Review, 7*(1), 25–60.

Cooper, A. (1988). *Sharecropping and sharecroppers' struggles in Bengal 1930–1950.* K. P. Bagchi & Company.

Dasgupta, S., & Bhaumik, S. K. (2014). Crop diversification and agricultural growth in West Bengal. *Indian Journal of Agricultural Economics, 69*(1), 108–124.

District Human Development Report (2010). District Human Development Report-North 24 Parganas, Development and Planning Department, Government of West Bengal, Kolkata.

District Human Development Report (2011). District Human Development Report-Hooghly, Development and Planning Department, Government of West Bengal, Hooghly, 2011, pp 25.

Ghosh, B. K., & Kuri, P. K. (2007). Agricultural growth in West Bengal during 1970–71 to 2003–04: A decomposition analysis. https://www.researchgate.net/publication/5105196_Agricultural_Growth_in_West_Bengal_from_1970-71_to_2003-04_A_Decomposition_Analysis

Government of West Bengal (2007). Economic Review 2006-07-Statistical Appendix, Bureau of Applied Economics & Statistics, Development & Planning Department, Government of West Bengal, Kolkata.

ICSSR (Indian Council of Social Science Research). (2015). The factors causing agrarian crisis in India: A study from four agro-ecological regions in India. https://doi.org/10.13140/RG.2.2.34664.57605

Islam, S. (1979). *The permanent settlement in Bengal: A study of its operation, 1790–1819.* Bangla Academy.

Klein, I. (1972). Malaria and mortality in Bengal 1840–1921. *Indian Economy and Social History Review, 9*(2), 132–160.

Mukherjee, R. (1938). *Changing face of Bengal: A study in riverine economy.* University of Calcutta.

Saha, A., & Swaminathan, M. (1994). Agricultural growth in West Bengal in the 1980s: A disaggregation by districts and crops. *Economic & Political Weekly, 29*(13), A2–A11.

Sarkar, S., & Ghosh, T. K. (2017). Agricultural development in West Bengal: An inter-temporal analysis. *Economic Affairs, 62*(3), 483–493.

Sekar, I., & Pal, S. (2012). Rice and wheat crop productivity in the Indo-Gangetic Plains of India: Changing pattern of growth and future strategies. *Indian Journal of Agricultural Economics, 67*(2), 238–252.

Chapter 6

Agricultural Growth in Gujarat

M. Dinesh Kumar, Nitin Bassi and V. Niranjan

6.1. INTRODUCTION

Gujarat was never known for vibrant agriculture. However, in the recent past, the state's agriculture sector has received a lot of attention for the extensive adoption of cash crops (fibre, oilseeds, spices, fruits and vegetables) and large-scale adoption of modern irrigation technologies, including drips and sprinklers. Historically, the state is known more for occurrence of droughts and drinking water scarcity (IRMA/UNICEF, 2001). Famines were also reported during the pre-Independence era (Shukla, 1980).[1] A large part of the state is affected by frequent droughts due to highly variable and erratic rainfall (IRMA/UNICEF, 2001). As seen in Chapter 3, the highly erratic growth which the agricultural GDP of the state witnessed for several decades (Jagadeesan & Kumar, 2015; Kumar et al., 2010, 2014) is mostly explained by the variability in annual rainfall. The state has four distinct regions, South Gujarat, Central and North Gujarat, Saurashtra and Kachchh. In terms of per capita renewable water resource availability, South Gujarat is water-rich, and the rest three regions are water-scarce (IRMA/UNICEF, 2001; Jagadeesan & Kumar, 2015; Kumar, 2002).

---

[1] Shukla (1980) narrates the Chumutaro famine of 1718 AD, which brought widespread starvation, diseases and death.

The South Gujarat region, by virtue of being water-rich and with several large irrigation schemes, has been agriculturally prosperous and is much less prone to droughts when compared to the other three regions, except some of the undulating eastern parts, whereas the other three regions had a long history of droughts due to poor dependability of annual rainfalls as a result of high inter-annual variability (IRMA/ UNICEF, 2001; Kumar, 2002). Nevertheless, groundwater irrigation had changed the trajectory of agriculture in the state. The alluvial tracts of Central and North Gujarat had witnessed intensive groundwater development since the early 1960s with energized open wells and later on deep tube wells. The area under well irrigation expanded remarkably in this region, and most of the irrigation expansion in the region during the period came from wells.[2] With this, groundwater resources also started depleting throughout the alluvial part of the region, with a consistent decline in water levels (Kumar, 2002).

With limited access to surface irrigation, the farmers of Saurashtra and Kachchh started exploiting groundwater through open wells, though the hard rock aquifers underlying most parts of these regions did not provide favourable conditions for intensive groundwater exploitation. The unscrupulous digging of wells had led to several problems including seasonal depletion of groundwater and acute summer water scarcity (Kumar, 2002). With very high inter-annual variability in monsoon rains, the overall water situation in these two regions also changed drastically between the hydrological years (Kumar et al., 2010, 2014). Excessively high rainfall meant more inflows into the surface reservoirs and increased recharge to groundwater and reduced water requirement for irrigation during kharif season. The situation was just the opposite in dry years, with limited surface water and poor groundwater recharge and an increase in irrigation requirement of crops.

---

[2] Overall, the net area under irrigation more than quadrupled from 6.82 lakh ha to 30.478 lakh ha during the three and a half decades (GOG, 1985–1986, as cited in Bhatia 1992; GOG, 1996/1997; GoI, 1971–1972 to 1992–1993). The contribution of public canals to this dramatic increase had only been 23 per cent. At the same time, groundwater contributed to 76.9 per cent of this growth (Kumar, 2002).

6.2. AGRICULTURE IN GUJARAT: RECENT EXPERIENCE

Gujarat witnessed one of the worst droughts of the last century for three consecutive years from 1985 to 1987 (Bhatia, 1992). Drinking water had to be transported to Rajkot by train, the cost of which was more than the cost of desalination of seawater at that point in time. It is also known that the state witnessed another severe drought for two years from 1999 to 2000. A graphical representation of the value of agricultural outputs in Gujarat for the period from 1960–1981 to 2008–2009 is given in Figure 6.1. It shows that agricultural growth in Gujarat was highly erratic, with annual growth rates varying widely with negative growth rates in some years.

Monsoon vagaries and agricultural and socio-economic droughts had attracted a lot of scholarly attention during the past three decades. The attempts to find a permanent solution to the socio-economic problems caused by frequent and severe droughts through a large-scale project involving the construction of a major reservoir on Narmada river in the water-rich South Gujarat and transfer of water to the dry regions of North Gujarat, Saurashtra and Kachchh witnessed fierce opposition from the social and environmental activists (Jagadeesan & Kumar, 2015; Patel, 2001), who advocated for the construction of small, decentralized water harvesting and watershed development as alternatives to large water systems for drought-proofing of the state (Dharmadhikary, 1993).

Although the Sardar Sarovar Project (SSP) started delivering water for irrigation in the largely rainfed areas of Gujarat by the year 2002 itself, and irrigation from SSP covered significant areas in South, Central and North Gujarat by the year 2008–2009, efforts were made to downplay the contribution of the project in stabilizing agricultural production and boosting rural growth and the sudden jump in the agricultural GDP of the state during 2000–2002 to 2007–2008 was primarily attributed to factors like decentralized water harvesting and groundwater recharge taken up by the state government since 1999 (see Shah et al., 2009).

In order to have a nuanced understanding of agricultural growth in the state, the data for 11 years from 1988–1989 (corresponding to the

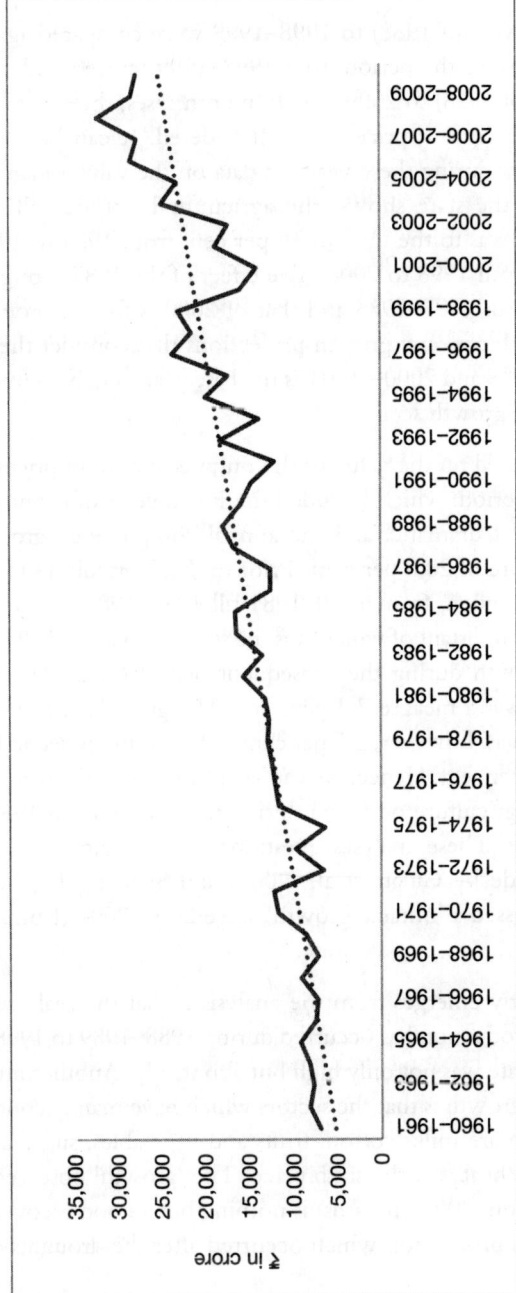

Figure 6.1 *Agricultural GDP in Gujarat at Constant Prices (1960–1961 to 2009–2010)*

Source: Based on authors' own analysis of primary data.

good rainfall year of 1988) to 1998–1999 were compared against the growth figures for the period from 1998–1999 (corresponding to the normal year of 1998) to 2009–2010. In both cases, the constant prices as well as the current prices were considered. It can be seen from Figure 6.1 that during these years, as data on the value of agricultural output from the state shows, the agricultural outputs fell remarkably. The fall was to the tune of 56 per cent from 1984 to 1987, and 30 per cent from 1998 to 2000. The effect of the 1987 drought is for the crop year of 1987–1988 and that of 2000 is for the crop year of 2000–2001. Hence, any growth projections that consider these years (i.e., 1987–1988 and 2000–2001) as the base year can give a misleading picture of the growth scenario.

Analysis based on the value of the outputs at current prices during the 11-year period, which included the initial years of economic liberalization, was dramatic, and the annual compounded growth rate clocked a figure of 20.8 per cent. Prior to that, agriculture in Gujarat did not grow much, from 1980–1981 till 1987–1988, due to several factors, most important of which was the severe drought of 1985–1987. Also, the growth during the subsequent period (i.e., 1998–1999 to 2009–2010) was a meagre 7.4 per cent. The growth in real terms in the first case was, however, 2.5 per cent, whereas in the second case, it was only 1.7 per cent. Hence, we can safely argue that the real 'growth' in Gujarat's agriculture occurred during the decade from 1988–1989 to 1998–1999. These analyses questioned the validity of the recent argument made by Gulati et al. (2009) and Shah et al. (2009) that Gujarat witnessed a 'miracle growth' since 2000–2001 (Kumar et al., 2010, 2014).

What clearly emerges from the analysis is that the real growth in agricultural production has occurred during 1988–1989 to 1998–1999. The growth rate was not only high but also steady. Another important fact vis-à-vis growth is that the sectors which have mainly contributed to this growth are milk, cotton, fruits and vegetables, sugarcane, and groundnut. Wheat is at the sixth place. The 'growth' observed in the recent past (from 2002 onwards) is nothing but a good recovery from a major dip in production which occurred after the droughts of 1999 and 2000.

Two important factors have contributed to this recovery: (a) the occurrence of four successful monsoons in the state after 2000 and (b) the steady expansion in area irrigated by the SSP canals, which have started supplying water to the water-scarce regions of North Gujarat. We will elaborate on this in the subsequent paragraphs.

Analysis of past growth trends for three important crops shows that with good monsoons, agriculture in Gujarat had grown substantially with steady expansion in either cropped area or yield growth. As against this, in drought years, the production has always suffered from shrinkage in the area under irrigated winter crops and a sharp reduction in yield of kharif crops, including cotton and groundnut. In other words, the 'criticality' of rainfall to sustain agricultural production in Gujarat is even higher as compared to the pre-Green Revolution period. The four consecutive years of good rainfall remarkably improved groundwater recharge, increased the storage in surface reservoirs throughout the state and improved soil moisture conditions. The reduced pressure on aquifers for irrigation due to availability of water from surface reservoirs reduced irrigation water requirement for crops due to improved soil moisture regime, and increase in replenishment together made a huge positive impact on groundwater balance, making more water available for subsequent years (Kumar et al., 2014).

Second, the import of water from Sardar Sarovar reservoir through canals under SSP had boosted the agricultural production at least in a few districts of South (Bharuch, Baroda and Narmada districts) and north Gujarat (Ahmedabad and Gandhinagar). Although the distribution and delivery canals were not ready for the delivery of water to the fields in the entire command (of 1.8 Mha), the length of the completed network is reasonable enough for farmers in many areas to tap water from the system (Kumar et al., 2010, 2014).

The total volume of water utilized from the Narmada Canal system in the initial phase of the command as of March 2008 was 1,800 MCM. The gross area irrigated by this could be in the range of 2.4–3.27 lakh ha, depending on an assumed delta of a maximum of 30 inches (750 mm) to a minimum of 22 inches (550 mm). In addition to this, Narmada Main Canal discharges water into several rivers of Central and

North Gujarat en route Rajasthan. They are Heran, Orsang, Sherdi, Dhadhar, Saidak, Watrak, Mesho, Sabarmati, Khari, Rupen, Banas, Pushpawati and Saraswati (Desai & Joshi, 2008). To exploit the situation, farmers put up engines to lift water from the canals and rivers and transport it to the fields. The area under wheat and cotton in the area around Narmada Main Canal has dramatically gone up during the past few years. The bumper production in cotton and wheat achieved in recent years is a testimony to this. Narmada waters have also started producing several indirect benefits by replenishing the aquifers and raising the water table, as the rivers that are receiving Narmada water are in the alluvial basin with dewatered aquifers.

What a project like SSP can do to the semi-arid, alluvial areas of the state which are expected to receive water from its canal network for irrigation can be guessed from a quick assessment of the agricultural scenario in South Gujarat. It is agriculturally one of the most prosperous regions of India and is also socio-economically forward. What characterize the region's agriculture are the two water-abundant gravity irrigation schemes, namely Ukai–Kakrapar and Mahi. With the introduction of canal water, the farmers of the region have taken up cultivation of paddy wheat, cotton wheat and perennial cash crops such as sugarcane and banana. The irrigation from canals has augmented the groundwater. The farmers who do not receive canal water are able to dig shallow tube wells and use groundwater for irrigation. The two schemes together irrigate around 5.20 lakh ha of land. Hundreds of thousands of farmers in the area purely depend on canal water for irrigation. The paddy, sugarcane and cotton yields are some of the highest in the region. The continuous replenishment of groundwater enables farmers' easy access to well water for irrigation, as the water table is very shallow. In years of reduced inflows into the reservoirs, or the area not receiving sufficient rains, the farmers could still grow the traditional and high-valued crops using the groundwater, which is available in plenty (Kumar et al., 2010, 2014).

As noted by Kumar et al. (2010, 2014), while the actual area irrigated by canals built under the SSP was nearly 0.4 Mha confined to South Gujarat and Central Gujarat, significant results were produced by the water which was carried through Narmada Main Canal that goes to Kachchh and Rajasthan. Farmers who have agricultural land located on both sides of the main canal and the rivers pump out water from them to irrigate their fields. It is not uncommon to find farmers who are using rubber pipes as long as 5–6 km to carry water to distant fields. The large investments which farmers made for the conveyance of water from the source to their farms show the high value they attach to this new water source.

For the farmers who have been using groundwater tapped from the deep confined aquifers using expensive tube wells, the availability of surface water became a boon. Besides being low cost, the quality of water available from canals is very good. Canal water, unlike the groundwater from tube wells, is free from salts, contains some micro nutrients and is cooler. It is highly suitable for growing crops such as paddy, banana and vegetables. In a study looking at the socio-ecological impacts of groundwater degradation in the Sabarmati river basin, Kumar et al. (2001) found that due to an increase in salinity of tube well water, well irrigators in the alluvial Central Gujarat had to abandon the cultivation of vegetables (Kumar et al., 2001).

With the introduction of canal water, the farmers in South and Central Gujarat have taken up cultivation of irrigated paddy, banana, potato and other vegetables on a large scale. With the dilution of groundwater in the alluvial aquifers, the well irrigators are also benefited by surface water import. As noted in a national daily,

Production of the fruit and vegetables registered a robust growth of 12.8 per cent between 2001 and 2008, which is more than double of that in the 1990s. The share of cotton in Gujarat's agricultural output has doubled, increasing from 6 per cent to 12 per cent of the gross cropped area within seven years. (*Business Line*, 2009)

When canal water is supplied to an area facing groundwater overdraft, apart from augmenting surface irrigation, it can reduce the stress on aquifers and do 'groundwater banking' for bad years. The two additional benefits are the economic value of the outputs that can be generated from the replenished groundwater and the positive externalities it induces on the cost of groundwater abstraction and the environment by raising the water table (Shah & Kumar, 2008). This argument was reinforced by the empirical analysis of indirect impacts of SSP on groundwater and well irrigation in its command area involving the use of field data (Jagadeesan & Kumar, 2015).

The foregoing discussions reemphasize the importance of successful monsoon and surface water import in ensuring agricultural prosperity in Gujarat. The impact of surface water imports and rainfall on groundwater rejuvenation in Gujarat was recently established through an empirical analysis by Kumar and Perry (2019). Having got good irrigation infrastructure (reservoir and canal networks and wells), with the occurrence of good monsoon, the supply of water for irrigation from the local reservoir-based irrigation schemes and wells can also be increased owing to good run-off from the reservoir catchments and good groundwater replenishment (Kumar & Perry, 2019).

6.3. THE STUDY LOCATION

6.3.1. Physiography

Banaskantha district is situated in the north port of Gujarat. The district is encompassed by 23.03–24.45 north latitude and 71.21–73.02 east longitude. The district is surrounded by Rajasthan state in the east-north, Mehsana in the south and Patan and Kachchh districts in the west. The geographical area of the Banaskantha district is 1,270,300 ha. The district is divided into 12 talukas. It is rich in respect of mineral resources. The important minerals in the district are marble, rubble, limestone, granite block, granite rubble, quartzite and ordinary sand.

6.3.2. Climate

North Gujarat is semi-arid to arid, with an average annual rainfall of about 735 mm. The region lies in alluvial plains and has sandy loam to sandy soils. The region is endowed with high-yielding alluvial aquifers, where groundwater occurs under unconfined, semi-confined, confined and free-flowing artesian conditions. However, due to overexploitation of groundwater in the region (stage of groundwater development is

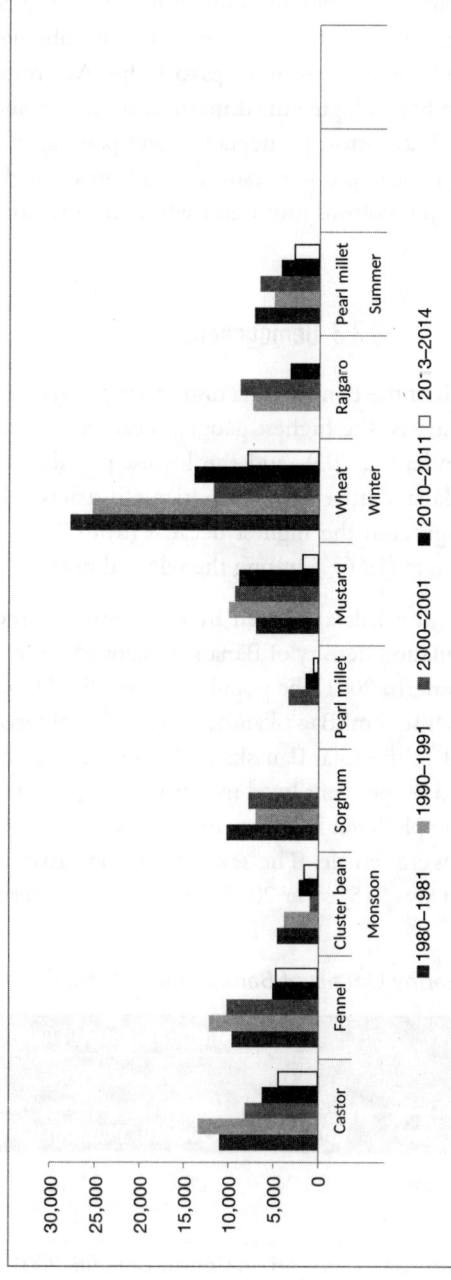

Figure 6.2 *Change of Input Cost over Time, North Gujarat (₹/Acre)*

Source: Based on authors' own analysis of primary data.

101%), both unconfined and confined aquifers have shown a decline in water levels at alarming rates of 3–5 m per year. The tube well yields have also considerably reduced from 35 lps to 15 lps. As a result, many farmers in the region have adopted the drip irrigation system and mainly grow cash crops such as castor, pomegranate and papaya, in order to make judicious use of scarce water resources and obtain high returns from agriculture. Bajra, cotton, jowar and wheat are the other major crops grown in the region.

6.3.3. Demography

Demographic details of the Banaskantha district are given in Table 6.1. Among selected districts, the highest geographical area (in sq. km) is of district Banaskantha (12,703), and the lowest population density was observed in Banaskantha and Chandrapur districts. However, Banaskantha has registered the highest decadal (from 2001 to 2011) population growth rate (19.6%) among the selected districts.

The initial provisional data released by the Census of India 2011 shows that the population density of Banaskantha district for 2011 was 290 people per sq. km. In 2001, the population density of Banaskantha was at 233 people per sq. km. Banaskantha district administered 10,743 sq. km of area. Out of the total Banaskantha population according to the 2011 Census, 13.30 per cent lived in urban regions of the district. In total, 414,915 people lived in urban areas, of which 216,638 were male and 198,277 were female. The sex ratio in the urban region of Banaskantha district was 915 as per 2011 Census data. As per the 2011

Table 6.1 Demography Details of Banaskantha District

		Population (Selected District)			
Region Covered	District Selected	2001 (in Lakh)	% to Region's Overall	2011 (in Lakh)	% to Region's Overall
North Gujarat	Banaskantha	25.04	28.01	31.16	30.25

Source: Authors' own analysis based on Census of India (2001, 2011).

Census, 86.70 per cent of the population of Banaskantha district lived in rural areas of villages. The total Banaskantha district population living in rural areas was 2,705,591, of which males and females were 1,393,741 and 1,311,850 respectively. In rural areas of Banaskantha district, the sex ratio was 941 females per 1,000 males.

6.3.4. Changing Land Use

The land use details of Banaskantha district are presented in Table 6.2. Total geographical area of the state is about 1,044.4 ('000 ha). It can be seen that the total cultivable area (including cultivable waste) is 83 per cent of the total area, and forest covers 11 per cent of the total geographical area. The gross cropped area is 1,033.4, with a cropping intensity of 138.8, and 75 per cent of irrigated area depends on bore wells.

Table 6.2 Land Use Pattern of Banaskantha Area (in '000 ha)

S. No.	Category	Area ('000 ha)
1	Total geographical area	1,044.4
2	Forests	110.6
3	Barren and uncultivable land	30.9
4	Land put to non-agricultural uses	52.9
5	Cultivable waste	17.5
6	Permanent pastures and other lands	65.1
7	Land misc. tree crops and groves	–
8	Other fallow lands	–
9	Current fallows	23.4
13	Net sown area	744.0
14	Gross cropped area	1,033.4

Source: https://agricoop.nic.in/sites/default/files/GUJ1-Banaskantha%20 3.2.2011.pdf

Table 6.3 *Landholdings in Banaskantha, North Gujarat*

Region	Total No. of Landholdings (in 000')		Total Area of Landholdings (in 000' ha)	
	2000–2001	2010–2011	2000–2001	2010–2011
North Gujarat	942	1,101	2,059	2,071

Source: ICSSR (2015).

6.3.5. Changes in Operational Holding

The details of landholdings in North Gujarat are given in Table 6.3. The details of changes in landholding patterns for different farming segments of the region are given in Table 6.4. In North Gujarat, households with small and marginal ownership holdings account for 69.2 per cent of all households and cover 88.8 per cent of all area owned. Semi-medium ownership accounts for 20.5 per cent of landholdings with a total area of 30.4 per cent which is larger than other landholdings.

6.3.6. Agricultural Situation

6.3.6.1. Cropped Area and Irrigated Area

The gross cropped area is 28.19 lakh hectares, of which 51 per cent of the area is gross irrigated and the percentage of the gross irrigated area depending on ground water is 92 per cent. The major sources of contributors are bore wells (75.3%) and open wells (22.7%), respectively.

6.4. RESULTS AND DISCUSSION

6.4.1. Income and Expenditure

The details of average annual household income, percentage income from agriculture and average annual expenditure as a percentage of annual income for North Gujarat region for the period from 1980–1981 to 2013–2014 are given in Table 6.5. The average annual income of households from 1980–1981 to 2013–2014 had increased from ₹22,120 to ₹225,693 per household, while the agricultural income had

Table 6.4 *Size Class-wise Details of the Operational Landholding in North Gujarat*

S. No.	Landholding Size Class	Particulars	North Gujarat	
			2000–2001	2010–2011
1	Marginal	% to total no. of landholdings	34.2	41.5
		% to total area	8.3	10.7
		Avg. size (ha)	0.5	0.5
2	Small	% to total no. of landholdings	28.5	27.7
		% to total area	18.9	21.3
		Avg. size (ha)	1.4	1.4
3	Semi-medium	% to total no. of landholdings	23.4	20.5
		% to total area	30.0	30.4
		Avg. size (ha)	2.8	2.8
4	Medium	% to total no. of landholdings	12.8	9.6
		% to total area	33.5	28.7
		Avg. size (ha)	5.7	5.6
5	Large	% to total no. of landholdings	1.2	0.7
		% to total area	9.3	8.9
		Avg. size (ha)	17.2	23.0

Source: ICSSR (2015).

proportionately decreased from 69 per cent to 49 per cent. However, during the same period, the expenditure as a percentage of the annual household income had increased consistently from 45 to 88.

The details of household expenditure for the same period are given in Table 6.6. The expenditure on food as a percentage of the total household expenditure decreased from 21 to 16, whereas that on agri inputs increased from 21 to 23, though not consistent with time. However, the major increase in the percentage expenditure was on

Table 6.5 *Income and Expenditure in North Gujarat Region*

S. No.	Time Period	Particulars (Average per Household	Districts Covered Banaskantha
1	1980–1981	Average annual income (₹/HH)	22,120
		% agricultural income	69
		% expenditure	45
2	1990–1991	Average annual income (₹/HH)	46,633
		% agricultural income	69
		% expenditure	64
3	2000–2001	Average annual income (₹/HH)	75,313
		% agricultural income	60
		% expenditure	70
4	2010–2011	Average annual income (₹/HH)	164,067
		% agricultural income	58
		% expenditure	65
5	2013–2014	Average annual income (₹/HH)	225,693
		% agricultural income	49
		% expenditure	88

Source: ICSSR (2015).

durable goods. Between 1980–1981 and 2010–2011, it became almost double before again coming down slightly in 2013–2014. This increase in expenditure is an indication of improvement in the households' living standards.

6.4.2. Changes in Cropping Pattern and Irrigated Area

In Banaskantha, a comparatively large number of crops are grown in the monsoon season (Table 6.7). Between 1980–1981 and 2013–2014, the proportion of total cropped area during monsoon season had increased substantially. It went up from 66 per cent to 70 per cent. The major increase was in the area under castor and fennel which fetch

Table 6.6 *Expenditure (Current Prices) on Major Items by Surveyed Households, North Gujarat*

S. No.	Particulars	Time Period	Average Expenditure per Household (% to Total) Banaskantha
1	Food items	1980–1981	21
		1990–1991	13
		2000–2001	14
		2010–2011	16
		2013–2014	16
2	Agri inputs	1980–1981	21
		1990–1991	25
		2000–2001	25
		2010–2011	21
		2013–2014	23
3	Children education	1980–1981	10
		1990–1991	8
		2000–2001	5
		2010–2011	10
		2013–2014	9
4	Healthcare	1980–1981	9
		1990–1991	14
		2000–2001	12
		2010–2011	5
		2013–2014	9
5	Household items and durable goods	1980–1981	15
		1990–1991	18
		2000–2001	23
		2010–2011	29
		2013–2014	25

Source: ICSSR (2015).

Table **6.7** Cropping and Irrigation Pattern of Surveyed Households, North Gujarat

Season	Crop	Proportion of Cropped Area under Different Crops (%)					Proportion of Cropped Area Which Is Irrigated (%)				
		1980–1981	1990–1991	2000–2001	2010–2011	2013–2014	1980–1981	1990–1991	2000–2001	2010–2011	2013–2014
Monsoon	Castor	17	16	23	22	24	74	72	76	65	76
	Fennel	5	10	13	10	11	100	100	100	100	100
	Cluster bean	22	21	17	22	22	0	100	0	0	0
	Sorghum	9	9	7	–	–	0	100	0	–	–
	Pearl millet	14	11	12	17	19	9	100	11	7	7
	Overall	66	66	72	70	76	28	100	44	35	41
Winter	Mustard	14	9	9	10	5	100	100	100	100	100
	Wheat	8	8	6	6	8	100	100	100	100	100
	Rajgaro	–	3	2	3	–	–	100	100	100	–
	Overall	22	20	17	19	13	100	100	100	100	100
Summer	Pearl millet	12	13	11	11	10	100	100	100	100	100

Source: ICSSR (2015).

high market prices. For fennel, the increase was more than double. However, the proportion of cropped area under winter crops had come down substantially, especially in the case of mustard. In summer, it was almost the same. Further, a high proportion of cropped area under castor and fennel, which are important cash crops, was reported to be irrigated. This is because the varieties grown are of long duration (seven–eight months), and crops extend far beyond the monsoon season. But overall, only 41 per cent of the area under monsoon crops was irrigated. Nevertheless, all the winter and summer crops were fully irrigated (Table 6.7).

6.4.3. Changes in Agricultural Inputs

The estimates of input costs for various crops for 1980–1981, 1990–1991, 2000–2001, 2010–2011 and 2013–2014 are presented in Table 6.8. Their graphical representation is given in Figure 6.2. Between 1980–1981 and 2013–2014, the average input cost for all crops had reduced substantially (Table 6.8). It reduced to one-third for wheat,

Table 6.8 *Agri Input Cost at Real Prices (2013–2014) for the Surveyed Households, North Gujarat*

| Season | Crop | Input Cost (₹/Acre) | | | | |
		1980–1981	1990–1991	2000–2001	2010–2011	2013–2014
Monsoon	Castor	10,979	13,387	8,165	6,242	4,512
	Fennel	9,632	12,141	10,198	5,109	4,810
	Cluster bean	4,587	3,836	971	2,176	1,669
	Sorghum	10,226	7,001	7,810	–	–
	Pearl millet	–	–	3,354	1,475	655
Winter	Mustard	6,998	10,022	9,341	8,881	1,865
	Wheat	27,703	25,273	11,733	13,911	8,023
	Rajgaro	–	7,390	8,819	3,257	–
Summer	Pearl millet	7,246	5,023	6,636	4,256	2,851

Source: ICSSR (2015).

cluster bean and mustard, and half for castor and fennel. However, both irrigation dosage and quantum of fertilizer used had increased. Average irrigation hours increased from 20 per acre to 26 per acre, whereas average fertilizer application increased from 48 kg/acre to 86 kg/acre. This indicates that a growing subsidy for irrigation (mainly on energy use) and on fertilizer had reduced the input cost. In fact, between 1980–1981 and 2013–2014, the average real cost of irrigation had reduced from ₹72/hr to ₹14/hr and fertilizer cost had reduced from ₹29/kg to ₹11/kg (adjusted to 2013–2014 prices). Thus, it had offset the actual rise in the cost of inputs to a great extent.

6.4.4. Changes in Crop Yield and Returns

The average yield of all the crops, except for fennel and monsoon pearl millet, had increased between 1980–1981 and 2013–2014 (Table 6.9). In the case of fennel and monsoon pearl millet, the yield had reduced by almost half. This can have a significant bearing on house-hold earning.

Table 6.9 *Crop Yield for the Surveyed Households, North Gujarat*

| Season | Crop | Crop Yield (kg/Acre) | | | | |
		1980–1981	1990–1991	2000–2001	2010–2011	2013–2014
Monsoon	Castor	693	740	871	648	981
	Fennel	1,480	524	525	525	703
	Cluster bean	316	408	219	522	325
	Sorghum	419	488	546	–	–
	Pearl millet	–	–	469	412	296
Winter	Mustard	623	656	963	851	926
	Wheat	1,398	1,302	1,921	1,912	1,817
	Rajgaro	–	700	900	750	–
Summer	Pearl millet	971	1,299	938	1,166	1,080

Source: ICSSR (2015).

Table 6.10 *Net Return from Various Crops in Real Prices (2013–2014) for the Surveyed Households, North Gujarat*

Season	Crop	Net Return (₹/Acre)				
		1980–1981	1990–1991	2000–2001	2010–2011	2013–2014
Monsoon	Castor	35,245	31,747	51,873	19,768	19,722
	Fennel	369,131	67,008	40,566	27,716	44,402
	Cluster bean	23,247	12,939	18,961	32,163	12,437
	Sorghum	18,702	22,449	21,717	–	–
	Pearl millet	–	–	9,323	5,102	2,309
Winter	Mustard	30,197	21,536	21,789	9,388	16,606
	Wheat	37,974	20,009	37,337	23,029	23,174
	Rajgaro	–	20,802	68,640	25,666	–
Summer	Pearl millet	21,161	31,727	8,927	9,997	11,625

Source: ICSSR (2015).

Interestingly, even after the low input cost and better yields, the average net return per acre declined for all the crops, except sorghum, between 1980–1981 and 2013–2014 (Table 6.10). Net return from fennel declined by almost 10 times. The main reason appears to be the low farm gate prices for the crops being offered to the farmers. Between 1980–1981 and 2013–2014, real farm gate prices (adjusted to 2013–2014 prices) had decreased from ₹67/kg to ₹25/kg for castor; ₹256/kg to ₹70/kg for fennel; ₹88/kg to ₹43/kg for cluster bean; ₹60/kg to ₹20/kg for mustard; ₹47/kg to ₹17/kg; and ₹29/kg to ₹13/kg for summer pearl millet.

Figure 6.3 shows the graphical representation of the changes in net income per acre of land for the major crops grown in the area over time from 1980–1981 to 2013–2014.

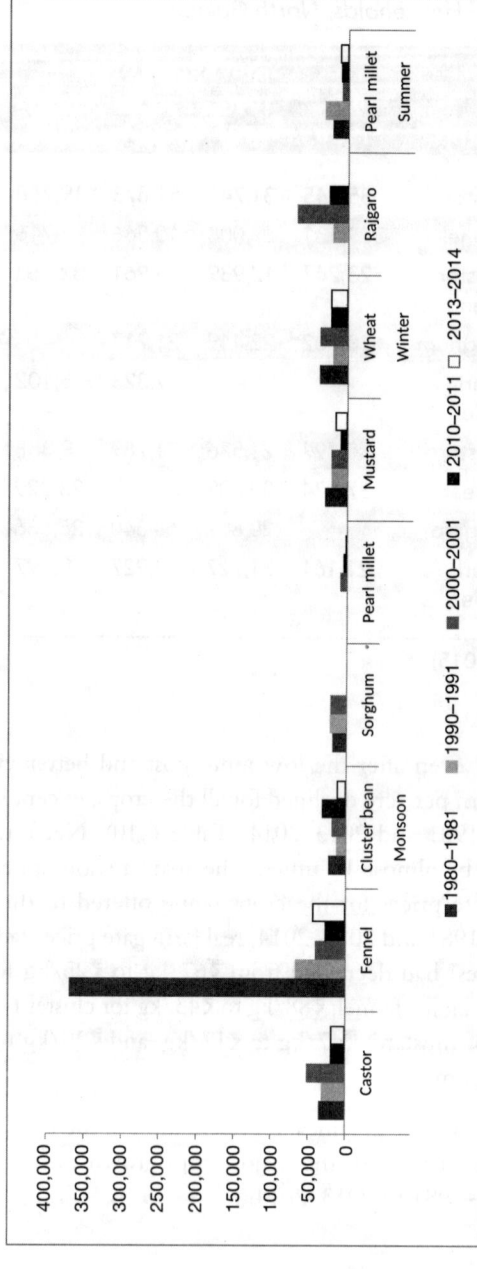

Figure 6.3 *Changes in Average Net Return from Various Crops over Time, North Gujarat (₹/Acre)*

Source: Based on authors' own analysis of primary data.

6.4.5. Changes in Livestock Holding and Milk Yield

Banaskantha is known for the well-developed rural dairy cooperatives which are supported by the District Dairy Union located in Palanpur, the district headquarters. Between 1980 and 2013, the number of cross-bred cows had increased by a substantial proportion for the surveyed households, whereas the number of buffaloes had decreased (Table 6.11). Nevertheless, there was an overall increase in the number of milch animals. Livestock holding for cattle in the non-milch category also shows a similar trend. The average annual milk yield of crossbred cows had increased by almost four times, which also explains households' preference for more numbers of such cattle. Accordingly, the amount of milk being sold per household had increased by a substantial proportion between 1980 and 2013.

Milk prices in the region were also revised from time to time to take care of the inflation and increasing cost of input for dairy farming. Due to the combined effect of high milk yield and increase in procurement prices, the average revenue earned per day by the households had also gone up to four times (Table 6.11).

6.4.6. Net Income from Farming

In the case of North Gujarat, the net income from farming was the highest in 1980–1981, and it witnessed a major drop during the first decade itself, from ₹181,135 in 1980–1981 to ₹98,687 in 1990–1991. Although there was some significant improvement in income during the third decade, as it jumped to ₹129,673, it witnessed a major drop to approximately ₹77,000 within a span of three years (Figure 6.4). This semi-arid, medium rainfall region with alluvial aquifers is heavily dependent on well irrigation for crop production in the absence of major surface irrigation schemes. The region also experiences very high inter-annual variability in rainfall. The drop in annual income during the short time span could be due to the changes in cropping conditions due to rainfall variations, with large areas under kharif cropping and good kharif yield during high rainfall years and better irrigation owing to improved groundwater availability during the winter season.

Table 6.11 Number of Animals and Milk Yield of Households Owning Livestock, North Gujarat

S. No.	Particulars	Animal Type	Year				
			1980	1990	2000	2010	2013
1	No. of milch animals	Crossbred cow	42	172	394	349	506
		Buffalo	299	459	345	223	181
2	No. of non-milch animal	Crossbred cow	0	75	245	365	264
		Buffalo	435	395	260	136	226
		Goat	0	1,101	1,244	1,073	0
3	Milk yield (lit/annum) per milch animal	Crossbred cow	3,562	5,170	10,502	9,552	12,979
		Buffalo	3,413	4,176	4,162	3,924	3,114
4	Average amount of milk sold (lit/day/HH)		6.43	16.76	23.65	21.94	27.03
5	Revenue from selling milk (₹/day/HH) at real prices (2013–2014)		222	534	540	622	778

Source: ICSSR (2015).

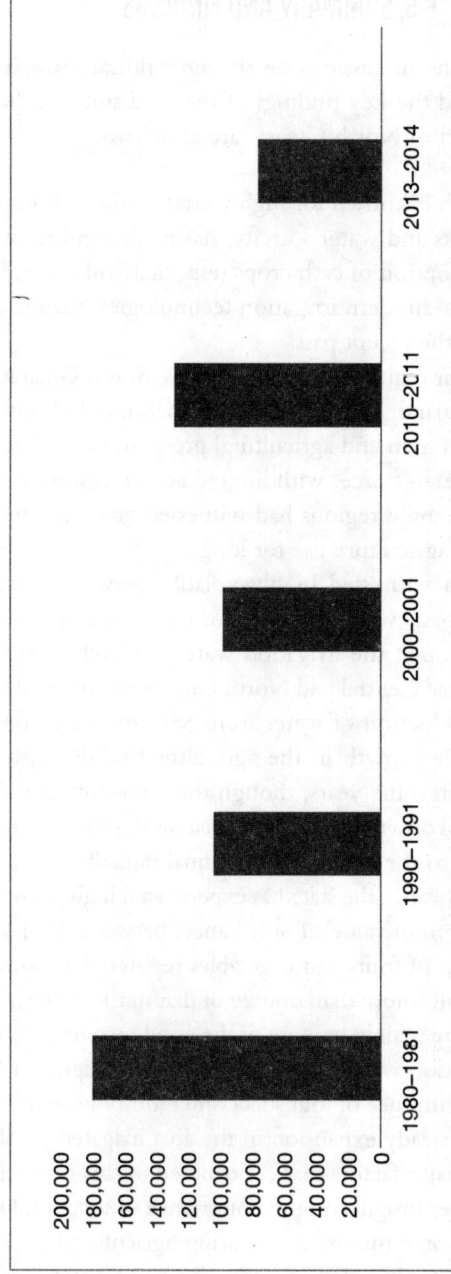

Figure 6.4 Net Annual Income (₹) from Farming for the Surveyed Households in North Gujarat (1980–1981 to 2013–2014)

Source: Based on authors' own analysis of primary data.

6.5. SUMMARY AND FINDINGS

The summary of the discussions on the agricultural growth scenario of Gujarat state and the key findings of the field study carried out in Banaskantha district of North Gujarat are as follows:

1. Gujarat, which is known for highly erratic rainfall leading to frequent droughts and water scarcity, has made significant progress in terms of adoption of cash crops (especially oil crops, fruits and vegetables) and modern irrigation technologies (mainly drips and sprinklers) in the recent past.

2. Out of the four regions in Gujarat, that is, South Gujarat, Central and North Gujarat, Saurashtra and Kachchh, only South Gujarat region is water-rich and agricultural prosperous. The other three regions are water-scarce, with limited access to surface water. As a result, these three regions had witnessed groundwater overexploitation for agriculture use for long.

3. The state had witnessed highly volatile growth in agricultural GDP in the past, with very sharp drops during years of severe drought. Although the irrigation water availability (especially in the water-scarce Central and North Gujarat region) had improved after the introduction of water from SSP, the state continues to witness volatile growth in the agricultural GDP, with negative growth rates in some years, though the inter-annual fluctuations have narrowed down slightly. The analysis shows that such a trend is mostly due to the variability in annual rainfall.

4. From 2002 onwards, the state has experienced high growth in agriculture (in terms of value). For instance, between 2001 and 2008, the production of fruits and vegetables registered a robust growth of 12.8 per cent (more than double of that in the 1990s). The high growth rates are mainly because of the good recovery from a major dip in production which occurred after the droughts of 1999 and 2000. The occurrence of four successful monsoons in the state after 2000 and the steady expansion in the area irrigated by SSP canals are the two major factors that contributed to this recovery.

5. To have further insights on the importance of successful monsoon and surface water import in ensuring agricultural prosperity in Gujarat, a case study in Banaskantha district of water-scarce North

Gujarat region was undertaken. The region is semi-arid to arid, with an average annual rainfall of about 735 mm, has sandy loam to sandy soils, and is endowed with high-yielding alluvial aquifers.

6. Due to the groundwater exploitation over the past many years, tube well yields had reduced considerably in the region (from 35 lps to 15 lps). As an adaptation strategy to make judicious use of available water, many farmers in the region had adopted the drip irrigation system for growing cash crops such as castor, pomegranate and papaya and had obtained high returns from these crops. Pearl millet, cotton, sorghum and wheat were the other major crops grown in the region.

7. Agriculture in the region was mostly dominated by small and marginal farmers (having less than 2 ha of land) who together owned about 69 per cent of the total agricultural landholdings. However, the medium farmers (having 2 ha or more but less than 10 ha) and large farmers (having 10 ha or more) accounted for 68 per cent of the total area owned by the farmers.

8. In the Banaskantha district of North Gujarat region, the net sown area was about 7.44 lakh ha, which is about 71 per cent of the district's geographical area. With a gross cropped area of 1,033,400 ha, the cropping intensity in the district was on the higher side (139%). About 75 per cent of the total irrigation (in terms of area) was through groundwater.

9. A large number of crops were grown in the monsoon season in Banaskantha district. Between 1980–1981 and 2013–2014, while the proportion of total cropped area during the monsoon season had increased substantially, it decreased under winter crops (mainly mustard). The major increase during monsoon was under castor (by 41%) and fennel crop (120%), which fetched a high market price. All the winter and summer crops were fully irrigated. Also, the fennel that was grown during the monsoon was fully irrigated.

10. Between 1980–1981 and 2013–2014, the average inputs cost per unit of cultivated area had reduced substantially, owing to high subsidies offered by the government for electricity (used for abstracting groundwater) and fertilizers. Hence, in spite of the increase in the application of irrigation (from 20 to 26 hours per acre) and the quantum of fertilizers (from 48 to 86 kg per acre), the input cost had reduced.

11. Between 1980–1981 and 2013–2014, the yield for all the crops (except fennel and pearl millet grown during monsoon) had increased. In spite of irrigation, the yield of fennel had reduced by almost half (from 1480 to 703 kg per acre). Further, even after low input cost and better yields for most of the crops, the average net return per acre had declined mainly due to low farm gate prices being offered to the farmers. For fennel, the prices (adjusted to 2013–2014 prices) declined to almost one-third and for some of the other crops (castor, cluster bean, mustard and pearl millet) by more than half.

12. Banaskantha district is known for intensive dairy farming and cooperatives engaged in the dairy business. In the case of the surveyed households, there was an increase in the number of milch animals between 1980–1981 and 2013–2014. Farmers preferred high-yielding crossbred cows (increased from 42 to 506 for the surveyed households), as the average annual milk yield of such cattle had increased by almost four times (from 3,562 to 12,979 l). The average daily revenue (adjusted to 2013–2014 prices) for a household selling milk had become nearly four times (₹222 to ₹778).

13. Over the years, the households' net annual return from farming was highly variable. It dropped consistently between 1980–1981 and 2000–2001, increased in 2010–2011 and then again dropped in 2013–2014. At the time of the survey, the average annual net return per household was about ₹77,000. The variation in annual income was attributed to the changes in cropping conditions due to rainfall variations. Nevertheless, between 1980–1981 and 2013–2014, the share of agriculture to annual household income decreased from 69 per cent to 49 per cent.

REFERENCES

Bhatia, B. (1992). Parched throats and lush green fields: Political economy of groundwater in Gujarat. *Economic & Political Weekly*, 27(51/52), A142–A170.

Business Line. (2009). Gujarat emerges a silver lining. 8 August.

Desai, S. J., & Joshi, M. B. (2008). Narmada water plays its role: Capturing initial trends from Gujarat [Presentation]. Sardar Sarovar Narmada Nigam Ltd.

Dharmadhikary, S. (1993). Hydropower from Sardar Sarovar: Need, justification and viability. *Economic & Political Weekly*, 28(48), 2584–2588.

Government of Gujarat (1996/97). Season and Crop Report, Department of Agriculture, Gandhinagar, Gujarat.

Government of India (1971–72 to 1992–93). Indian Agricultural Statistics, Directorate of Economics and Statistics, Department of Agriculture and Cooperation, Ministry of Agriculture, New Delhi.

ICSSR (Indian Council of Social Science Research). (2015). The factors causing agrarian crisis in India: A study from four agro-ecological regions in India. https://doi.org/10.13140/RG.2.2.34664.57605

Gulati, A., Shah, T., & Shreedhar, G. (2009). Agriculture performance in Gujarat since 2000: Can Gujarat be a 'Divadandi' (lighthouse) for other states? New Delhi: IWMI and IFPRI.

IRMA/UNICEF (Institute of Rural Management Anand/United Nations International Children's Emergency Fund. (2001). White paper on water in Gujarat. Report submitted to the Government of Gujarat. Gandhinagar.

Jagadeesan, S., & Kumar, M. D. (2015). The Sardar Sarovar project: Assessing the economic and social impacts. SAGE Publications.

Kumar, M. D. (2002). Reconciling water use and environment: Water resources management in Gujarat resource, problems, issues, options, strategies and framework for action [Report of the Hydrological Regime Subcomponent of the State Environmental Action Programme supported by the World Bank]. Gujarat Ecology Commission, Vadodara.

Kumar, M. D., Narayanamoorthy, A., Singh, O. P., Sivamohan, M. V. K., Sharma, M. K., & Bassi, N. (2010). Gujarat's agricultural growth story: Exploding some myths [Occasional Paper No. 2]. Institute for Resource Analysis and Policy, Hyderabad.

Kumar, M. D., Narayanamoorthy, A., Singh, O. P., Sivamohan, M. V. K., & Bassi, N. (2014). Unraveling Gujarat's agricultural growth story. In M. D. Kumar, N. Bassi, M. V. K. Sivamohan, & A. Narayanamoorthy (Eds.), The water, energy, food security nexus: Lessons from India for development (pp. 19–38). Routledge/Earthscan.

Kumar, M. D., & Perry, C. J. (2019). What can explain groundwater rejuvenation in Gujarat in recent years? International Journal of Water Resources Development, 35(5), 891–906.

Kumar, M. D., Singh, K., & Singh, O. P. (2001). Groundwater degradation and its socio-ecological consequences in Sabarmati river basin [Monograph No. 2]. INREM Foundation.

Patel, A. (2001). Resettlement in the Sardar Sarovar project: A cause vitiated. Water Resources Development, 17(1), 315–328.

Shah, T., Gulati, A., Hemant, P., Shreedhar, G., & Jain, R. C. (2009). Secret of Gujarat's agricultural miracle after 2000. Economic & Political Weekly, 44(52), 45–55.

Shah, Z., & Kumar, M. D. (2008). In the midst of the large dam controversy: Objectives, criteria for assessing large water storages in the developing world. Water Resources Management, 22(12), 1799–1824.

Shukla, J. R. (1980). The famines of Gujarat in the 18th century. In Proceedings of the Indian History Congress, 41(1980), 619–626.

Chapter 7

Agricultural Growth in Coastal Andhra Pradesh

V. Niranjan, K. Siva Rama Kishan,
M. V. K. Sivamohan and Nitin Bassi

7.1. INTRODUCTION

Andhra Pradesh, known as the 'rice bowl' of India, is agricultural in character. Since the backbone of the economy is agriculture, drastic changes in monsoon, frequent floods and cyclones often impact the GDP of the state adversely. It has 62 per cent of its population or about 46 lakh families dependent on agriculture and allied sectors. The growth of agriculture, though uneven in different regions, show upward economic mobility of these families. Andhra Pradesh, formed as a linguistic state of Telugu-speaking people, was again bifurcated into two states, with the Telangana region forming a separate state and Coastal Andhra and Rayalaseema forming the new state of Andhra Pradesh in 2014. The unified state had three distinct regions, namely Andhra, Telangana and Rayalaseema.

The undivided Andhra Pradesh witnessed a growth rate of 5.3 per cent during 1970–2010. This was mainly because of the contribution of the service sector emanating from the city of Hyderabad. For more than half a century, the overall growth rate registered in Andhra Pradesh had been 2.88 per cent.

The newly formed state of Andhra Pradesh had two distinct regions, Coastal Andhra and Rayalaseema. Rayalaseema is land-rich but severely water-scarce, whereas Coastal Andhra is relatively water-rich, with a large network of canals in Krishna district, East and West Godavari districts and Guntur. Agriculturally, West Godavari region is considered to be one of the prosperous regions in Andhra Pradesh due to the intensive cultivation of paddy made possible through the supply of canal water and presence of nutrient-rich deltaic soils. However, in recent decades, with extensive groundwater development, farmers of the water-scarce Rayalaseema region are now increasingly moving to high-value horticultural crops such as mango, sapota, lemon, banana and sweet lime, and several vegetables.

In this chapter, following a detailed analysis of changing landscape of irrigated agriculture in the state, with a focus on regional trends, we examine the changes in farming enterprise of the coastal region of the state with regard to cropped area, livestock holding, cropping pattern, input use, crop and milk yields, agricultural outputs, produce prices and net income from farming, based on primary data collected from farmers for the period from 1980–1981 to 2012–2013.

7.2. CHANGES IN AGRICULTURAL LANDSCAPE OF ANDHRA PRADESH SINCE THE 1970S

Andhra Pradesh had a long history of tank irrigation (especially in the Rayalaseema region) and some of the oldest canal irrigation systems in the country. In fact, the Rayalaseema region is dotted with several cascade tanks, many of which existed for hundreds of years. It also had a substantial area under public canal irrigation much before many states started developing surface irrigation. The greatest change in the irrigation landscape of the region is the large-scale introduction of well irrigation in a region. During the period from 1970–1971 to 2012–2013, the net well-irrigated area in the region went up consistently from 0.35 Mha to 1.15 Mha, a net increase of 0.80 Mha, which is a significant area for a region of the size of the newly carved Andhra Pradesh state, with energization of wells and use of deep drilling technology (especially in the hard rock terrain). Here again, there have been changes in the type of groundwater abstraction structures. The deep bore wells had replaced open wells in many hard rock areas, and shallow tube wells had replaced open wells in the alluvial belt.

Figure 7.1 shows the net area irrigated by different sources in Andhra Pradesh during 1970–1971 to 2012–2013. The net irrigated area in Andhra Pradesh had grown by only 0.46 Mha over the last four decades. Canals and wells were the major sources of water for irrigation in the state. Reallocation of water from surface irrigation sources for drinking water supply over the years and increasing incidence of lifting of water from canals and rivers and reservoirs by farmers, with access to pump sets, had led to a decrease in the share of canal irrigation by gravity.[1] The area irrigated by canals had come down from 1.35 Mha in 1970–1971 to 1.18 Mha in 2012–2013. Groundwater played an important role in irrigation in Andhra Pradesh, which is reiterated by the fact that over the years a substantial growth in well irrigation is seen.

Groundwater reduced farmers' reliance on rainfall and hence, with a decline in canal irrigation, area under well irrigation had picked up. In the year 2012–2013, about 41 per cent of crop land was irrigated through wells. Several hydrological, socio-economic and institutional factors had contributed towards a decline in area under tank irrigation. A 50 per cent reduction was noted between 1970–1971 and 2012–2013. According to a recent study by Kumar and Vedantam (2016), intensive groundwater draft in the catchments and commands could significantly affect irrigation potential of tanks by reducing the inflows of water into and increasing the infiltration of water from tanks.

The region-wise changes in net irrigated area are presented in Figure 7.2. It shows that well-irrigated area had gone up in all except North Coastal Andhra Pradesh. The area under tank irrigated had declined in all the regions, and more drastically in Rayalaseema.

The gross irrigated area in the state was around 3.71 Mha, which included irrigation from wells, canals, tanks, lift irrigation schemes and sources such as ponds and springs. There had been only a marginal increase in gross irrigated area in the state during the 12-year period from 2000–2001 to 2012–2013, that is, from 3.67 Mha to 3.71M ha (Figure 7.3; Directorate of Economics and Statistics, 2013). This is in spite of the fact that many new schemes had been built in the past one

---

[1] The area irrigated from lifting of water from canals, rivers and reservoirs gets reported under other sources of irrigation.

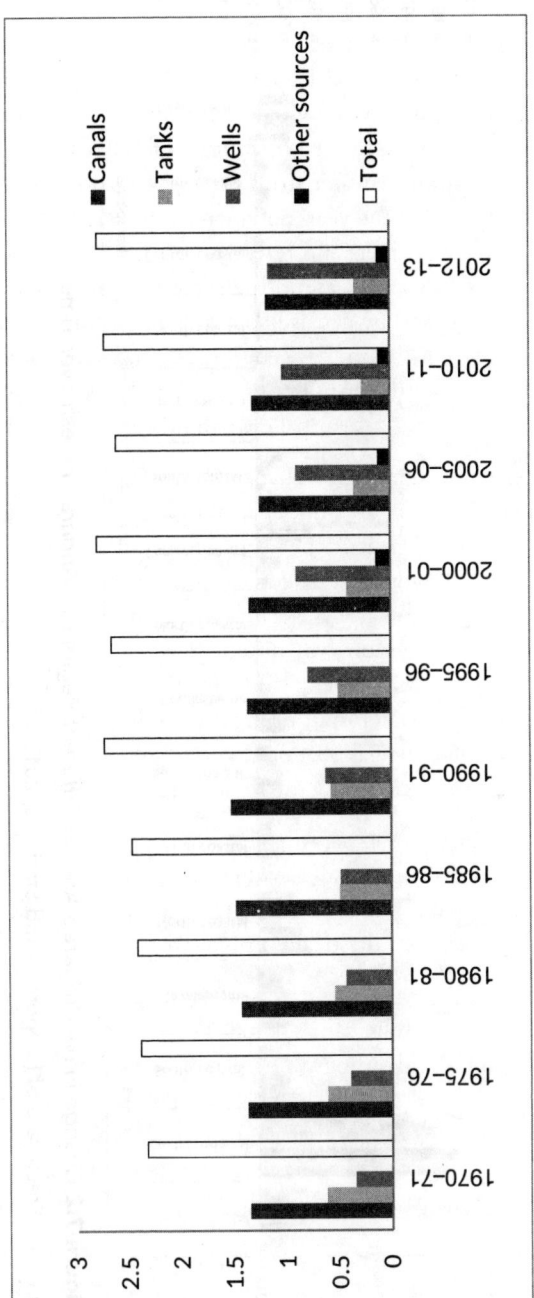

Figure 7.1 *Change in Net Irrigated Area by Source over Time (1970–1971 to 2012–2013)*

Source: Directorate of Economics and Statistics, 2013.

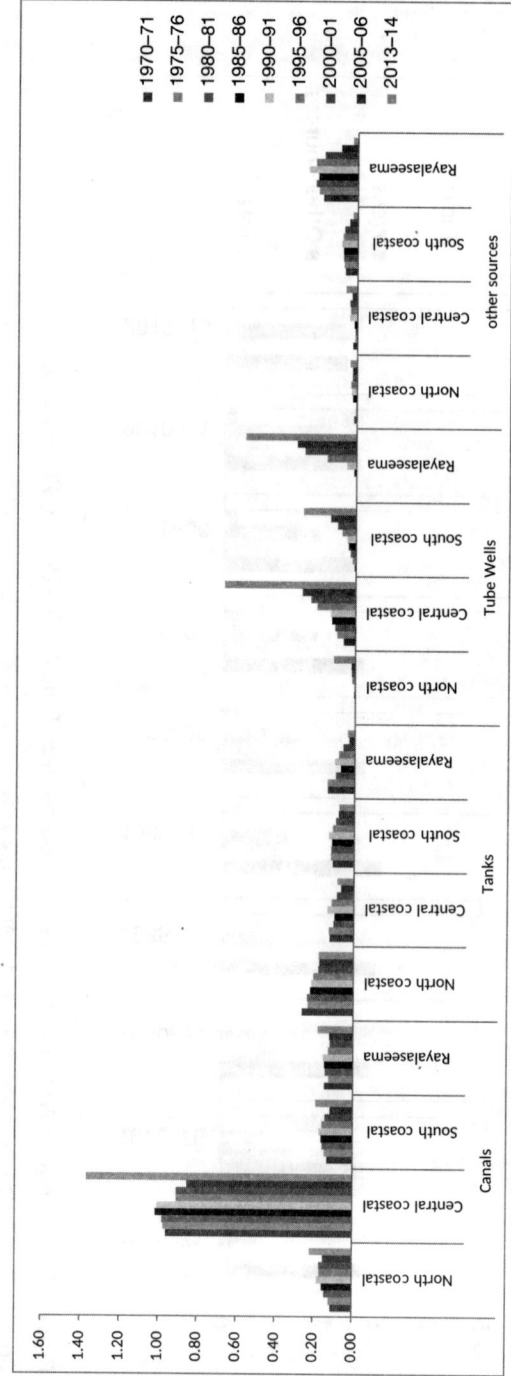

Figure 7.2 *Change in Net Irrigated Area in Different Regions of Andhra Pradesh over Time*

Source: Directorate of Economics and Statistics, 2013.

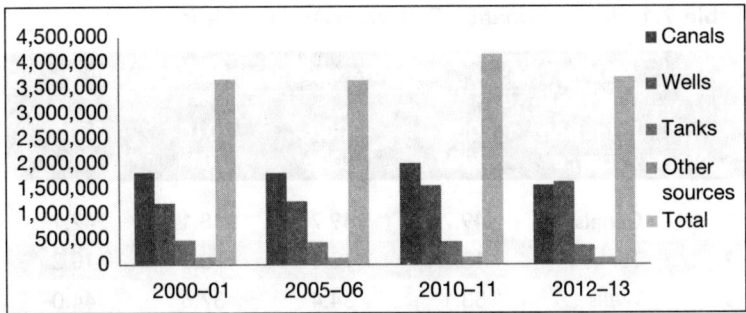

Figure 7.3 *Gross irrigation from various sources in Andhra Pradesh: 2000–01 2012–13*

decade or so in the public sector, and several hundreds of thousands of wells had been drilled with private investment. We would explain the reasons for this in the next section. Interestingly, it was highest during 2010–2011, with a gross area of 4.15 Mha. Such inter-annual variation could be explained by the variability in rainfall, which directly impacted irrigation potential of the sources, more so in the case of surface sources such as tanks and canal systems based on reservoirs and diversion structures.

However, as Table 7.1 shows, though there had been no notable increase in gross irrigated area, the pattern had changed. While canals accounted for 49.7 per cent of the irrigation in 2000–2001, it came down to 42.1 per cent in 2012–2013. The area under surface irrigation came down from 67 per cent to 56 per cent during the 12-year period.

An important factor determining the utilization of irrigation potential in the state is the increasing preference of farmers to go for paddy, after receiving water under gravity. Paddy is a staple crop in Andhra Pradesh, and good market support for paddy (with good procurement system and price) motivates the farmers to go for this crop. Also, growing paddy with well water is not viable in hard rock areas, with limited groundwater potential and poor-quality power supply. Our analysis shows that paddy accounts for a lion's share of the irrigation from canals and tanks.

Figure 7.4 shows the area irrigated from two distinct sources, namely surface irrigation and groundwater irrigation for the major irrigated

Table 7.1 *Shift in Irrigation Pattern in Andhra Pradesh*

S. No.	Name of the Irrigation Source	Percentage Area under Irrigation			
		2000–2001	2005–2006	2010–2011	2012–2013
1	Canals	49.7	49.7	48.1	42.1
2	Tanks	13.2	12.1	10.9	10.2
3	Wells	33.1	34.4	37.6	44.0
4	Other sources	4.1	3.8	3.5	3.6
5	Gross irrigated area (ha)	3,674,558	3,644,000	4,156,000	3,711,209

Source: Directorate of Economics and Statistics, 2013.

crops in Andhra Pradesh. It shows a clear pattern. The water-intensive crop (in terms of amount of irrigation water applied) of paddy mostly receives its irrigation from surface sources, which includes canals, tanks, river and canal lifts and other sources. A very small portion of paddy is irrigated from groundwater-based sources, whereas a large percentage of the irrigated area of less water-intensive crops such as jowar, bajra, ragi and maize receive irrigation from groundwater-based sources.

The pattern, therefore, is that surface irrigation sources are mostly used for irrigating highly water-intensive crops, and groundwater-based sources are used for irrigating lower water-consuming crops. The only exception is sugarcane, in which case, the area irrigated from surface sources (80,000 ha) is just 40 per cent of the area irrigated from groundwater-based sources (2.0 lac ha). Yet, overall, paddy accounts for 76.5 per cent of the total irrigated area of six major crops in the state. It could be argued that the presence of surface irrigation from canals, river/canal lifting and other sources accounts for 56 per cent of the gross irrigated area. From another angle, out of the total surface irrigated area, 91 per cent goes to paddy irrigation (Figure 7.5), and only 9 per cent goes to the other five major crops. The increasing preference for paddy is one factor that put a major constraint on the area under irrigation from surface systems.

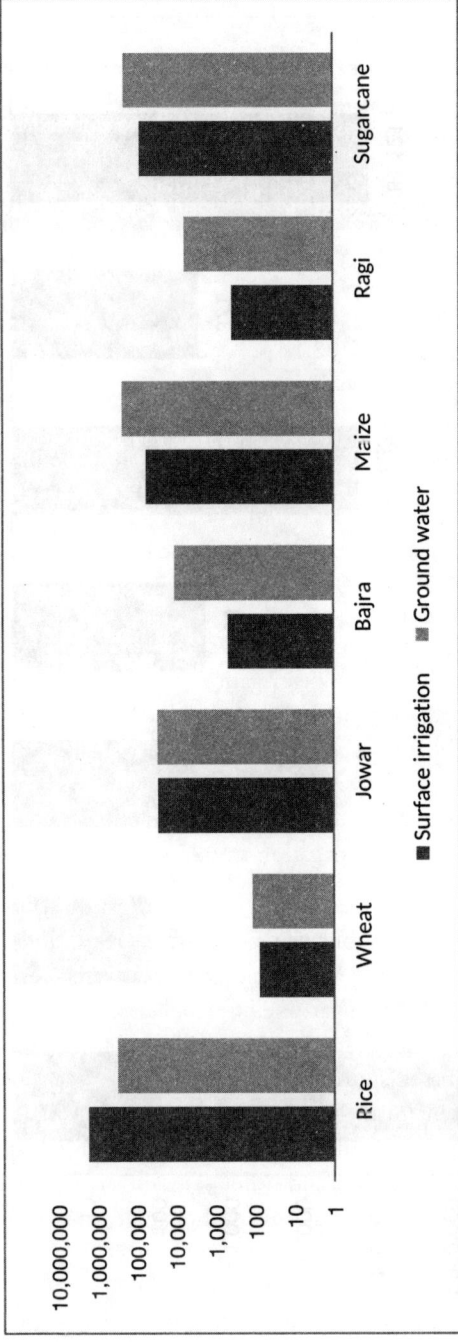

Figure 7.4 *Irrigated Crop Area under Two Distinct Sources*
Source: Directorate of Economics and Statistics, 2013.

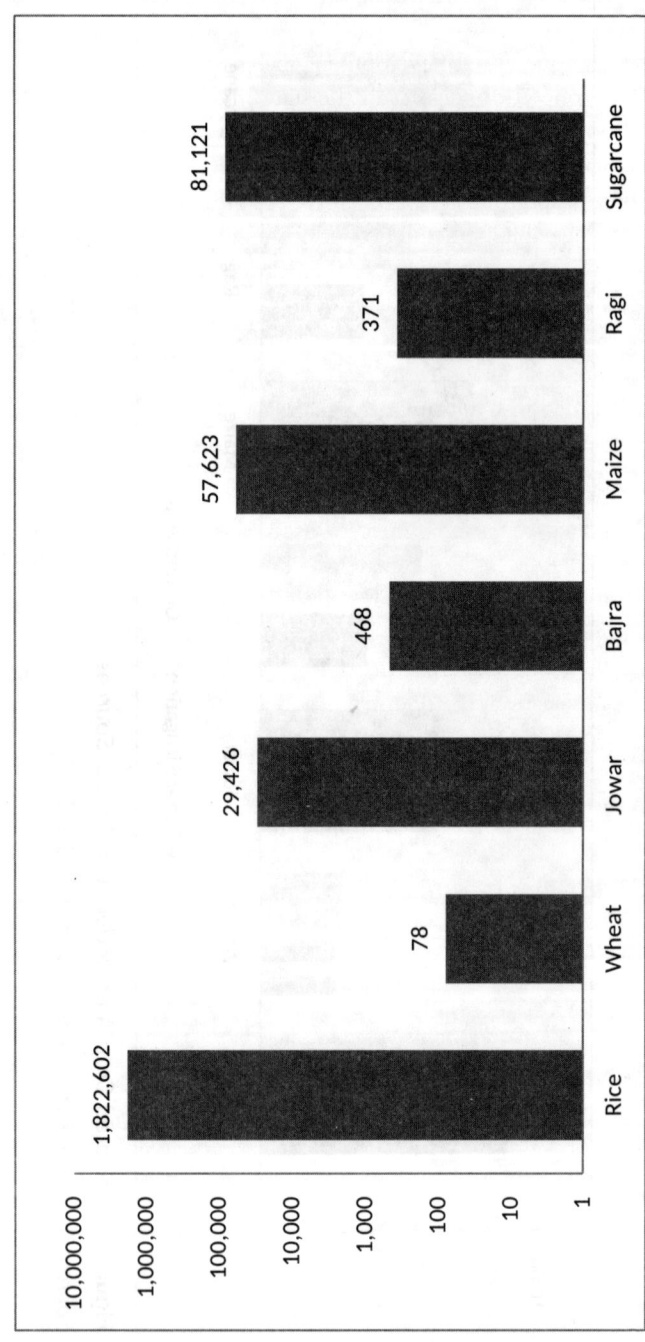

Figure 7.5 *Major Crops under Surface Irrigation (2012–2013)*
Source: Directorate of Economics and Statistics, 2013.

A study on agricultural development in Andhra Pradesh (Reddy et al., 2014) grouped the district in the state into high, medium and low categories based on absolute area under crops grown during the above-said period and analysed crop shifts in terms of major crop groups. These crop groups are: (a) cereals; (b) pulses; (c) oilseeds; and (d) fruits and vegetables. The highest positive shift (from low to high) was in Karimnagar for cereals and in the districts of Kadapa, Krishna, Kurnool, Mahbubnagar and Medak for pulses. While the coastal districts of East Godavari, Guntur, Krishna, Nellore and West Godavari remained in the high group for cereals, significant downward movement was recorded in Chittoor and Srikakulam for cereal production and East Godavari in pulses.

The state is a leading producer of cereals such as rice, maize and jowar and cash crops such as tobacco, groundnut, chilies, turmeric, cotton, sugar and jute. Rice dominates the cropping pattern of Andhra Pradesh. Horticulture contributes 4 per cent of the agricultural GDP and is an important segment in the agricultural sector of Andhra Pradesh. Among different crops, fruit crops are also significant, constituting a major share in the country's fruit production (Table 7.2).

In oilseeds, three Rayalaseema districts, namely Anantapur, Chittoor and Kurnool remained in the high group in both 1956 and 2011. In the matter of fruits, East Godavari, Khammam, Visakhapatnam and

Table 7.2 Fruit Crops in Districts of Andhra Pradesh

Fruit	Main Producing Areas
Mango	Chittoor, Krishna, Vijayanagaram, Khammam, Cuddapah, West Godavari
Sweet orange	Prakasam, Ananthapur, Khammam,
Banana	East and West Godavari, Guntur, Vijayanagaram, Cuddapah and Kurnool
Papaya	Cuddapah, Ananthapur, Prakasam
Lemon/lime	Nellore, Cuddapah, West Godavari
Sapota	Guntur, Prakasam, Ananthapur

Source: Rabo India Finance Pvt. Ltd. (2005).

West Godavari remained in the high group, and four Telangana districts, namely Adilabad, Hyderabad, Karimnagar and Medak remained in the low group. Overall, coastal districts dominated in cereals and fruits in both periods, while Rayalaseema districts dominated in oilseed production. Pulses expanded in Telangana and coastal districts due to the expansion of area under short-duration varieties for rice fallows.

According to NSSO (2010), the non-agricultural workers were higher in Coastal Andhra (42%) but less in both Rayalaseema and Telangana regions in 2007–2008. The share of farmers in Rayalaseema was more than the agricultural labourers because the agricultural land which had low productivity was owned mostly by poor households for their subsistence survival. In coastal areas, the opposite trend was observed. The people from coastal areas only were benefited by the productivity, enhancing technology during the Green Revolution period (paddy) and commercialization of agriculture (fruits, vegetables, milk and meat). This was mainly due to the abilities of the region with better resource endowment and eventual public and private investments in the agricultural sector. The revolution of crop production started with paddy in all the regions, but it started early in coastal districts and reached its zenith during 1980. In Rayalaseema, there was little scope for increasing the area under paddy except in the Kurnool–Cuddappah Canal (KC Canal) area spreading in the two districts (Reddy et al., 2014) of Kurnool and Cuddappah. Large-scale mechanization efforts were underway in KC Canal command areas ever since the 1990s. Irrigated area (NIA) in Rayalaseema remained stagnant without any increase. There was low cropping intensity in Rayalaseema.

A process of convergence was seen among the districts of Andhra Pradesh in agricultural growth, but the less developed districts were left out of the convergence process. Based on the respective resource endowments, both the agricultural intensification and diversification strategies played a crucial role in the development of districts (Table 7.3; Reddy, 2011). Overall total factor productivity (TFP) growth in agriculture and allied activities in Telangana was 13 per cent per decade, 11 per cent per decade in Coastal Andhra and stagnant in Rayalaseema.

The bifurcation of the state brought in its wake some impacts on agriculture in the Andhra and Coastal regions constituted by nascent

Table 7.3 Shifts in Relative Position of Districts in Production of Crop Groups between 1956 and 2011

Shift from	Cereals	Pulses	Oilseed	Fruits and Vegetables
High to low	Chittoor (R) Srikakulam (C)	East Godavari (C)	–	–
Medium to low	Anantapur (R) Kadapa (R)	Nellore (C) Visakhapatnam (C)	Karimnagar (T)	Nizamabad (T) Srikakulam (C)
High to medium	–	Anantapur (R)	Kadapa (R) Guntur (C) Mahbubnagar (T) Nalgonda (T)	Kadapa (R) Guntur (C) Kurnool (R)
Low	Adilabad (T) Hyderabad (T)	Chittoor (R) Karimnagar (T) West Godavari (C)	Hyderabad (T) Khammam (T) Medak (T) Nellore (C) Nizamabad (T)	Adilabad (T) Hyderabad (T) Karimnagar (T) Medak (T)
Medium	Kurnool (R) Mahbubnagar (T) Nizamabad (T) Visakhapatnam (C)	Khammam (T) Nalgonda (T) Srikakulam (C) Warangal (T)	Karimnagar (T) Warangal (T)	Nellore (C) Warangal (T)
High	East Godavari (C) Guntur (C) Krishna (C) Nellore (C) West Godavari (C)	Guntur (C)	Anantapur (R) Chittoor (R) Kurnool (R)	East Godavari (C) Khammam (T) Visakhapatnam (C) West Godavari (C)
Low to high	Karimnagar (T)	Kadapa (R) Krishna (C) Kurnool (R) Mahbubnagar (T) Medak (T)	–	–
Low to medium	Khammam (T) Medak (T) Warangal (T)	Hyderabad (T) Nizamabad (T)	Adilabad (T)	Mahbubnagar (T) Nalgonda (T)
Medium to high	Nalgonda (T)	Adilabad (T)	East Godavari (C) Srikakulam (C) Visakhapatnam (C) Warangal (T)	Anantapur (R) Chittoor (R) Krishna (C)

Source: Reddy (2011).

Note: (T) Telangana, (R) Rayalaseema and (C) Coastal Andhra.

Andhra Pradesh state. In the united Andhra Pradesh, there was only one agricultural university located in Hyderabad city in Telangana state, and the residual Andhra Pradesh had to fortify the agricultural research infrastructure. Although it had a total cultivated area of 6.35 Mha, crop productivity remained low and stagnant and the cost of cultivation increased. Agriculture, the primary sector in 2014–2015 in Andhra Pradesh, contributed 27.83 per cent in the state's GSDP, and it was poised to increase (GOAP & ICRISAT, 2015).

7.3. THE STUDY LOCATION

7.3.1. Physiography

The district consists of three very dissimilar natural divisions, namely (a) delta, (b) upland and (c) the Eastern Ghats. The upland area, which is an undulating plain broken by low ranges, covers parts of Chintalapudi, Kovvur, Eluru and Tadepalligudem mandals. This portion lies between the delta and the agency areas. Polavaram agency is traversed by the Eastern Ghats broken by the Papikonda range of hills. This area is covered by scattered hills and spurs rising from the lower uplands. The highest peak in the area is Peddakonda, and it rises to a height of 1,364 m above sea level.

7.3.2. Climate

Coastal Andhra, with an average annual rainfall that varies from 996 mm towards the south and 1128 mm in the north, has a semi-arid to dry sub-humid climate. Major soils include deltaic alluvium, coastal alluvium, red loamy and red sandy types. The thickness of alluvium is several hundred metres near the mouths of the major rivers like Cauvery and Krishna, and it decreases inland to a few metres where crystalline rocks occur (CGWB, 2014). Groundwater occurs under semi-confined conditions in the recent alluvium and under confined conditions in the underlying Rajahmundry/Gondwana sandstones. The water levels are shallow, but groundwater development is limited and is confined only to certain fresh water zones. As a result, the stage of groundwater development is only 47 per cent. Most of the deltaic area is under surface water irrigation projects. Major crops in the region include rice, cotton, jowar, bajra, tobacco, groundnut, ragi and sesame.

7.3.3. Demography

The district occupies an area of 7,742 sq. km, with a density of 508 per sq. km. It accounts for 2.81 per cent of the total area of the state. There are as many as 883 revenue villages in the district, of which 845 villages are inhabited, while the balance 38 villages are uninhabited. The physical characteristics, natural resources and potentialities of the mandals in the district are not homogeneous. As per the 2011 Census, the total population of the district is 39.37 lakh. It accounts for 4.65 per cent of the total population of the state. The female population of the district is 1,972,048, and this forms 50.09 per cent of the district and 4.68 per cent of the state's female population (Census of India, 2011).

The decennial growth of population in the district from the 2001 Census to the 2011 Census was 3.5 per cent. The density of the population according to the 2011 Census was 508 per sq. km, whereas it was 308 per sq. km for the state. The literacy rate of the district was 74.32 per cent, which was higher than the state literacy rate of 67.66 per cent. The sex ratio of the district was 986 females per 1,000 males as against 978 of the state. The number of workers as arrived at in the 2011 Census was 1,534,166, forming 38.97 per cent of the total population of the district and 3.37 per cent of the state population (Census of India, 2011).

7.3.4. Changing Land Use

The total geographical area of the district is 7.79 lakh ha, and the land utilization particulars are given in Table 7.4. The net sown area forms 55 per cent of the geographical area. About 14.92 per cent of the land is put to non-agricultural purposes in the district. Current and other fallows have a very limited area under them. Due to good irrigation coverage, nearly 63 per cent of the total sown area is put under a second crop. Hardly 10 per cent of the area is under forests.

7.3.5. Changes in Operational Holding

The cultivable land in the district is mostly under the ownership of small and marginal farmers. Between 2000–2001 and 2010–2011, the total landholding area had declined marginally (Table 7.5). The

Table 7.4 Land Utilization Particulars for 2012–2013 of West Godavari District

S. No.	Category	Area in Ha
1	Total geographical area	774,200
2	Forests	81,166
3	Barren and uncultivable land	37,642
4	Land put to non-agricultural Uses	115,477
5	Cultivable waste	13,352
6	Permanent pastures and other Lands	13,355
7	Land misc. tree crops and groves	7,872
8	Other fallow lands	7,900
9	Current fallows	24,471
10	Net area sown (11–12)	425,943
11	Total cropped area	694,812
12	Area sown more than once	268,802
13	Fish and prawn culture	47,021

Source: District Census Handbook West Godavari.

Table 7.5 Landholding Details of Coastal Andhra

Region	Total No. of Landholdings (in 000')		Total Area of Landholdings (in 000' ha)	
	2000–2001	2010–2011	2000–2001	2010–2011
Coastal Andhra	4,771	5,152	4,629	4,600

Source: Authors' own analysis based on Agricultural Census of India (2000–2001 and 2010–2011).

category-wise number and area of operational holdings in the region are presented in Table 7.6. While the marginal farms dominate the landholdings in terms of number, medium-size holdings account for a major share of the land owned in terms of area in Coastal Andhra.

Table 7.6 *Size Class-wise Details of the Operational Landholdings in the Coastal Andhra*

S. No.	Landholding Size Class	Particulars	Coastal Andhra	
			2000–2001	2010–2011
1	Marginal	% to total no. of landholdings	70.6	72.7
		% to total area	30.1	33.4
		Avg. size (ha)	0.4	0.4
2	Small	% to total no. of landholdings	17.8	17.3
		% to total area	25.7	27.0
		Avg. size (ha)	1.4	1.4
3	Semi-medium	% to total no. of landholdings	8.6	7.6
		% to total area	23.9	22.7
		Avg. size (ha)	2.7	2.7
4	Medium	% to total no. of landholdings	2.8	2.2
		% to total area	16.0	13.7
		Avg. size (ha)	5.6	5.5
5	Large	% to total no. of landholdings	0.3	0.2
		% to total area	4.3	3.2
		Avg. size (ha)	16.8	15.7

Source: Authors' own analysis based on Agricultural Census of India (2000–2001 and 2010–2011).

The number of holdings in the 'marginal' category, as a proportion of the total number of operational holdings, had increased over a decade from 2000–2001 to 2010–2011, while that under small, semi medium, medium and large holding categories had reduced.

7.3.6. Agricultural Situation

7.3.6.1. Cropped Area and Irrigated Area

In Coastal Andhra Pradesh, 60 per cent of the gross cropped area is irrigated and nearly 68 per cent of the irrigation is from surface water, especially canal water (Table 7.7).

7.4. RESULTS AND DISCUSSION

7.4.1. Income and Expenditure

West Godavari is one of the districts in the state with high agricultural potential. The economy of the district is primarily agrarian. Nearly 70 per cent of the population in the district depends on agriculture for their livelihoods. While the average annual household income (at current prices) increased from ₹17,548 to ₹59,667 consistently during the period from 1980–1981 to 2013–2014, the percentage income from agriculture declined consistently from 65 to 40. The expenditure as a percentage of annual income increased from 33 to 166. The reported annual expenditures during 2010–2011 and 2013–2014 were more than the annual income (Table 7.8). Thus, households were unable to have any savings.

As Table 7.9 indicates, the major household expenditure was on household items and durable goods, and expenditure on food items and agri inputs had decreased over time. However, between 1980–1981 and 2010–2011, expenditure on children's education and durable goods

Table 7.7 Cropped and Irrigated Area in Coastal Andhra

Region	Gross Cropped Area (Lakh ha)	Gross Irrigated Area (GIA) as % of GCA	Groundwater Irrigated Area as % of GIA
Coastal Andhra	54.42	60	32

Source: Authors' own analysis based on Agricultural Census of India (2000–2001 and 2010–2011).

Table 7.8 *Income and Expenditure (Current Prices) Pattern of Surveyed Households, West Godavari*

S. No.	Time Period	Particulars (Average per Household)	Districts Covered West Godavari
1	1980–1981	Average annual income (₹/HH)	17,548
		% agricultural income	65
		% expenditure	33
2	1990–1991	Average annual income (₹/HH)	22,778
		% agricultural income	58
		% expenditure	53
3	2000–2001	Average annual income (₹/HH)	35,681
		% agricultural income	41
		% expenditure	72
4	2010–2011	Average annual income (₹/HH)	50,178
		% agricultural income	34
		% expenditure	111
5	2013–2014	Average annual income (₹/HH)	59,667
		% agricultural income	40
		% expenditure	166

Source: Authors' own analysis based on Agricultural Census of India (2000–2001 and 2010–2011).

had increased consistently. It appears that the surveyed households were taking personal loans to meet such expenses.

7.4.2. Changes in Cropping and Irrigation Pattern

Paddy was the main crop for the surveyed households in the West Godavari district of Coastal Andhra (Table 7.10). Between 1980–1981 and 2013–2014, the proportion of total cropped area under paddy had remained almost the same, with a majority of the crop being grown in monsoon and winter seasons. About one-sixth of the cropped area was under perennial crops such as banana, casuarina, coconut, lemon and

Table 7.9 *Expenditure (Current Prices) on Major Items by Surveyed Households, West Godavari*

S. No.	Particulars	Time Period	Average Expenditure per Household (% to Total) West Godavari
1	Food items	1980–1981	29
		1990–1991	27
		2000–2001	17
		2010–2011	15
		2013–2014	18
2	Agri inputs	1980–1981	40
		1990–1991	28
		2000–2001	23
		2010–2011	14
		2013–2014	19
3	Children education	1980–1981	0
		19901991	4
		2000–2001	14
		2010–2011	19
		2013–2014	15
4	Healthcare	1980–1981	15
		1990–1991	18
		2000–2001	12
		2010–2011	8
		2013–2014	11
5	Household items and durable goods	1980–1981	7
		1990–1991	5
		2000–2001	23
		2010–2011	40
		2013–2014	29

Source: ICSSR (2015).

Table 7.10 *Cropping and Irrigation Pattern of Surveyed Households, West Godavari*

Season	Crop	Proportion of Cropped Area under Different Crops (%)					Proportion of Cropped Area Which Is Irrigated (%)				
		1980–1981	1990–1991	2000–2001	2010–2011	2013–2014	1980–1981	1990–1991	2000–2001	2010–2011	2013–2014
Monsoon	Paddy	45	46	42	43	41	97	98	98	98	97
Winter	Paddy	42	41	40	38	39	97	97	98	97	98
Summer	Paddy	0.4	0.4	0.3	0.3	0.3	100	100	100	100	100
Perennials	Banana	1	1	1	1	1	100	100	100	100	100
	Casuarina	2	2	2	2	2	100	100	85	90	100
	Coconut	10	10	13	14	15	100	100	100	100	100
	Lemon	0.0	0.0	0.0	0.5	1.0	–	–	–	100	100
	Mango	0.4	0.4	0.8	0.8	0.8	100	100	100	100	100
	Overall	13	13	17	18	19	100	100	98	99	100

Source: ICSSR (2015).

mango, and it had increased only marginally between 1980–1981 and 2013–2014. Almost the entire paddy crop was irrigated. Also, most of the area under perennial crops was irrigated.

7.4.3. Changes in Agricultural Inputs

The surveyed households provided agri input details for only paddy crops which occupy the major proportion of total cropped area which are presented in Table 7.11. The graphical representation of the same is provided in Figure 7.6. Between 1980–1981 and 2013–2014, input cost (adjusted to 2013–2014 prices) per acre had actually decreased for paddy grown during the monsoon season, whereas for winter paddy it had increased. However, in comparison to 20002001, input cost for winter paddy had also reduced. The reduction in input cost, though both irrigation (mainly groundwater) and fertilizer application had increased, indicates that the price of fertilizer and irrigation had actually not increased in accordance with the inflation rates. In fact, electricity for farm use was supplied at a highly subsidized rate in the whole region which lowered the cost associated with irrigation. Nevertheless, the average irrigation hours increased from 32 to 175 hours per acre during monsoon and 52 to 265 hours per acre during the winter season, whereas fertilizer application was more than double from 24 to 53 kg per acre during monsoon and from 31 to 73 kg per acre during the winter season.

Table 7.11 *Agri Input Cost at Real Prices (2013–2014) for the Surveyed Households, West Godavari*

Crop	Season	Input Cost (₹/Acre)				
		1980–1981	1990–1991	2000–2001	2010–2011	2013–2014
Paddy	Monsoon	13,995	15,954	9,519	9,580	11,551
	Winter	17,195	16,117	29,282	17,159	20,280

Source: ICSSR (2015).

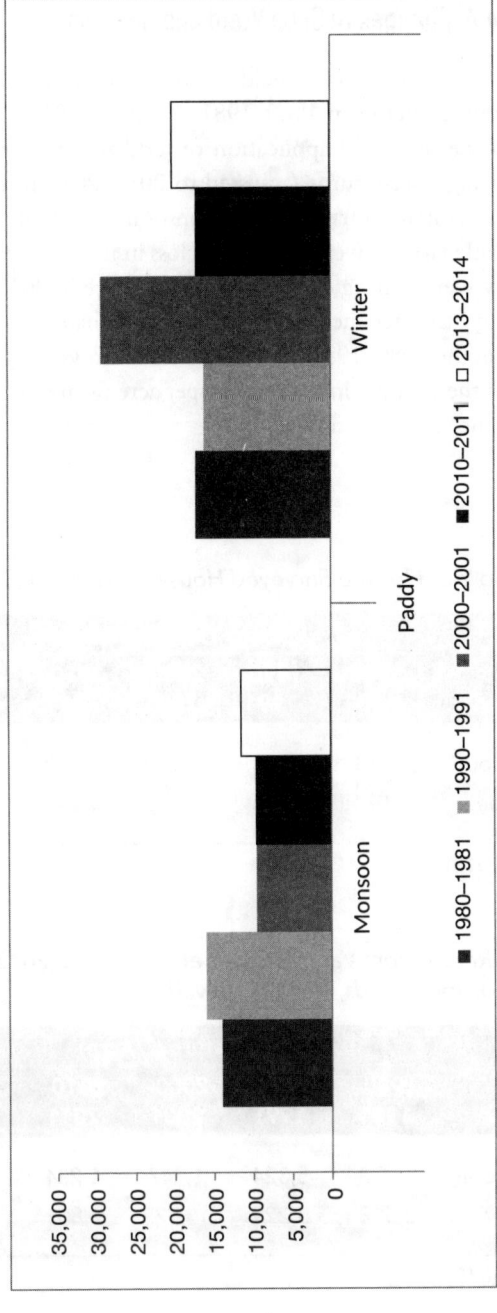

Figure 7.6 *Change of Input Cost over Time, Andhra Pradesh (₹/Acre)*

Source: Based on authors' own analysis of primary data.

7.4.4. Changes in Crop Yield and Returns

As Table 7.12 shows, the average yield of both monsoon and winter paddy almost doubled between 1980–1981 and 2013–2014. This can be attributed to the increased application of fertilizer and irrigation. Accordingly, average net returns (adjusted to 2013–2014 prices) had also gone up substantially for both the monsoon and winter paddy (Table 7.13). While farmers were incurring a loss in monsoon paddy in 1980–1981, they were getting close to ₹4,000 per acre in 2013–2014. For winter paddy, the net income return per acre had increased to almost three times the 1980–1981 levels. Figure 7.7 shows the graphical representation of the changes in net income per acre of land for various crops grown in the area over time.

Table 7.12 *Crop Yield for the Surveyed Households, West Godavari*

		Crop Yield (kg/Acre)				
Crop	Season	1980–1981	1990–1991	2000–2001	2010–2011	2013–2014
Paddy	Monsoon	481	738	703	878	849
	Winter	824	856	1,108	1,212	1,484

Source: ICSSR (2015).

Table 7.13 *Net Return from Various Crops at Real Prices (2013–2014) for the Surveyed Households, West Godavari*

		Net Return (₹/Acre)				
Crop	Season	1980–1981	1990–1991	2000–2001	2010–2011	2013–2014
Paddy	Monsoon	–73	5,324	1,347	1,234	3,935
	Winter	2,518	3,229	15,522	4,801	7,165

Source: ICSSR (2015).

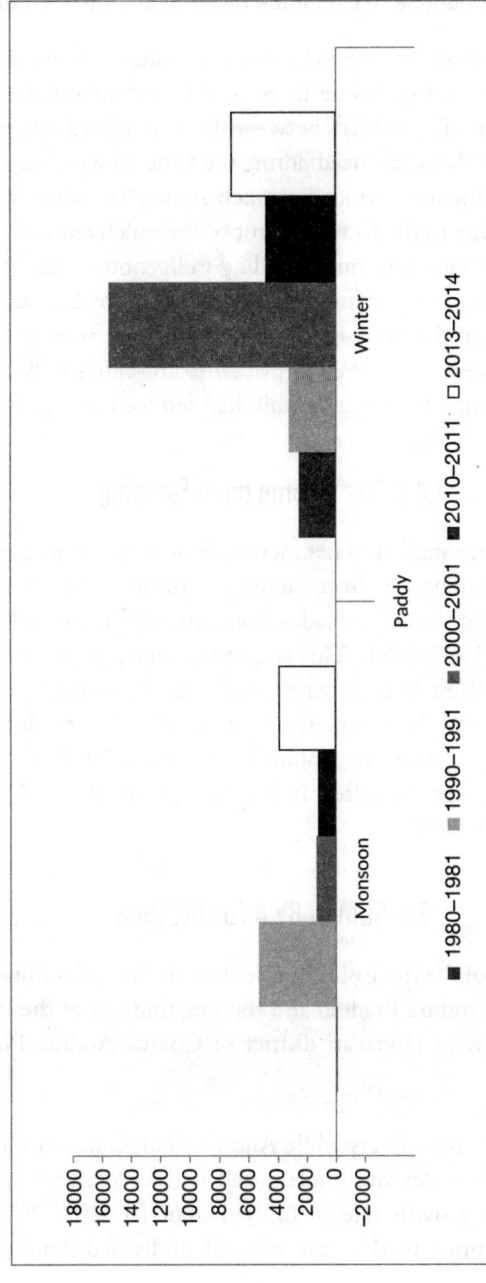

Figure 7.7 *Net Return from Various Crops over Time, Andhra Pradesh (₹/Acre)*

Source: Based on author's own analysis of primary data.

7.4.5. Changes in Livestock Holding and Milk Yield

There was significant growth in livestock keeping in the district of West Godavari (Table 7.14). While there was a substantial increase in the total number of milch animals between 1980 and 2013, the number of non-milch animals had reduced during the same time period. However, the annual production of milk per milch animal had come down. This was primarily due to the fact that most of the milch animals owned by the households were low-milk-yielding indigenous cattle. As a result, amount of milk sold per household had also decreased substantially (almost half). This led to a significant reduction in average household earnings (adjusted to 2013–2014 prices) from selling milk. The daily household revenue from selling milk had reduced to one-fifth.

7.4.6. Net Income from Farming

The results of the analysis of net income from farming are presented in Figure 7.8. As can be seen from Figure 7.8, the annual income went up drastically during the two decades from around ₹4,700 in 1980–1981 to ₹28,500 in 1990–1991. This is quite contrary to what was found in the case of West Bengal, where the annual income from farming drastically dropped during the first two decades. Although the annual income sharply declined to around ₹9,400 by 2000–2001, there was some improvement thereafter. It stood at approximately ₹15,790 per annum in 2013–2014.

7.5. SUMMARY AND FINDINGS

The summary of the discussions presented on the agricultural scenario in the state of Andhra Pradesh and the key findings of the field study conducted in West Godavari district of Coastal Andhra Pradesh are as follows:

1. Since the division of erstwhile Andhra Pradesh in 2014, the newly carved state of Andhra Pradesh had registered an average annual agricultural growth rate of 6.7 per cent (at 2011–2012 prices). However, prior to that, the state of undivided Andhra Pradesh

Table 7.14 *Number of Animals and Milk Yield of Households Owning Livestock, West Godavari*

S. No.	Particulars	Animal Type	Year				
			1980	1990	2000	2010	2013
1	No. of milch animals	Indigenous cow	89	94	64	198	194
		Buffalo	151	143	126	261	258
2	No. of non-milch animal	Indigenous cow	1	1	4	1	2
		Buffalo	0	0	2	8	9
		Bullock	22	14	22	6	6
3	Milk yield (lit/annum) per milch animal	Indigenous cow	1,190	1,061	957	843	806
		Buffalo	1,699	1,595	1,225	1,039	1,017
4	Average amount of milk sold (lit/day/HH)		16.27	15.65	11.92	8.50	7.51
5	Revenue from selling milk (₹/day/HH) at real prices (2013–2014)		1,260	840	480	312	275

Source: ICSSR (2015).

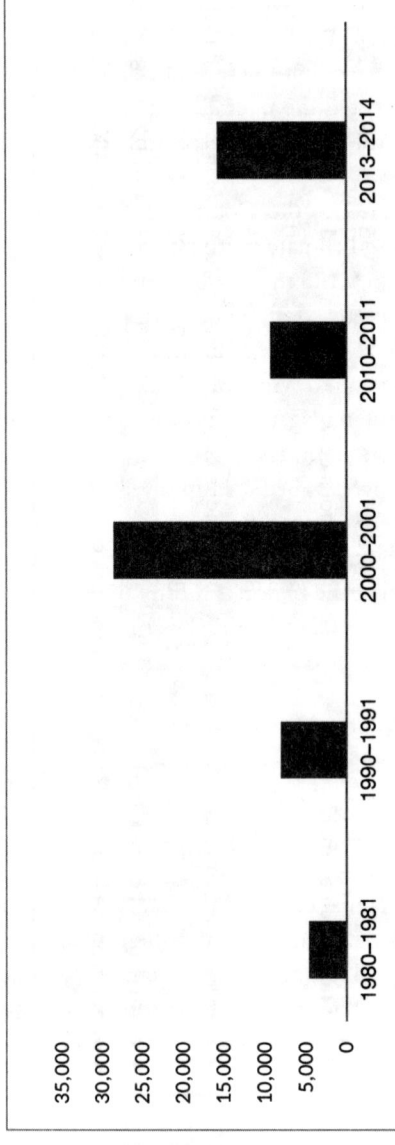

Figure 7.8 *Net Annual Income (₹) from Farming for the Surveyed Households in Coastal Andhra Pradesh (1980–1981 to 2013–2014)*

Source: Based on authors' own analysis of primary data.

registered a very meagre agricultural growth rate of only about 3 per cent (from 2004–2005 to 2013–2014 at 2004–2005 prices). One reason can be that between 2008–2009 and 2013–2014, the irrigated area under paddy which was the most dominant crop in the state (undivided Andhra Pradesh), declined to almost half and hence adversely affected the overall paddy production. The same trend was seen in the case of oilseeds and cotton, the two other major crops.

2. West Godavari district of the Coastal Andhra region has a semi-arid to dry sub-humid climate, with rainfall ranging from 996 mm towards the south to 1,128 mm in the north. Groundwater occurs under semi-confined to confined conditions. Groundwater levels are shallow but its abstraction is limited and is confined only to certain fresh water zones. Most of the deltaic area in the region is under surface water irrigation. Paddy, cotton, sorghum, pearl millet, tobacco, groundnut, ragi and sesame are the major crops of the region. The gross cropped area in the district is about 54 lakh ha, out of which 60 per cent is irrigated. Out of the total irrigated area, only 32 per cent is under groundwater irrigation.

3. The cultivable land in the region is mostly under the ownership of small and marginal farmers (owning less than 2 ha), who together account for 90 per cent of the total number of landholdings and 60 per cent of the land area that is fit for cultivation.

4. West Godavari is one of the districts in the state with high agri-cultural potential. The net sown area is about 55 per cent of the total geographical area of the district. Due to excellent irrigation coverage, nearly 63 per cent of the total sown area is put under a second crop.

5. There was no substantial change in the cropping pattern between 1980–1981 and 2013–2014. Paddy was the main crop in all seasons (monsoon, winter and summer) and was entirely irrigated. Further, in 2013–2014, about one-sixth of the cropped area was under per-ennial crops such as banana, casuarina, coconut, lemon and mango, and this was also fully irrigated.

6. Between 1980–1981 and 2013–2014, the average input cost per unit of cultivated area had decreased substantially for summer paddy and increased for winter paddy (though it also reduced for the latter

in comparison to 2000–2001). The reduction in input cost could be attributed to high subsidies offered by the government for electricity used for abstracting groundwater and fertilizers. Thus, in spite of a substantial increase in the application of irrigation (from 32–53 to 175–265 hours per acre) and quantum of fertilizers (from 24–31 to 53–73 kg per acre), the input cost had decreased.

7. The average yield and return for both monsoon and winter paddy had increased between 1980–1981 and 2013–2014. While yield for both monsoon and winter paddy got doubled (to 849 and 1,484 kg/acre, respectively), the net return per acre increased almost three times (₹7,165 per acre in 2013–2014) for winter paddy. In the case of monsoon paddy, while farmers were making a loss during the 1980s, they were getting close to ₹4,000 per acre in 2013–2014.

8. Dairy farming is not so popular in West Godavari. While between 1980–1981 and 2013–2014, the number of milch cattle had increased, they were of low-milk-yielding varieties. As a result, both milk yield per animal and the average amount of milk sold per household had come down.

9. The net annual income of the surveyed households from farming increased consistently from 1980–1981 to 2000–2001 but declined in 2010–2011. However, it again increased in 2013–2014 (was about ₹15,790 per household). Nevertheless, between 1980–1981 and 2013–2014, the percentage contribution of agriculture to the average household income declined consistently from 65 to 40.

REFERENCES

Census of India (2011). District Census Handbook West Godavari Village and Town Wise Primary Census Abstract (PCA), Directorate of Census Operations Andhra Pradesh, https://censusindia.gov.in/2011census/dchb/2815_PART_B_DCHB_WEST%20GODAVARI.pdf

CGWB (Central Ground Water Board). (2014). *Dynamic ground water resources of India (as on 31st March 2011).*

Directorate of Economics and Statistics (2013). Season and Crop report 2012–13, Directorate of Economics & Statistics Government of Andhra Pradesh, http://ecostat.telangana.gov.in/PDF/PUBLICATIONS/Season_crop_2012-13.pdf

GOAP, & ICRISAT. (2015). *Raithu Kosam primary sector development status.* Strategy and Action Plan submitted to NITI Aayog, New Delhi.

ICSSR (Indian Council of Social Science Research). (2015). The factors causing agrarian crisis in India: A study from four agro-ecological regions in India. https://doi.org/10.13140/RG.2.2.34664.57605

Kumar, M. D., & Vedantam, N. (2016). Groundwater use and decline in tank irrigation? Analysis from erstwhile Andhra Pradesh. In M. D. Kumar, A. J. James, & Y. Kabir (Eds.), *Rural water systems for multiple uses and livelihood security* (pp. 145–182). Elsevier.

National Sample Survey Organisation (2010). Education in India, 2007–08: Participation and Expenditure. NSS Report No. 532. National Sample Survey Office, National Statistical Organisation, Ministry of Statistics and Programme Implementation, Government of India, New Delhi.

Rabo India Finance Pvt. Ltd (2005). National Horticulture Mission Action Plan for Andhra Pradesh, report prepared for Ministry of Agriculture, Govt. of India, September 2005.

Reddy, A. A. (2011). Dynamics of the agricultural economy of Andhra Pradesh, India since the last five decades. *Journal of Development and Agricultural Economics*, 3(8), 394–410.

Reddy, A. A., Reddy, G. P., Rani, C. R., Reddy, A. N., & Bantilan, M. C. S. (2014). *Regional disparities in rural and agricultural development in undivided Andhra Pradesh, India* [Working Paper Series 47]. ICRISAT, Hyderabad.

Chapter 8

Agricultural Changes in Maharashtra

Nitin Bassi, K. Siva Rama Kishan,
M. Dinesh Kumar and M. V. K. Sivamohan

8.1. INTRODUCTION

Maharashtra is one of the very few Indian states which had been earning foreign exchange of export of agricultural produce (grapes, banana and pomegranate). The state is also known for some of the most celebrated experiments with watershed development in the 'rainfed areas', since the early 1990s. The state also has a great history of cooperative movement in agriculture since Independence. Yet the state has never been known for a vibrant farming culture. Instead, it is known for droughts and scarcity of water for irrigation and drinking water supplies, affecting large areas. More than one-fourth of the drought-prone districts of the country are in the state of Maharashtra.

The state's agriculture and water administration are often under attack from civil society groups for focusing on investments in large canal irrigation systems (with major and medium irrigation projects) that manage to irrigate hardly 20 per cent of the total cultivated area of the state despite heavy investments made so far. Out of the total cultivable area of 23.5 Mha, the net sown area is 17.5 Mha, and the total irrigated area is 3.95 Mha (GoM, 2019a). More importantly, the state continues to face criticism for the regional disparity in public investments in agriculture, and the disproportionately high allocation of water from the public irrigation systems for irrigating sugarcane, which is a water-guzzling crop given the low-to-medium rainfalls and semi-arid climatic conditions in the areas where the crop is largely grown.[1]

That said, it is an undisputable fact that the regional disparities in growth are high in Maharashtra. Vidarbha region, with a large tribal population, continues to be the most backward region in the state and is low on key human development indicators such as education, life expectancy and per capita income. The facts that Maharashtra state also has the unique distinction of having the highest reported cases of farmer suicides in the country (mostly from Vidarbha region), which is often attributed to crop failure (due to lack of water for irrigation) and acute drinking water shortage during summer months in certain parts like Marathwada, have given some credence to this criticism of this state's undeclared policy with regard to water allocation.

Nevertheless, it is generally argued that agricultural growth has been somewhat sluggish in Maharashtra, while it is a well-established fact that the state continued to make significant strides in other sectors of the economy, especially the tertiary and service sectors. A comprehensive analysis of agricultural sector performance, looking at how the income of farmers has changed over time, had never been attempted. Some of the relevant questions are: How have the cropped and irrigated areas in the state changed over time in relation to the changes in rural population? How has the cropping pattern changed over time? How has the net income per unit of cropped area changed over time, as a result of cropping pattern shift and change in cost of inputs and market price of produce? And finally, what has been the change in cropped area of individual farm households over time and how has that impacted their net income?

---

[1] Some civil society groups had long argued that Maharashtra should reallocate water from sugarcane to low-water-intensive coarse grains such as sorghum and pearl millet to improve water use efficiency (Shah et al., 2021), though least attention has been paid to the economic logic that drives farmers to sugarcane cultivation that the returns per hectare of sugarcane is far greater than that of jowar and bajra.

The chapter presents an overview of the performance of the agricultural sector in Maharashtra and then takes a closer look at Chandrapur district of Vidarbha region, particularly how it has been changing over the three plus decades, and examines how factors such as crop technology changes, change in the cropping pattern and farming system modifications, irrigation expansion, changing input use and cost of inputs and changing market conditions contribute to this trend.

8.2. AGRICULTURE IN MAHARASHTRA

The Maharashtra state grows rice, jowar, bajra, wheat, tur, green gram, black gram and other pulses. The state is a pioneer in onion production and also grows cash crops such as cotton, sugarcane, turmeric and vegetables. However, owing to the limitations imposed due to limited access to irrigation (when compared to the total cultivated land) and sharp regional variations in water resource endowments, the state is not very conducive to intensive farming. This has resulted in low yields of crops compared to all-India figures. The growth of the agricultural sector did not remain uniform across the state. There are five distinct regions in Maharashtra, each one having a unique topography, climate and water resource endowment. The names of these regions and districts falling in those regions are given in Table 8.1.

Table 8.1 *Five Regions of Maharashtra and Their Districts*

Region	Districts
Western Maharashtra	Pune, Satara, Sangli, Sholapur, Nasik, Kohlapur and Ahmednagar
Marathwada	Aurangabad, Beed, Nanded, Osmanabad, Parbhani, Latur and Jalna
Khandesh	Dhule and Jalgaon
Konkan	Mumbai, Thane, Ratnagiri, Raigad and Sindhudurg
Vidarbha	Akola, Amaravati, Buldana, Bhandra, Chandrapur, Gadchiroli, Nagpur, Wardha and Yavatmal

Source: Authors' own knowledge of the State.

Large areas of western Maharashtra are hilly and mountainous, and most parts of the region receive very high rainfall, with some districts (such as Pune and Ahmednagar) falling in the rain shadow area. The hilly regions with excessively high rainfall (above 2,500 mm) are also cold and humid. They form the upper catchment of the part of the Krishna river basin falling in the state. Geologically, the region is underlain by hard rock formations of basalt origin. Sholapur and Kolhapur districts have large areas under sugarcane cultivation. Nashik is quite well known for large-scale adoption of horticultural crops such as banana, pomegranate and grapes.

The Konkan region also receives very high rainfall (3,000 mm in certain parts) and has both hilly and flat areas. Geologically, it has a mix of basalt, laterite and alluvium. The region is drained by many west-flowing rivers and is the most water-rich among all the five regions. Socio-economically, the region is the most developed among all the regions in Maharashtra, being high on the human development indicators. Some parts of Konkan (such as Ratnagiri) are also known for large-scale cultivation of premium variety mangoes (Alphonso variety). Although water-rich, the region is not well-endowed in terms of land that can be brought under crop production (GoM, 2019b).

Although Vidarbha region receives relatively high rainfall (average above 1,000 mm), because of the undulating topography and the hard rock terrain (basalt and crystalline formations), the region faces water scarcity during the summer months. The region is tribal-dominated and is also known for severe droughts, crop failures and farmer suicides. Agriculture in the region is still very backward. The region has large areas under cotton, grown in both rainfed and irrigated conditions.

Marathwada is naturally the most water-scarce region in Maharashtra, with low-to-medium rainfalls and poor groundwater potential. It also experiences the highest frequency of droughts due to the high variability in monsoon rains and poor natural endowment of groundwater. However, because of the presence of large number of irrigation reservoirs and intensive groundwater development, agriculture has prospered in the region. Aurangabad is particularly known for its adoption of high-value crops such as sugarcane and pomegranate.

The region, which has a large share of the cultivable land of the state, is water-scarce. The spatial mismatch in the availability of land and water (GoM, 2019b) had acted as a barrier for agricultural development through conventional water resources development schemes.

About a quarter of India's drought-prone districts are in Maharashtra, with 73 per cent of its geographic area classified as semi-arid. The drought-affected districts of Maharashtra are mainly Ahmednagar, Solapur, Nashik, Pune, Sangli, Satara, Aurangabad, Beed, Osmanabad, Dhule, Jalgaon and Buldhana, which account for 60 per cent of the net sown area and lie in the rain shadow region, east of the Sahyadri mountain ranges in Maharashtra and the adjacent Marathwada region. The cropped area in the state for the last two decades is around 20.16 Mha. The area and production under principal crops during kharif and rabi seasons during last two years (2018–19 and 2019–20) are given in Table 8.2.

8.2.1. Dairy Development and Animal Husbandry

Dairy is a supplementary activity to agriculture, which has the potential for generating additional income and employment opportunities for the rural households besides improving nutritional levels. During 2018–2019, there were 107 milk-processing plants, 142 chilling centres and 898 bulk milk coolers with a capacity of 94.03 lakh litre and a chilling capacity of 44.16 lakh litre per day under the government and cooperative sectors together. The average daily collection of milk by the government and cooperative dairies were 1.79 lakh litre and 49.14 lakh litre, respectively, during 2018–2019 and 1.24 lakh litre and 39.16 lakh litre, respectively, during 2019–2020 up to October. There were 158 cold storages with a capacity of 11,613.84 MT. Of which, 150 cold storages with a capacity of 11,174.65 MT were with private sector (GoM, 2020).

Animal husbandry plays an important role in the rural economy. It is a supportive occupation which not only supplements farm income but also generates gainful employment. It provides essential nutrients at a low cost to livestock-rearing families. As per the results of the

Table 8.2 Area and Production of Principal Crops

Crop (Kharif)	Area ('000 ha)			Production ('000 MT)		
	2018–2019	2019–2020 (Tentative)	Percent Change[c]	2018–2019	2019–2020 (tentative)	Percent Change[c]
Total cereals	3,392	3,505	3	5,386	5,854	9
Total pulses	2,196	1,928	(–)12	1,234	1,275	3
Total food grains	5,588	5,433	(–)3	6,620	7,130	8
Total oilseeds	4,374	4,276	(–)2	4,830	4,899	1
Cotton lint[a]	4,219	4,431	5	6,593	8,141	24
Sugarcane[b]	1,163	822	(–)29	89,770	57,548	(–)36
Total sown area	**15,344**	**14,961**	**(–)3**	**–**	**–**	**–**

(Continued)

Table 8.2 (Continued)

Crop (Rabi)	Area ('000 ha)			Production ('000 MT)		
	2018–2019	2019–2020 (Tentative)	Percent Change[c]	2018–2019	2019–2020 (Tentative)	Percent Change[c]
Total cereals	2,958	2,902	(-)2	2,401	3,430	43
Total pulses	1,804	2,147	19	1,448	1,780	23
Total food grains	4,762	5,049	6	3,849	35	5,210
Total oilseeds	55	39	(-)29	19	15	(-)24
Total sown area	**4,817**	**5,087**	**6**	**–**	**–**	**–**

Source: GoM, 2020.

Notes: 1. [a] Production of cotton in '000 bales of 170 kg each; [b] Harvested area; [c] Calculated on the basis of actual figures.
2. Figures for 2018–2019 are based on final estimates and for 2019–2020 are based on second advance estimates. Figures may not add up due to rounding.
3. Kharif season cereals include rice, jowar, bajra, ragi, maize and other cereals. Pulses include tur, moong, black gram and other pulses. Oilseeds include soyabeans, groundnut, sesamum, niger seed, sunflower and other oilseeds.
4. Rabi season cereals include jowar, wheat, maize and other cereals. Pulses include gram and other pulses. Oilseeds include safflower, sunflower, sesamum, linseed, rapeseed and mustard.

GoI, 2019, the state ranks seventh at the national level, with total livestock of about 3.31 crore. The state ranks fifth at the national level, with a poultry birds' population of about 7.43 crore (GoM, 2020; GoI, 2019).

The Government of Maharashtra is one of the pilot states to implement a National e-Governance Programme (NeGP) in the agricultural sector as a mission mode project (MMP). By providing relevant information through different delivery channels, the project assists the farmer in making rational decisions for raising farm productivity and farm income.

The overall development model adopted by Maharashtra was attuned towards non-agricultural sectors (Dev, 1996) which had led to distress and prolonged stagnation in the agriculture sector. In tune with the happenings of the pan-Indian phenomenon, Maharashtra's share of agriculture in the state's gross domestic product is declining yet alarmingly. At present, this stands at 9.97 per cent. Agriculture in Maharashtra is currently going through a critical phase, with farmer suicides continuing, unabatedly signifying the agrarian crisis. Further, this is coupled with threatening stagnation in productivity and farm income (Shaha et al., 2020). Only among oilseeds, the productivity seen is permissive in the growth rates.

8.3. The Study Location

8.3.1. Physiography

Chandrapur is located on the eastern edge of Maharashtra in the 'Vidarbha' region. It is located between 19.30'N to 20.45'N latitude and 78.46'E longitude. The district is bound by Nagpur, Bhandara and Wardha on the northern side, Yavatmal on the western side, Gadchiroli on the eastern side and Adilabad district of Andhra Pradesh on the southern side. Physiographically, the district is situated within the Wainganga and Wardha river basins, respectively, flowing on the eastern and western boundaries of the district which are the tributaries of Godavari river.

8.3.2. Climate

Vidarbha, with an average annual rainfall of about 1,400 mm, has a dry sub-humid to moist sub-humid climate. However, rainfall is erratic with an average number of annual rainy days varying from 44 in the western part to 65 in the eastern part of the region. The soils are red sandy, red and yellow type. As most of the region is underlain by hard rocks (mainly basalt) which are characterized by poor primary porosity, groundwater yield is very low. Therefore, in spite of the safe stage of groundwater development (39%), water availability from wells is severely limited, especially during the summer months. Major crops that are grown include rice, wheat, jowar, cotton, orange, grams and chilli.

8.3.3. Demography

The demographic details of Chandrapur district are given in Table 8.3. In 2011, Chandrapur had a population of 2,204,307, of which males and females were 1,123,834 and 1,080,473, respectively. In the 2001 Census, Chandrapur had a population of 2,071,101, of which males were 1,062,993 and remaining 1,008,108 were females.

Chandrapur district population constituted 1.96 per cent of the total Maharashtra population. In the 2001 Census, this figure for Chandrapur district was at 2.14 per cent of Maharashtra's population. There was a change of 6.43 per cent in the population compared to the population as per 2001. In the previous Census of India 2001, Chandrapur district recorded an increase of 16.88 per cent to its population compared to 1991.

8.3.4. Changing Land Use

Table 8.4 shows the details of the land use pattern of Chandrapur district. The total geographical area of the district is 10,919 sq. km. The total cultivable land is 51.45 per cent of the total areas. The next highest area (33.44%) is under forests. The land which is neither available nor suitable for cultivation amounts to 12.68 per cent, and the area not used for cultivation is about 5.56 per cent.

Table 8.3 *Demography Details of Chandrapur District*

Description	2011	2001
Actual population	2,204,307	2,071,101
Male	1,123,834	1,062,993
Female	1,080,473	1,008,108
Population growth	6.43%	16.88%
Area sq. km	11,443	11,443
Density/km^2	193	181
Proportion to Maharashtra population	1.96%	2.14%

Source: GoI, 2011.

Table 8.4 *Land Use Pattern of Chandrapur District, 2010*

S. No.	Category	Area in 000' Ha'
1	Total geographical area	1,092.0
2	Forests	388.2
3	Barren and uncultivable land	26.3
4	Land put to non-agricultural uses	91.7
5	Cultivable waste	36.6
6	Permanent pastures and other lands	56.0
7	Land misc. tree crops and groves	12.0
8	Other fallow lands	13.6
9	Current fallows	16.0
10	Cultivable land	451.5

Source: GoM, 2011.

8.3.5. Changes in Operational Holding

Agriculture is the main economic activity of the district. The cultivators and agricultural labourers together account for 65.7 per cent of the workers in the district. Table 8.5 provides the details of landholdings in Chandrapur for the period 2000–2001 and 2010–2011.

Table 8.6 presents the landholding details as per different size classes in 2000–2001 and 2010–2011. In this region, the proportion of small

Table 8.5 *Landholdings in Vidarbha Region*

Region	Total No. of Landholdings (in '000)		Total Area of Landholdings (in '000 ha)	
	2000–2001	2010–2011	2000–2001	2010–2011
Vidarbha	2,359	3,024	5,160	5,172

Source: ICSSR (2015).

Table 8.6 *Size Class-wise Details of the Operational Landholding in Vidarbha*

S. No.	Landholding Size Class	Particulars	Vidarbha	
			2000–2001	2010–2011
1	Marginal	% to total no. of landholdings	30.3	35.9
		% to total area	9.0	12.2
		Avg. size (ha)	0.6	0.6
2	Small	% to total no. of landholdings	35.6	37.1
		% to total area	25.4	30.8
		Avg. size (ha)	1.4	1.4
3	Semi-medium	% to total no. of landholdings	23.0	19.8
		% to total area	30.7	30.8
		Avg. size (ha)	2.7	2.7

S. No.	Landholding Size Class	Particulars	Vidarbha	
			2000–2001	2010–2011
4	Medium	% to total no. of landholdings	10.1	6.7
		% to total area	28.3	21.7
		Avg. size (ha)	5.7	5.6
5	Large	% to total no. of landholdings	1.0	0.5
		% to total area	6.7	4.6
		Avg. size (ha)	13.7	14.6

Source: ICSSR (2015).

and marginal holdings had increased during this period. Small and marginal farmers were increasingly depending on small landholdings to earn their livelihoods.

8.3.6. Agricultural Situation

8.3.6.1. Cropped Area and Irrigated Area

The gross cropped area in Vidarbha region was 60.92 lakh ha, and the gross irrigated area was 18 per cent of the gross cropped area, and groundwater accounted for 62 per cent of the irrigated area in Vidarbha region.

8.4. RESULTS AND DISCUSSION

8.4.1. Changes in Income and Expenditure

Table 8.7 gives details of the average annual income and expenditure of the households in the region for the period from 1980–1981 to 2012–2013. Unlike other regions, in Vidarbha, the agricultural

Table 8.7 *Income and Expenditure in Chandrapur*

S. No.	Time Period	Particulars (Average per Household)	Districts Covered Chandrapur
1	1980–1981	Average annual income (₹/HH)	14,552
		% agricultural income	100
		% expenditure	41
2	1990–1991	Average annual income (₹/HH)	16,108
		% agricultural income	100
		% expenditure	48
3	2000–2001	Average annual income (₹/HH)	17,844
		% agricultural income	100
		% expenditure	51
4	2010–2011	Average annual income (₹/HH)	18,285
		% agricultural income	100
		% expenditure	53
5	2013–2014	Average annual income (₹/HH)	45,341
		% agricultural income	100
		% expenditure	67

Source: ICSSR (2015).

income still accounted for 100 per cent of the total family income of the surveyed households. The household expenditure as a percentage of the family expenditure however kept increasing like the sample households in the other three regions. From 41 per cent of the household's average annual income in 1980–1981, it increased to 67 per cent in 2013–2014.

As regards the break-up of the family expenditure (Table 8.8), the expenditure on food kept reducing consistently from 1980–1981 to 2012–2013, whereas that on agri inputs kept increasing during the same period, though not consistently. The percentage expenditure on children education had also shown a consistent increase.

Table 8.8 *Expenditure (Current Prices) on Major Items by Surveyed Households, Chandrapur*

S. No.	Particulars	Time Period	Average Expenditure per Household (% to Total) in Chandrapur
1	Food items	1980–1981	46
		1990–1991	41
		2000–2001	38
		2010–2011	42
		2013–2014	28
2	Agri inputs	1980–1981	14
		1990–1991	8
		2000–2001	10
		2010–2011	12
		2013–2014	32
3	Children education	1980–1981	1
		1990–1991	6
		2000–2001	10
		2010–2011	7
		2013–2014	8
4	Healthcare	1980–1981	4
		1990–1991	12
		2000–2001	10
		2010–2011	8
		2013–2014	9
5	Household items and durable goods	1980–1981	9
		1990–1991	10
		2000–2001	11
		2010–2011	12
		2013–2014	11

Source: ICSSR (2015).

8.4.2. Changes in Cropping Pattern and Irrigated Area

As Table 8.9 indicates, the proportion of area cropped was highest during the monsoon season and no crop was grown during the summer. Further, between 1980–1981 and 2013–2014, the area under cotton crop had increased by remarkable proportion. The increase was more than 1.5 times during this period. It is also observed that over the years, the proportion of area under winter crops (mainly under sorghum and pearl millet) had declined. This was largely due to the limited availability of water (groundwater being the major resource) for irrigation. As Table 8.9 shows, a large proportion of cropped area during the monsoon season was irrigated. However, it had come down post 2000 mainly for cotton and soyabean crops. Further, though the whole of the winter crops was irrigated, the number of watering was less as the groundwater got exhausted by the middle of the winter season.

8.4.3. Changes in Agricultural Inputs

Table 8.10 provides the input cost for the major crops grown in the area for different time periods, that is, 1980–1981, 1990–1991, 2000–2001, 2010–2011 and 2013–2014. The graphical representation of the same is provided in Figure 8.1. In comparison to 1980–1981, the input costs had dropped for all the crops by 2013–2014. The major decrease was for winter crops; it became almost one-fourth for maize and sorghum. The main reasons appear to be reduction in the number of irrigation hours per unit of land area; growing energy subsidies which further lower the cost of irrigation using groundwater; and lower fertilizer cost. The expenditure might also have been reduced due to lower returns, which will be discussed in subsequent subsections.

8.4.4. Changes in Crop Yield and Returns

As Table 8.11 indicates, for all the crops, the yield had gone up substantially after the 1980s. The most significant change was in cotton yield which increased by almost 10 times between 1980–1981 and 2013–2014. The major reason for this was the use of Bt cotton seed for sowing. Although this variety is resistant to many of the pest attacks, it is susceptible to damages during climate extremes.

Table 8.9 Cropping and Irrigation Pattern of Surveyed Households, Chandrapur

Season	Crop	Proportion of Cropped Area under Different Crops (%)					Proportion of Cropped Area Which Is Irrigated (%)					
		1980–1981	1990–1991	2000–2001	2010–2011	2013–2014	1980–1981	1990–1991	2000–2001	2010–2011	2013–2014
Monsoon	Cotton	28	29	29	34	45	100	100	100	92	81
	Soya bean	27	26	26	26	28	96	100	100	95	85
	Pulses	10	10	10	9	6	100	100	100	100	100
	Overall	65	65	65	69	78	98	100	100	94	84
Winter	Maize	2	2	2	2	1	100	100	100	100	100
	Sorghum	19	19	19	17	12	100	100	100	100	100
	Pearl millet	14	14	14	13	9	100	100	100	100	100
	Overall	35	35	35	31	21	100	100	100	100	100

Source: ICSSR (2015).

Table 8.10 *Agri Input Cost at Real Prices (2013–2014) for the Surveyed Households, Chandrapur*

Season	Crop	Input Cost (₹/Acre)				
		1980– 1981	1990– 1991	2000– 2001	2010– 2011	2013– 2014
Monsoon	Cotton	25,262	44,179	22,722	13,722	15,773
	Pulses	33,513	43,666	22,463	17,485	14,677
Winter	Maize	39,678	25,797	15,798	7,076	10,316
	Sorghum	34,832	24,345	11,573	8,470	8,874
	Pearl millet	32,559	25,059	13,952	9,939	10,378

Source: ICSSR (2015).

The reduction in input cost and yield increase was not reflected in the net returns for the farmers. In fact, the net returns from all crops except cotton had declined from the 1980s to 2013–2014 (Table 8.12). This implies that farmers were not able to give optimal inputs for the level of crop yields which could bring more income for them. Nevertheless, cotton had emerged as the major profit-giving crop for the farmers. In fact, cotton was not a profitable crop in the 1980s. However, it generated good returns in 2000–2001, and thereafter the income from the crop started declining. Nevertheless, it returned a profit of about ₹8,500 per acre in 2013–2014. However, its production was entirely dependent on good monsoons and during droughts (which are experienced frequently in the region), the crop suffered damage. Figure 8.2 shows a graphical representation of the changes in net return per acre of land for various crops over time.

8.4.5. Changes in Livestock Holding and Milk Yield

As Table 8.13 indicates, dairy farming was not well developed in the area. Most of the households had low-milk-yielding indigenous cattle and buffaloes. As the production was low, milk was mainly used for households' own consumption, and there was no marketable surplus.

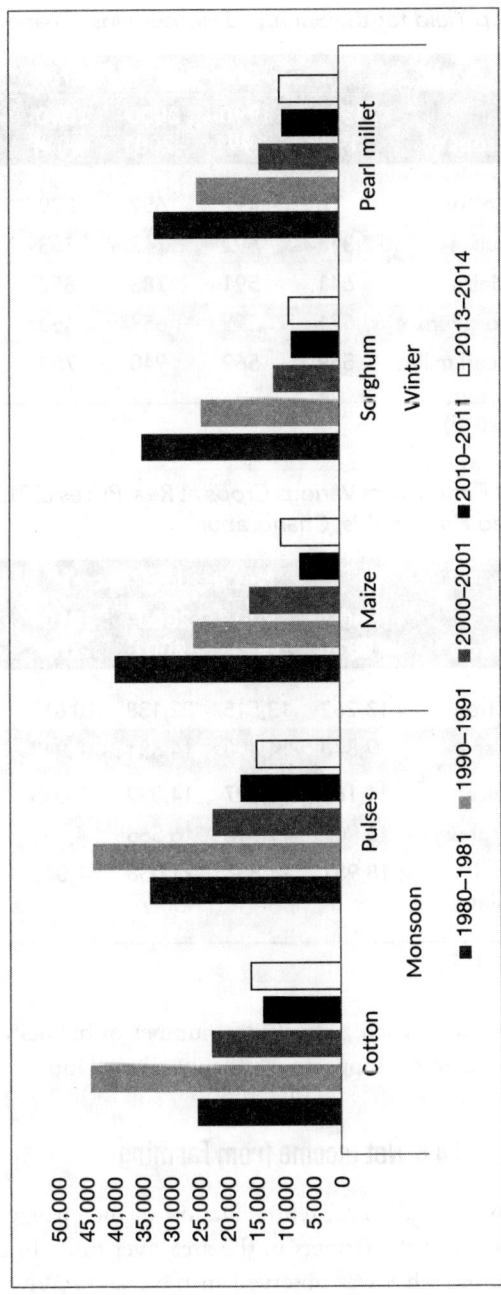

Figure 8.1 *Changing Input Costs over Time, Maharashtra (₹/Acre)*

Source: Authors' own analysis using field data.

Table 8.11 *Crop Yield for the Surveyed Households, Chandrapur*

Season	Crops	Crop Yield (kg/Acre)				
		1980–1981	1990–1991	2000–2001	2010–2011	2013–2014
Monsoon	Cotton	76	492	652	579	716
	Pulses	315	692	742	763	748
Winter	Maize	641	591	783	852	810
	Sorghum	571	595	657	650	665
	Pearl millet	559	569	940	759	664

Source: ICSSR (2015).

Table 8.12 *Net Return from Various Crops at Real Prices (2013–2014) for the Surveyed Households, Chandrapur*

Season	Crop	Net Return (₹/Acre)				
		1980–1981	1990–1991	2000–2001	2010–2011	2013–2014
Monsoon	Cotton	–13,262	13,515	22,138	10,619	8,446
	Pulses	9,870	14,408	14,381	2,940	333
Winter	Maize	11,163	15,027	14,099	7,035	97
	Sorghum	46,907	19,598	16,566	4,851	2,738
	Pearl millet	18,981	14,838	21,038	–1,006	24

Source: ICSSR (2015).

The households also owned a significant number of bullocks, which might have been used for supporting agricultural operations.

8.4.6. Net Income from Farming

Figure 8.3 shows the graphical representation of the changes in the average net income of the farmers in the area over time. In the case of Vidarbha, unlike what was observed in the case of West Bengal

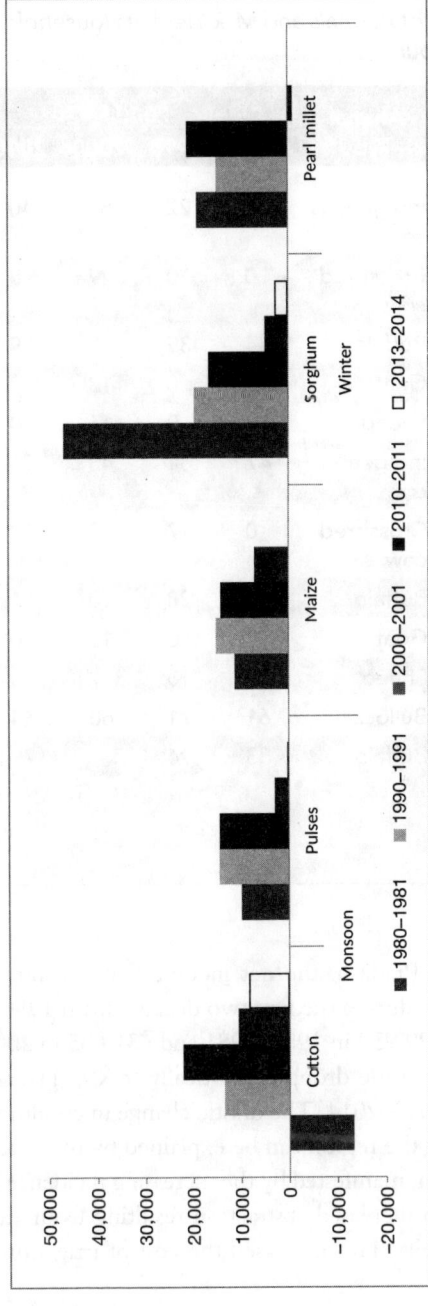

Figure 8.2 *Net Return from Various Crops over Time, Maharashtra (₹/Acre)*

Source: Authors' own analysis using field data.

Table 8.13 *Number of Animals and Milk Yield of Households Owning Livestock, Chandrapur*

S. No.	Particulars	Animal Type	Year				
			1980	1990	2000	2010	2013
1	No. of milch animals	Indigenous cow	43	22	54	40	51
		Crossbred cow	0	10	29	0	0
		Buffalo	44	39	0	59	49
		Goat	17	0	13	10	0
		Sheep	0	0	16	0	0
2	No. of non-milch animal	Indigenous cow	47	61	48	36	51
		Crossbred cow	0	17	32	13	0
		Buffalo	45	28	0	61	48
		Goat	15	0	13	0	0
		Sheep	0	10	7	0	0
		Bullock	61	71	60	64	65
3	Milk yield (lit/annum) per milch animal	Buffalo	83	94	–	79	103

Source: ICSSR (2015).

and Coastal Andhra Pradesh, the net income from farming did not witness much change during the first two decades from 1980–1981 to 2000–2001. It was ₹29,950 in 1980–1981 and ₹31,665 in 2000–2001. But thereafter, the income dropped drastically to ₹9,111 and further down to ₹7,330 in 2013–2014. The drastic change in conditions of the farming enterprise of the region can be explained by the deteriorating groundwater situation, manifested by the increasing incidence of failure of open wells due to increased abstraction resulting from an increase in the number of wells. This increased the cost of irrigation and also

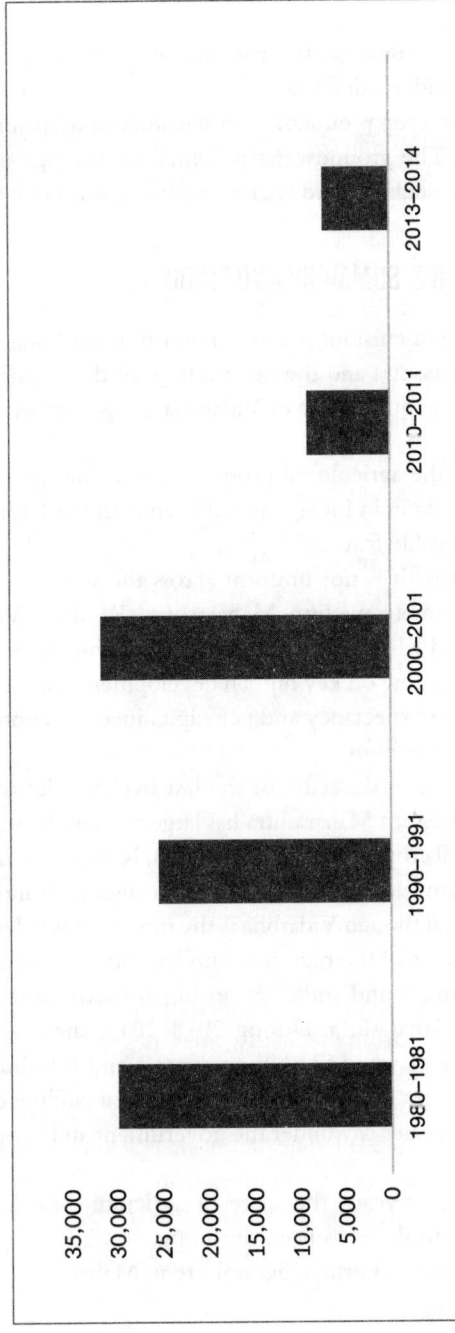

Figure 8.3 *Net Annual Income (₹) from Farming for the Surveyed Households in Chandrapur (1980–1981 to 2013–2014)*

Source: Authors' own analysis using field data.

reduced the availability of water for irrigation at the level of individual farmers. This semi-arid, medium rainfall region was heavily dependent on well irrigation for crop production, in the absence of major surface irrigation schemes. The groundwater potential of this region, which was underlain by crystalline, hard rock formations, was very poor.

8.5. SUMMARY AND FINDINGS

The summary of the discussions presented on the agricultural scenario of the state of Maharashtra and the key findings of the location study carried out in Chandrapur district of Vidarbha are as follows:

1. Maharashtra is the agricultural prosperous state and perhaps one of the very few states in India that had been at the forefront in the export of high value fruits.
2. Agricultural growth is not uniform across the state. Out of the five regions, namely western Maharashtra, Konkan, Vidarbha, Marathwada and Khandesh, Vidarbha, with a large tribal population and which is low on key human development indicators such as education, life expectancy and per capita income, continues to lag behind other regions.
3. The cropped area in the state for the last two decades is around 23.2 lakh ha. Western Maharashtra has large areas under sugarcane and horticultural crops (banana, grapes, etc.); Konkan is famous for mangoes; Marathwada has large areas under sugarcane and pomegranate; and even though Vidarbha is the most backward of all the regions, large parts of the region are under cotton cultivation.
4. The dairy farming and milk-processing infrastructure is well developed in Maharashtra. During 2018–2019, there were 107 milk-processing plants, 142 chilling centres and 898 bulk milk coolers with a capacity of 94.03 lakh litre, and a chilling capacity of 44.16 lakh litre per day under the government and cooperative sectors together.
5. Over the past few years, the share of agriculture in the state's gross domestic product has been declining, and it is 9.9 per cent at present (2019–20). Further, agriculture in Maharashtra is going

through a critical phase with stagnation in crop productivity and farm income.

6. To have further insights on the performance of the agricultural sector in the state, a field study was undertaken in Chandrapur district of the Vidarbha region. The region has a dry-to-moist sub-humid climate with an average annual rainfall of about 1,400 mm. However, because of the undulating topography and the hard rock terrain (basalt and crystalline formations), the region faces severe groundwater scarcity during the summer months.

7. In the Vidarbha region, the gross cropped area is 60.92 lakh ha, out of which only 18 per cent is irrigated. Groundwater accounts for 62 per cent of the total irrigated area. Paddy, wheat, jowar (sorghum), cotton, orange, grams and chilli are the major crops in the region. Although the small and marginal farmers (owning less than 2 ha of land) hold the maximum number of landholdings (73% of the total), the majority of cultivable land (53% of the total) is owned by medium farmers (owning 2 ha or more but less than 10 ha).

8. In Chandrapur district, agriculture is the major economy of the district, with cultivators and agricultural labourers accounting for about 66 per cent of the total workforce. However, only about 41 per cent of the total geographical area is cultivable. Farmers do not take any crop during summers, as water for irrigation (groundwater) is not available.

9. Mostly, the crops are grown during the monsoon and winter seasons. While cotton, soyabean and pulses are grown during the monsoon season, maize, sorghum and pearl millet are grown during the winter season. Between 1980–1981 and 2013–2014, while the proportion of cultivated area under cotton crop had almost doubled, it had declined for the winter crops. Nevertheless, all the crops were irrigated.

10. Between 1980–1981 and 2013–2014, the input cost for all the crops had reduced for the surveyed households. The reduction in the number of irrigation hours per unit of land area, and energy and fertilizer subsidies, are the main reasons for the same.

11. For the surveyed households, the yield for all crops had grown substantially between 1980–1981 and 2013–2014. For cotton,

it increased by almost 10 times, owing to the adoption of pest-resistant Bt cotton variety. Also, cotton had emerged as the most profitable crop for the farmers, as net returns from all other crops had declined. During 2013–2014, the average net return from cotton was 8,446 per acre of land.

12. Unlike the rest of Maharashtra, dairy is not well developed. Most of the surveyed households had low-milk-yielding indigenous cattle and buffaloes, and milk was mainly used for households' own consumption.

13. Between 1980–1981 and 2013–2014, the net annual income (adjusted to 2013–2014 prices) from farming had declined for the surveyed households (from ₹29,950 to ₹7,330 per household). Nevertheless, the agricultural income accounted for 100 per cent of the total family income of the surveyed households.

14. The major reason for low returns from agriculture in the district was the deteriorating groundwater situation, manifested by the increasing incidence of failure of open wells due to increased abstraction resulting from the increase in the number of wells. This resulted in a higher amount being spent by farmers in digging new and deeper wells which adversely impacted net returns from agriculture.

REFERENCES

Dev, S. M. (1996). *Agricultural policy frameable for Maharashtra: Issues and options.* Indira Gandhi Institute of Development Research.

GoI (Government of India). (2011). *Census of India 2011.* Office of the Registrar General and Census Commissioner, Ministry of Home Affairs, Government of India.

GoI (Government of India). (2019). *20th livestock census-2019, All India report.* Animal Husbandry Statistics Division, Ministry of Fisheries, Animal Husbandry and Dairying, Government of India, New Delhi.

GoM (Government of Maharashtra). (2011). *Scheme for timely reporting of agricultural intelligence: Land utilisation statistics 2010–2011.* Department of Agriculture, Government of Maharashtra, Mumbai.

GoM (Government of Maharashtra). (2019a). *Water conservation and saving in agriculture: Initiatives, achievements and challenges in Maharashtra.* Water Resources Department, Government of Maharashtra.

GoM (Government of Maharashtra). (2019b). *Maharashtra state water policy.* Water Resources Department, Government of Maharashtra.

GoM (Government of Maharashtra). (2020). *Economic Survey of Maharashtra, 2019–20.* Directorate of Economics and Statistics, Planning Department, Government of Maharashtra, Mumbai.

ICSSR (Indian Council of Social Science Research) (2015). The factors causing agrarian crisis in India: A study from four agro-ecological regions in India. https://doi.org/10.13140/RG.2.2.34664.57605

Shah, M., Vijayshankar, P. S., & Harris, F. (2021, 17 July). Water and agricultural transformation in India: A symbiotic relationship-I. *Economic & Political Weekly, 56*(29). epw.in/journal/2021/29/special-articles/water-and-agricultural-transformation-india.html

Shaha, K., Yogeswari, S., & Deshpande, R. S. (2020). Development challenges for agriculture in Maharashtra. *Economic & Political Weekly, 55*(26–27), 36–43.

Chapter 9

Agrarian Changes in Four Regions
Insights from Comparative Analysis

Nitin Bassi, M. Dinesh Kumar and V. Niranjan

9.1. INTRODUCTION

Agricultural production is dependent on several factors such as land and water availability, quality of the land put to cultivation in terms of drainage and soil moisture storage properties and presence of macro and micro nutrients, climatic conditions (especially precipitation, solar energy, temperature and its variations, relative humidity and wind speed), altitude and occurrence of natural disasters (floods, droughts, hailstorms, cyclones and excessive snowfall). Out of these several factors, rainfall, climate, soils and topography constitute agroecology. India's landmass displays wide heterogeneity in agroecology, with 15 different agroecological regions and many subregions within each. These factors together with micro-level conditions with respect to biodiversity and soil quality determine what crops can be grown and to what extent the yield potential of the crop can be realized, while technologies that control the production environment (to control humidity, temperature, etc.) can increase the opportunities for raising crops and livestock in climates which are otherwise not favourable.

That said, there are two factors, namely access to land and renewable water resources per capita (per capita cultivable land and per capita effective renewable water resources), which actually determine the agricultural production potential of a region and the surplus that a region can generate (Kumar et al., 2020), and both, or either of the two, are increasingly becoming a constraint for enhancing agricultural production in many regions. While in some (arable) land rich regions, water is becoming a major constraint, in some others, land is becoming a constraint (Kumar et al., 2012). In a few other regions, both are constraints. How these factors induce constraints on increasing farm surplus in different situations has not been analysed comprehensively on a time scale.

9.2. COMPARING AGRICULTURAL PERFORMANCE ACROSS REGIONS

Since farmers grow many crops and raise livestock, and allocate the inputs optimally to maximize the income from the whole farm rather than from individual plots and fields, analysis of the changes in income from individual crops alone has limited relevance. It is important to know how the farm as a whole has fared as an enterprise.

The average net returns at the farm level (adjusted to 2013–2014 prices) are presented in Table 9.1. It shows that average net returns at farm level for the surveyed households in Hooghly, North 24

Table 9.1 *Farm-level Net Return at Real Prices (2013–2014) for the Surveyed Households*

S. No.	Selected District	Net Return Farm (₹/Household)				
		1980–1981	1990–1991	2000–2001	2010–2011	2013–2014
1	West Godavari	4,669	8,047	28,583	9,328	15,790
2	Hooghly and North 24 Parganas	196,024	87,527	47,979	66,989	80,217
3	Banaskantha	181,135	104,472	98,687	129,673	76,998
4	Chandrapur	29,950	25,448	31,665	9,112	7,330

Source: Authors' own analysis using field data.

Parganas (both in Gangetic Plains, West Bengal) and Banaskantha (North Gujarat) are substantially higher than that in West Godavari and Chandrapur. The average farm income from crop production is lowest in Chandrapur (₹7,330/household per annum). One of the reasons is the diversified cropping pattern in both Gangetic Plains and North Gujarat, where farmers are found to be growing 10–11 different crops. In fact, after registering a decline, net farm returns have increased post 2000 in Hooghly and North 24 Parganas, owing to the introduction of new crops (mustard, red lentil and coriander). Further, farmers are able to adjust to the resource scarcity (water scarcity in North Gujarat and land scarcity in Gangetic Plains, West Bengal) by increasing the cropping and irrigation intensity.

However, farmers in Banaskantha, North Gujarat, have experienced a significant decline in their farm income which has reduced to half in 2013–2014 from the 1980–1981 level. The main reason, as discussed in the previous sections, is the low farm gate prices being offered to farmers. Nevertheless, there was a substantial increase in household earnings during 2010–2011 in comparison to the previous time period (before again declining in the subsequent period), as 1999–2000 was a drought year. In 2000–2001, farmers' earnings had also been affected in Hooghly and North 24 Parganas, as the gross cropped area per household reduced substantially. Further, in Chandrapur (Vidarbha), where the crop input (including irrigation) was suboptimal, earnings had reduced to about one-third in 2013–2014 from the 1980–1981 level. In fact, groundwater, which was the major source of irrigation in the region, was not available from the latter part of winter season, leading to insufficient irrigation and hence reduced yields. Hence, crop yields were dependent mostly on good monsoon. In West Godavari (Coastal Andhra), where paddy was the major crop, farm-level earning had increased. This was mainly due to availability of highly subsidized agri inputs (mainly irrigation and fertilizers) and a substantial increase in paddy yields.

Regarding the development of dairy as a major livelihood activity in the selected regions, North Gujarat is clearly a leader. Presence of infrastructure facilities (milk collection centres) at the village level and market-adjusted procurement rate of milk have made farmers consider

Table 9.2 Milk Prices in the Selected study Regions

S. No.	Selected District	Average Milk Price (₹/l)				
		1980–1981	1990–1991	2000–2001	2010–2011	2013–2014
1	West Godavari	7.57	10.66	16.36	27.61	36.65
2	Hooghly and North 24 Parganas	6.04	8.32	12.25	17.21	21.43
3	Banaskantha	3.37	6.33	9.29	21.33	28.8
4	Chandrapur	–	–	–	–	–

Source: Authors' own analysis using field data.

dairy as a serious livelihood activity (Table 9.2). Farmers in the region own high-milk-yielding cattle, and as a result, revenue from selling milk has increased substantially over the years. As a result, farmers' overall income is much higher than other selected regions.

In West Godavari, though there was an increase in the number of milch animals and milk price, most of them are low-yielding indigenous cattle and thus dairying no longer seems to be a profitable activity. Similarly, household revenue from dairy in the Gangetic Plains of West Bengal has declined, as the current milk procurement prices are comparatively low and there is no formal collection and marketing infrastructure (Table 9.2). In Vidarbha, dairy as an enterprise is a non-starter, as only a few of the surveyed households have cattle, and all the milk is used for households' own consumption.

9.3. FINDINGS FROM THE COMPARATIVE ANALYSIS

9.3.1. Where Is the Crisis Most Severe?

Both the nature and severity of agrarian crises change across regions. Among all the four regions, not only is the farm-level income the lowest in Vidarbha, but the degree of reduction in income over time is also the highest there. There is absolutely no doubt that the crisis is most severe in the Vidarbha region. This corroborates with the widely studied other manifestations of the agrarian crisis in the region in terms of farmer suicides and large-scale migration of farm workers to the urban areas.

In West Godavari, there is minimal crop diversification, and farmers entirely depend on paddy for their livelihoods. This can have serious implications for their earnings during an extremely wet or a dry year. During a year of below normal rainfall, the irrigated area will reduce (as most of the irrigation is by canals which in turn depend on releases from the reservoir), whereas floods can damage the entire standing crop. Dependence on just one crop and rainfall variability might be responsible for the decline of the contribution of agriculture to households' total income and reduction in milk yield, as the availability of green fodder becomes an issue. Nevertheless, the district has been able to register a substantial increase in farm income over a period of 35 years, but it remains one of the lowest among the selected regions.

In Hooghly and North 24 Parganas, a water-rich district of West Bengal, very small landholdings and difficulty in accessing irrigation water are having an impact on the earnings of small and marginal farmers. Starting from 1980–1981, the net farm income per household had declined drastically till 2000–2001 but picked thereafter. Although the farm-level income is the highest among the selected regions, rising fertilizer cost is resulting in a significant increase in input cost for rabi and summer crops. As a result, returns per unit cropped area have also started to decline. However, the reduction in net income per unit area is offset by the increase in cropping intensity, owing to expansion in irrigation. But the non-existence of proper infrastructure for milk procurement and marketing affects income from dairy farming.

In Banaskantha, a water-scarce district, returns from agriculture are seriously impacted due to low farm gate prices for most of the crops. However, dairy as an enterprise is booming and has emerged as a major livelihood activity for households. However, due to groundwater over-exploitation in the region, farmers' expenditure on either deepening wells or arranging for the alternate source of water for irrigation will rise. Although the farmers have also adopted micro irrigation technology (mainly drip systems), water use in agriculture has not reduced much as they bring more area under irrigation with the saved water.

In Chandrapur, most of the households depend on agriculture as the only source of income. However, farmers have to be content with growing crops in only two of the agricultural seasons. Water availability for irrigation during the winter season is a major limiting factor for achieving a higher crop yield. Availability of water in wells becomes a serious constraint during droughts, which recur in the region. Large-scale seasonal failure of agro wells is also reported. Average household income is one of the lowest, and agriculture is subsistence in nature. As the availability of water is an issue, most of the households do not own cattle.

9.3.2. What Are the Physical Factors Causing Crisis in the Agriculture Sector?

In Coastal Andhra, as most of the groundwater is saline, it is not used, and canals are the major source of irrigation. However, water availability from them depends on release from the reservoirs, which is again dependent on the occurrence of rainfall during a hydrological year. Thus, most of the irrigated agriculture in the region depends on the monsoon.

In North Gujarat, low rainfall and high aridity are the most significant physical factors affecting water availability and hence leading to a sort of agrarian crisis. As the average water consumption for crop production far exceeds the average rainfall in the region owing to intensive cultivation of crops that are grown during the non-rainy season, groundwater gets depleted. During drought years, groundwater replenishment drastically reduces, but overall water withdrawal for crop production increases. After droughts, farmers have to incur extra costs on well deepening. As per the household survey, the average depth to water level had gone up from 24 m in 1980–1981 to 49 m in 2013–2014. As a result, farmers had to spend a substantial portion of their net income on deepening the existing wells. A large proportion of the wells, that is, about 68 per cent, were deepened every year. The average depth of well had gone up from 33.5 m in 1980–1981 to 69 m in 2013–2014. The receding groundwater levels had also resulted in a decline in the average area irrigated per tube well from 17 acres in 1980–1981 to about 13 acres in 2013–14.

In Vidarbha, droughts resulting from monsoon failure are a major reason for farmers' distress. In combination with the region's geo-hydrology, it seriously affects the groundwater availability for irrigation. While during monsoon, water overflows from the large number of open wells tapping the un-weathered portion above the hard rock aquifers due to their limited storage potential, by late winters, most of the groundwater gets used up for irrigation or household consumption or flows out as base flows. Hence, by summers, most of the wells become dry.

In the Gangetic Plains of West Bengal, farmers have reported a reduction in soil fertility. This is mainly due to high cropping intensity and increased use of fertilizers, which deplete the soil of its essential micro-nutrients. Also, in a number of areas, groundwater is unusable as it is highly saline.

9.3.3. What Are the Socio-economic Factors Causing the Crisis?

In the Gangetic Plains of West Bengal, declining landholding size is a major problem. One of the major consequences of this is on the gross cropped area per household which had declined from 4.3 acres in 1980–1981 to 2.3 acres in 2013–2014. As a result, households' overall earning had declined. Further, the region has mainly marginal and small farmers, and their dependence on rented diesel pumps to lift ground-water for irrigation are quite high. Erratic electricity supply makes it difficult for even those who own electric pumps. This social set-up is leading to an agrarian crisis in the region which is further substantiated by the fact that close to 7 per cent of the surveyed households have confirmed that there is increased migration to the cities in search of better employment opportunities.

In Vidarbha, farmers are engaged in subsistence agriculture, which yields low returns and which is subject to vagaries of monsoon; easy availability of non-farm labour work under the Mahatma Gandhi National Rural Employment Guarantee Scheme (MGNREGS) further makes them disinterested in agriculture. Availability of wage labour for unskilled work in industries is also a deterrent for farmers to rely only on agriculture. Since no crops are taken during summer, farmers take up these works to supplement the household income. In the process, some even permanently migrate to nearby urban areas like Ballarpur (which is famous for the paper industry) for better earning opportunities.

In North Gujarat, there are problems with the farm gate price offered to farmers for some of their produce. Although the region has a large number of milk cooperatives, with every village having one dairy at least, and in some cases even two, there are no such influential cooperatives for selling agricultural crops, which can help farmers to get the right rate of their produce.

A considerably large proportion of the children from the households surveyed from North Gujarat, Gangetic Plains of West Bengal and Coastal Andhra are studying in schools. A high proportion of households in these regions want their children to take up jobs and migrate to cities. This indicates that there would be a great reduction in the number of people engaged in agriculture from these regions in the years to come.

9.3.4. What Are the Institutional and Policy Factors?

Subsidies on energy and fertilizers continue to play an important role in reducing expenditure on agricultural inputs for medium and large farmers in North Gujarat and Coastal Andhra, whereas they occupy a major proportion of the total input costs for small and marginal farmers in Gangetic Plains and Vidarbha. Nevertheless, electricity subsidy for agricultural pumping of groundwater is one of the factors responsible for the decline in groundwater levels in North Gujarat, which, in turn, has adversely affected farmers' income by increasing the cost of irrigation and expenditure on well deepening. Further, in Coastal Andhra, where farmers are content with mono-cropping, the current cultivation practices are producing low returns in comparison to other regions and can also affect the region's soil productivity in the long run.

Marginal and small farmers in the Gangetic Plains of West Bengal were found to be spending a high amount on fertilizers. As a result, farm income had declined substantially. Considering that the region is one of the largest producers of vegetables, the lack of policy initiatives to reduce input costs is detrimental to the sustainability of agriculture in the region.

In Vidarbha, which experiences frequent droughts, small farmers are unable to access a sustainable source of irrigation. The wells in this hard rock region are poor yielding and dry up much before summer. Therefore, farmers take less risk and apply agri inputs at a suboptimal level. As a result, both crop yields and returns are low. This has created a vicious cycle in the region where the farmer applies low inputs, gets low yields and returns and further reduces expenditure on crop inputs.

In dairy development, North Gujarat has a well-developed dairy structure which is supported by a professional milk marketing agency. However, the lack of infrastructure for milk procurement in Coastal Andhra and Gangetic Plains of West Bengal is making farmers disinterested in dairy farming as it yields low returns. Also, the milk prices offered to farmers in Gangetic Plains are lower than in other states.

9.4. CONCLUSIONS AND POLICY INFERENCES

The results of the study, which was undertaken in the four distinct agro-climatic regions of India, clearly show that the widespread perception about a growing agrarian crisis in India is largely true. However, the degree of crisis varies across regions—being highest in regions such as Chandrapur where natural endowment of water is poor; access to irrigation water is low; farmers have poor landholdings; and access to institutional credit and markets are also very poor. Also, the factors which act as drivers for this crisis vary from region to region. In the semi-arid, Coastal Andhra, North Gujarat and Vidarbha regions, physical factors, such as rainfall variability, overall scarcity of water, groundwater depletion and limited availability of groundwater, are causing stress on farming enterprise, whereas in West Bengal, socio-economic factors such as the declining size of landholding, migration and poor market conditions are the key factors. Non-availability of labours to work on farms, owing to large-scale migration of rural wage labourers to urban areas and engagement of a large number of those who are left behind in public works under the rural employment guarantee scheme, is also significant in the Vidarbha region.

But even within the same region, the crisis is not uniform across different segments of the farming community. The institutional and policy regimes governing the access to and use of water and distribution of input subsidies (electricity, diesel and fertilizer) ultimately decide how this crisis actually gets played out across different socio-economic segments. The existing energy and fertilizer subsidies are providing more benefit to large farmers in North Gujarat and Coastal Andhra Pradesh. For instance, in North Gujarat, the large and medium farmers who own wells are able to access groundwater at considerably low costs, which does not reflect the social cost of resource depletion because of heavy electricity subsidies, whereas small and marginal farmers who dominate the agricultural sector in the Gangetic Plains of West Bengal and Vidarbha continue to incur high input costs. Further, apart from North Gujarat where a proper infrastructure for milk collection, its distribution, processing and marketing are in place, dairy is unable to take off in other regions due to either low milk yields or low milk procurement prices. In Vidarbha, it is a complete non-starter. Therefore, a blanket policy across regions will not work in making agriculture a lucrative option, especially for small and marginal farmers.

In naturally water-scarce areas like North Gujarat, where groundwater is the major source of irrigation, establishing a system of water rights and efficient pricing of energy used for groundwater pumping would not only lead to resource (both water and energy) sustainability but also reduce farmers' expenditure on well deepening. It will also help small and marginal farmers, who are now dependent on water purchase, to secure water rights in the region (Kumar, 2005; Kumar et al., 2011). Further, a proper post-harvest marketing system to give farmers a fair return of their produce needs to be established. In areas which are largely under monocropping, such as Coastal Andhra, incentives in the form of easy availability of seeds and proper market for produce should be given to promote adoption of other remunerative crops. This will help in increasing farmers' income and also restore soil fertility.

In areas where rainfall variability is high, and groundwater resources, which act as drought buffer, are extremely limited due to the hard rock geology such as Vidarbha, an effective drought monitoring and prediction system needs to be established. It will help farmers in making a judicious decision on crop choice based on the information on the water availability during a particular hydrological year and help them reduce their losses. Along with this, long-term plans for investment in surface irrigation systems also will have to be explored with reservoirs, canal systems and lift irrigation from rivers/canals, provided they are economically viable. Only such measures can reduce the distress in the farming sector in such ecologically fragile regions.

In areas where water is abundant but land is scarce, such as the Gangetic Plains of West Bengal(based on CGWB, 2017; CWC, 2017), any policy intervention which is based on the strategy of intensifying land and water use will not work, unlike what some researchers have recently claimed, as land use intensity is already very high there. However, technological and institutional interventions to improve the economic access of small and marginal farmers to irrigation water can be explored such as the introduction of micro diesel engines and targeted subsidies for poor farmers. Simultaneously, a new policy for agricultural growth, which is driven by the strategy of enhancing the productivity of land and water and which is built on the concept of multiple-use systems, needs to be adopted (Kumar, Bassi et al., 2014).[1] Along with modifications in farming systems, the markets for high-value agricultural produce need to be strengthened, so as to encourage farmers to go for crop diversification. For dairy to become attractive in West Godavari and Gangetic Plains, a proper infrastructure for milk procurement needs to be established.

---

[1] As pointed out by Kumar, Bassi et al. (2014), the region needs farming systems that suit its agro ecosystem. The region has large areas under wetlands, including (a) areas that are under paddy, grown under submerged conditions; (b) areas that are inundated due to floods and tides; and (c) numerous wetlands that have water year round. Within the second type of areas, there are large low-lying areas in the coastal region of West Bengal that are likely to get inundated during tides. In addition, there are floodplains that are likely to get flooded due to river flooding, mostly in North Bihar. These areas are suitable for extensive shrimp farming, with very little farm inputs. While the first category of areas, which get water from tidal exchange, would be suitable for saltwater shrimp, the second type of areas would be suitable for freshwater shrimp and numerous varieties of native fish, along with paddy.

9.5. FUTURE OF AGRICULTURAL GROWTH IN ECOLOGICALLY FRAGILE REGIONS

In spite of the constraints induced by poor water endowment, Gujarat had achieved significant strides in agriculture through modernization, diversification, good infrastructure for production and marketing. This is particularly significant for milk, horticultural crops and cash crops. But the spurt in recent years (after 1998–1999) has become very erratic and vulnerable to droughts, with sharp falls in production in such years. The phenomenon throws up some very important lessons for other fragile agroecologies of India. The water and energy policy followed by the state for many decades has catalysed uncontrolled exploitation of groundwater with mining in many areas. The state has not put any serious thinking on the sustainable use of its water resource so far. In the process, it has used up all its renewable water resources, both surface and underground, and also most of the groundwater stock available in the alluvial basins of semi-arid areas. The 'criticality' of rains to the state's agriculture has become greater than ever before. This is a dangerous situation (Kumar, Narayanamoorthy et al., 2014).

The state's agricultural policymakers, for quite some time, believed that one way to protect the economic interest of the farmers is to subsidize electricity and provide good-quality power and subsidized canal water. The policy of providing subsidized electricity to the farm sector was a wrong one. Instead, there is a need to introduce metering and charging for every unit of electricity consumed (IRMA & UNICEF, 2001; Kumar, 2005). Only this can motivate farmers to use water and electricity efficiently. Findings of the research done in the past show that when confronted with a marginal cost of using electricity, farmers tend to use electricity and water more efficiently by improving physical efficiency of water use, by allocating water to crops that give higher returns from every unit of water and by improving the entire farming system, resulting in overall farming system water productivity (Kumar, 2005; Kumar et al., 2011, 2013). The recent decision of the state government to make the issuance of new power connections for agro wells contingent upon farming agreeing to install metres and pay on a pro rata basis is a welcome step to undo the damage. As a result of this new policy, around 60 per cent of the agricultural connections in the state are already under pro rata tariffs.

There is no doubt that the initiative of the state government to promote micro irrigation systems through its agency called Gujarat Green Revolution Company (GGRC) had paid good dividends. The area under micro irrigation systems had increased to around 4.07 lakh ha in 2010 (Sankaranarayanan et al., 2011) and then to 9.28 lakh ha in 2016–2017. Of this, 4.57 lakh ha were under drips alone.[2] The total area added to micro irrigation in the state during the period from 2001–2002 to 2004–2005 was less than 9,000 ha (Kumar, Turral et al., 2008). Electricity tariff reforms will change the situation altogether for the better, with much greater adoption of drips and sprinklers, as farmers would be concerned with the use of every drop of water they pump out from underground. While certain policies had fuelled agricultural growth in the entire state for more than a decade, it now appears that such growth would be unsustainable. Agriculture has become highly vulnerable to the occurrence of meteorological droughts. The state now has taken the major step of transferring water in bulk from the water-rich, land-scarce regions of South Gujarat to water-scarce, land-rich regions of North Gujarat and Saurashtra to reduce this vulnerability.

Such interventions to reduce drought vulnerability by improving water security positively impact human development and economic growth (Kumar, Narayanamoorthy et al., 2014). The strong correlation between annual GDP growth rates and rainfall in East Africa observed over a period of three decades illustrates the criticality of irrigation in boosting the rural economy and growth in semi-arid and arid tropics. As shown by Kumar et al. (2016), improving the water security of a region, expressed in terms of sustainable water use index, improves human development indicators by reducing mortality and malnutrition.

While groundwater was a 'drought buffer' in agriculturally prosperous semi-arid and arid regions, the depletion of the very resource due to its unsustainable use is now posing a threat to future agricultural growth. This is now also evident in many parts of Rajasthan, Punjab,

---

[2] https://pmksy.gov.in/microirrigation/AtGlance.aspx

Andhra Pradesh, Tamil Nadu, Karnataka and Madhya Pradesh. The yield of wells is declining sharply in hard rock areas, with an increase in the number of wells not adding to the well-irrigated area (Kumar, 2007). In Saurashtra, for instance, the well-irrigated area had declined in many districts. The situation is even more critical in areas that do not receive surface water resources.

To overcome its groundwater crisis, the Gujarat government launched a massive programme of decentralized groundwater recharge. This seems to have been driven by the general notion that more structures meant more water. There was no hydrological and economic consideration involved in planning water-harvesting systems in any of the basins. Most of these interventions were concentrated in basins which were already 'closed', leading to the dividing of the water rather than its augmentation. Often, structures are oversized (Kumar, Patel et al., 2008). Also, evaporation losses from impounded water increase due to an increase in reservoir area (Kumar et al., 2006). All these lead to poor economics.

The states like Gujarat which are facing groundwater depletion problems should look beyond such piecemeal solutions and try to tackle groundwater depletion through long-term, institutional and policy measures (Kumar, Narayanamoorthy et al., 2014).

While water harvesting, large water systems and water imports, all have a place in water management, the chances of achieving desired results from the same would depend on the basin-wide hydrological planning. The catchment and basin hydrology needs to be studied and the scale at which various small water harvesting systems and large water systems can be taken up in the basin needs to be assessed based on proper estimates of the dependable yield of the basin and the water demands. Potential for water demand management in agriculture, with the diversification of cropping system to accommodate water efficient crops, and use of micro irrigation systems also need to be explored. Further deficits can be filled through water imports. Only such an approach can ensure sustainable and equitable use of water resources for sustainable agricultural growth (Kumar, Narayanamoorthy et al., 2014).

Some of the regions in India which can follow the strategy adopted by Gujarat are Rayalaseema in Andhra Pradesh, Marathwada region of

Maharashtra and Western Rajasthan. Potential exists for the transfer of water to the first two regions. In the case of Rayalaseema, water can be transferred from the Godavari river to Krishna and then to the Pennar basin. Pennar basin which encompasses large parts of Rayalaseema is acutely water-scarce. The farming in the region is undergoing a big transformation, with a major shift towards high-value fruits and vegetables (mango, guava, sapote, brinjal, tomato and chilly) and adoption of precision irrigation technologies with mulching, water scarcity being one major driver for the shift. In the case of Marathwada, a possibility exists for the transfer of water from the water-abundant basins of west-flowing rivers of the Konkan region. While Marathwada has a large amount of un-irrigated cropped area, Konkan does not have sufficient amount of arable land for utilizing the water available in the basins of the region (GoM, 2019, p. 2). In western Rajasthan, water import through Indira Gandhi Nahar Project (IGNP) has already triggered an agricultural boom in the districts of Thar Desert, namely Ganganagar, Jaisalmer, Bikaner and Churu, the districts once known for acute water scarcity and frequent droughts.

REFERENCES

CGWB (Central Ground Water Board). (2017). *Dynamic ground water resources of India (as on 31st March 2013)*. Ministry of Water Resources, River Development & Ganga Rejuvenation, Government of India.

CWC (Central Water Commission). (2017). *Reassessment of water availability in India using space inputs*. Basin Planning and Management Organization.

GoM (Government of Maharashtra). (2019). *Maharashtra state water policy*. Water Resources Department.

IRMA & UNICEF (Institute of Rural Management Anand, & United Nations International Children's Emergency Fund. (2001). *White paper on water in Gujarat*. Report submitted to Department of Narmada, Water Resources and Water Supply, Government of Gujarat.

Kumar, M. D. (2005). Impact of electricity prices and volumetric water allocation on energy and groundwater demand management: Analysis from Western India. *Energy Policy, 33*(1), 39–51.

Kumar, M. D. (2007). *Groundwater management in India: Physical, institutional and policy alternatives*. SAGE Publications.

Kumar, M. D., Bassi, N., & Singh, O. P. (2020). Rethinking on the methodology for assessing global water and food challenges. *International Journal of Water Resources Development, 36*(2–3), 547–564.

Kumar, M. D., Bassi, N., Sivamohan, M. V. K., & Venkatachalam, L. (2014). Breaking the agrarian impasse in eastern India. In M. D. Kumar, N. Bassi, A. Narayanamoorthy, & M. V. K. Sivamohan (Eds.), *The water, energy and food security nexus: Lessons from India for development* (pp. 143–159). Routledge/Earthscan.

Kumar, M. D., Ghosh, S., Patel, A., Singh, O. P., & Ravindranath, R. (2006). Rainwater harvesting in India: Some critical issues for basin planning and research. *Land Use and Water Resources Research, 6*(2006), 1–17.

Kumar, M. D., Narayanamoorthy, A., Singh, O. P., Sivamohan, M. V. K., & Bassi, N. (2014). Unravelling Gujarat's agricultural growth story. In M. D. Kumar, N. Bassi, A. Narayanamoorthy, & M. V. K. Sivamohan (Eds.), *The water, energy and food security nexus: Lessons from India for development* (pp. 19–38). Routledge/Earthscan.

Kumar, M. D., Patel, A., Ravindranath, R., & Singh, O. P. (2008). Chasing a mirage: Water harvesting and artificial recharge in naturally water-scarce regions. *Economic & Political Weekly, 43*(55), 61–71.

Kumar, M. D., Saleth, R. M., Foster, J. D., Niranjan, V., & Sivamohan, M. V. K. (2016). Water, human development, inclusive growth, and poverty alleviation: International perspectives. In M. D. Kumar, A. J. James, & Y. Kabir (Eds.), *Rural water systems for multiple uses and livelihood security* (pp. 17–47). Elsevier Science.

Kumar, M. D., Scott, C. A., & Singh, O. P. (2011). Inducing the shift from flat-rate or free agricultural power to metered supply: Implications for groundwater depletion and power sector viability in India. *Journal of Hydrology, 409*(1–2), 382–394.

Kumar, M. D., Scott, C. A., & Singh, O. P. (2013). Can India raise agricultural productivity while reducing groundwater and energy use? *International Journal of Water Resources Development, 29*(4), 557–573.

Kumar, M. D., Sivamohan, M. V. K., & Narayanamoorthy, A. (2012). The food security challenge of the food-land-water nexus in India. *Food Security, 4*(4), 539–556.

Kumar, M. D., Turral, H., Sharma, B., Amarasinghe, U., & Singh, O. P. (2008). Water saving and yield enhancing micro irrigation technologies: When do they become best bet technologies? In M. D. Kumar (Ed.), *Managing water in the face of growing scarcity, inequity and declining returns: Exploring fresh approaches.* Proceedings of 7th Annual Partners' Meet. IWMI-Tata Water Policy Research Program, ICRISAT, Patancheru, Hyderabad.

Sankaranarayanan, K., Nalayani, P., Sabesh, M., Usharani, S., Nachane, R. P., & Gopalakrishnan, N. (2011). *Low-cost drip: Low cost and precision irrigation tool in Bt cotton* [Technical Bulletin No. 1]. Central Research Institute for Cotton.

PART III

Mitigating the Agrarian Crisis

Chapter 10

Efficiency of Input Delivery System in Agriculture

M. Dinesh Kumar

10.1. INTRODUCTION

Indian agriculture is undergoing a fast transformation. On the one hand, the cost (both the real economic cost and the costs incurred by the farmers) of conventional agricultural inputs such as fertilizers, pesticides, irrigation water, energy and labour and of throughputs such as land, irrigation equipment is on the rise. On the other hand, as the result of larger economic changes happening in the country—domestic economic growth, rise in per capita income, urbanization, changing consumption patterns and globalization of the economic system—the nature of farm economy is rapidly changing from subsistence to commercial and from traditional to modern, with many high-value crop outputs (MoAFW, 2016). Notably, the fluctuation in the price of such high-value produce has also become lesser over time, a clear indication of the growing demand for this produce throughout the year. While the former poses many constraints for the farming community, the latter offers many new opportunities and challenges.

In any case, the agricultural GDP in recent years has recorded impressive growth mainly due to diversification of the farming system and increasing proportion of high-value crops. An analysis by Rada (2013) showed a renewal of farm total factor productivity (TFP) growth in India following the economic reforms of the 1990s, led primarily by horticultural and livestock products and by southern and western parts of India. The high-input farming system championed by the Indian north has been outperformed by more diverse farming systems producing higher-valued commodities. Transitioning to higher-valued crops has accounted for 36.5 per cent of India's growth in aggregate crop production per hectare (Rada, 2013).

With the increasing demand for high-value produce such as vegetables and fruits, including exotic vegetables, flowers and spices in the Indian market including smaller cities and towns, farmers are tempted to diversify their farming systems to increase the profitability of agriculture. Even from the point of view of reducing rural poverty and increasing farmer incomes substantially, this is important. The agricultural component of the 'Three Year Action Plan' (as part of the Vision Document) for 2017–2018 to 2019–2020 prepared by the NITI Aayog of India envisions doubling of farmer incomes by 2022 (NITI Aayog, 2017, pp. 29–30). The key characteristics of the emerging farm economy in India are: (a) increasing role of capital and reducing role of labour in doing the farming operations; (b) increasing farm mechanization (for ploughing, application of inputs, weeding and harvest); (c) use of technologies for precision farming and production environment control; (d) increasing role of knowledge inputs on agronomic practices and produce marketing in the overall farm management; and (e) availability of freshwater increasingly becoming a constraint to crop production in some cases and good-quality land becoming a constraint in some. With this, the risk involved in farming is also on the rise. This farming system risk includes production risk (induced by weather and diseases), technology risk and market risk.

Resource-rich farmers increasingly use precision farming (automatic, weather-controlled irrigation), technologies for control of production environment (green house and polyhouse and polytunnel), efficient irrigation technologies (drip and sprinkler irrigation) and crop technologies to reduce the exposure of agriculture to weather-induced shocks and diseases (known as production-related shocks). However, to absorb the shocks induced by price fluctuations in the market, new approaches that involve a combination of technologies and institutional interventions are required. They include promotion of resilient farming system;

use of post-harvest technologies for storage and processing, group and corporate farming; creation of marketing infrastructure; and crop insurance. Adoption of such risky farming systems requires a greater deal of financial services which can help reduce the exposure of agriculture to these production- and market-related shocks (crop failure, yield losses due to crop damage, diseases and loss of revenue), and vulnerability of the farming communities to these shocks.

In this chapter, we discuss the drivers of future agricultural growth in India and the key features of the emerging farming systems; the technologies that act as drivers of change in agricultural output and are capable of reducing the production-related risks to sustain this growth; institutional approaches that can reduce the market risks; and, finally, the role of the financial sector in boosting technology adoption and reducing market risks in farming.

10.2. DRIVERS OF FUTURE AGRICULTURAL GROWTH IN INDIA

10.2.1. Increase in Area under Cultivation of High-value Crops

During the last decade, significant growth in Indian agriculture has come mainly from crop diversification with consistent growth in the area under high-value crops, comprising fruits, vegetables, spices and flowers in both aggregate and percentage terms (MoAFW, 2016). There is modest growth in the area under cereals, especially fine cereals such as wheat and paddy; there is relatively larger growth in the area under the high-value crops. On average, these crops fetch much higher prices in the market, though the price fluctuation is wide.

There are many factors that drive this agricultural transformation. First, there is a growing demand for the high-value crops in India, especially fruits, vegetables and flowers, owing to increase in per capita income and changing consumption pattern, and significant growth in consumption of fruits, vegetables and flowers is felt from cities and towns, with a perennial demand. Second, easier access to precision irrigation technologies and technologies for control of production environment which are required for raising some of these crops (foggers, drips and sprinklers, mulching, and fertigation), made possible through government subsidies and improved supply chain, had facilitated faster adoption of these crops and its penetration in the rural areas. Third, physical scarcity of groundwater in many areas (especially hard rock areas), which currently dominates irrigation in India, and the increase in the cost of production of water from underground sources had motivated farmers to grow crops that yield a high return per unit volume of water. So when the cost of production of water becomes high, it is put to high-value uses, that is, uses that give a very high incremental return per unit of water (Kumar, 2017). Fourth, the relatively higher degree of control over water application and access to pressurizing devices under well irrigation also enables farmers to grow high-value crops that are also water-sensitive.

It is correctly argued that the scarcity value of the resource is not felt by the farmers who use water for economic production functions due to inefficient pricing of water and energy that is characterized by heavy subsidies and zero marginal cost and lack of restrictions on volumetric water use. As a result, the efficiency of use of water and water productivity are very low in agriculture. Nevertheless, there are millions of farmers in different regions of India (including some of the water-rich regions of eastern India and North India and water-scarce regions of South Indian peninsular and western India) who purchase water from well owners and pay for water on an hourly basis (Kumar et al., 2010). These farmers are confronted with a positive marginal cost of using water and have an incentive to use water efficiently (Kumar et al., 2010, 2011). There are also farmers in the hard rock areas of India, whose primary source of water for irrigation is wells, and who have extremely limited access to water due to the limited groundwater potential. These farmers are confronted with an opportunity cost of using water and hence have the incentive to use water efficiently. Because of these reasons, they take the risk and allocate the expensive water for high-value uses while also using water and other inputs efficiently in order to obtain income returns large enough to recover the high input costs, which is again limited in quantitative terms. This enhances the return from farming.

The impact of induced water scarcity on the nature of farming enterprise and economic returns from farming is evident from the fact that in the water-rich areas, especially in areas that receive canal water, farmers prefer to grow cereals such as paddy, which fetch low value in economic terms. For instance, a recent analysis showed that in the newly formed state of Andhra Pradesh, around 85 per cent of the paddy irrigation is from surface sources and around 92 per cent of the surface irrigation is for paddy. While one reason for this bias towards paddy and such water-intensive crops like paddy is the lack of control over water delivery, the other reason is the access to cheap water.

10.2.2. Use of Water-saving Irrigation Devices Is Driving Area Expansion

Currently, micro irrigation systems cover nearly 5.95 Mha of India's irrigated land. Of this, around 3.15 Mha is under drip systems, used mainly for fruit crops, vegetable crops, flowers and some nuts (like coconut and areca nut).[1] Considering the fact that the area under irrigated crops which are amenable to water-saving micro irrigation systems is only nearly 8 Mha, this is a remarkable achievement (Kumar, 2016). A very large share of the area under micro irrigation systems including drips is in the semi-arid water-scarce regions of India, mainly covering the states of Maharashtra, Gujarat, Rajasthan, Karnataka, Andhra Pradesh, Tamil Nadu and Madhya Pradesh. With a deep water table, the use of drip irrigation systems with proper irrigation scheduling in such regions for distantly spaced row crops can surely lead to a reduction in consumptive use of water per unit area. One impact of this is the increase in crop yields as shown by many empirical studies involving primary data. The other impact is an increase in area under cropping (wherever water is relatively scarce in comparison to land), which is also shown by several studies as farmers reallocate the saved water for irrigating more area (Molle et al., 2004). As a coincidence, most of the areas witnessing the adoption of water-saving technologies have a small proportion of their arable land under irrigation, which enables area expansion easily.

---

[1] https://pmksy.gov.in/microirrigation/AtGlance.asp

10.2.3. Land Use Efficiency/Land Use Intensity

As per official statistics, the net sown area in the country has not been increasing. However, such findings are based on an analysis of official data on cultivable land in the country. With growing pressure on land as a consequence of the increasing number of operational holders, a large amount of area lying under wasteland, cultural fallows are being brought under cultivation. A lot of this land has low primary productivity. But access to well irrigation has enabled farmers to bring such low lands under cropping. There are large areas in the Thar Desert of Rajasthan which were lying fallow due to the presence of desert soils, high aridity and lack of access to good-quality water for irrigation. With access to canal irrigation under Indira Gandhi Nahar Project (IGNP), around a million hectares of this land are now under crop production.

With the current government's efforts to revive the idea of interlinking of rivers and to pass a National Framework Law on Interlinking of River to address the legal and social issues arising out of the decision to transfer water from one state to another, irrigation potential is likely to witness significant growth in the next few decades (NITI Aayog, 2017).[2] If that materializes, both land use efficiency and land use intensity would increase considerably, with many dry land areas receiving irrigation water.

In highly urbanized areas and peri-urban areas of agriculturally prosperous regions, there is a great market for horticultural crops in view of their proximity to cities which form a good market for horticultural produce, and entrepreneurs get low-quality land in these areas on lease for cultivating fruit trees and raising fruit and vegetable nurseries, as using high-quality land for such purposes will be economically unviable due to the astronomically high land prices. But they use such lands which were lying fallow for growing high-value commercial

---

[2] As per the NITI Aayog's action plan for sustainable management of water resources, the irrigation potential would increase by 35 Mha with the execution of water transfer links (comprising the Himalayan links and the peninsular links). The Minister of Water Resources, River Development and Ganga Rejuvenation has already tabled in the Parliament a draft National Framework Law on Interlinking of Rivers to expedite the work in this direction.

crops which find immediate uptake. Such practices are actually driving agricultural growth trends. Such trends were seen in the Rayalaseema region of Andhra Pradesh and western Rajasthan, which are highly water-scarce but with pockets having freshwater.

10.2.4. Fertilizer Use Efficiency

More than water saving, the adoption of micro irrigation devices has a great impact on fertilizer use efficiency, as most of the systems use fertigation devices called venture meters. The use of this equipment enables the direct application of fertilizer to the plants, increasing the nutrient use efficiency.

10.2.5. Use of Marginal-quality Water and Wastewater

When freshwater is becoming a major constraint for enhancing agricultural production in many areas, marginal-quality groundwater is being used for irrigation. This is the source of water for the future in coastal areas of arid and semi-arid regions and in some inland areas where there is plenty of marginal-quality groundwater (Kumar, 2017). Western Rajasthan and western parts of North Gujarat and Kachchh and Coastal Saurashtra have large areas underlain by saline aquifer formations (GoI, 2010). Currently, farmers in these regions are using this water for growing low-value cereals and some spices, oilseeds and other cash crops (cotton, cumin, castor, mustard and fennel), obtaining yields which are just half the yield obtained with good-quality water. Recent studies show that if freshwater is available, farmers in these regions will be able to grow some of the high-value fruits, vegetables, flowers and spices (including tomato, watermelon, coconut, kinnow orange, pomegranate, fennel, berry, marigold and gerbera flowers, and cucumber), obtaining very high returns per unit volume of water (Kumar, 2017).

One of the ways to reduce the salinity of groundwater in such areas is the careful and scientific introduction of canal water for irrigation. Return flows from canal-irrigated fields and seepage from canals would not only augment groundwater but also reduce the salinity levels in the water, thereby making it fit for irrigating vegetables and fruits. Through proper conjunctive use of canal water and groundwater, not only can the effective water availability be increased, but the problem of waterlogging in the canal command area can also be prevented. This is already happening in many canal commands, including the IGNP, the Sardar Sarovar Project and canal-irrigated areas of south-western Punjab. This has enabled farmers to grow vegetables and fruits which were not feasible earlier.

A recent survey showed pockets of fresh groundwater within the saline aquifer belts in arid parts of alluvial North Gujarat and western Rajasthan which are in the proximity of large reservoirs, with ground-water getting replenished from reservoir seepage. Farmers were found to be growing vegetables in these pockets (Kumar, 2017).

The use of untreated and partially treated wastewater in agriculture is becoming rampant in the peri-urban areas of many large and small cities. In Delhi and Kanpur, the municipal corporations are supplying treated wastewater to farmers in peri-urban areas at a fee (Amerasinghe et al., 2013). While growing economic power would enable large cities to invest in improved wastewater treatment technologies, the treated water would end up in the peri-urban areas for producing fruits, vegetables, flowers and forage crops on a much bigger scale than what is happening today around many cities. With greater willingness from the part of farmers in naturally water-scarce regions to pay for treated wastewater for irrigating these high-value crops, financially viable models in wastewater treatment and reuse would emerge in the future(Kumar, 2018a).

10.3. TECHNOLOGIES THAT RAISE AGRICULTURAL OUTPUTS AND REDUCE PRODUCTION RISKS

10.3.1. Crop Technologies and Seeds

For many high-value vegetables and flowers, the seeds used are of high-yielding varieties, mostly imported, and are not coming from the cultivars maintained by the growers. These high-quality seeds of high-yielding varieties ensure a very high rate of plant germination and uniform growth of the plants and simultaneous flowering of fruits and vegetable plants (brinjal, carrot, watermelon and papaya) and flower plants (for instance, marigold), most of which is essential for fetching premium prices in the market. Similarly, for some of the vegetables (such as tomato, cabbage and chilly), healthy saplings of uniform growth are available in the nurseries. For some of the fruit trees (pomegranate, sapota, mango, lemon, sweet lime, kinnow and berry), plants are mostly grafted hybrid varieties and are now available in the certified nurseries. Very few farmers have the knowledge to do grafting in their own farms. For banana, tissue-cultured plants are now available widely, and they ensure high-quality plants.

10.3.2. Technologies for Improving Water Use Efficiency

There is a whole range of technologies available in the market that help improve irrigation water use efficiency (kg/ET) in crop production. They include drip and sprinkler irrigation and plastic mulch. Drip irrigation system is amenable to wide range of crops such as distantly spaced mango (10 m × 10 m) to closely spaced brinjal, chilli, cabbage and Tomato (1.0 m × 4.0 m). For the same kind of crop, depending on the soil type, drip equipment are available with different types of emitters (in terms of discharge) with different emitter spacing. This versatility of the technology had actually driven the growth in the adoption of drip systems in India. In the case of sprinkler irrigation, the range of products available in the market include micro sprinklers to mini sprinklers to overhead sprinklers and guns. As a result, a wide range of crops are covered by sprinkler technology and include wheat, bajra, sorghum, mustard, maize, groundnut and potato.

Plastic mulching is far more effective in controlling soil evaporation and helps convert non-beneficial soil evaporation into beneficial transpiration for the plants, leading to higher yield, thereby increasing water use efficiency substantially (Xie et al., 2005). However, they are effective as a tool when used in conjunction with drip irrigation systems, as otherwise watering the plant becomes difficult once the soil is covered by the plastic sheet.

10.3.3. Technologies for Improving Land Use Efficiency

The advent of many new technologies has helped farmers to cultivate crops in terrains which otherwise were found unsuitable for cultivation due to the following reasons: (a) excessively high sand content in the soil, making fast percolation of water and nutrients and (b) undulating terrain making farming operations, especially irrigation, very difficult. The most important ones are sprinklers. The use of sprinklers has enabled farmers to cultivate undulating and sandy areas without doing land levelling, as well illustrated by cultivation in the desert areas covered by IGNP, reducing the cost of cultivation and labour required for irrigation. While drips can be used in sloppy terrains, they are not feasible in very sandy and undulating terrains. Today, hundreds of thousands of farmers in IGNP command use diggies (a large surface storage system for storing water), pumping machinery and sprinklers for irrigating cereals and oilseeds.

10.3.4. Technologies for Controlling the Production Environment

India's extreme climatic conditions in certain regions of the country (very cold winter resulting in frost formation in certain areas of the north and north-west to very hot climate with heat waves during summer in the north, north-west and western regions) make it necessary for use of plant protection technologies. The technologies for controlling the production environment include polyhouse and net house, generally known as green house, and polytunnels.[3] The first two are used in extremely hot and arid conditions to protect the plans from heat stress caused by excessive solar radiation and also to control other weather parameters (such as humidity and high winds), and the last one is used in very cold weather to protect the plants from frost formation. These technologies have now enabled the farmers to grow

---

[3] Drip systems are used inside the polyhouse and net house to water the plants which are cultivated on raised beds, and plastic mulching is also used to reduce evaporation or loss of water from the raised bed. To increase humidity, depending on the requirements, foggers are also used.

many weather-sensitive crops such as tomato, cucumber, chilly, cabbage, cauliflower and capsicum throughout the year. There is significant use of these technologies in north-western and western India and some arid pockets in the South Indian peninsula.

10.3.5. Technologies for Treating Marginal-quality Water

The marginal-quality water can also be desalinated using reverse osmosis systems at a cost much lower than that of seawater or brine, and the pH and other properties of water can also be controlled to suit the production of high value-fruits, vegetables and flowers which are sensitive to even small fluctuations in the acidity of water. Although the cost of desalination of marginal-quality water could still be quite high, the high income that can be derived from the production of high-value crops will motivate the farmers to adopt this technology. The other technology that is available is the multi-stage flash distillation (MSFD) process, which can be used when heat energy is available for free. Co-generation plants with thermal or nuclear power and desalination in the coastal areas can bring down the cost of desalination substantially. The heat produced from thermal and nuclear power plants is used to heat the brine, and the vapour is condensed into freshwater in the distillation chamber. There is already a thermal power plant with a desalination system in Jamnagar run by Reliance Industries Limited, supplying nearly 7 MLD of water to the city (Kumar, 2017).

10.4. COST IMPLICATIONS FOR NEW AGRICULTURAL TECHNOLOGIES

The new technologies that help farmers modify their farming systems to grow high-value crops have significant cost implications. Among all the technologies, micro irrigation is widely discussed. However, the emerging technology which changes the face of farming is the seed technology. The costs of seeds and plants used for high-value fruits, vegetables and flowers are given in Figure 10.1.

As recent field surveys carried out in western and north-western India showed, farmers are currently investing a substantial amount

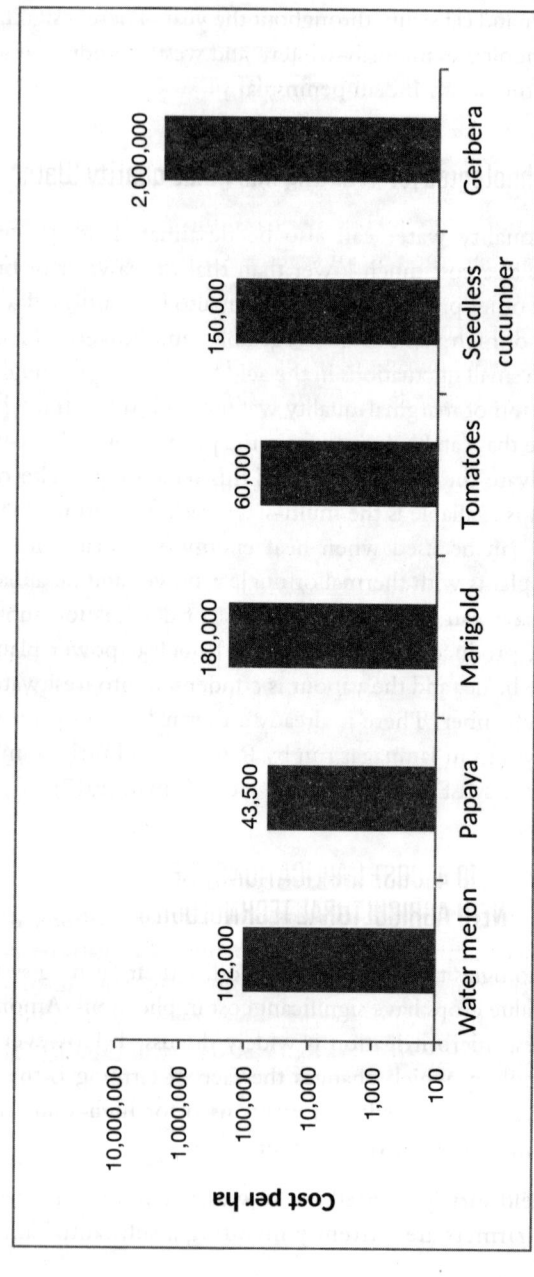

Figure 10.1 *Cost of Seed (₹) per Hectare*

Source: Kumar (2017).

of capital for seeds and seedlings of high-value vegetables (tomato and seedless cucumber), fruits (watermelon) and flowers (marigold and gerbera), in view of the fact that they help them obtain very high yields and produce of high quality. For watermelon, the cost of seeds is ₹34,000 per kg and the cost of seeds per ha of cultivation of the crop is ₹102,000. For papaya, the seedling cost is ₹43,500 per ha, @ ₹15 per seedling. The seed cost is ₹180,000 per ha for marigold cultivation and ₹ 60,000 per ha in the case of tomatoes. In the case of cucumber, the cost of seeds is ₹6 per plant, and with a plant density of 25,000 per ha, the cost is ₹150,000 per ha of planting. In the case of gerbera flowers, the seedling cost is ₹32.25 per plant, and with a plant density of 6 per sq. m, the initial investment for planting becomes ₹2,000,000 for a three-year life of the crop (Kumar, 2017).

The capital investment for technologies for control of production environment ranges from ₹422 per sq. m for polyhouse and ₹330 for net house, after a 50 per cent capital subsidy from the National Horticulture Mission. With an expected life of 10 years for the polyhouse and 8 years for the net house and a discount rate of 9 per cent, this works out to an annual cost of ₹654,000 per ha for polyhouse and ₹546,000 per ha for net house. Such high capital investment motivates the farmers to use the facility very intensely, taking crops throughout the year (Kumar, 2017). In addition to what has been shown in Figure 10.1, there are many crops whose seeds cost exorbitant amounts, like that of Bt cotton.

The high cost of seeds and saplings increases the financial risk in farming, and to cover this risk, farmers have to make further investments, in precision farming technologies or micro irrigation systems or technologies that control the production environment. Again, these add to the costs. The cost of drip irrigation systems for different plant spacing is given in Table 10.1. As one can see, when the lateral and dripper spacing becomes small, the cost increases substantially. For some of the vegetables such as tomato, chilli, brinjal and cabbage, in which case the dripper spacing is 0.4–0.45 m, the cost per ha will be higher than the highest figure in the table (i.e., ₹2.49 lakh).

Table 10.1 *Estimated Cost (₹) of Installing Drip Irrigation System for Different Plot Sizes*

Dripper Spacing (m × m)	Size of the Plot in ha					
	0.4	1	2	3	4	5
12 × 12	10,600	16,700	25,200	32,600	53,700	71,300
10 × 10	12,100	18,000	27,700	36,000	57,900	76,900
9 × 9	12,400	22,100	35,500	55,900	61,400	81,100
8 × 8	12,900	19,900	31,300	41,700	65,500	86,200
6 × 6	14,400	30,200	51,200	70,300	105,800	137,400
5 × 5	15,100	32,800	56,600	83,100	117,100	150,800
4 × 4	16,900	39,300	63,100	100,700	142,200	179,300
3 × 3	17,900	35,600	71,400	96,100	130,800	158,300
3 × 1.5	19,700	40,200	80,500	109,700	146,100	180,900
2.5 × 2.5	20,000	39,800	81,400	111,200	199,500	239,600
2 × 2	21,300	49,800	86,400	122,700	164,900	223,400
1.5 × 1.5	26,100	55,000	109,500	165,100	205,900	281,000
1 × 1	26,500	57,600	96,500	146,500	199,900	249,200

Source: Kumar (2018b).

An important input whose real cost is not borne by farmers many a time is the irrigation water. Water from public irrigation systems such as surface schemes is supplied to farmers almost free of cost and at times a nominal price per ha per watering is charged. This is even for the costliest irrigation schemes involving a huge river lift. But the economic cost or the cost incurred by the society for creating the irrigation infrastructure and supplying water at the farmers' fields is very high. These costs do not include the resource cost. These costs again vary from region to region, and one significant pattern which emerges vis-à-vis the cost of water is its relation with the water resources endowment of the regions where such systems are created.

If we leave states such as Mizoram, Jammu and Kashmir, Himachal Pradesh and Meghalaya, which are not known for investments in public irrigation, and Jharkhand whose irrigation schemes are ongoing, the subsidy varies from a highest of ₹103,962 per hectare in Andhra Pradesh to ₹2,995 per ha in the case of Chhattisgarh. The investment in per hectare terms is very high in Andhra Pradesh, and one of the reasons for this is the very high working expenses, owing to the large number of (river) lift irrigation schemes built recently by the erstwhile government of the state, incurring a substantial cost for energy for lifting water. The second highest irrigation cost in per hectare terms is in Maharashtra (₹68,498 per ha) which has the largest number of irrigation projects in the country, followed by Gujarat (₹63,543 per ha; CWC, 2015). Rajasthan, which is the second most important state in terms of canal-irrigated area, incurs considerably low expenditure on public irrigation. One important reason for this is that most of the irrigation is from the IGNP canal, which transfers water to irrigate more than 1 Mha of land from a barrage on Sutlej river in Punjab, whose cost was incurred by Punjab. A significant part of the project cost is not reflected in the capital expenditure against the state. In the naturally water-scarce regions, the cost of production and supply of irrigation water (per hectare) appears to be much higher than that of relatively water-rich regions (Kumar, 2017).

So far as groundwater is concerned, a common pool resource, but de facto a private property in India, the Indian farmers do not pay any price for using it in the form of resource fees or resource tax. The costs incurred by the well-owning farmers for abstracting groundwater are the costs of drilling the well and installing the pump sets, which are one-time costs, and the energy cost for pumping the water from underground. In many states, the energy used for pumping groundwater is charged on the basis of connected load, and only in a few states, electricity consumption is metered. In any case, electricity supply to the farm sector is heavily subsidized at the aggregate level (in terms of average subsidy per unit of electricity supplied), though the extent of the subsidy varies across states (see Table 10.2).

As Table 10.2 indicates, only Tripura state has an agricultural power tariff which is higher than the average cost of power supply. In all other states, there is a subsidy, which varies from ₹1.75 in Assam to ₹8.67 in Jharkhand. However, the average cost of power supply also varies across states. It is highest in Jharkhand (₹9.42) and lowest in Sikkim (₹3.19). In the states where power subsidy prevails, the extent of the subsidy varies from a highest of 100 per cent in Tamil Nadu, Punjab, Himachal Pradesh and Puducherry to a lowest of 28 per cent in Assam.

The heavy subsidy for electricity is available even in some of the water-scarce states, where groundwater resources are overexploited and the depth of pumping groundwater is high such as Tamil Nadu, Andhra Pradesh (undivided), Punjab, Haryana, Gujarat, Rajasthan and Maharashtra. This means that the actual economic cost of energy required for pumping a unit volume of groundwater is very high in those states. Over and above the energy cost, the cost of depletion of the resource, that is, water, is also high.

The high cost incurred by the society (the sum of the financial cost of production and supply of irrigation water and the cost of resource depletion) for every unit of water consumed in agricultural production in such water-scarce regions makes it all the more important that we maximize the economic returns per unit volume of water consumed in farming in such regions. While the pricing of irrigation water and electricity (used for groundwater) to reflect the scarcity value of the resource are fiscal instruments to improve the efficiency of use of water, they are not central to the theme of this chapter.

Table 10.2 *Power Subsidies in Agriculture in Indian States*

Name of State	Power Supply Cost (₹/KWhr)	Agricultural Power Subsidy (₹/KWhr)	Extent of Subsidy in Farm Power (%)
Undivided Andhra Pradesh	5.63	5.19	92.14
Assam	6.29	1.75	27.82
Bihar	7.85	3.74	47.67
Chhattisgarh	4.11	2.57	62.51
Gujarat	4.96	2.78	56.10
Haryana	6.46	6.00	92.80
Himachal Pradesh	5.26	5.25	99.78
Jammu and Kashmir	6.74	5.06	75.01
Jharkhand	9.42	8.67	91.96
Karnataka	5.05	1.98	39.24
Kerala	5.97	4.24	71.03
Madhya Pradesh	5.39	1.88	34.88
Maharashtra	5.84	3.26	55.78
Meghalaya	5.24	0.00	0.00
Punjab	5.78	5.78	99.99
Rajasthan	6.98	5.17	74.11
Tamil Nadu	6.46	6.46	100.00
Uttar Pradesh	7.06	4.82	68.25
Uttarakhand	5.10	2.82	55.18
West Bengal	6.13	1.98	32.26
Arunachal Pradesh	8.24	–	–
Goa	3.72	2.66	71.44
Manipur	8.55	7.14	83.51
Mizoram	7.41	0.00	0.00
Nagaland	9.06	–	–
Puducherry	4.06	4.03	99.22
Sikkim	3.19	–	–
Tripura	5.10	–0.44	–8.70

Source: Author's estimates based on GoI (2014), as provided in Kumar (2017).

10.5. INSTITUTIONAL APPROACHES THAT CAN REDUCE RISK IN FARMING

10.5.1. Promoting Resilient Farming Systems

It is generally argued that the introduction of high-value crops into the farming system would enhance the farm returns. Such arguments miss the point about risk. There are big risks associated with many of the high-value crops. These risks are related to production and markets (Kumar & van Dam, 2013). It is a well-known fact that some of the vegetables, fruits and spices are highly susceptible to diseases (pest attack and insect attack) and weather-related stresses (including heat stress and frost formation). These diseases can sometimes attack the entire field at an unimaginable speed in a sense that the crop is fully destroyed before any curative measures are undertaken by the farmer. On the other hand, market failure can also cause huge distress for the producer, given the fact that wide fluctuations in the price of some of the fruits and vegetables (especially the fast-perishing ones) within short time spans are quite common. Therefore, the crops introduced should be such that even in the event of production failures and market failures of the high-value crops, the farmers can still earn some income from other crops which are part of the farming system. Or else, the ability of the farmer to provide resilience against such risks needs to be taken cognizance of before such crops are introduced into the farming system.

From that perspective, it is important to know how resilient the existing farmer system is. The traditional farming systems are composite farming systems, with the outputs or by-products of crops being used as input for livestock/dairy farming and vice versa. Also, farmers grow many crops in their fields, of which only a few are high-risk (and high-value) ones and many are of low risk and low value (like paddy). Mostly traditional farming systems have a mix of cereals, pulses, cash crops and fodder crops. They fit into the agroecology of the area and are resilient to risks induced by natural calamities and changing market conditions (Choudhury and Sindhi, 2017). In the case of cereals such as paddy, bajra and sorghum, it is often found that even in the event of crop loss due to floods or water shortage towards the end of the growing season due to droughts, farmers use the leafy biomass from the damaged fields for feeding the dairy animals which provide some cash income. Such a system provides risk coverage, whereas in the case of vegetables and fruits, crop damage or price crash in the market can cause severe economic stress for the farmers.

10.5.2. Adopting a Cluster Approach

Often, isolated cases of farmers experimenting with certain high-value crops and earning high incomes are cited to build an argument that it makes more sense for a select few farmers to grow such crops, as that would reduce the market risk by preventing glut. But in many situations, such inferences are based on short-term observations. What is ignored is the fact that several of the input services for growing such high-value crops will be economically efficient only if a certain critical number of farmers grow these crops. Such inputs include the timely provision of high-quality seeds and good-quality saplings, provision of high-quality pesticides, insecticides and herbicides, and services of agronomists, horticulturists, scientists specialized in plant protection measures and precision farming experts. More importantly, the benefits of adopting high-value crops should reach a larger number of farmers, especially when the holding size is constantly reducing in the country, affecting profitability. Many of the successful cases of production and marketing of horticultural crops in India (from South Gujarat and Nasik and Nagpur divisions of Maharashtra) involve a cluster approach wherein a large number of farmers take up plantation of the same crop in considerable areas.

Even in the case of micro irrigation systems, the timely services of micro irrigation system suppliers, equipment assemblers and mechanics will be available only when large numbers of farmers from a locality adopt the system that it makes sense for these agencies to keep their outlets near the locality. If only a few farmers from a locality adopt such systems, services of input suppliers often get disrupted and can create dissatisfaction among the farmers with the use of such systems. Therefore, it makes sense to promote cluster approach for some of these inputs.

Last but not least, the suitability of the area's agro-climate for growing such crops and their potential adverse impact on ecology (especially on soils and crop species) need to be ascertained to prevent future catastrophe.

10.5.3. Creation of Marketing Infrastructure and Enabling Regulations

Lack of proper marketing infrastructure prevents farmers from remote areas from adopting many of the high-value crops, and the transaction cost of finding a market and taking the produce to the market regularly could be quite high. Therefore, the creation of marketing infrastructure has to be treated as an input for resilient farming. Marketing infrastructure to be created would include a place (yard) for grading, sorting, packaging and labelling, and vehicles for fast transportation of the produce from the place of produce to the market destination in order to ensure quality control and longer shelf life of the produce. This is important for gaining the confidence of the wholesaler.

There is also a need to amend the existing laws such as the Agricultural Produce Marketing Committee Act of the states that restrict the free movement of agricultural produce and make it mandatory for farmers to sell most of their produce in the local market, as argued by the Three Year Action Plan (2017–2018 to 2019–2020) for agriculture (NITI Aayog, 2017).

10.5.4. Adoption of Post-harvest Technologies

The post-harvest losses from fruit and vegetable production in India are one of the highest in the world. On the basis of production and wholesale market price in India, the estimated post-harvest losses in fruits and vegetables touched $33.745 billion in 2011–2012 (ASSOCHAM, 2013). For many crops, the produce needs to be processed for uniform ripening and appearance before they are sold in the market. Such crops include banana, mango and papaya. Some other crops which are fast perishing can also be processed for value addition (pineapple, mango, strawberry, papaya, cucumber, chilly and onion).[4] Crops such as potatoes and onions, which are seasonal crops[5] but are required for

---

[4] Chilly, cucumber and pineapple are kept under preservatives. Onions are dehydrated and kept for supply to restaurants. Mangoes are processed to make crush. Many fruits are processed to make juice and marketed in tetra packs.

[5] Onions are grown in two seasons (namely winter and summer), and potatoes are grown only in winter.

regular consumption in the households throughout the year, have to be kept in cold storages to prevent glut in the market and to ensure round-the-year supply. All these would require infrastructure, including expensive machinery for refrigeration, depending on the type of processing required.

10.5.5. Crop Insurance

Many of the high-value crops are susceptible to severe damage under unpredictable and extreme weather conditions which include untimely rains (for mango), rains under 'cloudburst', cyclone (of varying intensity), strong winds (banana plantation), avalanche and snowfall, and heatwave for most of the vegetable crops which are not raised under polyhouse. Some of these crops, especially in areas surrounding wildlife sanctuaries and national parks, are vulnerable to attack by wild animals. In such cases, insurance will be necessary to protect the economic interest of the farmers in a manner that they are able to service the loans taken from the banks and the basic minimum income is assured for survival till the next agricultural season.

10.5.6. Targeted Subsidies to Areas Where It Produces Maximum Welfare Benefits

Many technologies used in agriculture today produce welfare benefits. But it is a general tendency to offer subsidies for certain farm equipment (micro irrigation systems, precision farming system, polyhouse, net house and polytunnel) without taking into account the fact that such subsidies are essential when the private costs exceed the private benefits from the use of the system. However, there are significant positive externalities induced by the use of the system on the society due to which the social benefits exceed the social cost (private cost + negative externalities). In such cases, the subsidy can be structured in such a manner that the private cost becomes less than the private benefit. However, this principle is hardly followed in the agriculture sector today. Subsidies and lock, stock and barrel are being offered to farmers for purchase of micro irrigation equipment, polyhouse and net house, even when the private benefits are far higher than the private costs.

A major cause of concern is that in some situations, there are negative externalities such technologies can induce on the society. For instance, in a locality which experiences high rates of rural unemployment, mechanized farming of commercial crops including extensive use of irrigation equipment such as sprinklers and drips can take rural unskilled labour force out of farms, thereby creating more problems of unemployment. This is a negative externality, and the technology may not induce any positive externality. Therefore, subsidies in such situations will not be desirable from a societal point of view.

Subsidies should be advanced in areas where social benefits are high. For instance, in a water-scarce area, the adoption of water-saving irrigation equipment that actually produce real water-saving (if used for certain crops) should be encouraged through subsidies. Similarly, in a region that suffers from food insecurity due to low production, any technology which can boost the yields of cereals (be it a micro irrigation system or seed technology) but is too expensive for farmers to adopt, should be subsidized through government support if the social benefits (through a reduction in malnutrition problems or lowering of cereal prices) are large enough to exceed the social costs.

10.6. ROLE OF FINANCIAL INSTITUTIONS FOR BOOSTING TECHNOLOGY ADOPTION AND REDUCING MARKET RISKS

The basic character of farming in India is changing. Farming is increasingly getting commercialized, with a greater proportion of the farm outputs catering to the market, and with a greater share of the value addition coming from high-value crops. Accordingly, the nature of inputs and the level of investment required are also changing rapidly. The resource-rich and enterprising farmers are able to take high risks and increase their profit margins even in the harshest (climatic) conditions and even under a severe scarcity of fertile land and good-quality water. If the small farmers in the country have to take advantage of the new opportunities, their risk-taking ability has to increase. For this, the agricultural production system has to be resilient. In the coming years, financial institutions will have to support capital investments in desalination systems which treat marginal-quality groundwater, wastewater treatment systems, post-harvest technologies, marketing infrastructure, technologies for controlling the production environment and precision farming systems. Following are the few steps that need to be institutionalized by the financial sector.

10.6.1. Assess the Production and Market-related Risks

Farming risk is not uniform across the country. There are many regions which are historically known for their high incidence of droughts, and some are known for their high incidence of floods. Some regions are hit by cyclones, avalanche fall and hailstorm. Generally, the low-to-medium rainfall regions in India which are semi-arid to arid experience very high variability in annual rainfall and other climate parameters (temperature, wind speed and relative humidity) and are subject to climate extremes, whereas the high rainfall regions experience a much lower degree of inter-annual variability in weather parameters. Interestingly, the semi-arid and arid regions which experience high inter-annual variability in climate parameters are also agriculturally prosperous, and high-value agriculture is practised in these regions. Sometimes, these phenomena are also highly localized.

The risk involved in different farming systems in different agro-ecologies that capture the physical and socio-economic conditions of the region needs to be evaluated. Particularly, the risk determined by climate variability and climate extremes (droughts, floods and heat stress; Khan et al., 2009), disease attacks and changing market conditions; degree of exposure of the farming system to these shocks; the capacity of the farmers to insulate the farming system against such shocks and the 'adaptive capacity' need to be assessed.

Crop insurance based on assessment of weather risk has long been discussed in the Indian context (Golait & Pradhan, 2008). It is called weather-indexed insurance, when linked to the underlying weather risk, defined as an index based on historical data of rainfall, temperature, snow, heat stress, etc. (TERI, 2005).

The outcomes of such assessments, however, should not be used for stopping loans; instead, these should be used to take the necessary precautionary measures for protecting the interests of the banks and the farmers. This can be in the form of advice to farmers on the appropriate farming system for their farm which ensures a high degree of resilience. The general practice is to advance loans on the basis of an assessment of the repayment capacity of the applicant if sufficient collaterals are produced by them.

10.6.2. Linking Farm Loans to Crop Insurance

It is quite clear from the previous section that if the small and marginal farmers have to shift to high-value crops and modernize their farming systems, they would require a lot of capital. When loans are advanced to farmers for purchase and installation of equipment such as precision farming systems or micro irrigation equipment or for installing poly-houses or net houses or developing expensive horticultural plantations, crop insurance and insurance coverage for the equipment being pro-cured (irrigation equipment and technologies for control of production environment) should be made mandatory. It is all the more important for regions where the production and market risks are high. This would protect the interest of the farmers and financial institutions. The banks and insurance companies have to work in tandem.

10.6.3. Designing Insurance Products Based on Risk Assessment

The Ministry of Agriculture has a National Agricultural Insurance Scheme, administered through the Agriculture Insurance Corporation, which covers all farmers, introduced in 1999–2000. It operates on the basis of an 'area approach', that is, defined areas for each notified crop for widespread calamities and on an individual basis for localized calamities such as floods, hailstorms, landslides and cyclones. Although government crop insurance is subsidized, it has very low coverage as it suffers from many inadequacies (Golait & Pradhan, 2008; TERI, 2005).[6] The insurance companies need to design products for farmers,

---

[6] It fails to provide the right incentives to farmers, as crop yield is insured and not the investments. Conversely, farmers who have suffered losses as a result of

keeping in view the degree of farming risk, which goes far beyond weather risks. While risk is a function of the shock, exposure and vulnerability of the farm household, for the same weather conditions, the degree of risk would change depending on the nature of the farming system and the coping capacity of the farmer. As a general rule, the higher the production-related risk, the higher would be the premium to be paid by the farmer for the same amount of insurance cover. Therefore, it is important that the banks counsel the farmers to adopt farming systems which offer resilience to production risks, taking cognizance of the agroecology (soils, rainfall, climate, and drought and flood proneness) and plant diseases and market reality (access to market, demand, market behaviour, etc.), though the crop insurance will only cover production risks.

10.6.4. Research on Resilient Farming Systems

The financial institutions which advance loans for crops and various types of equipment need to have a greater understanding of innovative and resilient farming systems for different agroecologies and the average amount of income farmers can generate out of it, so as to be able to advise the client farmers to choose from a few options available. This calls for interdisciplinary research to generate knowledge for designs of resilient farming systems based on considerations of resource use efficiency, economic viability, and social and environmental sustainability for different agroecologies. For this, they would require a pool of experts who have knowledge of emerging crops and expertise in crop sciences, climate science, water management, agricultural economics and agricultural marketing.

---

weather-related disaster in a particular part of a district may not be eligible to benefit from crop insurance unless the entire district is declared disaster-affected. Finally, there are high administrative costs and, consequently, long delays in making claim payments (TERI, 2005).

10.6.5. Link Subsidies to Efficient Use of Technologies and Resources

The mode of provision of subsidies for the purchase of capital equipment in agriculture followed in the past in many states is that subsidy is paid to the manufacturers for every unit sold. In many situations, this has resulted in farmers procuring the system only to get the subsidy benefits and the manufacturers offering poor-quality products to the farmers, with no aftersales services being offered. The mode of administering subsidy should change in a way that the capital subsidy is paid to the farmers in instalments. This will make sure that the farmers make prudent use of the technology procured using the loan money borrowed from the banks. Many states are struggling hard to introduce metering of electricity in the farm sector, fearing repercussions from the farming lobby. One way to make it easier is to make it mandatory for farmers applying for capital subsidies to have installed electricity meters in their farms to be eligible for government subsidy. Gujarat has already tried this method of introducing metering of agricultural power connections successfully.

10.6.6. Special Incentives to Farming Clusters

The financial institutions including banks and insurance companies need to offer special incentives for promoting a 'cluster-based approach' to farming enterprises in order to make sure that the transaction cost of obtaining input delivery-related services is minimized, post-harvest technology adoption becomes viable and marketing of produce becomes feasible. NITI Aayog's action plan for agriculture also advocated group farming and contract farming in agriculture, with a view to increase the efficiency in input delivery (NITI Aayog, 2017). The financial institutions can directly work with a farmer organization promoted at the cluster level to advance loans for various initiatives. The banks should also be able to mobilize the services of agricultural scientists (soil scientists and crop scientists, horticulturists and post-harvest technology experts), water technologists and marketing experts to the cluster, and this should be part of the financial package. A cluster-based approach enhances knowledge transfer from farmer to farmer and increases the bargaining power of the producers in fixing produce prices, thereby increasing the ability to insulate against the weather- and market-induced shocks. The presence of such institutions would also increase the coping capacity of the farmers to the shocks induced by weather and the market.

10.7. CONCLUSION

The character of farming in India is changing. There is a slow and steady shift towards high-value agriculture, which even the small and marginal farmers will not be able to shy away from, given the economic pressures and the lure of big cash. Many of the investments are becoming long-term (especially for horticultural plantations), and continuous monitoring is required. Along with capital, the extent of knowledge inputs required to make the farming system resilient is increasing, be it about the crops having the least weather risk (Khan et al., 2009) or crops having high profitability or the level of inputs for getting optimum yield or about the marketing of the produce. This is particularly important as the biggest transformation is happening in the semi-arid and arid regions which are water-scarce and also subjected to high climatic variability and extreme weather conditions.

This transition needs to be properly negotiated. Technologies will have a role to play in terms of increasing the farm outputs, enhancing the input use efficiency and to a great extent reducing the production risks, and they come at huge costs which are unavoidable. While the adoption of micro irrigation technologies has already become extensive in the country, there are many new-generation technologies which have to find greater uptake. They include precision farming and technologies for control of the production environment. There are significant market risks in the production of high-value commercial crops which need to be tackled. The approaches for this are institutional in nature and include the following: (a) promoting resilient farming system; (b) adopting a cluster approach; (c) targeting subsidies to areas where they help maximize the social returns; (d) creating marketing infrastructure; and (e) adopting post-harvest technologies.

The banks and insurance companies have a huge role to play in improving the viability of the farming sector in the years to come. Their approach has to be more scientific and also more holistic. The banks need to mature themselves into a resource agency and not just a moneylender. The financial package has to include services of agricultural experts to ensure quality inputs to the growers for sustainable production and marketing and appropriate models for financing. The insurance companies have to be prepared to deal with the complex issues of 'farming risks', which are not very old in their lexicons. Greater coordination is required between banks and insurance companies to create synergies. Following are the interventions from the financial sector to make the recently witnessed growth in the farm sector sustainable and socially viable: (a) assessing the production and market risks; (b) linking farm loans to crop insurance; (c) designing insurance products based on production risk assessment; (d) undertaking research on resilient farming systems; (e) linking subsidies to efficient use of technologies and resources, especially water and energy; and (f) offering special incentives for promotion of farming clusters.

REFERENCES

Amerasinghe, P., Bhardwaj, R. M., Scott, C., Jella, K., & Marshall, F. (2013). *Urban wastewater and agricultural reuse challenges in India* (Vol. 147). International Water Management Institute.

ASSOCHAM (The Associated Chambers of Commerce and Industry of India). (2013). *Press releases: Post-harvest losses*. http://www.assocham.org/prels/shownews.php?id=4132

Choudhury, P. R., & Sindhi, S. (2017). Improving the drought resilience of the small farmer agroecosystem. *Economic & Political Weekly, 52*(32), 41–46.

CWC (Central Water Commission). (2015). *Financial aspects of irrigation projects in India*. Information System Organization, Water Planning and Projects Wing.

GoI (Government of India). (2010). *Ground water quality in shallow aquifers of India*. Central Ground Water Board, Ministry of Water Resources.

GoI (Government of India). (2014). *Annual report (2013–14) on the working of State power utilities & electricity departments*. Power and Energy Division, Planning Commission.

Golait, R. B., & Pradhan, N. C. (2008). Relevance of weather insurance in Indian agriculture. *CAB Calling*, 37–41. http://www.weathersecurepro.com/_content/Research/pdf/Relevance%20of%20Weather%20Insurance%20in%20Indian%20Agriculture.pdf

Khan, S. A., Kumar, S., Hussain, M. Z., & Kalra, N. (2009). Climate change, climate variability and Indian agriculture: Impacts vulnerability and adaptation strategies. In S. N. Singh (Ed.), *Climate change and crops* (pp. 19–38). Springer.

Kumar, M. D. (2016). Water saving and yield enhancing micro irrigation technologies: Theory and practice. In P. K. Viswanathan, M. D. Kumar, & A. Narayanamoorthy (Eds.), *Micro irrigation systems in India: Emergence, status and impacts* (pp. 13–36). Springer.

Kumar, M. D. (2017). *Market analysis: Desalinated water for irrigation and domestic use in India.* Paper prepared for Securing Water for Food: A Grand Challenge for Development in the Center for Development Innovation, U.S. Global Development Lab.

Kumar, M. D. (2018a). Future Water Management: Myths in Indian Agriculture in Biswas, A. K., Tortajada, C., Rohner, P. (Eds) *Assessing Global Water Megatrends,* Springer Water Resources Development and Management Series, Singapore.

Kumar, M. D. (2018b) Input Delivery System in Agriculture Including Irrigation and Other Services and their Efficiency: The Role of Finance Sector. *Indian Journal of Agricultural Economics, 73*(1): 17–37.

Kumar, M. D., Scott, C. A., & Singh, O. P. (2011). Inducing the shift from flat-rate or free agricultural power to metered supply: Implications for groundwater depletion and power sector viability in India. *Journal of Hydrology, 409*(1–2), 382–394.

Kumar, M. D., Singh, O. P., & Sivamohan, M. V. K. (2010). Have diesel price hikes actually led to farmer distress in India? *Water International, 35*(3), 270–284.

Kumar, M. D., & van Dam, J. C. (2013). Drivers of change in agricultural water productivity and its improvement at basin scale in developing economies. *Water International, 38*(3), 312–325.

MoAFW (Ministry of Agriculture and Farmer Welfare). (2016). *Horticulture statistics at a glance 2015.* Oxford University Press.

Molle, F., Mamanpoush, A., & Miranzadeh, M. (2004). *Robbing Yadullah's water to irrigate Saeid's garden: Hydrology and water rights in a village of Central Iran* (Vol. 80). International Water Management Institute.

NITI Aayog. (2017). *India three-year action agenda 2017–18 to 2019–20.*

Rada, N. E. (2013). Agricultural growth in India: Examining the post-green revolution transition. Paper presented at the Agricultural & Applied Economics Association's 2013 AAEA & CAES Joint Annual Meeting, Washington DC.

TERI (The Energy and Resources Institute). (2005). *Insuring climate risk in India: Are we prepared?*

Xie, Z. K., Wang, Y. J., & Li, F. M. (2005). Effect of plastic mulching on soil water use and spring wheat yield in arid region of northwest China. *Agricultural Water Management, 75*(1), 71–83.

Chapter 11

Future Growth in Indian Agriculture

M. Dinesh Kumar, M. V. K. Sivamohan, Nitin Bassi and V. Niranjan

11.1. INTRODUCTION

While the government continues to make huge investments in irrigation-related infrastructure, of late, there has been an overemphasis on augmentation of groundwater resources and conservation of water in small water bodies, with a consequent focus on decentralized water harvesting and local groundwater recharge, in schemes such as National Rural Employment Guarantee Act (NREGA; Bassi & Kumar, 2010). But there are no long-term strategies for supporting large-scale irrigation development or promoting productivity in agriculture insight.

While small water harvesting structures would no doubt provide reliable local water supplies in high rainfall areas, in most parts of India, this would not make much hydrological sense and sound economic proposition (Kumar, Patel et al., 2008). As a result, many negative impacts are observed, particularly on the agricultural front, distorting labour markets (Bassi & Kumar, 2010). Added to this, the policies governing the use of water in agriculture are degenerative, driven by political considerations, and promote inequity in accessibility and inefficient use of water. They defeat the very goal of sustainable agricultural production.

In this chapter, we would examine the effectiveness of current policies and programmes of the government for agricultural growth. For this, an analysis of the performance of the agriculture sector in recent times and scientific evidence available from recent research on the topic in India are taken into account. In the subsequent section, long-term strategies for improving the sustainability of agricultural production which involve physical strategies for improving the supply of water for irrigation and improving the efficiency of use of water in agriculture for both water-abundant and water-scarce regions are discussed. This is followed by a discussion on the institutional and policy measures for promoting efficiency, equity and sustainability in water use and water demand management in agriculture.

11.2. RECENT STRATEGIES FOR AGRICULTURAL GROWTH AND FOOD SECURITY

The Eleventh Plan strategy of inclusive growth rests upon a substantial increase in the plan allocation for agriculture, and irrigation and water management. While the allocation for agriculture and the allied sectors (at 2006–2007 prices) was ₹54,801 crore (US$1 equals ₹50), for irrigation and water management, it was ₹3,246 crore. Since irrigation is a state subject, there was a major contribution from state plan allocations to the tune of ₹182,050 crore. In addition, the contribution from schemes such as Accelerated Irrigation Benefits Programme stood at ₹47,015 crore (GoI, 2008, pp. 42–62). Hence, the total plan allocation for irrigation was ₹232,311 crore. This was far higher than the allocations during the Tenth Plan period for irrigation and flood control, which was only ₹84,692 crore. Similarly, in agriculture and allied sectors, the plan expenditure was only ₹19,175 crore (GoI, 2008).

But in spite of the substantial increase in plan allocation for agriculture and irrigation, agricultural growth rates have not shown any encouraging trend. While the growth rate in sectoral GDP was 2.47 per cent during the Tenth Plan period (GoI, 2008, Table 1.1, p. 4), during the first two years of the Eleventh Plan period, the average growth rate was only 3 per cent. This was in spite of the fact that there had been a threefold increase in plan allocation. There are two important reasons for this. First, while irrigation is the key to boosting agricultural growth in India, the overall progress in public (surface) irrigation development is poor, owing to cost and time overruns in project completion, which results in a very high capital cost of bringing one hectare of cultivable area under irrigation. Second, while some additional irrigation is achieved through the new schemes, there is a gradual decline in the performance of old schemes due to dwindling of reservoir capacity and lack of proper un-keep of water distribution and delivery infrastructure, which offset the gains. As pointed out in the second chapter of this book, the other reasons could be increased diversion of water from surface reservoirs for urban domestic uses and reduced flows into reservoirs due to intensive water harvesting and watershed development in the upper catchment areas.

Ever since 2007–2008, there has been substantial investment under the National Rural Employment Guarantee Scheme (NREGS), when it was first implemented in all districts of the country. On average, the government allocates around US$5.5– US$6 billion (₹40,000– ₹45,000 crore) every year for this scheme. The activities being undertaken under NREGA are: drought proofing (afforestation and tree plantation); water conservation and water harvesting; construction and cleaning of minor irrigation canals; renovation of water bodies; flood control and protection works including embankments; and land development and creation of irrigation facility for poor Scheduled Caste and Scheduled Tribe households. Although started as a social welfare scheme aimed at rural employment generation, with many components purely on water management, it is promoted as a strategic intervention for agricultural growth in rainfed areas (Kumar et al., 2012).

Barring the construction of roads, a large chunk of the infrastructure created under NREGS directly affects the rural water sector (Bassi & Kumar, 2010) and, therefore, agriculture and allied activities. However, planning of this work, done in a decentralized format, does not have considerations of hydrology, geo-hydrology, topography and agro-climate of the localities concerned (NCAER & PIF, 2009) and cost-effectiveness (Kumar & Bassi, 2011). A major proportion of the funds is spent on road building in areas which are most suitable for watershed development (Ambasta et al., 2008). Recharge structures are built in hard rock areas without considering the geological and geo-hydrological features, which heavily influence the performance of such structures (Bassi & Kumar, 2010). Tree plantation is taken up in semi-arid and arid low-rainfall areas (Tiwari et al., 2011) without much attention being paid to the availability of water for providing protective irrigation. The cost per cubic metre of water for these structures is not worked out and compared against that for other options.

The analysis shows that the NREGA interventions cause more negative welfare effects than positive ones, the most important among them being an artificial scarcity of agricultural wage labour and unprecedented increase in wage rates (Bassi & Kumar, 2010; Panagariya, 2009). As noted by Bassi and Kumar (2010), in naturally water-scarce basins, indiscriminate construction of water conservation structures such as ponds and check dams and desilting of existing village water bodies are causing negative impacts on the overall water economy as a result of reduced inflows into downstream reservoirs, meant for irrigation, domestic and industrial purposes. The water harvesting structures built in these regions are cost-ineffective owing to low annual rainfalls, high inter-annual variability which causes disproportionately higher variability in run-off, high potential evaporation, low infiltration rates and poor groundwater storage potential (Kumar, Patel et al., 2008). The land-based NREGA interventions lack proper scientific planning based on hydrological considerations and technical supervision of the work execution impacting on their overall effectiveness (Bassi & Kumar, 2010).

In the recent past, micro irrigation has also received great attention from India's Union Ministry of Agriculture (Ministry of Agriculture & Farmers Welfare) under the Pradhan Mantri Krishi Sinchayee Yojana (PMKSY) as a technology to achieve more 'crop per drop' of water and boost agricultural production. Accordingly, the budgetary allocation to cover the capital subsidies for micro irrigation has also increased. Although the area under micro irrigation systems, especially drip systems, had increased substantially—with their extensive adoption for many high-value fruits and vegetables and other cash crops, namely sugarcane, cotton, potato, castor and groundnut—to touch around

3.15 Mha by 2016–2017,[1] there was hardly any analysis done to assess its actual impact on agricultural water productivity at the macro level. Intuitively, with no marginal cost of using water and electricity in most situations, it is quite unlikely that the adoption of these technologies alone would always ensure improved water use efficiency and water saving, as reduced water and energy use would not lead to input cost saving for the farmers.

That said, the real source of the agricultural growth in recent years is not food grain crops, but the high-valued fruits, vegetables, milk and fish. Over the years, the contribution of these high-valued crops to the agricultural output in value terms has been increasing with an increase in the production of fruits, vegetables, milk and fish (Nandakumar et al., 2010; Rada, 2013). In fact, the per capita availability of food grain over the triennium has been on the decline since 1990. It declined from 172.5 kg per year in 1990 to 159.2 kg per year in 2008 (provisional). Against this, the per capita availability of milk, egg, fish, fruits and vegetables has been increasing over the years. Some scholars argue that the food security issue is not so much about the availability (physical access) of food grains but about access. However, subsequent analysis would show that this is not true. For instance, one of the arguments put forth by the scholars to discard the food availability argument is the changing consumption pattern, with increasing preference for animal products (chicken, egg and milk), fruits and vegetables (see, for instance, Nandakumar et al., 2010). While it is expected that such changes in consumption pattern would reduce the pressure on cereals for direct consumption, it would prove to be costly if one ignores the fact that even increased production of egg, milk, poultry and inland fish would require a large quantum of cereals in the form of animal and poultry feed (Amarasinghe et al., 2007). This would place an additional burden on cereals, whose production is already threatened. This accelerating rise in the price of cereals would mainly impact the poorer sections of the society.

Food security of hundreds of millions of poor people would be at risk if we do not increase the per capita production of cereals in

---

[1] https://pmksy.gov.in/microirrigation/AtGlance.aspx

proportion to the growing population. To enhance the production of food grains at the national level, the regions that are land-rich but experiencing water scarcity and groundwater depletion would require more water from exogenous sources. On the other hand, with increasing farmer preference to allocate more area for high-value horticultural crops and spices in these water-scarce regions, it is important that the water use efficiency is improved substantially in crops and areas in which such improvements are technically feasible so as to keep sufficient water for growing food grains to address food security concerns and high-value cash crops to meet the growing demands of the market. Also, the issues of growing inequity in access to water, especially groundwater in certain regions (including groundwater abundant eastern India), need to be addressed. Merely introducing micro irrigation technologies will not result in water use efficiency improvements, leave alone water reallocation from one farm to another and water demand management in agriculture. Affecting such changes would require institutional and policy reforms for the allocation and efficiency of water (Gulati et al., 2020).

11.3. PHYSICAL STRATEGIES FOR SUSTAINABLE AGRICULTURAL PRODUCTION AND FOOD SECURITY

The strategy should include improvement in productivity in the use of the scarce resource and an effective increase in the availability of utilizable water for irrigation. But water-abundant regions have very little arable land which can be brought under irrigated production and are dependent on food import from land-rich, water-scarce regions, which maintain high levels of productivity.

Hence, the future irrigation development in India lies in the appropriation of surface water in the water-abundant basins and its export to and use in water-scarce river basins which are endowed with sufficient amounts of arable land. This would help boost agricultural production, along with improving the sustainability of groundwater use. But this will not be possible everywhere due to topographical and engineering limitations. In water-scarce regions, the emphasis should be placed on improving water productivity in agriculture. Hence, the focus should be on economic instruments such as water and energy pricing. But too much reliance on this will also have its problems such as excessive preference for high-valued crops which use less water, with long-term negative consequences for cereal production. In the long run, large-scale water imports would be required in the semi-arid and arid regions, which are agriculturally prosperous, for saving these regions from droughts and sustain irrigated agriculture. In water-abundant regions, policies and programmes should be designed to encourage more intensive use of water.

11.3.1. Technologies to Change the Trajectory of Irrigation Development

11.3.1.1. Manually Operated Pumps and Micro Diesel Engines in Water-abundant Regions

Several regions have abundant groundwater supplies such as Assam, parts of Bihar, Odisha, West Bengal and Jharkhand (CGWB, 2017). These regions accommodate the largest number of poor people in the country (Shah et al., 2000). The groundwater resources in these regions largely remain underutilized in spite of the fact that public irrigation facilities are very poor (CGWB, 2017). As a result of the conventional (energized) water abstraction structures and mechanisms prevalent, the trajectory of development of groundwater resources in the region is likely to be very low.[2] In order to spur the development process, these regions need simple technologies which involve very little capital investment and which can absorb the surplus labour force. The region can thus promote equity in access to groundwater for irrigation while increasing its utilization. For the poor, small and marginal farmers, who are exploited by the rich for irrigation water (Kumar, 2007), this would provide relief. Although expansion in irrigation through the manual pump is not expected to be significant, a remarkable achievement would be in the provision of water security for millions of marginalized farmers.

---

[2] Due to extremely low rural electrification and high cost of fuel to run diesel engines.

A treadle pump, a manually operated pump, requires very low capital investments while being much more energy efficient than traditional water lifting devices such as *Denkul* and *Shena*. The pump, with costs in the range of ₹1,000– ₹1,400, is highly suitable for millions of poor farmers in the region who have tiny holdings. It can provide them the water security essential for their livelihoods. In eastern India, the adoption of treadle pumps leads to expansion in irrigated area, cropping intensities, enhanced crop output and yield, and a significant rise in income through farming while farmers move from subsistence agriculture to wealth-creating irrigated farming practices (Kumar, 2000b; Shah et al., 2000).

Studies conducted in Odisha also throw enough hard empirical evidence to show that pump adopter households enjoy greater food and nutritional security. Treadle pump irrigation ensures increased output from irrigated crops, more importantly, vegetables. The surplus production sold in the market fetches cash income. Other essential commodities are purchased using the surplus cash (Kumar, 2000b). Another aspect of household food security is the nutritional value of the food consumed. Study find that the introduction of treadle pump has directly contributed to growth in vegetable production from farms.

In addition to treadle pumps, effective rural electrification, easy access of farmers to farm power connections and availability of credit facilities/subsidy for purchase of pump sets would improve the access of small and marginal farmers to groundwater irrigation through two different routes: (a) Increase in the number of pump owners would reduce the monopoly power of pump owners, who otherwise charge exorbitant hourly rates for irrigation (Kumar, 2007). (b) Instead of purchasing water, more farmers would opt for power connections and electrification of their shallow wells, making groundwater irrigation cheap for a larger constituency of farmers.

Recently, some arguments are put forward that three factors have created conditions unfavourable for increased adoption of treadle pumps. They are increased employment opportunities in rural areas, especially after the launching of NREGA; subsequent increase in wage rates for labourers; and increased availability of Chinese micro diesel engines in eastern Indian states. While several treadle pump owners have shifted to diesel engines in the recent past, it is going to be a temporary phenomenon. In fact, the increasing fuel prices would once again attract the small and marginal farmers towards the treadle pumps. Another reason to opt for treadle pumps would be the rising prices of vegetables and the large increase in the small urban centres in the country. Research amply shows that even in the traditional paddy growing areas, the treadle pump owners grow high-valued vegetables and root crops and transport and sell them in the nearest towns, maximizing the returns from the labour and other inputs they use. The foregoing analyses suggest that treadle pump irrigation would be highly profitable for households which have very small holdings and surplus labour.

11.3.2. Technologies for Water Productivity Improvement

So far as harnessing more and more water from the natural systems is concerned, technologies described above have their limitations. The other option available to enhance food production is to improve the efficiency of use of water (Kijne et al., 2003; Kumar, 2010). Worldwide, micro irrigation technologies are promoted to save water and get increased efficiency of water use in agriculture (Postel, 1992; Postel et al., 2001). There are several technologies which help farmers save irrigation water (Kumar, Turral et al., 2008). While micro irrigation systems have seen a relatively rapid adoption rate over the past one decade in India, the overall adoption level is still quite low. Drip and sprinkler irrigation systems cover less than 6 per cent of the global irrigated area, and in the case of India, they cover 3.88 Mha, with 1.46 Mha under drips and 2.42 Mha under sprinklers.

But these technologies have great bias. To enable farmers to take full advantage of them in terms of water saving, they should install them in large fields. However, in areas (states) where power pricing is dependent on the pump horsepower, both the capital cost of the pumping per unit area and the operating cost per unit area will be higher for resource-poor farmers who adopt the system for smaller areas. The farmers who adopt the system for larger areas can reduce the cost per unit area significantly (Kumar, 2003, 2009). These systems involve high capital investments. Further, installing these systems for small fields would increase the cost per unit area. Further, the maintenance requirements for these irrigation systems are very high. The drip system, which is the most water efficient of these technologies, is most suitable for horticultural plantations for cost effectiveness. Thus, they are best suited to resource-rich, large farmers, who can spare part of their land for horticultural crops and can wait for three–four years for returns. Another important issue involved in the adoption of pressurized irrigation systems is the lack of economic incentives. In many Indian states, where depletion problems are encountered and groundwater resources are abundant, only power supply is limiting the farmers' access to groundwater. Examples are the alluvial areas of North Gujarat, Punjab, western Uttar Pradesh and Haryana. In these situations, groundwater supply potential is higher than what the available power supply could deliver (Kumar, 2009; Kumar, Turral et al., 2008).

The large static storage of the aquifers permits the farmers to keep pumping water, even though it causes excessive drawdown. Following are the reasons. First, either cost of electricity for pumping unit volume of water is extremely low or the marginal cost of energy for pumping is negligible. Second, there are no limits on the volumetric pumping by well owners, and no payment is required for the water (Kumar, 2003, 2009). Since pressurized irrigation systems need extra power to run, the well output could drop with the installation of the system. As the farmer is already utilizing the power supply fully, the total water output from the well would drop. Thus, the farmer will not be able to capitalize on the benefit accruing from water saving in the form of increased area under irrigation. Hence, the only economic opportunity available with pressurized irrigation technologies is yield increase. However, the ability to secure higher yields through water-saving devices depends heavily on management practices, including agronomic practices (Kumar, 2003).

The situation would be vastly different in hard rock areas facing depletion problems. Currently, farmers are not able to utilize the power supply fully due to a shortage of water in wells in these areas. In such situations, pressurized irrigation systems could benefit the farmers by enabling them to run the pump for longer hours, maintain the same level of total well output and irrigate a larger area. Water-saving technologies to suit the requirements of many millions of the poor, small and marginal farmers do exist in the country. They are the mini sprinkler systems and micro tube drip systems (Kumar, 2003, 2009).

One important factor which limits the adoption of micro irrigation technologies is the small-sized fields (Kumar, 2009). Micro irrigation systems are most suited to fruit crops, vegetables, tubers and flowers. The area under these crops is limited in India, with fruits accounting for 6.506 Mha, vegetables 10.259 Mha, flowers 0.324 M ha and plantation crops 3.744 Mha (MoAFW, 2018, pp. 9–11). But the water-saving impact of micro irrigation systems depends on a variety of factors, namely crops, type of micro irrigation technology, soil type, climate and geo-hydrology. Water saving is likely to be more in the case of widely spaced crops, under sandy soils and semi-arid to arid climate, with deep groundwater table, with drip or trickle irrigation (Kumar, 2009; Kumar, Turral et al., 2008). We need to keep in mind the fact that a large proportion of the area under fruit crops and plantation crops is located in water-abundant areas where farmers are unlikely to adopt micro irrigation systems. It cannot be assumed that micro irrigation system adoption for any of these crops would result in water-saving benefit, irrespective of the technology used, and soil type, climate and geo-hydrology of the area in which they are grown.

Going by this argument, the (real) water saving from micro irrigation systems should be relatively high in naturally water-scarce regions and low in naturally water-rich regions, characterized by high rainfall, humidity and shallow groundwater table conditions. It is already pointed out that naturally water-scarce regions also experience physical scarcity of water, and because of this correlation, the social benefit accrued from water saving would be very high in naturally water-scarce regions. As Kumar, Turral et al. (2008) argue, these are the regions where micro irrigation systems need to be subsidized.

Central funds allocated for subsidizing micro irrigation systems are very meagre in comparison to what is required to boost micro irrigation adoption in the country. A significant portion of the funds that are utilized for NGREA in naturally water-scarce regions, particularly the water conservation and drought-proofing activities, should be reallocated for subsidizing micro irrigation systems to have a significant impact on water use efficiency in crop production and overall agricultural productivity.

11.3.3. Transfer of Water from Abundant to Scarce Regions

One of the new sources for growth in aggregate demand for water in the country is the increasing need for meeting ecological water demands in river basins. While agricultural water demand management would remain the prime concern of future water demand management in India, this alone will not solve the growing water-scarcity problems in many river basins to produce food. The reasons are many, the most important being the limited potential of micro irrigation technology. While micro irrigation technologies are best amenable to high-valued fruits, vegetables and roots, the area under these crops cannot be expanded beyond a limit, as it would curtain the area under food crops. The total (real) water-saving possible through micro irrigation systems for five major crops which are amenable to micro irrigation systems would be 44.5 billion cubic metres at the current cropping pattern (Kumar, Turral et al., 2008), whereas the gap between water demand from various competitive use sectors and supplies would be 208 billion cubic metres. The scope for a major shift in cropping patterns to low water-intensive and highly water-efficient crops is extremely limited due to food security concerns (Kumar et al., 2012; Kumar and van Dam, 2013).

In order to meet the deficit, physical transfer of surface water from water-rich regions to water-scarce regions would be crucial. There are two major gains from physical water transfer. First, there would be a significant increase in utilizable fresh water resources, as the naturally water-rich regions of eastern India are short of arable land where the surplus water could be utilized for agricultural production. The naturally water-rich regions are net importers of food from agriculturally prosperous water-scarce regions. An increase in the area under irrigated crop production in the water-importing regions would lead to greater agricultural surplus, increasing farmers' ability to export food to the water-rich regions (Kumar & Singh, 2005). Second, the economic value of water use in agriculture is higher in water-scarce regions than in water-rich. Hence, incremental value is realized through physical transfer of water (Kumar, Malla et al., 2008).

There are other benefits of physical water transfer for irrigation. As seen in the case of the Sardar Sarovar Project, gravity irrigation using the imported water in the water-scarce regions led to increased recharge of groundwater through irrigation return flows. This improved the sustainability of well irrigation in the regions which were facing problems of overdraft. The reduced pressure on groundwater owing to an alternate source of water for irrigation further improved the groundwater balance. A rise in water levels would also reduce the economic cost of energy for groundwater pumping in irrigation. The positive externalities of gravity irrigation were estimated to be quite substantial (see Jagadeesan & Kumar, 2015).

There are many regions in India which are agriculturally prosperous but facing an acute shortage of water for agricultural production. They are: (a) western India, comprising the western part of Rajasthan, North and Central Gujarat, Saurashtra and Kachchh; (b) western part of Central India including parts of Madhya Pradesh and Maharashtra; and (c) most parts of southern Indian peninsula, covering almost the entire Andhra Pradesh except the coastal areas, most parts of Karnataka barring the Western Ghat region, and almost the entire Tamil Nadu. They are located in water-scarce river basins.[3] The current water utilization scenario in the basins encompassing these regions shows that the future of agriculture could be in great jeopardy if additional water resources are not provided to them. The main reason for this is that groundwater resources, which were the backbone of the agricultural economy in these regions, have been depleting alarmingly (Kumar, 2007).

Data from Andhra Pradesh indicate that well irrigation has started showing declining trends in the hard rock areas. The contribution of open wells, which used to be an important source of irrigation to the state's irrigated area, started declining since the early 1990s with a steep

---

[3] The only exception is the Godavari river basin, passing through Maharashtra and Andhra Pradesh, which is water-abundant.

drop after the late 1990s. On the whole, there has been hardly any increase in the net and gross area irrigated by wells in Andhra Pradesh since 2004–2005. Such alarming trends are showing up in many hard rock areas in India. It appears that the only way to sustain well irrigation in these regions is through the import of surface water, as the social consequences of groundwater depletion will be very severe. Depletion of groundwater puts the livelihoods of millions of poor farm households from these regions at risk. Rural–urban migration and increasing indebtedness of farmers are some of the immediate consequences. It is quite noteworthy that the regions with high rates of farmer suicides coincide with those having problems of groundwater mining and rampant well failures. Sustaining well irrigation would therefore be essential in maintaining the social fabric of the rural areas (Kumar et al., 2012).

Transferring water to these regions from water-abundant basins through inter-basin water transfers requires complex engineering solutions, in addition to addressing more complex social, economic, financial, legal and ecological questions involved in interregional bulk water transfers. Ecologists and environmentalists have already raised alarm signals about a possible 'ecological disaster' in the donor basins in the wake of water transfers from water-rich basins of eastern India (Ganges and Brahmaputra) to water-scarce basins in the west and the south. The other stakeholders of such interventions are the states which have to part with their water resources, and the issues involved here are of political nature. The political parties and governments in the concerned states try to take mileage out of the decisions emerging in favour or against them. As the basins are interstate and international, there are issues of livelihoods of millions of people living in the lower riparian states and countries.

Theoretically and also practically, what can hasten the decisions to engage in water transfers is the fact that the opportunity cost of not undertaking such projects would be prohibitive. The social benefits which are likely to accrue from them, if executed, would be enormous for the transformation of the countryside. But from a political economy perspective, the pressure for large-scale water transfers in the future would spring from the urban areas. The metros located in naturally water-scarce regions are dependent on water imported from far-off reservoirs for meeting lion's share of their water requirements. Today, the real urban growth is happening in water-scarce western, north-western and southern regions, comprising cities such as Delhi, Jaipur, Ahmedabad, Indore, Nagpur, Rajkot, Hyderabad, Pune, Bengaluru, Vijayawada and Chennai and hundreds of other fast-growing towns/ cities. By virtue of being the engines of growth, the socially and politically influential urban areas are likely to put great pressure on the state and federal governments to provide water for their needs. The dire need for providing water to the influential metros would ultimately help manage the politics involved in water transfer projects (Kumar et al., 2012).

Once this becomes socially and politically feasible, the next challenge would be to ensure that water is stored and used optimally. While it is evident that importing water from a large distance is going to be a costly affair, making such projects economically viable requires that water is put to the most efficient use from an economic perspective. In other words, the productivity of use of water has to be very high. Water control would be the most critical element in determining the productivity of the precious water.

11.3.3.1. Groundwater Banking and (Intermediate) Tank Storage

Gravity irrigation has several limitations due to inadequate control over water under this method. Due to the poor reliability of water supply and lack of proper control over water delivery, canal commands generally favour water-intensive crops such as paddy, banana and sugarcane, which are not highly sensitive to excessive watering. But these crops have low water use efficiency in economic terms (rupee per cubic metre). Therefore, alternatives to gravity irrigation are required when the cost of importing surface water for irrigation becomes prohibitively expensive. 'Groundwater banking' is a viable option for effectively increasing water availability in areas where sufficient aquifer storage space is available (Contor, 2009; Hostetler, n.d.).[4] Groundwater banking

---

[4] It is a process by which surplus run-off or surface water during times of surplus is stored in aquifers for use in times of shortage. Water can also be overdrawn with the understanding that it would be replenished later (Hostetler, n.d.).

here refers to intentional infiltration of surface water and incidental recharge from irrigated crop land. This can become a good strategy in north-western and western India, as the overexploited alluvial aquifers in these areas would provide storage space for the imported water. In the south, since the hard rock aquifers have limited storage potential, the infrastructure, which transfers water in bulk from the eastern basins, has to be integrated with hundreds of thousands of small and large water bodies spread all over the three states of the southern peninsula, namely Andhra Pradesh, Karnataka and Tamil Nadu.

Since conventional artificial recharge structures would be highly expensive, the cultivated land could be used as an infiltration basin in the alluvial areas by transferring the flood water during monsoon to the land covered by the standing kharif crops for incidental recharge.

When the recharge basin is large, with soils having good hydraulic conductivity, the recharging process would be effective during the rainy season (Watt, 2008). Also, this would not involve additional costs. The natural recharge from rainfall in the region plus the additional recharge from irrigation return flows would give sufficient water for irrigating winter crops. Groundwater irrigation also encourages the use of efficient irrigation technologies, which gravity irrigation is not amenable to. In the south, less water would be required to be put into the hard rock aquifers through the mechanism explained above, as most water could be stored in the tanks. Since most of the tanks do not receive adequate natural inflows from their catchments, as indicated by their poor performance, storage space will not be a problem in most years (Kumar et al., 2012).

11.3.4. Water Harvesting in the Hills

There are regions that are naturally water-rich (receiving excessively high rainfall and are cold and humid) yet face shortages of water to meet domestic and irrigation needs for short time periods. They include parts of Western Ghats and the hilly and mountainous areas of the northeast comprising seven hill states. In spite of the catchments in these regions having excessively high run-off rates (CWC, 2017), water shortage occurs due to inadequate infrastructure to store water to meet the demands during the lean season when the water demands peak and the natural availability sharply reduces. Since groundwater potential in the hilly tracts of these regions is extremely low due to the consolidated formations (CGWB, 2017), communities in these regions have to depend on streams and springs for meeting domestic and agricultural needs. However, the flows in these streams are highly variable, with a lion's share of it occurring during the monsoon and winter months. The plantation and horticultural crops (mainly fruit crops such as orange, banana, kiwi, mango, dragon fruit, citrus, areca nut and coconut) of these regions face water shortage during the two months of April and May as evapo-transpirative demand goes up. Due to water stress, though experienced for a short duration, the yield of these crops suffers. Small dams can be built in these regions for storing the flows during the high flow season in locations where good strata are available for foundation and can be lifted or transported down through gravity pipes for irrigating plantation crops and fruit trees depending on the location of the plots. Springer and drip irrigation can be introduced for irrigating these high-value crops, as these micro irrigation systems are amenable to these crops (Kumar, Turral et al., 2008).

11.4. INSTITUTIONAL CHANGES FOR CHANGING THE TRAJECTORY OF WATER USE IN AGRICULTURE

11.4.1. Promoting Equity and Productivity in Water Use

The growing competition and concomitant conflicts between different sectors are major issues that need to be addressed in water allocation. The fundamental challenges are promotion of economically efficient uses while adequately compensating the agriculturists for the losses they suffer due to transfer of water for other efficient use sectors and equitable access to water from canals and groundwater within the agriculture sector (Kumar, 2010). Saleth and Dinar (1999) point out that concerns in the water sector, which once revolved around water development (and quantity), now revolve around water allocation. Markets and regulations can be sought as instruments for water allocation (Rosegrant & Binswanger, 1994; Rosegrant & Gazmuri, 1995). But both markets and regulatory approaches are likely to fall short of satisfying all these criteria for efficient and effective water allocation (Frederick, 1993). The enormous geographic and temporal diversity in water supply and demand situations suggest that no single institutional arrangement is likely to be preferred in all instances (Frederick, 1993). While Howe et al. (1986) have argued that markets meet all the criteria for effective water allocation better than any likely alternative, this is not true for Indian situations (Kumar, 2003).

The absence of well-defined property rights regimes is a major source of uncertainty about the negative environmental impacts of resource use, leading to inefficient and sustainable use (Kay et al., 1997). This has been evident in the case of both groundwater and canal water supplied for irrigation. In the Indian context, many researchers in the recent past have suggested the establishment of property rights as a means to build institutional capacity to ensure equity in allocation and efficiency in the use of water across sectors (Kumar, 2000a). But if the rights are allocated only to use water, it can create incentives to use it even when there is no good use of it (Frederick, 1993). Therefore, water rights have to be tradable (IRMA & UNICEF, 2001; Kumar & Singh, 2001). Establishing privately owned property rights which are tradable is critical to establishing conditions under which individuals will have opportunities and incentives to develop and use the resource efficiently or transfer it to more efficient uses (Frederick, 1993; Rosegrant & Binswanger, 1994; Rosegrant & Gazmuri, 1995).

Empirical evidence collected on the functioning of groundwater irrigation institutions in North Gujarat show that under a system of fixed volumetric water use rights, farmers prefer to grow highly water-efficient crops (Kumar, 2005, 2010). Tradable private property rights need to be enforced for groundwater and water supplied from public reservoirs for irrigation. In the case of groundwater and canal water supplied for irrigation, as individuals enjoy access to the resource, private property rights for individual users are envisioned.

Fixing norms for allocation of volumetric water rights across individual sectors, namely agriculture, industry and domestic front, should involve considerations such as physical sustainability of the water resource system and environmental sustainability. The total water allocated from any region/basin, therefore, should not exceed the difference between annual renewable freshwater and the ecological demand, or the utilizable freshwater, whichever is less. Going by such norms, the regions where water resources are abundant by nature such as the eastern part of Uttar Pradesh, Bihar, Odisha and West Bengal, the volumetric water rights of individual sectors and users, especially farmers, would be very high. In these regions, land availability would continue to be an important factor in deciding returns from agriculture (Kumar, 2003). The farmers will, therefore, have to choose crops which are more water-intensive and which would encourage intensive use of the same piece of land. In states like Bihar and Uttar Pradesh, water rights would not mean much for a large number of cultivators who have marginal holdings or no land.

In such situations, the allocation norms in agriculture need to be carefully designed, if equal opportunities are to be given to all types of cultivators to improve their own farm economies. In water allocation, the food security needs of the families could be given priority, rather than the farm size. This will result in a disproportionate allocation of rights in favour of small and marginal farmers. This can induce inter-locked land, pump and water markets, wherein the rich, well-owning farmers will offer pump services to farmers who do not have their own irrigation sources and can, in return, use a portion of their water rights. This will force the rich well owners to charge less for the pump irrigation services they provide, thereby promoting greater equity in access to groundwater in these regions. They may also enter into sharecropping arrangements with landless farmers. A good economic opportunity lies for landless, small and marginal farmers in transferring water in bulk to water-scarce regions, or cities and industrial areas, which are concentrated points of large demands for water, as they are likely to have excess water. Physical conditions for transfer of water from rich areas to water-scarce areas exist in many regions (Kumar, 2003; Kumar & Singh, 2001).

While the physical allocation of water rights for surface water from public systems would be technically possible, there are legal, institutional and technology challenges which need to be overcome for establishing and enforcing property rights system for groundwater, given the invisible nature of the resource, the pattern of its use and the legal status vis-à-vis ownership of the resource. The proposed water rights system, if designed to address concerns of the current inequity in access to the resource, can rebalance access. With many millions of farmers in remote rural areas accessing groundwater, monitoring volumetric resource use by individual farmers required for tracking water allocations, however, would require new institutions with the associated transaction costs (Kumar, 2018).

The process of establishing water rights[5] and restricting water use by farmers is feasible in areas where farmers use electricity supplied by the state electricity utility, as the energy consumption is used as proxy for groundwater abstraction. Restricting farmers' energy use for pumping groundwater is analogous to rationing groundwater withdrawal for irrigation volumetrically, and hence energy rationing can be equivalent to a functional water rights system. This can be done through prepaid electricity meters as previously described. As shown by Kumar (2005) through a comparative analysis of well owners who are confronted with zero marginal cost of using electricity and water and farmers who have fixed water entitlements, farmers would allocate a greater proportion of the available water to economically more efficient crops besides improving the physical efficiency of water use when confronted with volumetric water rationing. Restricting energy use will have a positive impact on the efficiency of groundwater use by all categories of farmers. More importantly, it will help achieve sustainable groundwater use, if the energy quota is fixed by taking into account the sustainable yield of the aquifer. In such cases, it is important that the consumers are informed about their energy quota and the approximate number of hours for which they could pump water from their wells well in advance of the agricultural season. Such information helps them choose the crops depending on the availability of power (and hence water) over the cropping season(s) of the year. Here again, the energy quota will have to be decided on the basis of the geo-hydrological environment prevailing in the area and the lower optimum irrigation requirements (Kumar, 2018).

---

[5] These are not absolute ownership rights over water but rights to use water defined in volumetric terms and can also be called 'water entitlement' or 'quota'.

However, there are governance challenges in implementing this idea. First, the utility has to frame rules/norms regarding the allocation of energy quota among the farmers, which will have to be based on groundwater rights/entitlements. The decision on these entitlements should use sound criteria based on principles of access equity and resource sustainability. Framing such rules can be politically sensitive because the decisions would ideally result in the allocation of water rights/entitlements to many farmers who currently do not enjoy direct access to groundwater and limits to the use of groundwater by many large and medium farmers. Politicians and bureaucrats are generally averse to taking decisions, which have potentially large social ramifications (Kumar, 2018).

11.4.2. Encouraging Efficient Use of Water in Agriculture

11.4.2.1. Pricing of Irrigation Water

In spite of the recommendations of the Second Irrigation Commission, state irrigation bureaucracies have failed to raise water charges which make economic sense due to the potential social and political ramifications (MoIP, 1972). The failure has its roots in the absence of institutional capability to improve the quality of irrigation services and correctly monitor the water use, lack of institutional arrangements at the lowest level to recover water charges from individual farmers, and enforced penalties on free riders (Kumar, 2010). A few successes have been seen in areas where the Participatory Irrigation Management (PIM) programme was implemented, where farmers have shown the willingness to pay more for the irrigation services to the Water User Associations (Gandhi et al., 2020; Kumar, 2010).

The recent past has shown significant debates over the usefulness of irrigation water pricing as a way to regulate water demand, with some arguing for (Tsur & Dinar, 1995) and some others arguing against pointing out shortcomings at both theoretical and practical levels (Perry, 2001). There are three major and important contentions of those who argue against pricing: (a) They question the logic in the proposition that 'if the marginal costs are nil, farmers would be encouraged to use large quantities of water before its marginal productivity becomes zero, consuming much more than the accepted standards and needs' (Molle & Turral, 2004). (b) The demand for irrigation water is inelastic to low prices, and the tariff levels at which the demand becomes elastic to price changes would be so high that it becomes socially and politically unviable to introduce (Perry, 2001). (c) There are no reasons for farmers to use too much water, which can cause overirrigation (Molle & Turral, 2004).

However, as noted by Kumar (2010), these arguments have weaknesses. What is the most important issue is in linking irrigation charges and demand for water (see Perry, 2001). Merely raising water tariffs without improving the quality and reliability of irrigation will not only make little economic sense but would also find few takers. As returns from irrigated crops are more elastic to the quality of irrigation than its price (Kumar & Singh, 2001), poor quality of irrigation increases farmers' resistance to pay for irrigation services they receive. Therefore, the 'water diverted' by farmers in their fields does not reflect the actual demand for water in a true economic sense, so long as they do not pay for it. In other words, the impact of tariff changes on irrigation water demand can be analysed only when the water use is monitored and farmers are made to pay for the water on a volumetric basis. The above arguments also lead us to the conclusion that the rates for canal water can be increased to substantially higher levels, provided the quality of irrigation water is enhanced.

But water pricing for irrigation can impact poor farmers adversely, if pitched at higher levels (Frederick, 1993). One of the ways to reduce the negative impacts on access equity is to introduce a progressive pricing system. An appropriate pricing structure for water followed by clearly recognized private property rights and good-quality irrigation service could help achieve the desired effect of pricing changes on demand management. It also means that if positive marginal prices are followed by improved quality, the actual (aggregate) demand for irrigation water might go up depending on the availability of land and alternative crops that give a higher return per unit of land. This is because the tendency of the farmers would be to increase the volume of water used to maintain or raise the net income (Kumar & Singh,

2001). Hence, water rationing is important to affect demand regulations in most situations (Perry, 2001).

11.4.4.2. Subsidy Removal and Correct Pricing of Electricity

Foster et al. (2017) presented the results of a laboratory experiment conducted in the city of León, Guanajuato, México, to study the groundwater extraction decisions of stakeholders under alternative subsidy structures. They analysed the performance of two traditional policy interventions, that is, elimination and reduction of subsidy, and then a novel policy—decoupling the subsidy from the electricity rate by replacing it with a lump sum transfer. Their results suggested that the rate of water extraction and the level of water in the aquifer may be improved significantly by altering the subsidy structure. An important finding for policymakers is that decoupling leads to outcomes similar to those of eliminating the subsidy, however, with fewer political economy conflicts.

In the Indian context, research studies carried out in North Gujarat (Kumar, 2005), and North Gujarat, eastern Uttar Pradesh and South Bihar (Kumar et al., 2011, 2013) had shown that the energy prices at which the farmers start responding to tariff changes in terms of reducing the demand for these inputs would be socio-economically viable.

Kumar et al. (2011) showed that the farmers who were confronted with the marginal cost of using electricity and water, which included farmers who paid for electricity on the basis of consumption (in North Gujarat), buyers of water from electric well owners who paid for irrigation services on an hourly basis (in eastern Uttar Pradesh and South Bihar), diesel well owners who incurred positive marginal costs for every hour of pumping and water purchasers from diesel well owners who paid for irrigation services on an hourly basis (in eastern Uttar Pradesh and South Bihar),[6] secured not only higher water productivity

---

[6] Here, buyers of irrigation water, who pay for irrigation services on an hourly basis, are considered to be the proxy for pro rata pricing of electricity. This is because the effect of both pro rata pricing of electricity and volumetric irrigation water charges in terms of marginal cost of irrigation would be the same.

Table 11.1 *Impact of Electricity Prices and Volumetric Water Charges on Water Productivity and Net Income from Farming and Groundwater Use per Unit Area*

Region	Type of Well Command	Type of Farmer	Water Productivity in Economic Terms (₹/m³)	Total Farm-level Income (₹) with Crops and Dairying	Farm-level Income per Unit Land (₹/Ha)	Average Irrigation Pumping per Ha (Hours)
Eastern Uttar Pradesh	Electric well	Well owner	10.98	131,740	24,880	175.00
		Water buyer	11.18	60,803	27,570	184.00
	Diesel well	Well owner	8.67	82,194	14,528	222.00
		Water buyer	12.89	68,584	18,075	148.00
North Gujarat	Electric well	Flat rate pricing	6.30	768,287	57,531	444.00
		Pro rata pricing	7.90	669,250	56,882	304.00
South Bihar	Electric well	Well owner	9.28	130,770	210,345	330.00
		Water buyer	10.13	76,024	190,031	250.00
	Diesel well	Well owner	11.97	150,064	191,387	231.00
		Water buyer	12.43	84,043	197,895	198.00

Source: Kumar et al. (2011, 2013).

in economic terms (₹/m³ of water) but also higher net income per unit area of land (₹/ha) than farmers who paid for electricity on the basis of flat rate or got free electricity supply in these regions (fourth and sixth columns, respectively, of Table 11.1). The rate of groundwater pumping per unit of irrigated land (hour/ha) was less for the farmers who were confronted with a positive marginal cost of using electricity/water (seventh column of Table 11.1). The extent of reduction in irrigation water demand possible without causing any reduction in the net income is roughly 20 per cent.

This is because they are able to improve the efficiency of use of irrigation water and other farm inputs and also modify their farming systems when confronted with the positive marginal cost of electricity and higher unit tariff, with the result that they get not only higher water productivity but also higher net income per unit area of land. Therefore, one should arrive at the ideal unit price for electricity for different regions which would be most efficient in terms of demand reduction, affordable for farmers, and also improve the viability of the power sector (Kumar et al., 2011, 2013). The studies also showed that the shift from free power or flat rate (based on connected load) to pro rata pricing would not have any effect on the price at which water is traded in the market (Kumar et al., 2013).

On that note, the argument of increasing inequity in access to groundwater due to rise in the market price of water as a likely impact of pro rata pricing (Mukherji et al., 2009) missed the point that under flat rate pricing of electricity, the large well owners, whose implicit cost of irrigation is very low and return from crop production high, may enjoy monopoly power and decide the price at which water should be sold in the market. Conversely, the smallholders owning wells, whose implicit cost of irrigating their own farm is high, are left without much choice but to look for buyers to whom they could sell water to earn extra income, at a price decided by the market as they will have limited bargaining power. Such prices obviously offer high profit margins for the large farmers but not for the small farmers (Kumar, 2018).

If electricity is charged on a pro rata basis, both small and large farmers from the same locality will incur the same unit cost of pumping water, and the large farmers will not enjoy a comparative advantage over small farmers. In view of the fact that there are no fixed costs of keeping pump sets, the small landholders are not under pressure to sell water at a very low price to stay in the market. Hence, both large and small farmers would have equal incentives to invest in wells and sell water and have equal opportunities to make profits in the shallow groundwater areas. This will lower the price at which water would be sold in the market (Kumar, 2018).

But given the sharp variations in water table conditions across India (CGWB, 2017), electricity tariff fixation has to be done carefully in different regions. The pro rata tariff should be an inverse function of the depth to groundwater table to make sure that the cost of electricity to abstract a unit volume of groundwater remains more or less the same across geo-hydrological environments (Kumar, 2018).

However, the price for electricity would also have to be a function of what farmers would be willing to pay. The willingness to pay would be a function of the economic surplus generated from the use of water for irrigation or the value of water use in irrigation (Dinar et al., 1997; Young, 1996). This is a function of the cropping system which is feasible under the given climate, the wherewithal available with the farmers to adopt the technologies needed to raise the crops and the market demand for the crop. These factors need to be considered while fixing the price for electricity.

The question is: What should be the actual unit charge for electricity to affect reduction in demand for groundwater, without causing adverse effects on the economic prospects of farming? The experience in West Bengal and Gujarat shows that within the same locality, a uniform tariff (unit charges) for electricity can be followed, irrespective of the total electricity consumption by individual farmers. In the case of North Gujarat, where the water table is very deep (often 400–500 feet below the ground), the charge levied by the electricity utility on farmers is ₹0.70 per kWhr, whereas in West Bengal, where the groundwater table is very shallow, it is ₹4.10 per kWhr. In both states, this mode of charging electricity is working for many years.

11.4.4.3. Reducing the Transaction Costs of Metering

The State Electricity Boards and policymakers recognize the importance of metering electricity in the farm sector. But they are also struggling with the idea of carrying out metering in a way that makes it foolproof as well as cost effective (Kumar, 2018). Today, technologies exist not only for metering but also for controlling energy consumption by farmers. The prepaid electronic meters operated through scratch cards can work on satellite and Internet technology and are ideal for remote areas to monitor energy use and control groundwater use online from a centralized station. Over the past 15 years, there has been a remarkable improvement in the quality of services provided by Internet and mobile (satellite) phone services, especially in the rural areas (Kumar et al., 2011).

Prepaid meters prevent electricity pilferage through the manipulation of pump capacity. They can be operated through tokens, scratch cards, magnetic cards or recharged digitally through the Internet and SMS, and can be used by an electricity company to restrict the use of electricity. The company can decide on the 'energy quota' for each farmer on the basis of reported connected load and total hours of power supply per unit of irrigated land. Farmers can pay and obtain an activation code through mobile SMS (Zekri, 2008). Alternatively, automatic metering infrastructure, which are used to meter electricity and in many cases water supply, can be used (Aarnoudse et al., 2016). All these will reduce costs and theft (Zekri, 2008). Prepaid meters are now used for agro wells in some countries, including China (Aarnoudse et al., 2016) and Bangladesh (Schmidt-Rosen, 2016).

As regards the cost of introducing such a system, the modern electricity metering technology with farm-level metering combined with the establishment of ICT would cost around US$250 per well (Gulati & Pahuja, 2015). The cost of a prepaid meter (including the cost of installation) works out to be only US$90 approximately (Singh, 2020).

11.5. FUTURE AREAS OF ACTION IN AGRICULTURE

To conclude, strategies and policies for agricultural growth in India have to be region-specific, considering the unique problems each region poses and the opportunities they provide. Promotion of low-cost, energy-efficient water-harnessing technologies such as treadle pumps and micro diesel pumps, through the supply of information, materials and services, can enable poor farmers in the agriculturally backward eastern and north-eastern parts of our country, to gain access to irrigation water. This will create millions of micro economies with sustainable utilization of water resources in the water-abundant regions (Kumar, 2003; Postel, 1999; Shah et al., 2000). Low-cost, water-saving technologies will enable the poorest sections of the communities to practise irrigated agriculture with very limited water in water-scarce regions. Land-based interventions for drought-proofing, water harvesting and artificial recharge under NREGA should be planned carefully, after proper consideration of hydrological and economic aspects, so as to improve the overall water economy and to reduce the negative welfare effects on the society (Bassi & Kumar, 2010).

In naturally water-scarce regions, where such interventions are likely to create negative welfare effects, the funds should be earmarked for providing subsidies for micro irrigation (Bassi & Kumar, 2010). In those regions, the said welfare gains would be substantial due to the following reasons: (a) real water saving through micro irrigation would be possible and (b) the value of saved water would be high in these regions owing to its physical scarcity. This would, to an extent, help reduce groundwater overdraft in some of these regions along with raising crop outputs, whereas in other regions, the impact would be only increased agricultural output (Kumar et al., 2012).

If India has to expand its irrigation potential for agricultural growth on a sustainable basis and sustain intensive well irrigation in the naturally water-scarce regions, transfer of water from water-abundant regions to water-scarce regions would be essential. Inter-basin or inter-regional water transfer is a natural choice for irrigation expansion and groundwater replenishment because of the following two reasons. The water-scarce regions have the natural advantage of being able to produce more crops, if irrigation water is available, as a sufficient amount of arable land remains uncultivated and unirrigated, whereas water-abundant regions face an acute shortage of arable land in addition to ecological constraints to crop production induced by floods. This calls for designing an entirely new water management system, which would promote efficient use of water in agriculture and improved recharge of groundwater at no extra costs (Kumar et al., 2012).

In alluvial areas of western and north-western India, the depleted aquifers can be effectively replenished through the diversion of water for irrigation during the rainy season, with a large amount of land available for infiltration and good hydraulic conductivity of the dewatered zone. Conjunctive management of groundwater and surface water is already being practised in alluvial areas of North Gujarat wherein excess monsoon flow from the Narmada river is being diverted through the Narmada Main Canal (NMC) and the distribution canals for recharge of the overexploited alluvial aquifers of the region, through decentralized storage systems such as village ponds and tanks and the sandy beds of the several river channels which the NMC crosses (Jagadeesan & Kumar, 2015), whereas in hard rock areas of peninsular India, the hundreds of thousands of tanks, which dot the region, could be integrated with the infrastructure which transfers the water to this region. As many of them do not receive sufficient inflows from their catchments, they can store a portion of the imported water, while the remaining water could be diverted to the agricultural land (Kumar et al., 2012).

Enforcement of private and tradable water rights in water supplied from public reservoirs and water drawn from aquifers can together bring about a significant increase in farm outputs with a reduction in aggregate demand for water in agriculture. It will also bring about more equitable access to and control over the water available from canals and groundwater for producing food and to ensure household–level food security. In overexploited areas, allocation of water use rights for groundwater will be possible through energy rationing using prepaid meters, as most farmers in such areas would be using electric pumps for abstracting groundwater. This has to be complemented by volumetric pricing of canal water and pro rata pricing of electricity in the farm sector with improved quality and reliability of the supplied power. Metering and pro rata pricing of electricity has to receive priority in naturally water-scarce regions, which also experience groundwater overdraft, whereas in groundwater-abundant regions, the pricing structure should be designed in such a way that it encourages greater use of groundwater for agricultural production (Kumar, 2018).

REFERENCES

Aarnoudse, E., Qu, W., Bluemling, B., & Herzfeld, T. (2017). Groundwater quota versus tiered groundwater pricing: Two cases of groundwater management in north-west China. *International Journal of Water Resources Development*, *33*(6), 917–934.

Amarasinghe, U. A., Shah, T., & Singh, O. P. (2007). *Changing consumption patterns: Implications on food and water demand in India* (Vol. 119). International Water Management Institute.

Ambasta, P., Shankar, P. V., & Shah, M. (2008). Two years of NREGA: The road ahead. *Economic & Political Weekly*, *43*(8), 41–50.

Bassi, N., & Kumar, M. D. (2010). *NREGA and rural water management: Improving the welfare effects* [Occasional Paper No. 3]. Institute for Resource Analysis and Policy, Hyderabad.

CGWB (Central Ground Water Board). (2017). *Dynamic ground water resources of India (as on 31st March 2013)*.

Chowdhury, A. (2011). Food price hikes: How much is due to excessive speculation? *Economic & Political Weekly*, *46*(28), 12–15.

Contor, B. (2009). *Groundwater banking and the conjunctive management of groundwater and surface water in the Upper Snake River basin of Idaho*. Idaho Water Resources Research Institute.

CWC (Central Water Commission). (2017). *Reassessment of water availability in India using space inputs*. Basin Planning and Management Organization.

Dinar, A., Rosegrant, M. W., & Meinzen-Dick, R. (1997). *Water allocation mechanisms: Principles and examples*. The World Bank.

Foster, E. T., Rapoport, A., & Dinar, A. (2017). Groundwater and electricity consumption under alternative subsidies: Evidence from laboratory experiments. *Journal of Behavioral and Experimental Economics*, *68*(2017), 41–52.

Frederick, K. D. (1993). *Balancing water demands with supplies: The role of management in a world of increasing scarcity*. The World Bank.

Gandhi, V. P., Johnson, N., Neog, K., & Jain, D. (2020). Institutional Structure, Participation, and Devolution in Water Institutions of Eastern India. *Water 2020*, *12*, 476; doi:10.3390/w12020476.

GoI (Government of India). (2008). *Eleventh five-year plan 2007–2012, Vol. III: Agriculture, rural development, industry, services, and physical infrastructure*. Planning Commission.

Gulati, A., Kapur, D., & Bouton, M. M. (2020). Reforming Indian agriculture. *Economic & Political Weekly*, *55*(11), 35–42.

Gulati, M., & Pahuja, S. (2015). Direct delivery of power subsidy to manage energy–ground water–agriculture nexus. *Aquatic Procedia*, *5*(2015), 22–30.

Hostetler, S. (n.d.). *The Australian water bank: The bank we have to have*. Bureau of Rural Sciences, Australian Government.

Howe, C. W., Schurmeier, D. R., & Shaw, Jr, W. D. (1986). Innovative approaches to water allocation: The potential for water markets. *Water Resources Research, 22*(4), 439–445.

IRMA, & UNICEF (Institute of Rural Management Anand & United Nations International Children's Emergency Fund). (2001). *White paper on water in Gujarat.* Report prepared for the Government of Gujarat.

Jagadeesan, S., & Kumar, M. D. (2015). *The Sardar Sarovar Project: Assessing economic and social impacts.* SAGE Publications.

Kay, M., Franks, T., & Smith, L. (1997). *Water: Economics, management and demand.* E. & F.N. Spon.

Kijne, J. W., Barker, R., & Molden, D. (2003). Improving water productivity in agriculture: Editors' overview. In *Water productivity in agriculture: Limits and opportunities for improvement* (pp. xi–xix). CABI Publishing in Association with International Water Management Institute.

Kumar, M. D. (2000a). Institutional framework for managing groundwater: A case study of community organisations in Gujarat, India. *Water Policy, 2*(6), 423–432.

Kumar, M. D. (2000b). *Irrigation with a manual pump: Impact of treadle pump on farming enterprise and food security in coastal Orissa* [Working Paper No. 148]. Institute of Rural Management Anand.

Kumar, M. D. (2003). *Food security and sustainable agriculture: India's water management challenge* [Working Paper No. 60]. International Water Management Institute, Colombo.

Kumar, M. D. (2005). Impact of electricity prices and volumetric water allocation on energy and groundwater demand management: Analysis from Western India. *Energy Policy, 33*(1), 39–51.

Kumar, M. D. (2007). *Groundwater management in India: Physical, institutional and policy alternatives.* SAGE Publications.

Kumar, M. D. (2009). *Water management in India: What works, what doesn't?* Gyan Books.

Kumar, M. D. (2010). *Managing water in river basins: Hydrology, economics, and institutions.* Oxford University Press.

Kumar, M. D. (2018). Institutions and policies governing groundwater development, use and management in the Indo–Gangetic Plains of India. In K. G. Villholth, E. Lopez-Gunn, K. Conti, A. Garrido, & J. van Der Gun (Eds.), *Advances in groundwater governance* (pp. 443–462). CRC Press/Balkema.

Kumar, M. D., & Bassi, N. (2011). *Maximizing the social and economic returns from Sardar Sarovar Project: Thinking beyond convention.* In R. Parthasarathy & R. Dolakhya (Eds.), *Sardar Sarovar Project on the River Narmada: Impacts so far and ways forward* (pp. 747–776). Concept Publishing.

Kumar, M. D., Malla, A. K., & Tripathy, S. K. (2008). Economic value of water in agriculture: Comparative analysis of a water-scarce and a water-rich region in India. *Water International, 33*(2), 214–230.

Kumar, M. D., & Patel, P. J. (1995). Depleting buffer and farmers response: Study of villages in Kheralu, Mehsana, Gujarat. In M. Moench (Ed.), *Electricity prices: A tool for groundwater management in India?* VIKSAT-Natural Heritage Institute.

Kumar, M. D., Patel, A., Ravindranath, R., & Singh, O. P. (2008). Chasing a mirage: Water harvesting and artificial recharge in naturally water-scarce regions. *Economic & Political Weekly*, *43*(35), 61–71.

Kumar, M. D., Scott, C. A., & Singh, O. P. (2011). Inducing the shift from flat-rate or free agricultural power to metered supply: Implications for groundwater depletion and power sector viability in India. *Journal of Hydrology*, *409*(1–2), 382–394.

Kumar, M. D., Scott, C. A., & Singh, O. P. (2013). Can India raise agricultural productivity while reducing groundwater and energy use? *International Journal of Water Resources Development*, *29*(4), 557–573.

Kumar, M. D., & Singh, O. P. (2001). Market instruments for demand management in the face of growing scarcity and overuse of water in Gujarat, India. *Water Policy*, *5*(3), 86–102.

Kumar, M. D., & Singh, O. P. (2005). Virtual water in global food and water policy making: Is there a need for rethinking? *Water Resources Management*, *19*(6), 759–789.

Kumar, M. D., Turral, H., Sharma, B., Amarasinghe, U., & Singh, O.P. (2008). Water saving and yield enhancing micro irrigation technologies: When do they become best bet technologies? In M. D. Kumar (Ed.), *Managing water in the face of growing scarcity, inequity and declining returns: Exploring fresh approaches*. Proceedings of 7th Annual Partners' Meet. IWMI-Tata Water Policy Research Program, ICRISAT.

Kumar, M. D., & van Dam, J. C. (2013). Drivers of change in agricultural water productivity and its improvement at basin scale in developing economies. *Water International*, *38*(3), 312–325.

Kumar, M. D., Vedantam, N., Narayanamoorthy, A., & Bassi, N. (2012). Future strategies for agricultural growth in India. In M. D. Kumar, M. V. K. Sivamohan, & N. Bassi (Eds.), *Water management, food security and sustainable agriculture in developing economies*. Routledge/Earthscan.

MoAFW (Ministry of Agriculture & Farmers' Welfare). (2018). *Horticultural statistics at a glance 2018*. Department of Agriculture, Cooperation & Farmers' Welfare, Horticulture Statistics Division, Ministry of Agriculture and Farmers' Welfare, Government of India.

Ministry of Irrigation and Power (MoIP) (1972). Report of the Irrigation Commission, Volume I, Ministry of Irrigation and Power, New Delhi.

Moench, M. (1995). *Electricity pricing: A tool for groundwater management in India?* [Monograph]. VIKSAT-Natural Heritage Institute, Ahmedabad.

Molle, F., & Turral, H. (2004). Demand management in a basin perspective: Is the potential for water saving overrated? Paper presented at the International Water Demand Management Conference, Dead Sea, Jordan.

Mukherji, A., Das, B., Majumdar, N., Nayak, N. C., Sethi, R. R., & Sharma, B. R. (2009). Metering of agricultural power supply in West Bengal, India: Who gains and who loses? *Energy Policy, 37*(12), 5530–5539.

Nandakumar, T., Ganguly, K., Sharma, P., & Gulati, A. (2010). *Food and nutrition security status in India: Opportunities for investment partnerships* [ADB Sustainable Development Working Paper Series No. 16]. Asian Development Bank.

NCAER, & PIF (National Council of Applied Economic Research & Public Interest Foundation). (2009). *NCAER–PIF study on evaluating performance of National Rural Employment Guarantee Act.* National Council of Applied Economic Research.

Panagariya, A. (2009). More bang for the buck. *The Times of India,* 19 September.

Perry, C. (2001). Water at any price? Issues and options in charging for irrigation water 1. *Irrigation and Drainage, 50*(1), 1–7.

Postel, S. (1992). *The last oasis: Facing water scarcity.* World Watch Environmental Alert Series. Earthscan.

Postel, S. (1999). *Pillars of sand: Can the irrigation miracle last?* Norton/World Watch Book, W. W. Norton & Co.

Postel, S., Polak, P., Gonzales, F., & Keller, J. (2001). Drip irrigation for small farmers: A new initiative to alleviate hunger and poverty. *Water International, 26*(1), 3–13.

Rada, N. E. (2013). *Agricultural growth in India: Examining the post green revolution transition.* Paper presented at the *Agricultural & Applied Economics Association's 2013 AAEA & CAES Joint Annual Meeting,* Washington, DC.

Rosegrant, M. W., & Binswanger, H. P. (1994). Markets in tradable water rights: Potential for efficiency gains in developing country water resource allocation. *World Development, 22*(11), 1613–1625.

Rosegrant, M. W., & Gazmuri S. R. (1995). Reforming water allocation policy through markets in tradable water rights: Lessons from Chile, Mexico, and California. *Cuadernos de Economía, 32*(97), 291–315.

Saleth, R. M. (1997). Power tariff policy for groundwater regulation: Efficiency, equity and sustainability. *Artha Vijnana, 39*(3), 312–322.

Saleth, R. M., & Dinar, A. (1999). *Water challenge and institutional responses (a cross country perspective)* [Policy Research Working Paper Series 2045]. The World Bank, Washington, DC.

Schmidt-Rosen, M. (2016). *Prepayment metering in Bangladesh: How to improve electricity delivery and eliminate theft.* Global Delivery Initiative, German Development Cooperation.

Shah, T., Alam, M., Kumar, M. D., Nagar, R. K., & Singh, M. (2000). *Pedalling out of poverty: Social impact of a manual irrigation technology in South Asia* (Vol. 45). International Water Management Institute.

Singh, R. K. (2020). Rs 1.5 lakh crore: The bill India is set to pay for the coming power gamechanger, *The Economic Times,* New Delhi. https://economictimes.indiatimes.com/industry/energy/power/rs-1-5-lakh-crore-the-bill-india-is-set-to-pay-for-the-coming-power-gamechanger/re_show/74329268.cms

Tiwari, R., Somashekhar, H. I., Parama, V. R. R., Murthy, I. K., Kumar, M. S. M., Kumar, B. K. M., Parate, H., Varma, M., Malaviya, S., Rao, A. S., Sengupta, A., Kattumuri, R., & Ravindranath, N. H. (2011). MGNREGA for environmental service enhancement and vulnerability reduction: Rapid appraisal in Chitradurga district, Karnataka. *Economic & Political Weekly*, *46*(20), 39–47.

Tsur, Y., & Dinar, A. (1995). *Efficiency and equity considerations in pricing and allocating irrigation water* [Policy Research Working Paper Series 1460]. The World Bank, Washington, DC.

Watt, J. (2008). *The effect of irrigation on surface-ground water interactions: Quantifying time dependent spatial dynamics in irrigation systems* [Thesis submitted for the Degree of Doctor of Philosophy]. School of Environmental Sciences, Faculty of Sciences, Charles Sturt University.

Young, R. A. (1996). *Measuring economic benefits for water investments and policies* [Technical Paper No. 338]. The World Bank, Washington, DC.

Zekri, S. (2008). Using economic incentives and regulations to reduce seawater intrusion in the Batinah coastal area of Oman. *Agricultural Water Management*, *95*(3), 243–252.

Chapter 12

Summary and Conclusions

M. Dinesh Kumar, M. V. K. Sivamohan and Nitin Bassi

Research on agrarian change in India is vast and rich. The phenomenon of agrarian change in India has been analysed in the past from various perspectives. They include problems and challenges induced by different agrarian structures (feudal, ryotwari, permanent settlement, etc.); various modes of production (feudal, capitalist and socialist); challenges posed by unfavourable situations vis-à-vis various factors of production such as water scarcity, land scarcity, limited access to inputs and production technologies; environmental externalities impacted on production; externalities induced by the changing market conditions; long-term growth trends; long-term change in stability of agricultural productivity and production; regional growth disparities; and growing risks and indebtedness among farmers.

There is an enormous volume of work done during the past five decades or so looking at the agrarian change from the perspective of modes of production and agrarian structure which existed during the colonial and precolonial eras. However, there were too few comprehensive analyses of the problems which factor in the changing conditions with respect to the factors of production, the changing technology environment, the changing economic dynamics of farming with respect to the cost of various inputs affected by the changing subsidy structure and overall socio-economic change, and the externalities induced by the changing environmental and market conditions. The limited analysis lacked empirical depth and academic rigour.

While the former required the use of perspectives from sociology and anthropology, the latter required systematic engagement with life sciences, agricultural economics, agronomy and water management. The latter also required comparative analysis of regions taking into account the distinct physical, socio-economic environment (overall economic conditions of the farmers and infrastructure and market conditions), as all of them have bearing on the profitability of farming. This essentially meant that analysis carried out for one region, no matter how rigorous it was, would not hold good for another region. In that respect, too much regional bias in such studies was also noticeable.

Researchers were preoccupied with the question of agrarian crisis in India (Aerthayil, 2008; Chakrabarty, 2013; Mishra, 2008) and the agricultural stagnation (also called as 'agrarian impasse') in the eastern region (particularly Bihar and West Bengal; Kishore, 2004; Mukherji et al., 2012; Shah, 2016). A good amount of academic interest was generated regarding the phenomenon of miracle growth in agriculture as claimed by a few researchers (Gulati et al., 2009; Kumar et al., 2010; Shah et al., 2009).

Agriculture in the Indian subcontinent is thousands of years old and was a way of life for its people. Even in the early civilizations, people in this part of the world were known to have evolved distinct agricultural ethos and practices such as tilling the soil and applying irrigation and natural manures to their fields for raising food crops. Hundreds of generations of people practising agriculture here had operated their farms under tyrannical regimes of colonial rulers (Arnold, 2005), as well as benevolent and cruel local rulers (Habib, 1999), though as pointed out by Chatterjee and Rudra (1989), too little was known about the production relations that existed during the precolonial era. Farming in India had survived severe droughts and even famines, often affecting large regions. The evolutionary development of agriculture ever since 1000–500 BC in the subcontinent through the medieval period to the post neoliberal times displayed its important role in the economy.

Chapter 1 of the book provided this backdrop of history and development of agriculture in India. It briefly discussed how the Mughal and British rule obscured the splendour and legacy of agriculture, whose growth came to experience restrictions due to the presence of several layers of taxation. They also discussed the creation of several development institutions, and the strategies and policies initiated by the national and provincial governments through Five-Year Plans to boost agricultural growth and the economy. The twists and turns which occurred in the agricultural sector ultimately led the country to surplus food production and technological upsurge. Yet the process of development had its own hitches, causing crisis situations in the agricultural sector of the country.

Chapter 2 presented the changing characteristics of India's agricultural sector since the early 1950s with regard to some key attributes. They are per capita land and water availability, land use, average growth rates in agriculture, cropping pattern, level of seed production, levels of fertilizers used for various crops, degree of farm mechanization and labour use, real wage rates, extent of agricultural subsidies, electricity consumption in agriculture, average crop and milk yields, and value of agricultural outputs in real terms.

The analyses pointed to the emergence of crises that came up from time to time as well as the opportunities for boosting agricultural growth in India. For instance, the rise in yield of major cereals was very impressive from 668 kg/ha in 1950–1951 to 2,462 kg/ha in 2012–2013 in the case of rice, and from 663 kg/ha in 1950–1951 to 3,119 kg/ha in 2012–2013 in the case of wheat. But the use of farm inputs also increased substantially. For instance, for a hectare of gross cropped area, the consumption of fertilizers went up from 0.52 kg to 137 kg during the same period. The electricity consumption per unit of gross irrigated area increased 160 times from 7 kWh/ha in 1950–1951 to 1,154 kWh/ha of gross irrigated area in 2006–2007. The extent of agricultural subsidies in real terms increased manifold from 1980–1981 to 2008–2009 in both aggregate terms (8.45 times) and per hectare of gross cropped area (7.5 times).

Another landmark change in Indian agriculture was in the contribution of the private sector to the production of quality seeds. By 2001–2002, the private sector developed 150 hybrid seeds of cotton compared to 15 by the public sector. Similarly, in maize, the number of hybrid varieties developed was 67, against three in the public sector. The overall production of certified seeds also increased over the years. The price of agricultural commodities also increased manifold in real terms: for rice from ₹22/quintal in 1975–1976 to ₹186/quintal in 2012–2013, and for wheat from ₹31/quintal to ₹201/quintal during the same period. The overall agricultural output in value terms grew by 450 per cent over the 65-year period from 1954–1955 to 2011–2012.

While, on the whole, Indian agriculture has grown steadily in medium and long terms, annual growth rates have been highly erratic, with negative growth rates often witnessed during years of severe droughts. India's economists and policymakers were always obsessed with predicting annual growth rates in agriculture, as much of the country's economy depended on agriculture. The agricultural growth prediction for a crop year mainly takes into consideration whether the rainfall would be normal or above or below normal. The annual agricultural growth rate is linked to annual rainfall, suggesting a good monsoon would ensure high agricultural growth rate during the year concerned. An extension of this logic was that a low annual growth rate in agriculture sector is attributed to the failure of monsoon during that year. More strangely, an impressive growth rate in agriculture in the medium term is attributed to the high performance of the sector in terms of technology adoption, policy frameworks and institutional interventions, without looking at the medium trends in the precipitation.

But there are two questions that need to be answered. First, is it is appropriate to link performance of the agriculture sector in terms of growth rate to aggregate predictions of monsoon rainfall in a country which has several rainfall zones? Second, even if the rainfall does influence agricultural growth rates, how can the average rainfall of a single year alone cause wide year-to-year fluctuations in the agricultural growth rate noticed in the country? In Chapter 3, an attempt was made to identify the key factors which drive annual agricultural growth rates using data on the weighted average of annual rainfall of the country for the period from 1954–1955 to 2011–2012 (obtained from India Meteorological Department), the extent of irrigation in different years and the agricultural outputs in value terms. The analysis was repeated using similar data for Gujarat.

It was found that the percentage difference in annual rainfall from the previous year is a major determinant of the annual agricultural growth rate. The second most important factor is the percentage difference in the irrigated area from the previous year. The rainfall (percentage change in rainfall of a year over the previous year) and irrigation (percentage change in the irrigated area of a year over the previous year) explained annual agricultural growth rate to an extent of 55 per cent. The greater the percentage increase in the rainfall in a particular year over the previous year's rainfall or growth in the irrigated area over the previous year, the higher are the chances of getting an increased agricultural growth rate.

While a positive change in the rainfall of a year over the previous year guaranteed a high growth rate, vice versa was not always found to be happening, though a decrease in rainfall resulted in a very low growth rate or sometimes negative growth.

The analysis suggested that annual agricultural growth rates can become high under two conditions. First, there is a high percentage increase in rainfall over the previous year. Second, there is a high percentage increase in the irrigated area over the previous year. As per the model, a 20 per cent increase in rainfall would ensure a 6 per cent higher growth in annual agricultural outputs in India. Similarly, a 5 per cent increase in irrigated area over one year would ensure a 2.35 per cent higher growth in agricultural output. Although the beta coefficient for irrigation growth was higher than that of rainfall difference (+ive), analysis of historical data showed that it was difficult to obtain such high annual growth rates in irrigated area, unlike in the case of rainfall. The maximum value of annual irrigation growth rate ever obtained in India since Independence was 8.6 per cent, whereas the maximum increase in rainfall obtained was 28.6 per cent. Adding two more variables, that is, deviation in rainfall from the mean annual rainfall and gross irrigated area, increased the value of the regression coefficient marginally to 0.575.

In Chapter 4, an extensive review of the published literature available on agrarian change in India was presented and synthesized by the authors. The review outcomes were summarized as follows. As a result of several factors, including irrigation expansion and technology advancements, a marginal decline in instability of agricultural output was observed at the national level. However, there were significant regional differences in agricultural productivity growth owing to differences in the level of use of inputs and adoption of crop technologies and agroecological factors, and this had culminated in major differences in current average crop yields among regions. During the period from 1980–1981 to 1996–1997, the regional differences in agricultural productivity and income had grown and the gap between underdeveloped and developed and poor and rich states had increased. The period from 1970–1971 to 2007–2008 was marked by a major shift in cropping pattern towards high-value crops and reduction in area under coarse cereals, while technological and institutional support for crops such as rice and wheat had resulted in an increase in area and output composition of these crops.

The scholarly studies seem to suggest that having limited potential for absorption of rural workforce in the rural non-farm sector, crop diversification can be an opportunity to increase farm revenues, given the impact of diversification on the poverty of farm households, especially smallholders. Nevertheless, its impact on farming risk from the point of view of technology, production and market is not yet fully understood. The strong and inverse relationship between farm size and farm income at the aggregate level shows the potential negative impact the increasing rural population will have on the income of the average agricultural households as a result of reducing the size of the landholding with time, unless there is a large-scale shifting of rural populations out of agriculture or significant opportunities are generated in the rural non-farm sector for absorbing this workforce.

Vast differences in agro-climatic conditions, resource endowment, socio-economic conditions and the landholding pattern among regions, and more importantly the differences in growth trajectory witnessed by these regions, make it imperative that research on agrarian crisis in the sector looked at individual regions rather than the aggregate-level scenario of the country. The dairy sector emerged as a major contributor to agricultural growth in India, and its contribution to farm income, especially that of small and marginal farmers, should be carefully assessed and considered. More importantly, the role of livestock in making the farming system resilient to production and market risks and averting a crisis in the farm sector needs to be carefully analysed.

Keeping in view these crucial aspects of agrarian change, the approach and the methodology was framed for the location studies undertaken in four states to have regional perspectives. The analytical tool was designed to capture the real change in farm income over a long-time frame.

Chapters 5, 6, 7 and 8 presented the findings of the studies undertaken in West Bengal, Gujarat, Maharashtra and Coastal Andhra Pradesh. Each region represented a unique agroecology and socioeconomic setting. The districts covered in West Bengal were 24 Parganas and Howrah. In Gujarat, Banaskantha was chosen for the field study. In Maharashtra, Chandrapur from Vidarbha was chosen. In Coastal Andhra, West Godavari was chosen.

The analysis included temporal changes (1980–1981 to 2011–2012) in yield of crops, level of use of inputs and input costs, cropping pattern and gross cropped area under different crops, livestock holding, net income per hectare of individual crops, net income from dairy production per unit of livestock and overall net income of the farm households. In terms of the change in net income from farming among the sample households, different states showed different patterns, while none of the four states had witnessed an increase in farm income in real terms. In the case of Vidarbha, the reduction in annual farm income was the sharpest and most consistent, while no consistent trend was seen in any of the other three locations.

Chapter 9 presented a synthesis of the results discussed in the previous four chapters and key findings from the location studies on agrarian crisis. The findings were with regard to the following: (a) the region that witnessed the most severe crisis in terms of declining farm income among all the four and (b) physical, socio-economic, and institutional and policy factors contributing to the distress. The concluding section of the chapter discussed what could be done from physical, institutional and policy fronts to mitigate the agrarian crisis in different study regions. Drawing on the experience from Gujarat and Madhya Pradesh, the measures that ecologically fragile regions of India should adopt to avert a crisis in agriculture from a production point of view were elaborated.

Chapter 10 argued that with the changing character of Indian farming with a shift towards high-value agriculture—along with capital—the extent of knowledge inputs required in farming to make the farming system robust and resilient is increasing. This is all the more important when we consider the fact that the biggest agrarian transformation is happening in the semi-arid and arid regions which are water-scarce and also subjected to high climatic variability and extreme weather conditions. Such conditions mean high production, technology and market risks for the farmers, along with high profits.

The chapter went on to discuss the drivers of future agricultural growth in India, and the key features of the emerging farming systems; the technologies that act as drivers of change in agricultural output and are capable of improving the input use efficiency and reducing the production-related risks to sustain this growth and their cost implications; the institutional approaches which can reduce the market risks associated with the emerging farming system; and finally the role of the financial sector in boosting technology adoption and reducing market risks in farming. The following interventions were suggested to make the growth in the agricultural sector economically sustainable and socially viable: (a) assessing the production risks induced by weather and other factors, and market risks, prior to advancing farm loans; (b) linking farm loans to crop insurance; (c) designing insurance products based on risk assessment; (d) undertaking research on resilient farming systems; (e) linking subsidies for efficient irrigation and fertilizer use technologies to efficient use of technologies and resource, especially water and energy; and (f) offering special incentives for promotion of farming clusters.

Chapter 11 argued that while in the past, irrigation expansion through large public irrigation schemes received a lot of attention from governments in India, of late, there has been an overemphasis on augmentation of groundwater resources and conservation of water in small water bodies, with a consequent focus on decentralized water harvesting and local groundwater recharge. Further, long-term strategies for supporting large-scale irrigation development or promoting productivity in agriculture are absent. More importantly, the larger concerns of growing inequity in access to resources and inefficient resource use are not being addressed by the current programmes.

Based on this premise, the chapter laid down some key technical, institutional and policy measures for improving the sustainability of agricultural growth in different agroecologies. The key technical solutions for improving the sustainability of agricultural growth were: low-cost irrigation technologies to change the trajectory of irrigation development in water-abundant regions; technologies to improve the productivity of use of water in agriculture in water-scarce regions; transfer of water from water-abundant regions to naturally water-scarce regions to expand gravity irrigation and to improve the sustainability of well irrigation; and water harvesting in the hills for supplementary irrigation of horticultural crops during summer. The institutional measures suggested for changing the trajectory of water use in agriculture were: enforcement of water use rights and water allocation for promoting equity and sustainability in water use and pro rata pricing of water and electricity for encouraging efficient use of water. Technological measures for reducing the transaction cost of metering electricity were also suggested.

The authors concluded that the strategies and policies for promoting agricultural growth in India have to be region-specific. Promotion of low-cost, energy-efficient water harnessing technologies such as treadle pumps and micro diesel pumps can enable poor farmers in the agriculturally backward eastern and north-eastern parts of our country access irrigation water. Low-cost, water-saving technologies will enable the poorest sections of the communities to practise irrigated agriculture with very limited water in water-scarce regions. Land-based interventions for drought-proofing, water harvesting and artificial recharge should be planned carefully, after proper consideration of hydrological and economic aspects, so as to improve the overall water economy and to reduce the negative welfare effects on the society.

In naturally water-scarce regions, the MGNREGA funds should be earmarked for providing subsidies for micro irrigation. In those regions, the welfare gains would be substantial due to the following reasons: (a) real water saving through micro irrigation would be possible and (b) the value of saved water would be high in these regions owing to its physical scarcity. This would, to an extent, help reduce groundwater overdraft in some of these regions along with raising crop outputs, whereas, in other regions, the impact would be only increased agricultural output.

With the transfer of water from water-abundant regions to water-scarce regions, the latter being land-rich would have the natural advantage of being able to produce more crops. This calls for designing an entirely new water management system, which would promote efficient use of water in agriculture and improved recharge of groundwater at no extra costs.

In alluvial areas of western and north-western India, depleted aquifers can be effectively replenished through the diversion of water for irrigation during the rainy season. Here, large amounts of land are available for infiltration and good hydraulic conductivity of the dewatered zone, whereas in hard rock areas of peninsular India, the hundreds of thousands of tanks, which dot the region, could be integrated with the infrastructure which transfers the water to this region. As many of them do not receive sufficient inflows from their catchments, they can store a portion of the imported water while the remaining water gets diverted to the agricultural land.

Enforcement of private and tradable water rights for water supplied from public reservoirs and water drawn from aquifers can together bring about a significant increase in farm output, with a reduction in aggregate demand for water in agriculture. It will also result in more equitable access to and control over the water available from canals and groundwater. In groundwater 'overexploited' areas, allocation of water use rights will be possible through energy rationing using prepaid meters. This has to be complemented by volumetric pricing of canal water and pro rata pricing of electricity in the farm sector, with improved quality and reliability of the supplied power. Metering and pro rata pricing of electricity have to receive priority in naturally water-scarce regions which also experience groundwater overdraft, whereas in groundwater-abundant regions, the pricing structure should be designed in such a way that it encourages greater use of groundwater for agricultural production.

REFERENCES

Aerthayil, M. (2008). Agrarian crisis in India is a creation of the policy of globalisation. *Mainstream, 46*(13). https://www.mainstreamweekly.net/article588.html

Arnold, D. (2005). Agriculture and 'improvement' in early colonial India: A prehistory of development. *Journal of Agrarian Change, 5*(4), 505–525.

Chakrabarty, A. (2013). *Trends in agricultural productivity in post land reform period: A study of the impact of agricultural productivity on employment and the economy of West Bengal* [Thesis submitted for the Doctor of Philosophy in Economics]. University of North Bengal, Raja Rammohunpur.

Chatterjee, S., & Rudra, A. (1989). Relations of production in pre-colonial India. *Economic & Political Weekly, 24*(21), 1171–1175.

Gulati, A., Shah, T., & Shreedhar, G. (2009). *Agriculture performance in Gujarat since 2000: Can Gujarat be a 'divadandi' (lighthouse) for other states?* IWMI and IFPRI.

Habib, I. (1999). *Agrarian system in Mughal India 1556–1707* (2nd rev. ed.). Oxford University Press.

Kishore, A. (2004). Understanding agrarian impasse in Bihar. *Economic & Political Weekly, 39*(31), 3484–3491.

Kumar, M. D., Narayanamoorthy, A., Singh, O. P., Sivamohan, M. V. K., Sharma, M. K., & Bassi, N. (2010). *Gujarat's agricultural growth story: Exploding some myths* [Occasional Paper No. 2]. Institute for Resource Analysis and Policy, Hyderabad.

Mishra, S. (2008). Risks, farmers' suicides and agrarian crisis in India: Is there a way out? *Indian Journal of Agricultural Economics, 63*(1), 38–54.

Mukherji, A., Shah, T., & Banerjee, P. S. (2012). Kick-starting a second green revolution in Bengal. *Economic & Political Weekly, 47*(18), 27–30.

Shah, M. (2016). Eliminating Poverty in Bihar: Paradoxes, Bottlenecks and Solutions. *Economic and Political Weekly, 51*(6): 56–65.

Shah, T., Gulati, A., Shreedhar, G., & Jain, R. C. (2009). Secret of Gujarat's agrarian miracle after 2000. *Economic & Political Weekly, 44*(2), 45–55.

About the Editors and Contributors

EDITORS

M. Dinesh Kumar is Executive Director of the Institute for Resource Analysis and Policy (IRAP), Hyderabad, a water policy think tank he established in 2008. He offers consultancy and advisory services to many international agencies, including the World Bank, FAO, ADB, USAID, ACIAR, UNICEF, international consulting firms, and many Indian government agencies. He did his BTech in civil engineering, ME in water resources management and PhD in water management. He has 30 years of professional experience in the field of water resources, agriculture, food security and energy. He has nearly 250 publications to his credit, including 8 books, 8 edited volumes, and several book chapters and international peer-reviewed journal articles. He is associate editor of *Water Policy* (since 2011); editorial board member of *International Journal of Water Resources Development* (since 2014) and *Frontiers in Water;* and section editor of *PLOS Water Journal* (since 2021). His internationally acclaimed research works are integrated water resources management in river basins; agriculture water productivity; global virtual water trade; integrated urban water management; methodology for assessing global water and food security challenges; climate risk in water, sanitation and hygiene; and socio-economic impacts of large water systems.

M. V. K. Sivamohan is a founding board member of IRAP, Hyderabad. He has rich experience working on the themes of participatory irrigation management, watershed development and management, and institutions. He has a BSc in biological sciences, MA in public administration and PhD in social sciences. For over

30 years (1969–2003), he was a senior faculty member, agriculture and rural development area, with the Administrative Staff College of India (ASCI), Hyderabad. He has been engaged as a specialist for research projects and consultancies by several organizations, including International Water Management Institute (IWMI); Natural Resources Institute, UK; Ford Foundation; Department for International Development (DFID); World Bank and UNICEF. To his credit, he has three books, two edited volumes, and several book chapters, journal articles and policy papers.

Nitin Bassi worked with IRAP, Hyderabad (Mar 2009–Feb 2022). He has over 15 years of experience undertaking research, consultancy and training in the field of water resources. He did BSc in botany, MSc in environment management and MPhil in natural resource management. His areas of work include river basin water accounting, agriculture water management, institutional and policy analysis in irrigation and water supply management, water quality analysis, climate variability analysis, climate-induced water risk assessment, and wetland management. He has been engaged as a specialist in projects, research studies and assignments supported by various national and international organizations. Some of these organizations include European Commission, World Bank, Deutsche Gesellschaft für Internationale Zusammenarbeit GmbH (GIZ), DFID, WRG 2030/IFC, UNICEF, WWF, IWMI, Sir Ratan Tata Trust (SRTT) and Sir Dorabji Tata Trust (SDTT). He has co-edited three books and has authored several book chapters and peer-reviewed journal articles. He regularly reviews manuscripts for *Water Policy; International Journal of Water Resources Development; Journal of Hydrology;* and *Journal of Hydrology: Regional Studies.* Presently, he works as Programme Lead with the Council on Energy, Environment, and Water (CEEW).

CONTRIBUTORS

Arijit Ganguly holds a bachelor's degree in environment and water management from Burdwan University, West Bengal, and a master's degree in environmental studies and resources management from

TERI University, New Delhi. He has more than six years of experience working in the fields of hydrological modelling for rivers, climate risk and resilience analysis, water quality management, water resources management, and analysis of environmental quality. He has worked with several organizations which include IRAP, Hyderabad; Ministry of Water Resources, RD & GR, GoI; and DHI (India) Water & Environment Pvt. Ltd, New Delhi. He has a working knowledge of many analytical, geographic information system (GIS) and hydrological modelling tools. His professional interests include integrated water resources management, climate variability analysis, GIS and environmental system analysis.

K. Siva Rama Kishan has a master's degree in social arthrology and more than 15 years of experience working in the fields of water resources, watershed management and sanitation. He worked with IRAP, Hyderabad, for more than five years, wherein he contributed to several research projects focusing on water, sanitation, hygiene and water quality management. He is an ardent field researcher and specializes in designing tools and instruments for the primary survey.

Saurabh Kumar is a PhD in forestry (forest ecology and environment) from the Forest Research Institute, Dehradun. He has worked on biodiversity assessment studies, environmental impact assessments (EIA) and the development of action plans for biodiversity conservation for CII-IBBI member companies related to automobile manufacturing, ports and harbours, agriculture, cement, and power. He worked as a researcher with IRAP, Hyderabad (2020–2021), and was engaged in the Pavitra Ganga Project which is financially supported by the DBT, GoI, and the European Commission. He has expertise in using MINITAB, SPSS, EstimateS, PC-Ord and Twin Span.

V. Niranjan has a master's degree in environmental management. He has nearly 14 years of experience in the fields of EIA, baseline environmental studies, water resources management and teaching. He has prepared EIA reports for many major industries in India and abroad. He has worked on irrigation efficiencies and water productivity in agriculture. He is experienced in performance evaluation of major, medium and minor irrigation projects. While working at IRAP (from 2010–2015), he was a part of two major projects, one 'Agrarian Crisis in India' sponsored by ICSSR and the other 'Drought Monitoring in Maharashtra' supported by UNICEF, Mumbai. He also played a major role in the research support for 'Multiple Use of Water Services to Reduce Poverty and Vulnerability to Climate Variability and Change', Maharashtra, supported by UNICEF, Mumbai.

Index

Index